Penguin Books

The Price of Glory

Winner of the Hawthornde

Verdun was the battle which lasted ten months; the battle in which at least 700,000 men fell, along a front of fifteen miles; the battle whose aim was less to defeat the enemy than to bleed him to death; the battle ground whose once fertile terrain is even now the 'nearest thing to desert in Europe'.

But this book is very much more than a chronicle of the facts of death. It is a profoundly moving, sympathetic study of the men who fought there, and one that shows Verdun to be the key to an understanding of the First World War – the key to the minds of those who waged it, to the traditions that bound them, and to the world that gave them the opportunity.

'For the student of human character, as well as of military endeavour and mismanagement, Verdun has everything to offer. *The Price of Glory* should help one to understand the true nature of war' – *Guardian*

About the author

Alistair Horne was born in London in 1925, and has spent much
of his life abroad, including periods at schools in the United
States and Switzerland. He served with the R.C.A.F. and the
R.A.F. in Canada in 1943 and ended his war service with the
rank of Captain in the Coldstream Guards in the Middle East.
He then went up to Jesus College, Cambridge, where he read
English Literature and played international ice-hockey.

Since leaving Cambridge, Alistair Horne has concentrated on
writing: he spent three years in Germany as correspondent for
the *Daily Telegraph* and speaks fluent French and German. His
books include *Back into Power* (1955); *The Land is Bright*
(1958); *Canada and the Canadians* (1961); *Small Earthquake in
Chile* (1972); and his widely praised trilogy on Franco–German
conflicts: *The Fall of Paris, 1870–71*; *The Price of Glory: Verdun
1916*; *To Lose a Battle: France 1940* (written in the 1960s). *A
Savage War of Peace: Algeria 1954–62*, won both the *Yorkshire
Post* Book of the Year Prize and the Wolfson History Award in
1978. It also earned for Mr Horne C. P. Snow's acclaim of being
'one of the best writers of history in the English-speaking world
. . . his new book shows him at the peak of his powers'. His
other publications include *Napoleon, Master of Europe
1805–1807* (1979), *The French Army and Politics 1870–1970*
(1984), which was awarded the Enid Macleod Prize in 1985 and
the highly praised two volume biography *Macmillan* (1988,
1989). He has founded a Research Fellowship for young
historians at St Antony's College, Oxford, and is a Trustee of the
Imperial War Museum.

Alistair Horne

The Price of Glory
Verdun 1916

Penguin Books

PENGUIN BOOKS

Published by the Penguin Group
Penguin Books Ltd, 27 Wrights Lane, London W8 5TZ, England
Viking Penguin, a division of Penguin Books USA Inc.
375 Hudson Street, New York, New York 10014, USA
Penguin Books Australia Ltd, Ringwood, Victoria, Australia
Penguin Books Canada Ltd, 2801 John Street, Markham, Ontario, Canada L3R 1B4
Penguin Books (NZ) Ltd, 182–190 Wairau Road, Auckland 10, New Zealand

Penguin Books Ltd, Registered Offices: Harmondsworth, Middlesex, England

First published in Great Britain by Macmillan 1962
First published in the United States of America by St Martin's Press, Inc. 1962
This specially abridged edition first published in Penguin Books 1964
10 9

Printed in England by Clays Ltd, St Ives plc
Set in Linotype Times

To Francis and Jacqueline

Contents

Maps and Plans

Acknowledgements

It would be nearly unthinkable to undertake any book on the First War without reference to the Imperial War Museum, and for their unstinting help I am greatly indebted; equally to the *Bibliothèque de Documentation Internationale Contemporaine* of the University of Paris, with its unique collection of First War books, and to the *Bibliothek für Zeitgeschichte* in Stuttgart, which made up in helpfulness for the material lost during the Second World War.

I should also like to record my appreciation to Captain Liddell Hart (almost as indispensable a *sine qua non* to writers on the First War as the Imperial War Museum) for his guidance and encouragement at an early stage; to General de Cossé-Brissac of the *Service Historique* of the French Army; to Lt-Colonel Morell of the *Militärgeschichtliches Forschungsamt* of the Bundeswehr; to General Robert Huré, Commandant of the *École d'Artillerie*, and Colonel de la Ruelle of the *École de Guerre*; to General Henry Blanc, Director of the *Musée de l'Armée* at the Invalides; to Colonel Goutard and Commandant Homant, Chaplain at the *Ossuaire de Douaumont*; to Major Diggle, late of the 9th Lancers, for accompanying me round some of the battlefields with a professional eye; to Mrs Philip Pollock for reading the manuscript; to Mrs Alvarez, who did much of the work on cross-referencing and typing; to Mrs St George Saunders for help on the bibliography (in the interests of compactness, the bibliography and source notes contained in the original edition have had to be excised in this edition), and to the Research and Information Bureau of Chambers's Encyclopaedia for some material on air/ground communication in 1916; and finally to the French Embassy in London.

For photographs I am grateful to the following: Weltkriegsbücherei, Stuttgart, for plate 1; Musée de la Guerre (Université de Paris) Vincennes, for plates 2, 5, 8, 9, 10, 11, 12, 13, 14, 15, 16, 18; Kurt von Klüfer, *Seelenkräfte im Kampf um Douaumont*, for plates 3 and 4; V. Wienskowski, *Falkenhayn* (Siegismund Verlag, Berlin 1937), for plate 6; Radio Times Hulton Picture Library, London, for plate 7; Imperial War Museum, London, for plate 17.

The maps and plans were drawn by W. Bromage.

This Western-front business couldn't be done again, not for a long time. The young men think they could do it again but they couldn't. They could fight the first Marne again but not this. This took religion and years of plenty and tremendous sureties and the exact relation that existed between the classes. The Russians and Italians weren't any good on this front. You had to have a whole-souled sentimental equipment going back further than you could remember. You had to remember Christmas, and postcards of the Crown Prince and his fiancée, and little cafés in Valence and beer gardens in Unter den Linden and weddings at the Mairie, and going to the Derby, and your grandfather's whiskers.... This was a love-battle — there was a century of middle-class love spent here.... All my beautiful lovely safe world blew itself up here with a great gust of high explosive love....

F. SCOTT FITZGERALD, *Tender is the Night*

1 La Débâcle

... *car la Revanche doit venir lente peut-être*
Mais en tout cas fatale et terrible à coup sûr
La Haine est déjà née, et la force va naître
C'est un faucheur à voir si le champ n'est pas mûr.
PAUL DÉROULÈDE

Three and a half years elapsed between the First Battle of the Marne, when the Kaiser's armies reached the gates of Paris, and Ludendorff's last-gasp offensive that so nearly succeeded in the spring of 1918. During this time the Germans remained on the defensive behind a brilliantly prepared and almost impregnable line, while the French and British wasted themselves against it in vain, at an unimaginable cost of human lives.

Only once did the Germans deviate from this strategy that paid so handsomely. In February 1916, they attacked in the Verdun sector, catching the French there thoroughly by surprise. Compared with the seven German armies that marched into France in 1914 and Ludendorff's sixty-three divisions that struck at Haig in 1918, this assault on Verdun with only nine divisions was but a small affair. A small affair; yet out of it grew what those who took part in it considered to be the grimmest battle in all that grim war, perhaps in History itself. Certainly it was the longest battle of all time, and during the ten months it lasted nearly three-quarters of the French Army were drawn through it. Though other battles of the First War exacted a higher toll, Verdun came to gain the unenviable reputation of being the battlefield with the highest density of dead per square yard that has probably ever been known. Above all, the battle was a watershed of prime importance in the First War. Before it, Germany still had a reasonable chance of winning the war; in the course of those ten months this chance dwindled away. Beyond it, neither the French nor the German army would be quite the same again; Verdun marked the point at which, among the Allies, the main burden of the war passed from France to Britain, and its influence upon America's eventual entry into the war cannot be overlooked.

In the aftermath, too, Verdun was to become a sacred national legend, and universally a household word for fortitude, heroism, and suffering; but it was also a modern synonym for a Pyrrhic victory. Long after the actual war was over, the effects of this one battle lingered on in France. Of the men to arise from the triumph of Verdun, one in particular will be forever associated with the appalling tragedy of a generation later, and today the marks of Verdun upon France and the French have not been eradicated. Behind the scribbles of *'De Gaulle ne passera pas'* on Algerian walls lies perhaps more than just the adaptation of a famous battle-cry.

'This Western-front business couldn't be done again,' declares Dick Diver in *Tender is the Night*. He was right, as 1940 proved; the nearest the Second World War came to it was at Stalingrad, often referred to as a Russian 'Verdun'. The explanation of why there was no 'Western-front business' in 1940, why the German Panzers went rolling round the Maginot Line with such ease, why there was a Maginot Line at all, cannot be explained without reference to the happenings at Verdun in 1916.

Similarly to see how the German forces came to stand before Verdun in 1916, why they chose to attack what was reputedly the strongest fortress in Europe, and why the French withstood their attack with such incredible steadfastness, one needs to hark back to yet an earlier war – to the fateful year of 1870.

*

Six weeks after France had declared war that summer, the last Emperor of the French, his face rouged to conceal the agonies caused by a monstrous bladder stone, was on his way to captivity in Germany. Within another four-and-a-half months, at Versailles in the great palace that bears the inscription *'à toutes les Gloires de la France'*, and beneath a painting of Frenchmen chastising Germans, the Prussian King had himself proclaimed Kaiser. When at last the peace was signed, the conquerors insisted that its terms embrace a triumphal march through Paris, only massed French citizens were able to prevent the Uhlans perpetrating the ultimate insult of riding through the Arc de Triomphe.

One would have to search diligently through the pages of history to find a more dramatic instance of what the Greeks called peripeteia, or reversal of fortune. Where before has a nation of such grandeur (indeed, *La Grande* Nation), brimming over with hubris and refulgent with material achievement, been subjected to worse humiliation within so short a space of time? And when has a military power as assured in traditions as soldierly prowess been more shamefully defeated? In July 1870, Louis Napoleon's forces had set off, optimistically entitled 'The Army of the Rhine', and lavishly equipped with maps of Germany, though none of France. After two minor defeats that were far from decisive, the French Army never ceased retreating. Old crones along the route jeered at the dispirited, bedraggled soldiery. The vigilant Uhlans pursued them; now like a pack of wolves, waiting for stragglers; now like beaters, driving the frightened coveys towards the guns. Finally, half the army under Bazaine was herded into Metz, where it surrendered after doing nothing for two months. Into the trap at Sedan, just forty miles downstream from Verdun, went the other half, under MacMahon and accompanied by the Emperor himself. '*Nous sommes dans un pot de chambre et nous y serons emmerdés!*' remarked General Ducrot. The words might have applied to the whole bitter sense of total disgrace felt by the French Army after 1870. It was a terrible slur to be faced by the heirs of Henri VI and Condé, Turenne and Saxe, not to mention the great Bonaparte – by soldiers who, down through the ages, had considered themselves to be *the* warrior race of Europe.

The results of Louis Napoleon's ill-advised declaration of war were to alter the character of war itself as much as they were to affect the future of all Europe. The employment of mass conscript armies and the merciless sieges where civilians had been indiscriminately blown to pieces by long-range guns introduced a new savagery into warfare, which for some centuries had been a reasonably gentlemanly affair. The harsh Prussian peace terms, requiring the surrender of two of France's richest provinces and the payment of reparations on an unprecedented scale – so that the war would cost the loser nearly ten times as much as the victors – instilled a new bitterness into European relations. And the French Army would never forget its degradation.

＊

In 1871, France was exhausted, bankrupt, demoralized; the countryside ravaged and torn by civil war of the most brutal kind. France has frequently astonished the world by her recuperative ability which stems from the intrinsic richness of a country twice as largé as the British Isles, and her great resources of human energy – so often dissipated in the boudoir and the political lobby. Never, though, has her recovery been so rapid or so remarkable as after the catastrophe of 1870–71. The legacy of the war was soon liquidated. A scapegoat to bear the collective disgrace of the army was speedily found in the form of Bazaine. Well ahead of schedule, the crushing £200,000,000 of reparations were paid off, and in September 1873 the last Prussian soldiers left French soil. The French economy began to flourish as never before; the Paris Exposition of 1878 showed Europe that the affluence of the latter-day Second Empire was back again, though now a more solid achievement lay beneath the glittering surface.

Nowhere was the renaissance more striking than in the army. A new type of dedicated young officer – like Ferdinand Foch who, as an 18-year-old student, had seen Louis Napoleon trail sick and defeated through Metz – strode forward to replace the fops of the Second Empire with their emulative Imperials. A new spirit ran through the whole army, determined to expunge the recent blots on its reputation. With it went a passion for study, replacing the traditions of the café and the vacuous routine of garrison life. It formed a marked contrast to the days when MacMahon had threatened: 'I shall remove from the promotion list any officer whose name I read on the cover of a book'. Penetrating studies were made of the 1870 campaign, and in their sweeping reorganization, the army leaders made no bones about imitating the conqueror. Three successive laws provided France for the first time with universal military service (of the exceptional length of five years) and a cadre of reserves. Under General Lewal a Staff College was created to lay the foundations for something better than the inefficient old General Staff disbanded by the reformers, and later, under General Miribel, the *État Major de l'Armée* was formed. In peace, its role was to prepare for war and – notably – to plan the details of mobilization in which France had been so deficient in 1870; in war, it was to provide the command of France's principal group of armies. Thus, in embryo, came to life the famous *Grand Quartier Général*, or G.Q.G. In 1886, the French army adopted the first model of the Lebel rifle that it would go to war with in 1914; about the same time were laid down the calibres of guns that were used in the war; and a few years later high explosive Lyddite replaced black powder as a filling for shells.

Of all the military reorganization undertaken by France after 1871, little concerns this story more than the defensive measures she carried out on her new frontier. (By a chain of cause and effect they were, moreover, to make inevitable Britain's participation in the First War; though this could hardly be foreseen at the time.) The War of 1870 had been fought, on paper, more or less between equals. But now any thoughtful Frenchman could reasonably predict that disparity between the two nations would grow with increasing rapidity; the Germans were breeding faster and, with the transfer of Alsace-Lorraine, their industrial power was bound to expand more rapidly. However successful the reorganization of the French army, it alone could now hardly suffice to protect France against Germany. In addition, the re-drawn frontier brought the hereditary enemy to less than two hundred miles from Paris, with no natural barrier like the Rhine or the Vosges in between. Thus a sapper general called Serré de Rivière was entrusted with the construction of a defensive system on a scale never before contemplated, and only to be outdone by Maginot. Instead of converting one or two cities into fortified camps, like Metz, which in 1870 had turned out to be an insidious trap, de Rivière built a continuous line of sunken forts; or rather, two continuous lines. On the Swiss frontier, the system was anchored on Belfort and ran uninterruptedly along the line of hills to Épinal. At the old fortress town of Toul on the Moselle the line began again, along the heights on the right bank of the Meuse, to Verdun. North of Verdun was the dense Argónne, and then the Ardennes, through which (until von Manstein showed the way in 1940) it was assumed no invading army could manoeuvre. Between the linchpins of Toul and Épinal, de Rivière ingeniously left a forty-mile gap in the defences, called the *'Trouée de Charmes'*. It was like a gateway in a wall, intended (perhaps a little naïvely) to entice within and canalize any German invasion, so that the French mass of manoeuvre lying in wait could then conveniently drive into both its flanks and eventually close in behind. Of course, the Belgian frontier was left unfortified, save for a few scattered fortresses like Lille and Maubeuge. It was Verdun, with its vital position, already fortified by Vauban – and indeed as far back as the Romans – that was both the principal strongpoint of, and key to, the whole system.

As 1914 came, morale in the army had never been higher. The pilot lamp that – despite all the distractions in the long years since 1871 – had been kept alight in its ranks by those dedicated to the ideals of *'La Revanche'* and of erasing the shame of the lost war, now flared high. The proportion of deserters on mobilization, which, it had been previously estimated would reach thirteen per cent, turned out in fact to be less than one and a half per cent, and during the first terrible winter only 509 French soldiers deserted. This time, in some respects at least, the French Army was genuinely, superbly ready. In fact, it was perhaps a little too ready.

When the Army had fully recovered its confidence after 1870, on the completion of de Rivière's defence system, it had begun increasingly to abandon its defensive thinking. Its studies of 1870 seemed to prove convincingly that the main reason above all others for France's defeat had been the lack of offensive spirit. There was much talk about the posture of attack being most suited to the national temperament; the spirit of the *'furia francese'* was evoked from as far off as the Battle of Pavia in 1525, as was Danton's exhortation to the defenders of Verdun in 1792 – *'il nous faut de l'audace, encore de l'audace, toujours de l'audace'*. The new mood was also well matched to the philosophy of Bergson that was now all the rage in France, with its emphasis on the *'élan vital'*. As the years moved further

away from the actual experience of war, so the philosophy of
the offensive moved ever further from reality. At pre-war
French manoeuvres, British observers with memories from the
Veldt were always struck by the antipathy to going to ground.
At the École de Guerre little study was made of the success of
the defence in the American Civil War, the Boer War, or in the
recent and more significant fighting in Manchuria. In fact, there
was little pragmatic study of any sort, and it was hardly surprising that in 1913–14 three hundred books on war were published in Germany, to only fifty in France.

During the critical years before 1914, the gospel of '*L'attaque
à outrance*', as it had become known, found its ultimate prophet
in Colonel de Grandmaison, Chief of the *Troisième Bureau*
(Operations) of the General Staff. He and his supporters had
engineered the downfall of the Commander-in-Chief, Michel,
whose approach to countering a German onslaught had been
a little too rational for their liking. In his place was installed
Joffre, who, because he was a sapper and had served most
of his career in the colonies, could be assumed to know
nothing of military theory and would make an excellent figurehead.

From top to bottom, the army was impregnated with de
Grandmaison's extravagant, semi-mystical nonsense: 'In the
offensive, imprudence is the best of assurances.... Let us go
even to excess, and that perhaps will not be far enough.... For
the attack only two things are necessary: to know where the
enemy is and to decide what to do. What the enemy intends to
do is of no consequence.' Young soldiers on joining up were
expected to learn by heart a catechism which incorporated the
following words: 'From the moment of action every soldier
must ardently desire the assault by bayonet as the supreme
means of imposing his will upon the enemy and gaining victory....' Another product of the de Grandmaison philosophy,
harking back to grim memories of the physical invasion of
France in 1870, was the rigid dogma that – should the enemy
dare to seize the initiative even for a moment – every inch of
terrain must be defended to the death, and, if lost, regained by
an immediate counter-attack, however inopportune. Enforced
by threat of court martial and disgrace, this was a dogma that
hardly encouraged tactical initiative among French army

leaders.[1] Even Foch, France's leading military intellect, followed the de Grandmaison line. Only a few, like Colonel Pétain, resisted, teaching that 'firepower killed' and that it might do terrible things to any '*attaque à outrance*' unsupported by heavy weapons; for which heresy his promotion had lagged. De Grandmaison's doctrine was to cost France hundreds of thousands of her best men, quite unnecessarily; later, discredited, he himself was to find death and '*La Gloire*' before the end of 1914 while trying to prove his theories at the head of a brigade.

The de Grandmaison doctrine naturally enough had a profound effect on the equipment of the army. In 1909, the General Staff representative on the Chamber of Deputies' Budget Commission declared: 'You talk to us of heavy artillery. Thank God, we have none. The strengh of the French Army is in the lightness of its guns.' In 1910 Foch, then Commandant of the Staff College, said: 'The aircraft is all very well for sport, for the army it is useless.' The St Étienne machine gun was brought into service that year, but, said the Inspector General of Infantry, it would 'not make the slightest difference to anything.' A complicated weapon, it was something of a headache to the troops, and though brought out on manoeuvres to impress journalists, was otherwise left behind at Company H.Q. Both machine guns and heavy artillery were deemed contrary to the Grandmaison spirit, and their withdrawal from the Army Estimates was joyfully supported by budget-conscious politicians. (The spirit was infectious and died hard; even after August 1914, Kitchener was telling General Murray that the British Army really should be able to take positions without artillery, instancing his own successes against the Fuzzy-Wuzzies!) Everything depended on what Foch called 'the Will to Conquer'; that, supported by the bayonet and the '75. The '75 was indeed a marvellous weapon; well ahead of its age,

1. Of this 'fatal doctrine of the conservation of ground' a French general wrote after the war: 'the humblest company, the humblest battalion in the front line had the order to retake any ground lost. Was it not essential, they said, to maintain the impetus of the soldier? This doctrine distracted our leaders from the manoeuvre that consists of withdrawing a few kilometres in order to lure the enemy out of his positions, and lead him to fall disorganized under our fire and under our counter-offensives.' (Percin, *Le Massacre de Notre Infanterie*). It will be seen later with what force the above applied to the Battle of Verdun.

quicker firing, more accurate, more mobile, and with longer range than any other field gun in service. To the de Grandmaison school it was 'God the Father, God the Son, and God the Holy Ghost', but as General Weygand later added irreverently: 'one would have liked to have seen it surrounded by a few saints.' Superb for fighting in the open field – the kind of war envisaged by de Grandmaison – it could not be used for plunging fire, like the howitzers possessed in plenty by the Germans, and its projectiles were too light to be effective against entrenchments. Nevertheless, the '75 saved France time and again during the war, and, for once, it was a weapon she had in sufficient numbers from the start. (Not so, alas, its ammunition, for Foch and the others had reckoned on a brief, brutal conflict of a matter of weeks.) Meanwhile, so that the enemy should see them clearly and be terror-struck by their furious numbers, the infantry went to war in the red *képis* and pantaloons of the Second Empire, despising the Germans for converting to the less martial, though more practical *Feldgrau*. And, just as in 1870, the army found itself once again with a dearth of maps of France, but plenty of Germany.

By de Grandmaison, out of Joffre, was hatched the General Staff's disastrous Plan XVII. On the outbreak of war, four out of five French armies, totalling 800,000 men, were to charge forward, with the main impetus directed towards the lost territories; objective, the Rhine. The strategic aim was to dislocate the ponderous German war-machine before it could carry out its plans. But the *Deuxième Bureau* (Intelligence) of the General Staff were good pupils of de Grandmaison and had indeed not troubled themselves unduly to find out what the enemy's intentions might be.

*

By the end of the old century, two new factors had forced a complete revision of strategy upon the German General Staff. One was General de Rivière's system of fortifications, which now meant that any attack on France along the traditional invasion route would involve extremely hard, prolonged fighting. The second was France's alliance with Russia, which meant that Germany would be faced with war on two fronts. Necessity bred one of Germany's greatest military minds and his equally famous plan: Graf von Schlieffen, who was Chief of the General Staff from 1891 to 1906. The Schlieffen Plan was to knock out France in a *Blitzkrieg* while Russia was still mobilizing, then turn with all force to the East. The weight of the French Army would be lured towards the Rhine by leaving this sector deliberately weak, while the main German force marched rapidly through Belgium to outflank the French. It would then execute a huge wheel to the west of Paris and eventually, from the rear, pin the French Army up against the Swiss frontier. The plan has been likened to a revolving door, and under their Plan XVII the French were in fact to add momentum to the door's rotation, thereby doing just what Schlieffen wanted.

Fortunately for France and unfortunately for Germany, Schlieffen's successor, Moltke, tampered with the master plan. Although the nephew of the great Moltke, the resemblance between them was roughly that of Louis Napoleon and his uncle. The younger Moltke was the first of the mediocre First War generals to bring disaster to his side by faint-heartedness and half-measures. Schlieffen's last words are reported to have been 'make the right wing strong', but Moltke was fearful of what might happen if the French pushed too hard on the revolving door. Consequently, as additional forces became available, he added eight divisions to the left wing but only one to the right. More disastrously, he weakened the covering force in the East, so that at the critical moment of the Battle of the Marne two army corps, that might have tipped the balance in favour of Germany, had had to be sent to save East Prussia from an unexpectedly strong Russian threat.

Although the German army of 1914 was a fearsome power, compared with that of 1870, it was a bludgeon to a rapier. It had had no dummy run against the Austrians at Sadowa. Whereas in the French army politics and religion had played their baneful role in promotion, in Germany the 'caste' system had tended to frustrate the rise of brilliant officers of humbler origins, such as Ludendorff. The idiotic sycophancy that surrounded the Kaiser, whereby at war-games the side commanded by His Majesty always had to win with a magnificent encirclement of the enemy, also had its effect. Moreover, the army that moved on France, a million and a half strong, the largest the world had ever seen, was far too big and unwieldy for a man of Moltke's calibre to command effectively. Its strength lay chiefly in the excellence of its N.C.O.s, in its reservist system (which completely deceived Joffre just as it had deceived Louis Napoleon), and the superiority of its weapons. Whereas the French had only six of the despised St Étienne machine guns per regiment, the Germans had highly efficient Maxims that were not relegated to the Company Quartermaster. The whole French Army possessed only 300 heavy guns; the Germans had 3,500. The French heavies were mostly elderly 120 millimetre guns built in the 1880s, with no recuperation system so that they had to run out up a ramp; they were outclassed in every way by the German 210s and 150s. For 'super-heavy' artillery, the French had to make do with a few 270 mm. mortars dating back to 1875, while the Germans had brand new 280s that could fire a shell weighing nearly 750 lb. over a distance of six miles. Finally, they had the monster 420 mm. 'Big Berthas' that Krupp had produced in great secrecy, which were to pulverize the 'impregnable' Belgian forts and which later were to become all too familiar to the defenders of Verdun.[1]

1. Contrary to popular belief, the super long-range gun that shelled Paris in 1918 was not called 'Big Bertha'. The true 'Big Bertha' (named after the Krupp heiress) were short-barrelled mortars with only limited range.

2   Joffre of the Marne

En avant! Tant pis pour qui tombe
La Mort n'est rien. Vive la tombe
Quand le pays en sort vivant.
        En avant!
    PAUL DÉROULÈDE

Down plunged the avalanche, sweeping away alike the midgets
that had been preparing its descent, as well as those that had
tried feebly to prevent it. The wind of its passage snuffed out
the age of unrivalled prosperity and unlimited promise, in
which even poor medieval Russia was beginning to take part,
and Europe descended into a new Dark Age from whose
shadows it has yet to emerge. For the next four years, it was to
seem as if the avalanche were the sole arbiter in the world,
with human leaders, political and military, reduced to impo-
tence in the face of a force infinitely greater than anything
they had ever foreseen and – in the gentle life of Edwardian
Europe – had ever been trained to handle.

Though, from a point of view of doctrinal and material shortcomings, France entered the war in a condition depressingly
similar to that of 1870, this time at least her mobilization functioned; for which much of the credit must go to Joffre, who had
made himself an expert on railways. Nearly two million men
were brought into position by 4,278 trains, and of all the trains
set in motion only nineteen ran late. It was a remarkable
achievement; however, the Germans mobilized even more efficiently. Reservists numbering 1,300,000 poured towards the
front and Joffre, deceived by the Kaiser's pledge that there
would be 'no fathers of a family in the first line', could not believe that reserve formations would take part in the initial
battles. The strength of the German armies that the French met
in executing their Plan XVII convinced Joffre that the enemy's
main weight lay in front; consequently he was completely taken
by surprise by the great phalanx that was swinging round by
Liège to hammer him in the back.

The two huge forces, the German and the French (supported by the four valiant divisions which were all Britain could provide at the time), met with a crash which will resound down through the centuries. On one side, the great grey, disciplined hordes strode vigorously forward, confident in their numbers and the superiority of their race, singing raucously:

> *'Siegreich woll'n wir Frankreich schlagen,*
> *Sterben als ein tapf'rer Held.'*

Perhaps a little more than other young men of Europe, after the long years of bourgeois prosperity they were yearning for the 'great experience'. As one of them noted, 'the war had entered into us like wine. There is no lovelier death in the world . . . anything rather than rest at home.' The spectacle of the first shattered corpses fascinated them, for 'the horrible was undoubtedly a part of that irresistible attraction that drew us to the war.' To their Crown Prince, watching them pass, they were 'joyous German soldiers with sparkling eyes'.

On the other side, young men filled with a mighty lust for revenge were marching up at that rapid staccato pace, accompanied by the regimental music and with the rather more melodious refrain of *'Mourir pour la Patrie est le sort le plus beau'* on their lips. Magnificent specimens, these French soldiers of 1914, thought the soldiers of General French's army, repeatedly astonished to find them bigger and tougher men than themselves. They ripped up the frontier posts in Alsace and sent them to be laid upon the grave of Déroulède. Then the enemy was located. The trumpeters sounded the call that sent a thrill more heady than wine through French veins:

> *Y a la goutte à boire là-haut!*
> *Y a la goutte à boire!*

All along the frontier the infantrymen in their red trousers and thick, blue overcoats, carrying heavy packs and long, unwieldy bayonets, broke into the double behind their white-gloved officers. Many sang the *Marseillaise*. In the August heat, sometimes the heavily encumbered French attacked from a distance of nearly half a mile from the enemy. Never have machine-gunners had such a heyday. The French stubble-fields became transformed into gay carpets of red and blue. Splendid cuirassiers in glittering breastplates of another age hurled their horses hopelessly at the machine guns that were slaughtering the infantry. It was horrible, and horribly predictable. In that superb, insane courage of 1914 there was something slightly reminiscent of the lemmings swimming out to sea. But it was not war.

For a whole week, as the censors released news of the capture of Mulhouse while suppressing such unpleasant details as casualties, France held her breath and thought Plan XVII might succeed. Triumphantly *Le Matin* proclaimed, *'Plus un soldat allemand en France!'* But, at Joffre's headquarters, courier after courier was arriving with news of identical disasters from all parts of the front. In the two weeks that the terrible Battle of the Frontiers lasted, France lost over 300,000 men in killed, wounded, and missing, and 4,778 officers – representing no less than one-tenth of her total officer strength. De Castelnau's Second Army, which was to have led the advance to the Rhine, reeled back on Nancy almost in a rout; in it, the *élite* XX Corps commanded by Foch was particularly hard hit. To the North, the swinging German right wing pushed the French and the B.E.F. back to the Marne. In 1870, such catastrophes might well have led to a débâcle as disastrous as either of the Sedans, but this was not the France of either Louis Napoleon or Lebrun. Von Kluck committed his historic blunder of wheeling inwards, on his own responsibility, thereby exposing the First Army's flank to the newly constituted army guarding Paris. Galliéni, the governor, spotted what had happened; Joffre made the retreating armies turn about; and the 'Miracle of the Marne' came to pass.[1] With it the Germans lost their one chance of an absolute victory (it had been a close thing) though it took the Allies another four bloody years to prove it to them. Their mighty impetus finally checked, they fell back, but the French were too exhausted to turn the retreat into a rout. Then, in the last flicker of the war of movement, there took place the side-

1. Russia's contribution to making the 'Miracle' possible at all should never be forgotten. Without waiting to complete her own mobilization, she had attacked unexpectedly in East Prussia, with the result that – at the most critical moment of the campaign in France – Moltke had been forced to transfer two badly needed army corps from the West to the East. As will be seen later, it was not the last time that Russia would come to France's rescue.

stepping motion towards the Channel, with each side trying to outflank the other in the so-called 'Race for the Sea'.

By the autumn of 1914, a continuous static front had been established from Switzerland to the Belgian coast. It was based not on natural features (the bastion of Verdun left in a precarious salient that bulged out like a large hernia was the striking exception), but on a line of exhaustion. The first five months of the war in the West had cost both sides more heavily than any other succeeding year; Germany, a total of approximately 750,000 casualties; France, 300,000 killed (or nearly a fifth more than Britain's total dead in the whole of World War II) and another 600,000 in wounded, captured, and missing. The horrors of trench warfare now began.

*

Out of the victory of the Marne, Joffre emerged as immeasurably the most powerful figure on the whole Allied side. Before the battle, when the German guns were heard in Paris and cynical American correspondents were openly betting that on the morrow it would have become 'a provincial city of Germany', the Government had left hastily for Bordeaux. Exaggerated rumours of the deputies' Capuan luxuries there soon reached the front, and for the rest of the war Bordeaux became a dirty word. The politicians sank to their lowest repute for many a decade. In the Government's absence, the *Grand Quartier Général* assumed reponsibility for the entire conduct of the war. As a Deputy remarked later, it had become a veritable 'ministry' in its own right. And never since Bonaparte had one Frenchman been so all-powerful or so popular as Joffre. Car-loads of gifts, boxes of chocolates and cigars, rolled in daily and his officers grew weary dealing with the copious fan-mail; all of which Joffre somehow found time to read with obvious enjoyment.

Joseph Joffre (his middle name, suspiciously enough, was Césaire) was the son of a humble cooper – one of a family of eleven – and, like Foch and de Castelnau, a Pyrenean. In 1870, as a student at the Polytechnic, he had been sent to Vincennes to learn how to fire a cannon, and, after his captain had collapsed with a nervous breakdown, found himself commanding a battery during the Siege of Paris. Soon after graduating from the Polytechnic as an engineer, he was sent to Indo-China, and there began a long career in France's new empire. In 1894, he led a column in conquest of Timbuctoo, and first made his mark by his efficiency in organizing the column's supplies. Aged thirty-three, he was then the youngest sapper Lieutenant-Colonel. Timbuctoo was followed by Madagascar, until Joffre was called home in 1904 to be Director of Engineers. Between 1906 and 1910 he commanded first a division and then a corps for brief periods; this was his only experience in commanding a large body of infantry. In 1910 he became a member of the War Council, and the following year, Chief of the General Staff; selected, as has been remarked earlier, more for his qualities as a 'good Republican' than for any military brilliance. It was to his credit, however, that between 1904 and 1914 there had been any improvements in the French fortresses and heavy artillery, and he had hammered through (just in time) the Conscription Bill of 1913. He was a talented organizer, but the dual role of Commander-in-Chief of France's main group of armies also required him to be a first-rate strategist and tactician. This he was not.

At the outbreak of war 'Papa' Joffre was a widower rising 63. According to Spears, who saw him frequently during 1914,

his breeches were baggy and ill-fitting. The outfit was completed by cylindrical leggings. ... His chin was marked and determined. The whiteness of his hair, the lightness of his almost colourless blue eyes, which looked out from under big eyebrows, the colour of salt and pepper, white predominating, and the tonelessness of his voice coming through the sieve of his big, whitish moustache, all gave the impression of an albino. His cap was worn well forward so that the peak protected his eyes, which resulted in his having to tilt his head slightly to look at one. A bulky, slow-moving, loosely built man, in clothes that would have been the despair of Savile Row, yet unmistakably a soldier.

But the really outstanding (in more than one sense) physical feature of Joffre was his belly. His appetite was legendary; staff officers often observed him consume a whole chicken at a sitting, and one, explaining his taciturnity at table, remarked that he never left himself time to speak, even had he wanted to. Joffre maintained his appetite to his death-bed; in the final coma, when a hospital orderly tried to insert a few drops of milk between his lips, he opened his eyes abruptly, seized the glass and drained it, then went back to sleep. Once when criticizing a general he remarked, tapping his own, that the man 'had no stomach', and no doubt his own supremacy in this respect helped make him additionally acceptable to democratic politicians suspicious of the Cassius-type.

Joffre was a true viscerotonic, and this was the source of his principal strengths and weaknesses. He thought from his belly rather than with his mind, with the intuitive shrewdness of a peasant. Even one of his most loyal associates, and biographer, General Desmazes, comments on his extraordinary lack of intellectualism. Before the war he read little on military theory; afterwards he read not one of the books on the war in which he had played so large a role. He was totally lacking in curiosity and imagination. Haig remarked of him, patronizingly: 'the poor man cannot argue, nor can he easily read a map.' In at least two respects, however, Joffre closely resembled Haig. One was his reserve. (Indeed, it was a mystery how together they ever communicated at all.) But where with Haig this was due to inarticulateness, with Joffre it was more often than not that there was simply nothing in his mind. A Headquarters visited by Joffre, hoping for some vital guidance from him, was generally left still hoping when the great man departed. There was the famous episode of the gunner colonel, who had come to the Generalissimo with a grave problem; after listening for a while, Joffre dismissed him with a pat on the shoulder and a laconic 'You always loved your guns; that's excellent.' Joffre turned this taciturnity to good advantage when assaulted by politicians; like a hedgehog, he 'rolled himself into a ball', and his assailants went away, baffled.

Above all, Joffre's comfortable frame and healthy appetite provided him with utterly unshakable nerves and an almost inhuman calm. At Chantilly he lived a life of strictest routine. Nothing, certainly not a national disaster, was allowed to interfere with it. In the morning (not early), the duty officer briefed Joffre on the events of the night. At 1100 hours, the Major-General presented orders for his signature; 1200 hours, lunch, any delay in which incurred Joffre's quiet but terrible rage. Afterwards Joffre, accompanied later by Castelnau (on his appointment as Joffre's Chief of Staff), would go for a walk in the Forest of Chantilly, hands clasped behind his back, his left leg dragging a little. On reaching one particular bench, they would sit down; Castelnau meditating, Joffre dozing. Later in the afternoon, Joffre would receive visitors; at 1700 hours, the Major-General reappeared with the afternoon's orders; 1900 hours, dinner, and immediately afterwards the Generalissimo retired to bed. He slept the sound, guileless sleep of a child and, like Montgomery, gave strict orders that on no account, repeat *on no account*, was he to be disturbed. Joffre loathed the telephone because it was the one thing that could upset the rhythm of his work; even at the crisis of the Marne he had refused to have the President put through to him. Day and night Joffre's tranquillity was guarded over by two watch-dog orderly officers. One was the devoted Thouzelier, or as he was usually called by Joffre, *'sacré Tou-Tou'*; on the old man's fall from grace, the only one of his staff to follow him into exile. In a crisis, Joffre would sit in 'Tou-Tou's' room, astride a chair, while the two officers telephoned orders. The only sign he ever gave that things were bad was the ritualistic screwing and unscrewing of the cap of his fountain pen. Thus, for over two fateful years, were conducted the affairs of the greatest army in France's history.

In his memoirs, Field Marshal Alexander complains that throughout his service as a fighting soldier in the First War 'no commander above my Brigade Commander ever visited my front line.' Joffre was no exception to this rule, and on his rare visits to the forward areas, about the closest combatants below the rank of Corps Commander came to him was in a march past or a decoration parade. He could not bear to have his tranquillity upset by confrontation with the actual horrors of war. This was the second characteristic which he and Haig had in common; Haig, his son tells us, 'felt that it was his duty to refrain from visiting the casualty clearing stations because these visits made him physically ill.' After pinning the *Médaille Militaire* on a blinded soldier, Joffre said: 'I mustn't be shown any more such spectacles. ... I would no longer have the courage to give the order to attack.' It was in fact about the only emotion of this kind that he is recorded to have shown. In all his lengthy memoirs there is not one mention of the human element, not one word about the dreadful suffering of his soldiers. Like a peasant keeping account of his sacks of grain, Joffre in 1914 kept a little notebook in which he entered ammunition reserves still remaining. But it would have been better for France if he had also made accurate entries of the lives expended. As it was, so many First War generals, overwhelmed by the size of the forces suddenly placed under their command, tended to regard casualties as merely figures on a Quartermaster's return; and in Joffre, the engineer, the technician, this dismal characteristic was particularly accentuated.

To an excitable, impressionable race like the French, Joffre's greatest contribution, however, undoubtedly was this unusual degree of sangfroid. The Kaiser once predicted that 'the side with the better nerves will win,' and one French soldier summed up the feelings of the rest when he scribbled in his dairy that here was a leader whom 'not even the worst situations would disconcert ... this is what we did not have in 1870.' By not losing his head when his Plan XVII disintegrated about him, Joffre saved France. At the Marne, whereas the impetuous Foch might have attacked a day too early and the cautious Pétain a day too late, the unflurried Joffre (pushed by the inspired Galliéni) timed it correctly. But this great asset of Joffre's also concealed terrible dangers. His power of deep sleep had created a legend throughout the nation that 'if things were going badly he would not sleep.' It was a legend that often blinded both the nation, as well as Joffre himself, to just how bad things were. His confidence in himself was enormous and indestructible; in 1912 he had predicted 'there will be a war and I shall win it;' even in November 1914 he had turned down the first project to issue steel helmets, declaring 'we shall not have the time to make them, for I shall twist the Boche's neck before two months are up.' Worst of all, this confidence, this fat man's complacent optimism, was taken up and reflected back by the sycophantic *Grand Quartier Général*.

Through his long absence in the colonies, Joffre suffered from the same disadvantage as Auchinleck of the Indian Army when commanding in the Western Desert. Appointed to the supreme command, Joffre had insufficient knowledge of his officers' records to judge the good from the bad in the French Army, but when war had unmasked the inadequate he had acted with great ruthlessness. By the time of the Marne, two out of five Army

Commanders, ten out of twenty Corps Commanders, and forty-two out of seventy-four Divisional Commanders had been sacked or sent to Limoges; whence came a new word in the French language – *limoger*. Yet, when it came to pruning out de Grandmaison's satraps from the G.Q.G., he somehow seemed powerless. Perhaps the G.Q.G. was too strong for him, perhaps his own indifferent intellect found it more comfortable to be surrounded by mediocrities. And this he certainly was; the G.Q.G. could be blamed for many of Joffre's worst disasters, and the hostility it provoked in the country largely contributed to Joffre's eventual downfall.

Isolated in its palace at Chantilly, G.Q.G. lived amid an atmosphere of back-stabbing intrigue reminiscent of the court of Louis XV at Versailles. With the ambitious jockeying for position on every side, the different branches were distrustful of liaising too closely with one another. Each became a little moated castle on its own. The rare witty sally of Asquith's about the War Office keeping three sets of figures, 'one to mislead the public, another to mislead the Cabinet, and the third to mislead itself' applied with even greater force to G.Q.G. The *Deuxième Bureau* had a curious mathematical formula for computing enemy losses, based on some marvellous racial equation whereby it was assumed that if two Frenchmen had fallen then three casualties had been suffered by the Germans. It was, alas, nearly always the other way about. Deceived by the *Deuxième Bureau*, the *Troisième* planned its operations totally divorced from the realities of war beyond the ivory tower of Chantilly. The G.Q.G. also maintained its own vast propaganda system, designed to deceive the outside world and thus perpetuate its own existence. Perhaps most typical of all the G.Q.G. personalities was the liaison officer to President Poincaré, General Pénélon, aptly nicknamed 'April Smiles,' who could transmogrify the direct catastrophe into a triumph. Partially discredited and reduced in power, after 1914, the Government found it practically impossible to intervene in the mighty, sealed brotherhood that was the G.Q.G.

To sum up on Joffre, it might be said that the war was very nearly lost with him, but that it would almost certainly have been lost without him.

*

With the exception of the first gas attack at Ypres in April –
where the Germans came near to a breakthrough – 1915 saw
them on the defensive in France, attacking ferociously in
Russia. Meanwhile Joffre and the G.Q.G. pursued the simple-
minded, but murderously wasteful, strategy of what he called
'*grignotage*', or nibbling-away at the enemy; which has also
been described as 'trying to bite through a steel door with badly-
fitting false teeth'. A series of major battles took place, each
one aimed at a breakthrough, at forcing the Germans into the
open again. (In his optimism, Joffre was here reinforced by
Haig, who told Repington of *The Times* at the beginning of the
year that when sufficient shells were accumulated 'we could
walk through the German lines at several places'.) But all the
time the Germans just dug themselves a little deeper into the
hard chalk. The first attack was conducted by Foch with
eighteen divisions in Artois, in May; its only success was scored
by Pétain's XXXIII Corps, which advanced a bare two miles –
but the reserves were not there to follow it up. After the French
had lost 102,500, more than twice as many as the defenders, the
offensive was abandoned. In September, Joffre tried again. Now
he had the added excuse of coming to the rescue of the Russians, who had been dreadfully mauled by the Hindenburg-
Ludendorff offensives in the East. Joffre's September effort was
altogether more ambitious, with the French attacking both in
Artois and the Champagne and the British making their first
major effort of the war at Loos. A heavier bombardment
preceded the attacks, but so long in advance that all possibility
of surprise vanished. Whereas in Artois in the spring there had
been just one German line, in the Champagne the French penetrated the first only to be mown down from a second that had
been rapidly dug on the reverse slopes during the warning
bombardment. This time even Pétain failed, and about all his
corps had to show was the capture of one cemetery. In the
Champagne, Castelnau persisted in attacking, believing wrongly
that a breakthrough had been achieved, long after all hope had
evaporated. The casualty lists were larger than ever; 242,000 to
141,000, of which the British lost 50,380 to the Germans' 20,000
at Loos.

Each battle had failed largely due to the lack of heavy guns
and ammunition of all sizes. At Arras, Pétain had been limited

to 400 shells on a twelve-mile front, and, to make things worse, over a period of six months hastily manufactured shells burst 600 guns, killing many of their crews. The 75s barely scraped the surface of the German dug-outs, so that time and again the attacking French were mown down as they left the trenches by a solitary untouched machine gun. An officer who later fought at Verdun described one such typical occurrence in the autumn Artois offensive:

Three hundred men of our regiment lay there in sublime order. At the first whistling of bullets, the officers had cried 'Line up!' and all went to their death as in a parade.

Still in the de Grandmaison spirit, officers declined to make themselves inconspicuous by carrying a rifle; instead they led the way brandishing their canes and were picked off by the hundred. The attacks assumed a drearily stereotyped pattern. First came the preliminary bombardment and the agonizing wait in the front-lines; then the attack, with perhaps a fortunate few, generally very few, reaching the first German trenches to bayonet the survivors there; a brief pause, then the enemy's deadly barrage on their own captured positions, followed by the inevitable counter-attack; finally, the attackers, too few to hold their ground, driven back to their own trenches, decimated relics of the original force; the remaining three-quarters to nine-tenths dead, or dying with their bowels hooked on the wire of No-Man's-Land, knowing that unlike Gravelotte in 1870 there would be no truce to collect the wounded, and hoping only to attract the merciful attention of an enemy machine-gunner. Thus ended 1915, in a complete and bloody stalemate. France had by now lost fifty per cent of her regular officers, killed or disabled, and her dead already approached the total Britain was to lose in the whole of the war. And the only thing it had proved was that this was no way to win a war.

3 Falkenhayn

The World bloodily-minded,
   The Church dead or polluted,
The blind leading the blinded,
   And the deaf dragging the muted.
ISRAEL ZANGWILL, *1916*

. . . the celebrated tale of the man who gave the powder to the bear. He mixed the powder with the greatest care, making sure that not only the ingredients but the proportions were absolutely correct. He rolled it up in a large paper spill, and was about to blow it down the bear's throat. *But the bear blew first* –
WINSTON S. CHURCHILL, *The Second World War.*

Nineteen hundred and fifteen was the least successful year of the whole War for Allied arms; never again would the prospects seem so bright for the Central Powers as at its close. The costly failures in the West had been matched by worse disasters in the East. Realizing that there was no danger of a breakthrough in France, the Germans had been able to concentrate on pushing the pathetically ill-equipped Russians back across Poland, inflicting losses that would have sealed the fate of most European powers. By September Hindenburg and Ludendorff had captured 750,000 prisoners and come close to enveloping the main Russian army. Gallipoli, so brilliantly daring in conception, where, like many another undertaking of the First War, success seemed at times balanced on a razor's edge, had passed into the hands of receivers. Courageous Serbia, the nation over which the war had ostensibly begun, had finally been submerged; her gallant old king forced to flee over the Albanian mountains in a bullock cart. Nervously sheltering behind the anti-submarine nets, Jellicoe's formidable array of *Dreadnoughts* had won none of the sparkling naval victories that the British public and her Allies had expected. Instead, Scarborough and Hartlepool had been bombarded with impunity by Tirpitz's battle-cruisers, and there appeared to be no solution to the mounting submarine menace. The sinking in May of the *Lusitania* had stirred America, but had not persuaded her to join hands with the Allies. Even in East Africa, the elusive von Lettow-Vorbeck and his handful of *Askaris* continued to pin down ten times as many Empire troops. Nowhere could the Allies find consolation.

As '*L'Année Stérile*' drew to a close, both sides began to shape their plans for 1916. On 6 December Joffre held a historic conference of the Allied commanders at his H.Q. in Chantilly. It was the first attempt yet made by either side to coordinate war policy, and it was very much Joffre's conference. Not until catastrophe brought in Foch in 1918 was there to be a supra-natural commander like Eisenhower, but at the end of 1915 Joffre came closest to it. Of the men who had led Europe's armies into the war, Moltke had been replaced by Falkenhayn after the Marne; Grand Duke Nikolai Nikolaievich had been sacked and General Sir John French was about to be. Joffre alone remained, his dominion surer than ever; moreover, France was still bearing the greatest burden of the Allies. Under the influence of Joffre, the Allied representatives agreed that the only hope of a decisive rupture was for all-out offensives to be launched simultaneously in both East and West, accompanied by an Italian attack on the Austrians. With the perennial optimists of G.Q.G. at his elbow, Joffre spoke of the 'brilliant tactical results' of the Champagne and Artois offensives. Their failure was facilely explained away, while the G.Q.G. mathematicians declared that Germany was running out of reserves. For the Western end of the concerted offensives, it was agreed that 1915 should be repeated, but this time on a far bigger scale, with the British and French efforts linked, astride the River Somme. The plan was a simple and unimaginative one, which appealed to the mind of Haig, the new British commander. As the plan evolved in subsequent talks between Haig and Joffre, the French would attack with forty divisions on a twenty-five-mile front south of the Somme, the British with some twenty-five along the fifteen miles to the north. This time there was to be no question of the 'Big Push' going off at half-cock; they would wait until there was an abundance of heavy guns, and the ammunition for them, and until the new 'Kitchener Army' was quite ready. They would wait until the summer. *But the bear blew first.* ...

●

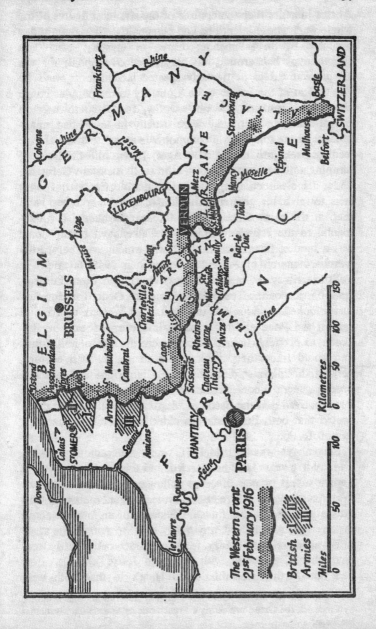

The Western Front 21st February 1916

British Armies

At this juncture there enters one of the strangest figures of the whole war, whose intentions and personality still remain today obscured by an astonishing degree of mystery. Erich von Falkenhayn's background was hardly unconventional, nor was his pre-war career particularly spectacular. In most ways he was typical of the Junker caste. Contrary to the popular image abroad, the Junkers were not wealthy, feudal landowners on a vast scale; in fact, they were usually impoverished small-holders whose sole asset in common was an aristocratic lineage leading back into the Middle Ages. It was the hardship of scraping a living from the poor, sandy soil of eastern Germany, under its bleak climate, that traditionally orientated Junker sons towards the greater attraction of a military career, and that, at the same time, fostered the spartan habits so funda-mental to the Prussian Army. The Falkenhayn family home was a modest farmhouse near Thorn, which, even before the westward march of Poland's frontiers in 1945, lay deep in Polish territory. In medieval days, Thorn had been the prin-cipal bastion of the Teutonic Knights, the Order that for cen-turies looked upon itself as the bulwark of Western civilization against the Poles and other barbaric eastern tribes. The Fal-kenhayns proudly claimed descent from the Teutonic Knights, and could trace their origins back to the twelfth century. Among the many soldiers the family had produced, one had been a general under Frederick the Great and had won the *Pour le Mérite*[1] at the Battle of Liegnitz. Thus it was not unex-pected that both Erich and his elder brother chose the army as a profession.

Falkenhayn was born in 1861, nearly a decade after Joffre. Twenty-five years later he married, and this is about all that is known of his private life. The following year he entered the War Academy. Both here and in his subsequent career his most sympathetic biographer finds no evidence of an intellect above the average; nor, indeed, any 'lively urge' to pursue the study of advanced military theory. It was a characteristic that Falken-hayn shared, evidently, with Haig and Joffre; and his career had one further resemblance to Haig's in that both were

1. The *Pour le Mérite*, Germany's highest decoration, was instituted by Frederick the Great, preferring a French title as he despised his mother language.

average officers whose later rise to the summit was greatly facilitated by the patronage of their Sovereign. At the age of thirty-two, Falkenhayn became a captain on the General Staff, and three years later, in 1896, he was posted to the German Military Mission to China. Before it had started work, the Mission collapsed under protest from the Russians, who were alarmed at the possible consequences of any militarization of the rickety Manchu regime. Falkenhayn, already in China, was given instead the post of chief instructor at Hankow Military School. After less than two years, however, he resigned – complaining that he had been able to achieve little, because of the extreme age of his pupils. Meanwhile, the Boxer Rebellion had broken out, and Falkenhayn (now a Major) found himself appointed by von Waldersee, the commander of the International Relief Force, to the provisional government in Tientsin. Here he displayed considerable efficiency, and some ruthlessness, in restoring order to the chaotic situation; it was he who demolished part of the ancient, sacred city wall of Peking to improve communications.

It was about this period that Falkenhayn's perceptive reports from China first caught the eye of the Kaiser. In 1902, he returned from the Far East to command – at the already advanced age of forty-one – a battalion of line infantry. In 1906 he was appointed Chief of Staff to the 16th Army Corps at Metz. General von Prittwitz, the Corps Commander, was an incompetent, panicky officer, whose command of the German forces in East Prussia in the first days of the war very nearly brought total disaster. Falkenhayn quickly saw his chance and allowed the work of the corps to centre more and more around his own person, cutting out his senior. Outsiders were left in no doubt as to von Prittwitz's dependence on his Chief of Staff, and it was Falkenhayn's mastery of the situation during summer manoeuvres that made its final, decisive mark on the Kaiser. From then on, Falkenhayn's rise was meteoric. By 1911 he, a line officer, had achieved what was as improbable in the German as in the British army of that day; the command of a Guards regiment. The following year saw him promoted Major-General, again a Chief-of-Staff, and again at odds with his superior. In 1913 he was on the verge of applying for a transfer, when the news came that he had been put

up another rank and appointed Minister of War. Nobody
(with the possible exception of his brother officers) was more
surprised than Falkenhayn. Finally, with the fall of Moltke in
September 1914, the ultimate plum fell into Falkenhayn's lap.
He was then a mere fifty-three.

Even more astonishing than the way in which the new Chief
of the General Staff had leap-frogged so many more senior
generals was the fact that for several months he still retained
his old post. By modern democratic standards this was as
extraordinary as if Alanbrooke had combined the offices of
C.I.G.S. and Minister of War, as well as most of the functions
of Minister of Defence. In his dual capacity, Falkenhayn had
far greater powers for the prosecution of the war than any
Allied leader, and his planning could encompass a wider arena
than just the conduct of war by land. At the same time, he
assumed this great responsibility with an experience of command and actual battle conditions even more remote than
Joffre's.

On first seeing a portrait of Falkenhayn, one's immediate reaction is: 'this is a typical Prussian general.' The hair is close-
cropped, the nose well-bred, the features vigorous and stern.
The eyes have that Prussian turn-down at the corners – a
suggestion that in some far-off age there was an infusion of
fierce blood from the Steppes into the Teuton stock. They flash
with hard intelligence, and imply a capacity for ruthlessness
and possibly cruelty. But when one comes to the mouth, partly
concealed under the aggressive military moustache, the whole
picture changes. It is not the mouth of a determined leader,
a man of action, but that of an indecisive, introversive man of
thought, and the sensitive, dimpled chin confirms the implications of weakness.

Here lies the vital key to Falkenhayn's character. The ruthless streak was there all right; before the war in Parliament he
had stood up strongly for duelling, as essential to the 'honour
of the army'; it was he who sanctioned the first use of gas at
Ypres, advocated unrestricted submarine warfare and promis-
cuous bombing in reprisal for Allied air raids. He had a true
Junker's contempt for the Press and the 'masses', and was
even less moved by casualty lists than either Haig or Joffre.
He drove himself and his staff with similar ruthlessness, and

his capacity for work seemed limitless; if anything, he erred by taking too much on his shoulders and trying to be in too many places at the same time. His strategic appreciations were often brilliant, and to Falkenhayn is due almost all the credit for bringing Germany out of the nadir of the disaster on the Marne to the high peak where her fortunes rested at the end of 1915.

Yet his ruthlessness lacked the tenacious purpose of a Ludendorff; too often indecision and excessive prudence turned his successes into only half-successes. When the surprise of the gas cloud at Ypres had torn a great hole in the British line, Falkenhayn was not prepared to risk a follow-up. When Ludendorff was on the verge of inflicting a greater defeat even than Tannenberg on the Russians, Falkenhayn thought the offensive too ambitious and nervously called it off. Temporary neutralization was achieved, instead of annihilation. Caution and indecision dictated his refusal of an early Austrian design for a tank and of a Turkish offer to send some of their magnificent troops to the Western Front, where they might well have provided the decisive reserves he lacked. He never took full advantage of Germany's one great asset; the ability to switch troops rapidly from East to West, thereby gaining a temporary superiority. His principle was to be secure simultaneously at all points, and in this, as Liddell Hart has aptly remarked 'his actions and his mental attitude were those of a Commander striving to ward off impending defeat rather than one whose mighty army had only missed decisive victory by a hair's breadth.' Even the disgraced Moltke had perceived the flaws in Falkenhayn's character, writing to the Kaiser in January 1915 that his successor presented 'a serious danger for the Fatherland ... despite an apparently strong will ... does not possess the inner forces of spirit and soul to draft and carry through operations of great scope. ...' But by then the Kaiser was totally under the Falkenhayn spell, and all Moltke received for his trouble was the coldest of Imperial rebuffs. Finally, in the eyes of Colonel Bauer, one of his ablest staff officers (though, admittedly, a disciple of his rival, Ludendorff, and writing *ex post facto*), Falkenhayn was 'all in all an unusual personality who would have made a brilliant statesman, diplomat, or parliamentarian, but least of all a general.'

Falkenhayn was what today would be known as a cold fish. Joffre may have been inarticulate, Haig too, and Pétain *repoussant* and imperious to his entourage, but we feel we know something about them as human beings. About Falkenhayn we know absolutely nothing. One of his biographers dubbed him 'The Lonely General', but his was a loneliness deliberately nurtured. He had no intimates, no confidantes, no coterie, and none of the popular appeal of Hindenburg and Ludendorff, so that when at last his potent influence over the Kaiser began to wane, he was finished. He guarded his thoughts like the Golden Fleece, repelling would-be Argonauts with a devastating, cold sarcasm. Supporting him in the role of Sleepless Dragon was the obstinate, slow-thinking Colonel Tappen, Head of Operations, whose biting tongue matched that of his superior, and of whom a colleague wrote 'seldom was an officer so hated by his subordinates as he.' Even Falkenhayn's war memoirs are written in a coldly impersonal third person, and from this aloof, almost inhuman reserve stemmed the mystery as to just what his intentions really were in attacking Verdun. One salient characteristic of Falkenhayn, indecisiveness, was to bring heart-breaking tragedy to both France and Germany at Verdun; the other, an almost pathological secretiveness that was a by-product of his withdrawn personality, would later play a vital part in the final defeat of his hopes there and go far to losing the war for the Central Powers.

Early in December 1915, Falkenhayn sat down to compose a lengthy memorandum to his Kaiser. It began with an impressive appreciation of the state of the war:

France has been weakened almost to the limits of endurance. .... The Russian armies have not been completely overthrown, but their offensive powers have been so shattered that she can never revive in anything like her old strength.

The reason the war continued at all, Falkenhayn deduced, was simply because of 'the enormous hold which England still has on her allies'. And here he singled out the arch-enemy – Britain. 'The history of the English wars against the Netherlands, Spain, France, and Napoleon is being repeated. Germany can expect no mercy. ...' Nor could she afford to maintain her defensive posture against Britain:

Our enemies, thanks to their superiority in men and material, are increasing their resources much more than we are. If that process continues a moment must come when the balance of numbers itself will deprive Germany of all remaining hope.

But how to strike at this deadly foe? The British homeland itself was beyond the reach of German troops. Victories in Mesopotamia, or even on the Suez Canal, would not prove mortal; while defeats might be disastrous to German prestige among her allies. On the Continent, Falkenhayn ruled out one after another the alternatives for decisive offensive; Flanders, because of 'the state of the ground'; south of Flanders, because it would require about thirty divisions, which – he claimed – would drain all other fronts of reserves 'to the last man'. Therefore there was nowhere a crippling blow could be struck directly at Britain. It was 'certainly distressing'.

But, argued Falkenhayn with some ingenuity, 'it can be endured if we realize that for England the campaign on the Continent of Europe with her own troops is at bottom a side-show. Her real weapons here are the French, Russian, and Italian Armies.' If these could be knocked out, Falkenhayn felt this might spell the end of Britain's 'lust for destruction'; but, before suggesting how, he first touched on the one weapon that *could* strike directly at Britain. 'The definite promises of the naval authorities that the unrestricted submarine war must force England to yield in the course of the year 1916' should be pursued to the limit. Even if this should bring the United States into the war, it would be too late.

Discussing, then, how to deal with 'England's tool on the Continent', Falkenhayn began by contemptuously dismissing Italy, whom his brother-in-arms, Austria-Hungary's Conrad von Hötzendorf, was itching to dispatch once and for all. Besides, Austrian troops were too badly needed on the Russian front. Turning to Russia, he estimated that 'even if we cannot perhaps expect a revolution in the grand style, we are entitled to believe that Russia's internal troubles will compel her to give in within 'a relatively short period.' With a good sense that might have benefited Hitler, Falkenhayn commented: 'an advance on Moscow takes us nowhere.' The Ukraine was the only worthwhile Russian objective, and this acquisition might bring Rumania in on the Allied side. Then, said the cautious general, communications towards the Ukraine were inadequate, and anyway there were not enough reserves for either operation. Russia would have to be left to stew in her own revolutionary juice.

Here one meets with the most controversial of all the arguments on German World War strategy. As in Britain, Germany had her 'Westerners' and her 'Easterners', equally ardent for their respective causes. By the end of 1915, Falkenhayn had become a 'Westerner'; whereas Hindenburg and Ludendorff and their supporters, backed by the disciples of Schlieffen who believed that to win Germany must concentrate overwhelmingly on one front at a time, saw Russia as the most promising place to exert the superiority with which Germany would enter 1916. After the war the 'Easterners' received vindication from Allied strategists ranging from Liddell Hart to Winston Churchill; in the words of the latter, 'one-half the effort, one-quarter the sacrifice, lavished vainly in the attack on Verdun would have overcome the difficulty of the defective communications in "the rich lands of the Ukraine".' Russia might have been knocked out of the war a year earlier; even if she staggered on, with the wheat and raw materials of the Ukraine tucked beneath their belt, the Central Powers could have prolonged the fight undismayed by the Royal Navy's blockade. But, fortunately for the Allies, it was Falkenhayn, not Ludendorff, who held the reins in 1916.

Falkenhayn's lengthy memorandum comes at last to the point:

There remains only France. . . . If we succeeded in opening the eyes of her people to the fact that in a military sense they have nothing more to hope for, that breaking point would be reached and England's best sword knocked out of her hand. To achieve that object the uncertain method of a mass breakthrough, in any case beyond our means, is unnecessary. We can probably do enough for our purposes with limited resources. Within our reach behind the French sector of the Western front there are objectives for the retention of which the French General Staff would be compelled to throw in every man they have. If they do so *the forces of France will bleed to death* [1] – as there can be no question of a voluntary withdrawal – whether we reach our goal or not. If they do not do

1. My italics.

so, and we reach our objectives, the moral effect on France will be enormous. For an operation limited to a narrow front, Germany will not be compelled to spend herself so completely. . . .

The objectives of which I am speaking now are Belfort and Verdun. The considerations urged above apply to both, yet the preference must be given to Verdun.

Falkenhayn terminated by giving a rather unconvincing explanation for this 'preference', in that a potential French offensive out of Verdun could constitute a grave menace to the whole German front; although not even the most half-witted planner at G.Q.G. had ever envisaged concentrating for an attack in a three-quarters encircled salient, where every inch could be raked by German gunfire.

Falkenhayn's memorandum made military history. Never through the ages had any great commander or strategist proposed to vanquish an enemy by gradually bleeding him to death. The macabreness, the unpleasantness of its very imagery could only have emerged from, and was symptomatic of, that Great War, where, in their callousness, leaders could regard human lives as mere corpuscles. Whether this unique strategy was right is for events to show.

Somewhere between 15 and 22 December, Falkenhayn, accompanied by the faithful Tappen, was received by the Kaiser at Potsdam. The lack of precision about the date of one of the most significant decisions of the war is typical of the mystery surrounding Falkenhayn. In the Kaiser's memoirs, there is a curious absence of any mention of either Falkenhayn or Verdun, and Tappen remained as uncommunicative as his master, but it is probable the interview took place on the 20th. As to its course, one can only surmise. After the retreat from the Marne, the Supreme Warlord – to the surprise, and probable satisfaction, of his General Staff – had interfered less and less in the conduct of the war. Murmuring (so it was alleged) as the holocaust spread, 'I never wanted this,' he had retreated into a dream-world of optimistic illusion, busying himself with irrelevancies. When at his Western operational H.Q. at Charleville-Mézières, his day was leisurely, consisting of chatting with, and decorating, heroes from the front, and taking frequent walks around nearby Sedan, where he liked to ruminate over the simpler glories of the past. In the evenings, at dinner, members of his staff were detailed off to feed him with the 'trench anecdotes' he so delighted in. Highly coloured, these anecdotes had to glorify feats of Teutonic heroism and demonstrate the ridiculousness of the enemy. To the more proximate realities of war the Kaiser closed his mind, and even the favourite, Falkenhayn, was not safe from reproof when he attempted to dissipate those rosy Hohenzollern illusions that had been the despair of poor Moltke. Increasingly Tappen and he became accustomed to doling out only selected titbits.

At the Potsdam meeting, one can visualize Falkenhayn, to break the ice, relating the latest 'trench anecdote' (though privately he despised them); the Supreme Warlord, astride the saddle-stool that gave him a much-needed sense of command even at his desk, his eyes glowing with approbation as Falkenhayn enlarged upon the memorandum. For Falkenhayn was not court favourite for nothing; experience had shown him just how to wrap up his parcel in paper pleasing to the Kaiser's eye. The long preamble about 'England, the arch-enemy' was highly, and deliberately, exaggerated; in 1915–16, Britain's relative power in the coalition was in fact obviously far less than in 1939–40. France was still very much the dominant partner. But Falkenhayn knew his Kaiser; knew of his antipathy to his English mother, of how he blamed the English 'quack' for the death of his adored father, of the real or imaginary slights suffered from debonair Uncle Edward, of how the Royal Navy had seemed to thwart his peacetime plans at every turn. By making it seem that he would be striking a blow against Britain, Falkenhayn was sure of a sympathetic hearing. Furthermore, by selecting Verdun instead of Belfort, his project was sure of assent for reasons near and dear to the Kaiser. For the army that would lead the victorious assault must inevitably be that of his own son, the Crown Prince, who had been battering against the walls of Verdun ever since September 1914. That very month the first signs of hardship and war-weariness had manifested themselves in Germany. None of it was yet very serious; nevertheless, the Social Democrats were growing increasingly troublesome, and domestic reasons alone made it attractive to win a dynastic triumph – especially if, as his Chief of the General Staff promised, it would be such a cheap one.

On the return journey from Berlin, Falkenhayn's train was boarded at Montmedy (about an hour's distance from General Headquarters at Mézières) by a General Schmidt von Knobelsdorf. While the Crown Prince was the nominal commander of the Fifth Army, it was Knobelsdorf, his Chief of Staff, who (in the German Army way of things) made the decisions. It was also Knobelsdorf who, it appears, had originally put the idea of an attack on Verdun in Falkenhayn's mind, but now for the first time he learned that it was to comprise Germany's main effort for 1916. When he passed on the news to the Crown Prince, the latter was ecstatic – but with qualifications (though one is entitled to wonder to what extent these emerged *ex post facto* in his memoirs):

My long-suppressed eagerness to lead my tried and trusted troops once more to battle against the enemy was now to be gratified. I was filled with happy anticipations; yet I could not regard the future with a confidence altogether serene. I was disquieted by the constantly repeated expression used by the Chief of the General Staff that the French Army must be 'bled white' at Verdun, and by a doubt as to whether the fortress could, after all, be taken by such means.

On the day after Falkenhayn's return, Christmas Eve, a flood of telegrams began, disguised under the foreboding code name of *'Gericht'*; meaning a tribunal, or judgement, or – more rarely – an execution place. Compared with Allied preparations for the Somme, things moved with astonishing speed. The first of the new army corps earmarked for the attack was transported in greatest secrecy from Valenciennes, and its commander, General von Zwehl, had arrived in his new headquarters by 27 December. By 27 January (the date was selected for auspicious reasons, it being the Kaiser's birthday), the final orders were published, and the attack scheduled to go in on 12 February.

In discussions that took place between Falkenhayn and the Fifth Army from 24 December to 27 January, two vital points of discord emerge. Firstly, Knobelsdorf and the Crown Prince wanted to attack simultaneously on both banks of the Meuse. But Falkenhayn insisted that he did not have the forces to spare; repeating again and again that at least one-third of the total available German reserves must be kept in hand to meet the relief counter-offensives the Allies were certain to launch on other parts of the line. The attack would have to be limited to the Right, or Eastern, Bank, and involve a modest enough outlay of only nine divisions. The cautious Falkenhayn's fears of Allied counter-attacks were by no means shared by other German leaders, perhaps in a better position to judge. On 7 January, General von Kuhl, the Chief of Staff of the Sixth Army which faced Haig, was summoned to Berlin, told of the forthcoming offensive, and warned of the certainty of an impromptu British riposte north of Arras. Falkenhayn added, generously, that after the repulse of this attack, a counter-offensive could be made in mid February for which eight divisions would be available. Von Kuhl replied in almost so many words that Falkenhayn's appreciation was nonsense, pointing (correctly) to the complete unpreparedness of the new Kitchener armies. On 11 February, the day before the curtain was due to go up at Verdun, Falkenhayn saw von Kuhl again and repeated that he hoped the expected Allied ripostes, when repulsed, would 'bring movement into the war once again'. When this was relayed to the Commander of the Sixth Army, Crown Prince Rupprecht of Bavaria, he commented that 'General von Falkenhayn was himself not clear as to what he really wanted, and was waiting for a stroke of luck that would lead to a favourable solution.' Such was the confusion Falkenhayn created about his own intentions.

The second point of discord in the German plan, perhaps its most curious feature of all, was what the shrewdest German critic on Verdun, Hermann Wendt, describes as its 'two conflicting components'. In his directives to the Fifth Army, Falkenhayn spoke only of 'an offensive in the Meuse area in the direction of Verdun'. But the Crown Prince in his Army Orders set forth the objective as being 'to capture the fortress of Verdun by precipitate methods'. When questioned by Herr Wendt years later as to whether Falkenhayn really intended to take Verdun in February 1916, Tappen replied emphatically that 'the seizure of Verdun was never represented as the real aim of the offensive, but it was the destruction of the French forces that we had to find there. If in the process Verdun fell into our hands, so much the better.' And this tallied completely with the famous memorandum – while the Fifth Army's design for a *Blitzkrieg* victory at Verdun ran quite contrary to any gradual, 'bleeding-white' process. Once France had lost Verdun, the carrot to lure the French Army into the abattoir would have been removed; the deadly salient itself where the actual bleeding was to take place would have been excised by the Fifth Army's advance.

Neither the Crown Prince nor Knobelsdorf had actually seen the original memorandum, yet, one asks at once, why did Falkenhayn approve the Fifth Army's plans which differed so much from his own? The answer, it seems, was: MORALE. The cold mind of Falkenhayn apparently calculated that troops would fight better if they went in believing that their objective was to seize France's strongest fortress, rather than knowing that they were only embarking on another long-drawn-out battle of attrition. (Even von Knobelsdorf later asserted that, had he originally known what Falkenhayn's true intentions were, he would never have supported them.) Meanwhile, to make quite certain the Fifth Army did conform to his will, Falkenhayn, while promising the Crown Prince that adequate reserves would be available, ensured that in fact they remained firmly under his control and *not* under the Fifth Army's. Two divisions, allegedly because of accommodation shortage, were kept two days' march away, and a further two in Belgium; none would be close enough to intervene in the battle at the crucial moment. Thus, as Wendt remarks, the supply of these vital reserves was used by Falkenhayn as a 'lever', the manipulation of which, and with what fateful consequences, will shortly be seen.

Seldom in the history of war can the commander of a great army have been so cynically deceived as was the German Crown Prince by Falkenhayn.

4   Operation Gericht

The highest form of generalship is to baulk the enemy's plans;
the next best is to prevent the junction of the enemy's forces;
the next in order is to attack the enemy's army in the field; the
worst policy of all is to besiege walled cities.... In war, the
way to avoid what is strong is to strike at what is weak –
SUN TZU (500 BC), *The Art of War*

The German national genius for organization had never shown
itself to better advantage. To supplement the roads across the
boggy Woevre that the French, in a rare piece of pre-war foresight, had left as poor as possible, the Fifth Army now built ten
new railway lines and some two dozen new stations. Seven spur
lines were established in the Forest of Spincourt alone, to provision the heavy guns that would be concealed there. Whole
train-loads of steam-rollers and road-building equipment were
shipped in. Day and night the little petrol locomotives chugged
forward on the sixty-centimetre railways to the front, pulling
long trains loaded with supplies for the pioneers. For one corps
alone, the quartermaster's list included 6,000 wire-cutters, 17,000
spades, 125,000 hand grenades, a million sandbags, 265,000 kilo-
grammes of barbed wire, etc., etc. Entire villages behind the
front were evacuated to make room for the 140,000 men
assembling for the attack. The few remaining French inhabitants watched in helpless horror at the endless lines of men
and material, at the great guns bringing death towards their
own people. Occasionally they found comfort in sallies of
Gallic humour as the stubby-barrelled mortars passed by;
whispering 'ours are longer'.

It was the artillery that absorbed the maximum German
effort. The whole German plan was based on the thesis that
their heavy guns would literally blast a deep hole in the French
lines, which the infantry would then occupy; with only slight
casualties, it was hoped. As successive French reinforcements
moved into the Verdun salient to stem the attack, they in their
turn would be ground to pieces by the devastating barrages. The

concentration of guns and ammunition represented the peak of the German arms programme launched in 1914; nothing like it had ever been seen in war before. Falkenhayn's lavishness in this respect certainly went far towards banishing any doubts lingering in the Crown Prince's mind as to whether he meant business or not. The area of attack itself would receive the attention of 306 field pieces and 542 heavies, supported by some 152 powerful mine-throwers. Additional artillery massed on the flanks brought the grand total to over 1,220; and all for an assault frontage of barely eight miles.

Day and night the great cannon flowed in, from as far away as Russia and the Balkans. In order of size there were the mighty 420-millimetre mortars, the 'Big Berthas' or 'Gamma Guns' – thirteen of them – evil instruments, looking like monstrous Guinness bottles. With a calibre of seventeen inches, and firing a shell standing nearly as high as a man and weighing over a ton, they were the biggest guns ever used in the First War. In order to transport them, the 'Big Berthas' broke down into 172 pieces, requiring twelve wagons, and took twenty hours to get into action. When they were fired, the concussion broke the windows of houses for two miles around. They were Herr Krupp's first great contribution to the war effort, and had been Germany's 'secret weapon' of 1914. With a roaring descent as noisy, prolonged, and demoralizing as a Stuka, the huge shells had shattered the allegedly impregnable forts at Liège, and the Germans hoped they would do the same at Verdun.

Then came two long-barrelled 380 mm. (15-inch) naval guns (also by Krupp) with immensely long range, tucked away safely in the Bois de Wapremont, well behind the front. There were seventeen stocky Austrian 305 mm. mortars, or 'Beta Guns', and there were masses of the quick-firing, easily transportable 210s, that for the French '*poilu*' were to become the most familiar and most feared weapon at Verdun. Next came the long 150s, the future nightmare of French artillerymen and supply troops, with their eternal probing and seemingly limitless range. There were the hated 130 mm. 'whizzbangs', whose flat trajectory gave you no time at all to duck, that preyed on unwary troops making for the latrines, or enjoying a game of cards behind the lines; and, in sharp contrast but equally disfavoured, there were the mine-throwers – crude instruments, throwing canisters

filled with over 100 lb. of explosive, as well as often being
packed with bits of alarm clocks to enhance their nastiness. You
could see them coming, tumbling slowly over and over in the
air; though it seldom did you much good as their gigantic blast
levelled whole sections of trench. At the bottom of the scale
came the 77 mm. field guns that could lay down a barrage
among attacking troops nearly – but not quite – as lethal as
the famous French 75s; and the light-infantry weapons, semi-
automatic 'revolver-cannons' and 'pom-poms'. Finally, there
was a new instrument of horror that was to make its debut at
Verdun: the flame-thrower.

Each class of gun had its own carefully appointed task. The
mighty Gamma and Beta mortars, hidden behind the hills of
Romagne and Morimont, with their superb observation points,
were to concentrate on the forts. One of the 380 mm. naval
guns was to drop a steady forty shells a day on Verdun itself;
the other to interrupt communications far away on the left
bank of the Meuse. The 210s – one battery to every 150 yards
of trench – were to pulverize the French first line. When that
was taken, they would lift and 'box off' the intermediary areas
with an impenetrable *cordon sanitaire* to stop French reinforcements coming up to counter-attack. Any strong-points that
somehow withstood the mortars would be administered the
coup-de-grâce by the close-in mine-throwers. As soon as the
attack succeeded, the lighter guns would first move up into new
prepared positions, covered by the heavies behind, which, in
their turn would move forward as soon as the light batteries
were ready to give covering fire. On D-Day, recognized French
battery positions would be deluged with gas by the howitzers
and field artillery, while special batteries of 150s stood by to
eliminate any new guns that might appear in the course of the
battle. Meanwhile, other long-range 150s would be constantly
raking all roads and tracks leading up to the front. 'No line is
to remain unbombarded,' ran the German gunners' orders, 'no
possibilities of supply unmolested, nowhere should the enemy
feel himself safe.' To supply this fearful bombardment, six days'
ammunition had been stocked near the guns. This added up to
2,500,000 shells, the transportation of which had required
some 1,300 munition trains. Yet, despite the appalling road
conditions, Major-General Beeg, G.O.C. Artillery to the Fifth

Army, could report on 1 February that the last of the twelve hundred guns was in position, on schedule – even though the supreme effort had cost him thirty per cent of his horses. In the woods ringing Verdun there was hardly room for a man to walk between the massed cannon and ammunition dumps.

No tiny detail was overlooked in the meticulous German plans; up in the front line emplacements were already being dug for the heavy howitzers to move into once the French first line had been taken; artillery telephone lines were spooled up in readiness to be run forward to overrun positions. There were special liaison troops equipped with large red balloons, to show the artillery just where the attacking infantry had reached in the dense woods.

Only more remarkable than the speed of the German preparations was their secrecy; here the influence of Falkenhayn had played its part. The rest of the German Army was kept in the dark about *'Gericht'* until the very last moment. Liaison officers from other armies were banned from the Fifth Army front, and even Colonel Bauer, Falkenhayn's chief artillery adviser, was not shown the plans until it was already too late for him to alter the artillery programme. Down at the far south of the line, General Gaede was allowed to go blithely ahead with preparations for 'Operation Black Forest,' an attack on Belfort that Falkenhayn had had no intention of consummating. To add weight to the deception, the Crown Prince made a well-publicized trip to Army Group Gaede, ostentatiously shaking hands with Swiss frontier guards. Elaborate diversionary bombardments were planned for several other sectors, and, when it was no longer possible to conceal that something was afoot at Verdun, German agents in various neutral countries spread rumours that this was only a feint, while the big attack would come elsewhere. Even nurses arriving at the vast new hospitals set up behind Verdun were told that they were simply 'for the treatment of internal illnesses'. To what extent the enemy were taken in by all this will be shown shortly; meanwhile Germany's ally, Austria, was hardly better informed – an astonishing error of diplomacy on the part of Falkenhayn that was to have its repercussions.

In their attempts to conceal the mammoth activities going on behind Verdun, the Germans were greatly helped by the broken

and heavily wooded country of the Meuse foothills, as well as
by the mists that so often hung there in winter. (Indeed, the
decision to attack from the covered North-eastern approaches
instead of along the perhaps more tempting Eastern axis, out of
the exposed Woevre, had been dictated almost exclusively by
the need for concealment.) What Nature supplied, German ingenuity supplemented. Franz Marc, the artist, was among those
set to work painting camouflage nets and canvases to cover the
guns. Where there were no trees, these were draped across all
roads, like great fishing nets hung out to dry. The installation
of the twelve-hundred cannon was accomplished with considerable finesse; when crews had reconnoitred positions, gun pits
were dug at night and immediately camouflaged; then the ammunition came up and finally when all was ready, the tell-tale
cannon themselves. Before the attack, only long-established
guns, that were assumed to be already pin-pointed on French
artillery charts, were permitted to reply to enemy fire.

But by far the most effective contribution to secrecy was the
great concrete *Stollen*, or underground galleries, hastily burrowed out all along the attack zone. In the futile offensives of
1915, the vital element of surprise had been lost each time by
the cramming of assault troops into the forward trenches, so
easily visible to a vigilant enemy. Not only had this at once
given the game away, but almost invariably led to hideous casualties from the counter-bombardment. The Allied generals never
learnt, but the Germans did, and at Verdun the assaulting infantry were housed in these capacious, shell-proof *Stollen*, some
of which could hold half a battalion of men, well out of sight
of French eyes. On D-Day, the infantrymen emerging from the
Stollen would have to cover not fifty, but often as much as
1,000 yards of No-Man's-Land. It was a calculated risk based
on the assumption that most of the French 75s would have
been knocked out by the German bombardment; and it was a
technique that was to be used against the British in March
1918 with even greater success.

Over all this terrestrial activity watched the first air umbrella
the world had ever seen. Up to 1916, the infant air weapon on
both sides had confined itself largely to single, gladiatorial
combats between heroic young men flying flimsy and primitive
aircraft. A start had been made on photographic reconnais-

sance (though viewed with gravest suspicion by the Army Staffs) and there had of course been the Zeppelin raids. But that was about all. Now, at Verdun, history was to be made in the air. For the first time aircraft were used *en masse* in support of ground tactics. Before the attack on Verdun, the Germans mustered there the main weight of their air strength – 168 planes, plus fourteen captive balloons and four Zeppelins. A huge force by First War standards, it was to provide a dawn to dusk 'aerial barrage' which would, in theory, prevent any French aircraft from spying out the German preparations as completely as the ground barrage was later to 'box off' French reinforcements. Once the attack had begun, the German 'aerial barrage' was to protect the vital observation balloons, the eyes of the artillery, from French aircraft. The days of the gladiators were numbered and the Battle of Britain a step closer.

*

Behind the city of Verdun lay a long and quite distinguished history in which, among the deities, Mars had had an unusually large interest. Even in Roman times, *Virodunum* was already an important fortified camp, and considered worth burning by Attila. In 843 the Treaty of Verdun was signed there by the three quarrelling heirs of Charlemagne; it divided Europe between them, and gave birth to Germany as a nation – hence part of the eternal mystique Verdun held for Teutonic minds. Although in theory the Treaty made Verdun part of France, in 923 it fell under German suzerainty where it remained until 'liberated' by Henri II in 1552. Just over a hundred years later Vauban confirmed France's title by turning Verdun into the most imposing fortress in his cordon protecting France. Besieged in the Thirty Years' War, the experience was repeated regularly once a century, up to 1916. In 1792 Verdun held out against Prussian guns until its commander, Beaurepaire, committed suicide, rather than surrender (or, as another version has it, was murdered by less patriotic burghers); in 1870, it was the last of the great French fortresses to fall, surviving Sedan, Metz, and Strasbourg. Thus on both sides there was plenty of symbolic and sentimental material on which to draw.

At the opening of 1916 Verdun was a sleepy, duller-than-average French provincial town, unassumingly modest about its noble past and strangely insouciant about the future. It was proud of its sugared almonds (they had replaced the rather less *bourgeois* trade in eunuchs, the city's principal commerce up to the seventeenth century); but not so proud of a climate that must be one of the rainiest, foggiest, and nastiest in all France. Considering that since September 1914 the enemy had been less than ten miles from the city gates, life in Verdun seemed remarkably little altered from pre-war days. The place was full of troops, but this was nothing new to the Verdunois, as it had always been a garrison town. The proximity of war and the spasmodic bombardments had reduced the population from somewhere under 15,000 to about 3,000. But those that remained had adapted themselves well, and had seldom had it so good.

From October 1914 until February 1916 the sector had been one of the quietest on the whole front. For Verdun was reputedly unassailable, the strongest fortress on earth, the Gibraltar-cum-Singapore of the First War. Its reputation had been thoroughly put to the test during the Battle of the Marne. The Crown Prince's Army had all but encircled the fortress, and Joffre – ever mindful of the fate of Bazaine, locked up in Metz with his huge useless army in 1870 – actually ordered its abandon. Fortunately the commander of the French Third Army, Sarrail, disregarded the order. Verdun stood like a rock against the Crown Prince's repeated assaults, forming a vital anchor and pivot for the whole left wing of the French Army falling back on Paris. Had it in fact been abandoned, Joffre's front would have been cut in two, the Miracle of the Marne could never have taken place, Paris – and probably the war – would have been lost. In 1914 the importance of Verdun was as simple as that.

After the Marne, the Germans had been forced to withdraw slightly on either side of the fortress, but surged back again to establish a bridgehead across the Meuse at St Mihiel, embarrassingly close to Verdun and severing one of its major railway links. Through 1915 new attempts had been made to cut off Verdun by thrusting into the salient on both flanks, at Vauquois in the Argonne and Les Éparges, culminating in some particularly savage mine warfare. By 1916, the front around

Verdun still formed a bulge like a large and vulnerable hernia.

On the ground, Verdun's defences looked dreadfully impressive. Surrounding it on all sides were the steep Meuse hills whose unusual concentric pattern itself formed an immense natural fort, with a radius of five to ten miles, the Keep at the centre of the fort being Verdun itself. In the vital north-east sector of the Right Bank there were four natural lines of defence along the ridges. Many of these were formed like the glacis of a fort, sloping gently away towards the enemy, but with steep reverse slopes, so that defenders could lie in wait in these relatively protected ravines, then move up to sweep an enemy advancing up the long glacis with withering fire. Forces trying to progress along the meandering Meuse valley would find themselves caught in enfilading fire first from the one side, then from the other, from the ridges that protruded, interlocking and overlapping, into the river bends. Little resemblance here to the featureless, open country of Flanders and the Champagne.

Moreover, the crest of each important hill or ridge in this great natural stronghold was itself studded with powerful forts, the outstanding feature of Verdun's defences and the derivative of General de Rivière's post-1870 line of fortifications. On the German 1914 maps alone, no less than twenty major and forty intermediary forts (or *'ouvrages'* as the French called them) were shown. The Right Bank forts lay roughly in an outer and two inner rings; the first containing Moulainville, Vaux, and Douaumont; the next, Tavannes and Souville, and the innermost ring, on the heights overlooking Verdun, Belrupt, St Michel, and Belleville. On the left bank there were two similar lines, but the most important was the outer one comprising five forts along the Bois Bourrus ridge, which lay interlocking with the Douaumont and Souville lines across the river. To the south of Verdun, but unconcerned in the great approaching battle, were still further clusters of forts. Of all, the most powerful, and indeed, the cornerstone, was Douaumont; which, from its 1,200-foot elevation, dominated the terrain at every point of the compass like a scaled-down Monte Cassino.

From the time of Vauban, French engineers have led the world in the ingenuity of their fortifications, and Verdun was no exception. Each fort was so sited that its guns could dislodge any enemy appearing on the glacis of its neighbour. The guns themselves, sometimes either a heavy 155 mm. or twin short-barrelled 75s, were housed under heavy steel carapaces in re-tractable turrets, and were invulnerable to all but a direct hit from the heaviest artillery. They were supplemented by equally well protected machine-gun turrets and ingeniously placed block-houses containing flanking guns that could repel an attack on the fort from any direction. The bigger forts con-tained a company of infantry or more underground, and the more modern were armoured with reinforced concrete up to eight feet deep under a thick layer of earth. They were in fact like ranks of immobile, but apparently indestructible tanks, or a flotilla of unsinkable monitors. Furthermore, as the battle had receded in 1914, the outer line of the forts had been left with a protective cordon of trenches in the foothills between them and the Germans, two or three miles deep; which the French had had a relatively undisturbed fifteen months to make as impreg-nable as might be.

In theory Verdun in 1916 should have been the strongest point of the whole Allied line. Yet, in practice, it was one of the weakest. Why?

In 1914 the ease with which the secret German 420s had shattered the legendary Belgian forts, and – worse still – had forced the surrender of France's own Manonviller, her biggest and most modern, had come as a terrible shock to the French High Command. At G.Q.G., the Grandmaisonites – ignoring Sarrail's success at Verdun – rapidly exploited these disasters to their own advantage (no doubt partly to re-establish their reputation tarnished by the Battle of the Frontiers). Forts are nothing but shell traps, they averred, and so we have always maintained; quite out of keeping with French offensive spirit. The French soldier's place was *en rase campagne*, if absolutely necessary in a trench, but certainly not hiding under a pile of concrete. And what had happened to Bazaine and MacMahon in the vaunted fortresses of Metz and Sedan during the last war? When the Allied 1915 spring offensives failed, owing to lack of artillery, G.Q.G. had rummaged through all its arsenals for every available gun. But why not tap the vast resources of cannon installed in all those useless fortresses at Verdun, sug-gested some bright disciple of de Grandmaison?

In July, General Dubail, commanding the Group of Armies East, in whose sector Verdun lay, told a visiting Army Commission delegation that, of course, G.Q.G. was quite right. The actual Governor of Verdun, General Coutanceau, disagreed and was promptly sacked for his temerity. The following month his successor, an elderly gunner called Herr, was instructed by Dubail (acting on direct orders from Joffre) that 'strongholds, destined to be invested, have no longer a role to play'. Verdun itself 'must *under no circumstances* be defended for itself, and the General commanding there must at *no price* allow himself to be invested there'. Meanwhile, to meet the needs of the forthcoming Champagne offensive, the Verdun forts were stripped of their guns; notably those in the flanking block-houses, and in fact virtually all but the cannon immovably fixed in the revolving turrets. By October the equivalent of forty-three heavy (plus 128,000 rounds) and eleven field-gun batteries had been removed. At a stroke the whole defence system of France's mightiest strongpoint was transformed; it was, in the words of one French military historian, 'an imprudence difficult to qualify'.

Meanwhile, General Herr, under orders from a High Command contemptuous of the fortresses on the Right Bank, began to prepare a line of defence on the Left Bank, i.e. *behind* Verdun. No sooner, however, had he asked the Corps Commander *in situ* for a defence plan than the corps was moved to the Champagne, and right up to February 1916 the unfortunate Herr was plagued by a shortage of hands, through forces being constantly withdrawn to feed other fronts. By 10 February, two days before the German attack was due to begin, the French were still preoccupied with works on the Left Bank; yet, towards the end of January as the German threat began to filter through to G.Q.G.'s consciousness, Herr's limited forces were called upon, in addition, to work on communications to Verdun and positions on the Right Bank. 'Everything had been started, and nothing finished.'

Not only were the numbers for the job grossly lacking, but the spirit was too. In contrast to both the British and the Germans, the French soldier has never been renowned for digging-in'. Then, the troops available to Herr were also either weary from the Champagne offensives, looking forward to a 'cushy'

life on a quiet front, or else 'old sweats' who had been too long
in the calm of Verdun to see any point in getting their hands
blistered for the whims of some new general. A visiting officer,
querying a soldier about the lack of communication trenches up
to the front line – those vital, life-saving arteries – was told: 'It
doesn't matter. One can pass very easily, the Germans don't
shoot.' The rot of the 'phony war' at Verdun had apparently
spread to high levels; 'In the Verdun zone of battle there was
not a communication trench, not one underground telephone
line, no barbed wire. But huge entanglements had been placed
around the ramparts of the city itself ... for the benefit of
visitors.' It was indeed *'un terrain à catastrophe'*; such was the
immediate reaction on taking up his command of General
Chrétien, the man whose corps was to bear the brunt of the
German onslaught a few weeks later.

General Herr, perhaps a little too mild-mannered and ineffectual, cannot be absolved for the lethargy of those under his
command, but he at least was alert to Verdun's terrible weakness. Repeatedly he pleaded in vain for reinforcements to carry
out the essential works. The poor man's despair is reflected in
his remark to an aide of Pétain in the autumn of 1915: 'Every
day I tremble; if I were attacked I could not hold; I've told the
G.Q.G., and they refuse to listen to me.' And later, to Galliéni,
the Minister of Defence: 'What was most terrible for me, was
the Young Turks of G.Q.G. At every demand I addressed them
for reinforcements in artillery, they replied with the *withdrawal*
of two batteries or two and a half batteries; "you will not be
attacked. Verdun is not the point of the attack. The German's
don't know that Verdun has been disarmed."'

So G.Q.G. remained blind to the danger threatening Verdun
and deaf to Herr's appeals, until quite unexpectedly Joffre's
Olympian calm was shaken by a mere lieutenant-colonel.

Émile Driant, however, was no ordinary colonel. Early in his
army career (at the time of Verdun he was over sixty), he had
been A.D.C. to General Boulanger, subsequently marrying his
daughter. A brilliant soldier, he had published several books on
war, including one called *La Guerre de Forteresse*, but, probably on account of his political connexions more than any other
reason, he found himself passed over for promotion in five
consecutive years. He finally decided to resign from the army,

and became Deputy for a constituency close to Verdun. During the pre-war years he had repeatedly attacked the weaknesses in the French Army, and the German manoeuvres he attended in 1906 so alarmed him that he wrote an article for *'L'Éclair'*, predicting 'we would be beaten as in 1870, but even more completely than in 1870 ...' In 1914 he at once rejoined his old unit, the *Chasseurs-à-pied*, as a reserve officer. He was attached to the staff of the Verdun garrison, but, despite his age, requested an active command and was given two battalions of Chasseurs.[1] After the Marne, his Chasseurs, the 56th and 59th, had been given the task of clearing the Bois des Caures to the north-east of Verdun, and there they had remained ever since.

The Bois des Caures was a wood about two miles long and half a mile wide, running north-east to south-west atop a small but dominant rise. In 1916 it comprised the centre of the Verdun first line on the Right Bank, and lay right across the axis of any direct German assault on the fortress. Thus Driant found himself entrusted with the defence of a key position of the first importance.

Like most of his rapid-marching, hard-fighting *Chasseurs*, Driant was a smallish man, but his fiercely aquiline, mustachioed face (a sub-specie of the race that by 1918 seemed to have become virtually extinct) radiated will-power. In a letter of January 1915, Driant declared the Germans 'will not make one further step forward; they will never penetrate to Verdun, even if they bring up all their 420s.' By July, obviously uneasy, he was complaining to his Brigade Commander that he would be unable to carry out the works ordered, while at the same time adequately manning the front line. On 22 August he was writing to his friend Paul Deschanel, President of the Chamber of Deputies, predicting:

The sledge-hammer blow will be delivered on the line Verdun–Nancy. What moral effect would be created by the capture of one of these cities! ... we are doing everything, day and night, to make our front inviolable ... but there is one thing about which

1. In both the French and German armies units tended to be commanded by lower ranks than in the British forces; thus a Battalion Commander is usually a Major (or *Commandant*), while a Regiment would be commanded by a Colonel, but more often in practice by a Lieutenant-Colonel.

one can do nothing; *the shortage of hands*. And it is to this that
I beg you to call the attention of the Minister (of Defence). If our
first line is carried by a massive attack, our second line is inadequate
and we are not succeeding in establishing it; *lack of workers* and
I add: *lack of barbed wire*.

The contents of Driant's letter reached the Minister of Defence (now Galliéni, the saviour of Paris, who had no high
opinion of Joffre), and in December a delegation of the Army
Commission was sent to Verdun. On its return it confirmed to
Galliéni all Driant had said. Galliéni passed the report to Joffre,
asking for his comment. The intervention threw Joffre into one
of his rare rages, and his reply, as Liddell Hart acidly remarked,
'might well be framed and hung up in all the bureaux of official-
dom the world over – to serve as the mummy at the feast.'

I cannot be a party [said Joffre] to soldiers under my command
bringing before the Government, by channels other than the hier-
archic channel, complaints or protests concerning the execution of
my orders ... It is calculated to disturb profoundly the spirit of
discipline in the Army ... To sum up, I consider nothing justifies
the fear which, in the name of the Government, you express in
your dispatch of 16 December. ...

Probably only Driant's heroic death saved him from the
ignominy of a court martial, securing for him instead immort-
ality among the French martyrs.

If Joffre, right up to the eleventh hour, persisted in his blind-
ness to Verdun's peril, it was partly because French intelligence
was able to offer little help in penetrating Falkenhayn's web of
secrecy. Unfortunately for the *Deuxième Bureau*, it seems that
just before Verdun the Germans had succeeded in breaking up
an important spy network, operated behind the lines by a courageous Frenchwoman, Louise de Bettignies. Over sixty agents
had vanished overnight, and a complete silence had descended.
In despair, and some humiliation, the French had been forced
to apply to the British for information, but it was not till late
in January that Royal Navy Intelligence was able to glean some
definite information from the indiscreet talk of a high German
official at a Berlin cocktail party. At Verdun itself, collation of
intelligence was equally ineffective. Few patrols were sent out
(the suspense of lying in wait in No-Man's-Land was in any

case about as alien to the French temperament as digging-in); instead, for intelligence at lower levels, the French depended largely on their not very reliable listening posts, that were occasionally able to pick up fragments of conversation from the enemy's crude trench telephone system.

Until 17 January, bad weather had virtually ruled out any aerial photography of the German lines. There were in fact three reconnaissance *escadrilles* in Verdun; but, alas, there was not one single officer on Herr's staff who could analyse air photographs. (Nor was any expert provided until four days before the actual attack, when – though perhaps a little late in the day – he was able to predict the exact location of the main thrust.) On 17 January, a French plane that was twice intercepted by Fokkers of the German 'barrage' and had its camera smashed, nevertheless brought back some revealing shots of German guns behind the Côte de Romagne. Six days later a full scale reconnaissance penetrated again to the Romagne area, but neglected to photograph the huge gun concentrations in the nearby Forest of Spincourt. Half-hearted as the French reconnaissance efforts were, they proved that the German 'aerial barrage' was not watertight. If the French aerial reconnaissance failed, it did so more owing to a combination of bad weather, the artillery bombardment of their airfields, and pure lethargy. Up to the time of the German attack, only seventy gun emplacements had been identified from the air, thus the French were never aware of the full extent of the artillery confronting them. What the reconnaissance planes did record, however, was the absence of any new 'jumping-off' trenches in the front line; and this, as indeed the Germans had hoped it would, entirely persuaded G.Q.G. that no attack could be imminent.

For all the shortcomings of French intelligence, evidence of the preparations for *Gericht* was piling up daily. Some of the first rumours percolating to the nervous French had been rather wild; the Germans were building, it was whispered, a long tunnel fourteen metres wide beneath the French lines south of Verdun, to enable them to attack from the rear. Then the deserters, many of them Alsatians, began to creep over in ever-increasing numbers – always a sign of an impending 'push'. With them they brought Herr details of the secret *Stollen*, the purpose of which he immediately comprehended. (But no, re-

plied G.Q.G., doubtless these are purely defensive installations.)
Early in January, observers noticed that church spires behind
the German lines, useful reference points for French counter-
battery fire, were disappearing. On the 12th, Herr's *Deuxième
Bureau* reported that the German artillery had begun 'ranging';
the 14th brought news of the establishment of new hospitals,
and the 15th disquieting details of heavy troop transports passing through Longwy. As February came, deserters told of all
leave being cancelled and voiced fears that 'something terrible'
was about to happen.

In Paris, the Army Commisson appeared less concerned at
the threat to Verdun than at the outrage to the capital perpe-
trated by a Zeppelin attack on 29 January (to the extent of
forcing the Under-Secretary of Air to resign); up to a few days
before the attack Joffre could still assure Haig that it was Russia
the Germans were planning to attack; while G.Q.G. maintained
that if there were an offensive in France the main blow could
be expected to fall in either Artois or the Champagne. But
alarm was in the air. A flood of visitors descended on the
harassed Herr. On 24 January, Joffre's right-hand man, de
Castelnau, arrived to dictate that all work be switched to com-
pleting the first and second lines on the Right Bank, and to
creating a new intermediary line between the two. Even President Poincaré, clad in his usual incongruous chauffeur's cap
and leggings, was there inspecting the front from a special little
rail car drawn by two mules. Finally the great Joffre himself
appeared; but by far the most important arrival of all was the
reinforcements Herr had been clamouring for over the past
six months. Time was running out fast. The two additional divisions were in fact only placed at Herr's disposal on 12 February
– the very day the Crown Prince's guns were due to begin their
dreadful work.

Across this strip of pleasant French countryside a few miles
long, over 850 German guns – including some of the heaviest
ever used in land-warfare – faced a motley collection totalling
270, most of them short of ammunition; seventy-two battalions
of *élite*, tough storm troops faced thirty-four battalions in half-
completed positions. Of the German assault troops, on the extreme right wing on the Meuse lay VII Reserve Corps; next to
it, between Flabas and Ville, XVIII Corps, and on its left III

Corps. Waiting in the wings were V Reserve and XV Corps. Facing this formidable array was simply General Chrétien's XXX Corps, described by one contemporary observer as 'composed of bric-à-brac', with – reading from the Meuse eastward – the 72nd Division, the 51st, and the 14th (which was to play only a minor role in the battle), with the 37th moving up in reserve.

All was ready. Had the attack gone in on schedule the French at Verdun would have been caught in the midst of moving house and a hideous disaster must have ensued. As it was, at the eleventh hour there occurred one of those rare miracles that alter the destinies of nations. In this case, it undoubtedly saved Verdun, and possibly France herself.

5   The Waiting Machine

> But the god of the weather suddenly took it into his head to derange all our plans – CROWN PRINCE WILLIAM, *My War Experiences*

> *La guerre, mon vieux, tu sais bien ce que c'était.*
> *Mais quand nous serons morts, qui donc l'aura jamais su?*
> JACQUES MEYER

During the night of 11 to 12 February, French troops of the forward line at Verdun were ordered to stand-to in the first serious alert to be proclaimed. This was no false alarm. From his headquarters at Stenay-sur-Meuse the Crown Prince had issued on the 11th, for publication on the morrow, a proclamation which began: 'After a long period of stubborn defence, the orders of His Majesty, our Emperor and King, call us to the attack!' But as the morning of the 12th dawned, weary French outposts gazed out on an opaque white landscape. It was snowing hard, and through the thick mist and blizzard one could barely perceive the enemy front-lines. Over the whole front an uncanny silence prevailed; no suspicious noises, no unusual movements. Grumbling a little at their lost night's sleep, the French troops resumed their normal positions. Their officers sighed with relief. On the other side of the lines, several hundred pairs of German eyes peering through artillery range-finders noted that 'less than a thousand metres away everything disappears into a blue-grey nothing.' Further back, generals anxiously studied the barometer; finally, at Stenay, the Crown Prince decided that both his proclamation and the offensive would have to be postponed twenty-four hours. If the all-important guns could not see, the battle could not proceed.

All the waiting German storm-troops heard of the postponement was when orders decreeing 'interior duties' were pinned up in the *Stollen*. On the day of the 13th, a second alert turned out the French, but once again they were stood-down on the morrow as the snow continued and the weather grew even colder. The notice of the previous day reappeared in the German *Stollen*, which the wags re-interpreted down the line as 'in case of bad weather the battle will take place indoors.' Day after day the same entries were noted down in unit diaries: 'snow again ... snow thaws, but fog ... rain and gales ... still rain and gales. Another day's respite ... rain and gales. Not a sound of a cannon ... wind and snow squalls ... misty and cold.' In its devotion to *la Patrie*, the perverse climate of Verdun could scarcely have shown more zeal.

By 1916 the infantryman had become, in the words of one of the great French war novelists, simply a 'waiting machine'. To this latest, most unnerving waiting game, daily extended, the opposing forces settled down in their different ways. A few keen young French officers tried to get their men to work on the dilapidated defences, but in the hard ground little could be achieved but the further exhaustion of already fed-up troops. For the most part the *poilus*, huddled in their oversize greatcoats, resorted to the time-honoured techniques for mitigating trench boredom. Some continued months'-old work on delicately engraved bangles; bracelets for a wife made from the copper driving band of a shell; a ring for a fiancée made from the aluminium of its fuse-cap, perhaps inset with the button off a German tunic; or a pen-cap for a child, made out of a spent rifle cartridge. Despite the crippling weight of his other kit, on his way to the front the *poilu* craftsman somehow always found room for his metal vice; his trinkets were capable of indefinite elaboration, often terminated only by a sniper's bullet. Some gambled away their paltry *sous* of pay in endless games of *piquet*. In the Bois des Caures, a lieutenant of the *Chasseurs* toyed exultantly with a new trench mortar he had invented. Others stepped up the tempo of rat-hunting, simply as a means of keeping warm. Anything to silence the deadly question of WHEN?

To the taut nerves of the German storm-troops the protracted wait was even more painful. The *Stollen* had simply been intended as temporary shelter, and there was not sleeping accommodation in them for more than a fraction of their inmates. The remainder had to march as much as seven miles back to their billets each night through the snow and freezing sleet. The *Stollen* themselves revealed one important omission in the all-impressive attention to detail of the German plan; under the foul weather they rapidly filled with water and there was a critical shortage of pumps. So the *élite* German infantry often spent their days in baling out the *Stollen*, knee-deep in icy water. Day by day they subsisted on a monotonously unhealthy fare of chocolate and canned food, drawn from their emergency rations. Wild rumours preyed on their nerves; a French spy dropped by parachute had been caught near Billy; reports that a French officer in German uniform was spying out the forward position gave rise to an order to arrest any 'suspicious-looking officers'. Far away to the North, Crown Prince Rupprecht wrote in his diary on 14 February – 'with any further delay there will not be much left of the intended surprise' – and his fear was shared by every man in the *Stollen*. After yet another postponement a priest, serving as an infantry subaltern, wondered 'Is this Gethsemane we are undergoing?' The Germans, *knowing* to what they were committed, found it harder than their opponents to gain distraction. Even the more fortunate, surfeited with writing letters home, could find only temporary refuge in nostalgic, homely thoughts; some prayed with an unwonted, desperate earnest; others indulged, for probably the first time, in tormented thoughts about the senselessness of war. Each day the number of cases of acute stomach trouble mounted; whether owing to nerves or to the foul conditions in the frozen trenches and *Stollen* is not revealed. It was hardly the best way of keeping shock-troops in peak fighting trim.

The French soldier of 1916 bore hardly a resemblance to the insouciant neophytes in their red pantaloons that had marched to war behind the regimental music in 1914. The *képi* had been replaced (despite Joffre's optimism) by the more practical steel helmet; in which, for once, the French were ahead of the Germans. Gone were the deadly pantaloons and gone was the pre-war-spit-and-polish, even among units normally as proud of their *chic* as the Chasseurs. A new uniform, the *horizon bleu*, was slowly being issued (it was a compromise; though still not as well camouflaged as the British khaki or the German *Feldgrau*, after a few days in the mud of the trenches it blended with surroundings as well as any other. And in its pristine state, as British troops relieved by French units frequently noted, the sight of the *horizon bleu* was a tremendous morale-booster to stained and jaded troops in the line.) But it was still not widespread; in the Bois des Caures the Chasseurs continued to wear a motley of tattered sheepskins and tunics so patched as to be no longer identifiable as anything military. Despite their outward dilapidation, in the manner of veterans of the trenches, they never omitted to put a cork in the muzzle of their rifles or to keep a handkerchief around the bolt.

Veterans they were, on both sides. After the initial losses had been made up, the front line soldiers were now comprised, in more or less equal parts, of survivors of twenty-five or thirty years old already wounded and repaired once or more times, of reservists in their forties, and boys of the new intakes of eighteen or twenty. Heavy unkempt beards (hence the ill-favoured nickname, *poilu*) gave these last the appearance of ageless veterans.

Most Europeans alive today can conjure up some picture of existence in the trenches, but even to those who actually experienced it the intervening years have mercifully softened the full memory of its miseries. Modern imagination quails at the thought of human beings living month after month like rodents below the earth, usually in several inches of water, frequently a foot deep; never completely dry, never free of the evil-smelling mud, and free from lice only for brief periods following a spell out of the line. Dugouts were shared with huge rats that – like bloated profiteers – seemed to be the only creatures that actually thrived on war. They scurried across the faces of men asleep, gnawing food from their packs, and gorged themselves on the flesh of the unburied. But apart from this last, there was little enough to distinguish between the existences of the two species. To the French *poilu*, next to the arrival of letters and rations, the greatest pleasure life held was the hole burrowed laboriously in the side of the trench during quiet moments (this was rigidly banned in the British and German lines). Although one near miss from a shell probably meant being buried alive, to be able to sleep out of the rain, to be relatively dry, were risks well worth taking. Even without the enemy, life in the trenches to a normal, civilized man must have been hell, but on top of it there was the eternal 'wastage' (as the staff so euphemistically described it); the daily casualties to snipers' fire, the men buried by the unexpected mortar blast, the ubiquitous stretcher-bearers carrying the muddy and bloody bundles to the rear, which nobody even glanced at any more.

Whether due to lack of organization or lack of material, or both, things usually seemed to be a little worse in the French trenches, and rather better than average in those occupied by Germans for any length of time. French carelessness about hygiene in the trenches never failed to shock visiting Britons; though, perhaps immunized by the rusticity of their normal peacetime sanitary arrangements, it rarely appeared to disturb the French. Even their squalid life in the trenches could not entirely repress the acute Gallic humour. With some envy, the immense fertility of the louse was noted; one born in the morning, the *poilus* swore, was a grandmother by the evening. The favourite quip on taking over flooded trenches was: 'It'll be all right so long as the U-boats don't torpedo us!'

These things could be put up with; provided, above all, the *pinard* (the rough red wine of the French Army) was good and abundant – and the same with the food. As might be expected, these considerations weighed perhaps more with French soldiers than with those of other nations. Yet so often, and generally through abysmal inefficiency, the catering system broke down. When, in December 1915, G.Q.G.'s propaganda section circularized a report describing in glowing terms how much better fed French troops were than the Germans, and claiming that 'our soldiers have always enjoyed two substantial meals a day,' two hundred thousand enraged letters were received from the front. Each company was supposed to be equipped with a mobile kitchen consisting of a stove and two great pots; but of a batch of three hundred thousand ordered, half were found to be unserviceable when they reached the line. Doubtless some factory owner had made a fat profit out of the Government. When the rations did arrive, with dreadful monotony they consisted of stringy and greasy tinned beef, known as '*singe*' to the troops, inadequately salted cod, or rubbery macaroni; all, as often as not, liberally mixed with mud and dirt.

Even out of the line, the French soldier's life was no sinecure. When he moved up, unacquainted with the luxuries of 'Company Transport' familiar to Western troops of World War II, he moved on his feet, weighed down by kit that made him resemble a deep-sea diver; two blankets rolled up in a groundsheet, a spare pair of boots, a sheepskin or quilted coat, a shovel or pair of heavy wire scissors, a mess tin and a large pail for rations, two litres of *pinard* in a large water bottle, rations for four days, 200 cartridges, 6 hand grenades, and a gasmask, as well as his personal belongings – all crammed into three cumbersome haversacks. On average, the *poilu*'s total burden weighed over eight-five lb. It was hardly surprising that tired soldiers slipping on the slimy paths of the approach route to the front got up 'less easily than a maybug that has fallen on its back'. When bivouacking out of the line, what accommodation existed was promptly occupied by the officers and N.C.O.s, and the other ranks were left to fend for themselves; often having to pay avaricious peasants out of their own miserable five sous a day. Even in the permanent 'Zones of Rest', provision of proper lavatories, showers, and kitchens was appallingly neglected, and – until Pétain's reforms in 1917 – soldiers frequently had to share their beds. The old British Army principle that the officer's first concern should be the welfare of his men seldom seemed to apply.

One of the more curious things about the French Army of the First War is that, although it was the only 'republican' force of the major combatants and – in theory – relationships between ranks ought to have been more democratic than in the other armies, in fact, the dichotomies dividing officers, N.C.O.s, and men were far more pronounced than in either the British or even the Imperial German Army. They were epitomized by the subtly differentiating signs to be found at French railway stations:

> *W.C. pour MM. les officiers*
> *Cabinets pour les sous-officiers*
> *Latrines pour la troupe*

The terrible gaps cut in the French officer corps during the first two years of the war (fifty per cent of the regular cadres) had been filled to a large extent by former Sergeants and *Adjudants* (Sergeant-Majors), and no one clung to their social distinctions more than these new officers. By 1916 the division between officers and men was probably wider than it ever had been. Contact was at a minimum, limited largely to the actual battle itself. Allied observers were often shocked at the way in which French commanders, after a successful attack, left their troops lying out on the destroyed enemy position for days and nights after they should have been relieved. It was an attitude of mind not only confined to the higher ranks. Though the comparison is obviously extreme, in the relationship of French officers to their men in the First World War there is something that reminds one of Lord Cardigan riding back to his yacht after the Charge, without pausing to inquire about the casualties sustained by the Light Brigade. Often it seemed as if French officers felt that, once the action was over, so was their responsibility to the troop. But what officers lacked in personal contact with their men out of the line, they made up with leadership in battle that was composed of selfless example and fantastic gallantry. Their prestige was reinforced by a discipline that struck even Prussian officers as savage. In September 1914 special *Conseils de Guerre* had been established to try men, and officers, accused of dereliction of duty. Death was the sentence usually passed on those found guilty; there was no appeal, and the sentence had to be dispatched within 24 hours. The supreme penalty was frequently awarded for offences that, by modern standards, seem trifling; for lesser offenders, the French Army still abided by the system of 'penal companies', earmarked for carrying out particularly dangerous tasks. When a regiment failed badly, its commander sometimes resorted to 'decimation' – that disgracefully unjust and draconian system – whereby men were selected from each company, often more or less at random, and were shot after a purely ritualistic court martial; *pour encourager les autres*. In 1917, a gross failure of leadership caused the devotion inspired by the French officers' personal bravery to flag for one disastrous moment, and then even this iron discipline could not maintain the cementing bond. But, meanwhile, at the opening of 1916, morale and discipline in the French Army were about as good as they could be.

The neglectfulness of his superiors seemed to dog the unhappy *poilu* even away from the army, on his rare spells of *permission*. No regular leave was instituted until the war was a year old, and even then the *permissionaire* wasted many valuable hours – sometimes days – travelling in crowded trains with broken windows. During his long waits on station platforms, there was nothing like the Y.M.C.A. or the various welfare organizations that cared for the British soldier. Canteens were rare, and anyway he had little enough money to spend in them. Occasionally, through unbelievable bureaucratic muddles over soldiers' passes, there were cases of soldiers not being able to get home to their families; instead, they frittered away their precious leaves in some strange and expensive big city. As compensation for all his miseries and discomforts, there was, finally, for the more fortunate *poilu* the benevolence of his 'godmother'. The *marraines de guerre* began as a scheme for women to adopt an unknown soldier, keeping him supplied with woollen comforters, and had grown into a powerful propaganda instrument. Sometimes frightened soldiers were prompted into action more by fear of their *marraines'* contempt than of their lieutenant's revolver. For the majority, the *marraine* was simply an unseen, unknown Beatrice who wrote her soldier beautiful letters telling him to be brave and die well; the happy minority also sometimes found her willing to share her bed with him on leave. (Once in a while, the admirable system defeated its own purpose; there was the sergeant who collected 44 *marraines*, eventually found that his leaves were never long enough to keep them all contented, and deserted.)

Of all the factors that had contrived to the education of the novices of 1914, obviously none was more fundamental – for both sides – than the sickening effect that the new weapons of the industrial revolution had on the bodies of men. It was bad enough to be wounded at all, but at least a bullet was a relatively clean agent. If you were hit by either a rifle or a machine gun, the chances were that either you were killed outright, or eventually you returned to life more or less in one piece. However, in contrast to World War II, bullet wounds were the minority; the greater part of casualties were caused by the terrible effects of shell-fire. Also, by 1939, the march of civilization had advanced metallurgy to a point where shells and bombs burst into smaller fragments; they killed more men with each burst, but they tended to do so more tidily. In the First War the crude iron of the shells (most of them many times bigger than anything used in the land battles of 1939–45) shattered into huge ragged chunks that sometimes two men would be unable to lift. The effect on the soft human carapace of impact with these whirling fragments may be imagined; Barbusse in *Le Feu*, one of the best French novels of the First World War, describes it in a manner that is not just a piling of horror on horror –

... men squashed, cut in two, or divided from top to bottom, blown into showers by an ordinary shell, bellies turned inside out and scattered anyhow, skulls forced bodily into the chest as if by a blow with a club ...

It was only astonishing how much of such mutilation flesh could suffer and still survive; Duhamel, a war doctor whose writings later brought him election to the Academy, tells of the riddled but living bodies, brought to his clearing station – 'they reminded us of disabled ships letting in water at every seam'. And then there was gas, many of whose victims (those that survived) were reminded of its choking, searing horror on damp winter days every year till they died; an experience mercifully altogether unknown to World War II combatants.

To cope with these mutilations on so massive a scale, medical services were singularly ill-equipped. In this respect – as in many others already mentioned – France in 1914 was notably, and notoriously, behind both Britain and Germany. She remained so throughout the war. Her Medical Service had been prepared in 1914 for a short sharp war, and was hopelessly caught out. Its doctors, inculcated in the de Grandmaison notions of war *en rase campagne* and clean bullet wounds, also reckoned on an 'aseptic' war. Their miscalculation possibly cost France an army corps of men; for, with wounds impregnated by dirt and debris from the explosion of shells, hideous 'gas gangrene' became the single largest mortality factor among the wounded. Almost unheard of in World War II, once it set in it was only curable by prompt and skilful surgery; both usually lacking in the First War.

If a badly injured man survived the brutal jolting in the two-man handcarts used by the French to collect the wounded, the crude attention of over-worked medicos in the clearing stations, and the long bumping about in the ambulances with their solid tyres and unyielding springs, even then his prospects were poor. At the beginning of the war Clemenceau's *L'Homme Libre* had violently denounced the insanitary railway cattle-trucks used to transport the wounded back to base hospital, in which many that had endured so far now contracted fatal tetanus. Though the paper was promptly suppressed by the censors, conditions improved only a little as the war went on. Even at the base hospitals the mortality rate was high. The surgery itself was often as crude as the steel that made it necessary. Over-worked surgeons operating under impossible conditions instantly divided the wounded into three categories; those who would die anyway, and were therefore not worth operating on: those who would probably survive, but would be of no further use to the war effort; and those who could eventually be returned to duty. On this third category, the doctors lavished most of their attention; this was known as the 'conservation of effectives'. The second category was just patched up as well as time would allow. The results were often horrifying; describing them, Duhamel says in one terrible sentence – '*Il y avait Sandrap, qui faisait ses besoins par un trou dans le côté. . . .*'

When the final reckoning on war casualties came to be made, it was hardly surprising that of the three Western Powers France led with easily the highest ratio of deaths to wounded; on top of a total of 895,000 killed in action, another 420,000 had died of their wounds or of sickness.

*

To a sociologist studying human behaviour during the First War one of the most astonishing revelations must be the extent to which the fighting men of all nations adjusted themselves to, and then accepted over so long a duration the mutilations, the indignities, the repeated displays of incompetence by the leaders, and the plain bestiality of life in the trenches. When, in the course of the ensuing battle, one reads of episodes where courage failed, and when one attempts to visualize just what the maintenance of courage might have involved at Verdun, one can only be amazed that these 'failures' did not happen more often, did not become the norm of human behaviour. Could we of the mid twentieth century, one asks oneself, stand one quarter of what the men of the First War had to put up with? Their stoical capacity to endure could undoubtedly be partly explained by the strong leavening of tough, hardy peasants in their ranks (and especially in France, where the strange solitude and emptiness of French villages today still testifies to their terrible losses). But all the men of 1914 had been conditioned under Scott Fitzgerald's 'tremendous sureties and the exact relation that existed between the classes', established by the long years of Victorian solidity and its continental equivalents. They had been brought up to *accept*. Steady convictions and the unquestioning 'theirs not to reason why' that imparted total confidence in the wisdom of superior powers were their inheritance; 'sureties' that were to be erased forever by the First War.

By 1916 'acceptance' was really the operative word. Those who in 1914 had groused about conditions had by now either vanished or submitted. For every individual who tortured himself trying to think out a reason for life under these conditions, there were ten who dumbly, helplessly, and unreflectingly accepted it as it was. In this mute acceptance of conditions there was a certain cynicism about the soldier of 1916, but it was a tough kind of cynicism. He no longer considered himself fighting for such noble symbols as Alsace, Belgium, the *Vaterland*, or rule of the seas. He fought simply out of a helpless sense of habit, to keep going, to keep alive. Eighteen months in the trenches had taken the edge off the fine ideologies of 1914. Nevertheless, it seemed as if the man at the front could continue to accept almost indefinitely. Physically and morally, both the French and the Germans had become toughened to the act of acceptance; as it were, inoculated against the afflictions of war. Cases of pneumonia in the snow-bound trenches were almost unheard of, as were disciplinary lapses requiring a court martial. The troops that faced each other at Verdun represented the peak that the war was to produce. Like steel that has been tempered for just the right length of time, they were hard and tensile, but not yet brittle; no longer the green enthusiasts of 1914, nor yet the battle-weary veterans of 1917–18. Verdun was to be the watershed; beyond it neither army would be quite the same again.

*

After over a week of waiting and alerts, nerves at Verdun were showing perceptible signs of strain. The volatile French had come to regard the enemy's exasperating passivity as all part of a diabolical campaign to wear down the strength of the defenders. On 17 February, there had been a mild morale-booster in the shape of news of a great Russian triumph against the Turks. But Erzerum was far away, and the French had long ago begun to take announcements of 'decisive victories' with the correct amount of salt. Still the bad weather continued. Then, on the 19th, the sun appeared and the mud slowly started to dry out. Joffre made a last visit to Verdun and congratulated Herr on his preparations. The night frost set in. The 20th was a radiant, almost spring-like day. Everyone knew it must be coming soon. At *Grand Quartier Général*, Colonel Renouard, Chief of the *Troisième Bureau*, was heard to remark gleefully: 'What a hornet's nest they will fall upon!' In the Bois des Caures, more realistically, Driant wrote in a last letter to his wife: 'The hour is near ... I feel very calm ... In our wood the front trenches will be taken in the first minutes. ... My poor battalions, spared until now!' And to a friend: 'As for me, I have always had such good fortune that it will not abandon me, and I hope to be writing to you when we have crossed the worst passage.' To encourage the nervous troops, at 1600 hours that afternoon, the French artillery opened up for the first time, with an hour's bombardment. General Herr issued his final orders to his troops, incorporating the formula that was almost standard among French First War Commanders: 'Resist whatever the cost; let yourselves be cut to pieces on the spot rather than fall back.'

Night fell. At Revigny, thirty miles behind Verdun, the vigilant crew of a 75 fired at, and brought down in flames a Zeppelin setting out to raid communications; an unprecedented feat. Meanwhile between the lines a superbly clear, cold moonlight had lit up the tranquil landscape. In the Bois des Caures the Chasseurs stood watch with an affected casualness, hands in pockets, gazing at the mysterious dark shapes of the woods to their front and wondering what would emerge from them on the morrow. Behind them in the shadows there was an occasional cracking of twigs and the murmuring of muffled voices as ration parties brought up the last supplies; otherwise silence. Far off the sleepless Chasseurs could hear the steady rumble of the German trains moving ammunition in the Forest of Spincourt. Closer, over a No-Man's-Land made beautiful by the flattering moonlight that erased the blemishes of war, there came a sound of German soldiers singing.

6   The First Day

Il n'y a que la première gorgée qui coûte.
PAUL CLAUDEL, *Ballade*

When I knew it [war] I passionately loved it. ... I shall not
cease to love it, for all the splendour in which it has clad the
most humble – CAPTAIN LA TOUR DU PIN, *Le Creuset*

Deep in a wood near Loison one of Herr Krupp's naval guns
raised its immense barrel slowly through the camouflage netting. For the tenth time the sleepy crews went through their
drill. They were getting fed up with being tumbled out night
after night in the bitter pre-dawn cold – and all to no purpose.
But today it seemed to be the real thing. Once again the battery
commander lovingly checked the fuse on the shell that stood
nearly as high as himself. There was a ring on the field telephone. The long-awaited order had arrived. The monster projectile was hoisted up and rammed into the breech. The crews
turned their backs to the muzzle, raised their hands to their
ears, and braced themselves as the officer shouted 'FEUER!'

Nearly twenty miles away the shell exploded with an earth-
shaking roar in the courtyard of the Bishop's Palace in Verdun,
knocking a corner off the cathedral. After all the repeated gun
drill of the past days, it was not a good shot; instead of hitting
one of the vital Meuse bridges it merely provided Allied
propaganda with yet another example of German 'frightfulness'. Somewhere in the vast labyrinth of Vauban's Citadel
where once British P.O.W.s had been lodged during the Napoleonic Wars, a bugler sounded a warning to take cover. The
shells began to fall at a steady tempo. Another 380 millimetre
gun firing on Verdun station was rather more successful than
its sister piece; after a few shots the rails of the marshalling
yard were standing in the air like twisted fragments of wire.
Operation 'Execution Place' had begun.

In the Bois des Caures, most of Colonel Driant's Chasseurs
slept on oblivious of what was going on behind them. Some

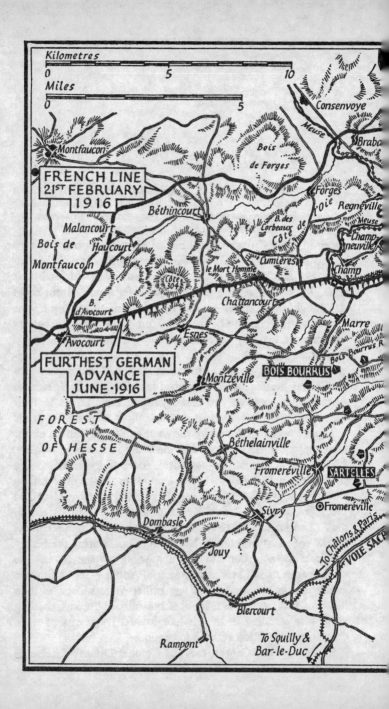

Flabas
Ville
Azannes
Bois le Comte
Bois d'Haumont
Bois de Ville
Gremilly
Haumont
Bois des Caures
B. la Wavrille
B. Herbebois
les Jumelles d'Ornes
Beaumont
Mormont Fm
Côte 344
Bois des Fosses
B. les Chaume
Ornes
Maucourt
Louvemont
Côte du Poivre
la Vauche
Bezonvaux
Vacherauville
Haudromont Quarries
Douaumont
Bezonvaux
B. d' Hardaumont
Lorient
Hardaumont
Bras
Thiaumont
DOUAUMONT
N. D. de Lorette
la Caillette
Vaux
PLAIN OF
Froideterre
Cheminées
Fleury
B. Fumin
VAUX
Damloup
Abaucourt
Damloup Battery
R. des Vignes
Meuse
SOUVILLE
Laufée
WOEVRE
BELLEVILLE
St MICHEL
TAVANNES
Fix
Belleville
Eix
Sta
MOULAINVILLE
VERDUN
Moulainville
Manesel
Regret
Barracks
BELRUPT
FOREST
Chatillon
Belrupt
OF
SOMMEDIEUE
Meuse
Haudainville
ROZELLIER
HAUDAINVILLE

FRONT LINE
26TH FEB. 1916
FRONT LINE
15TH DEC. 1916
Fort   VAUX   Ouvrage ◎   Railway ┼┼┼┼   Roads ✕

three hours later, Corporal Stephane – known as *'Gran'père'* because of his forty-six years – was gently awakening, to the homely sound of a coffee-grinder nearby. With it came the voices of two men arguing in the grumbly, good-natured way of soldiers in the early morning. From *'Gran'père'* Stephane's dugout the day looked much like any other; if anything it promised to be better than the filthy weather one had had during the past few weeks. With all this talk about a German attack, a fine clear day like this might seem a bit ominous; yesterday evening, for the first time in a long while, there had been the unusual, and rather menacing spectacle of a German plane flying between the lines. But there had been these rumours almost non-stop since Christmas, and nothing had yet happened. One could almost believe it was all invented by the staff back in Verdun, just to get a little more work out of the poor sods of *biffins*. Lying between sleep and waking – a pleasurable state, were it not for the numbing cold – Corporal Stephane's thoughts were all of the immediate problems of getting up and the more distant prospects of a leave that was due shortly.

Suddenly, the whole world seemed to disintegrate around him. With the conditioned alacrity of old soldiers, the two men with the coffee-grinder disappeared below ground, cursing in unprintable French 'why couldn't the ...... wait till I had finished my coffee!' The air in the Bois des Caures seemed solid with whirling material. To Corporal Stephane, it was as if it were swept by 'a storm, a hurricane, a tempest growing ever stronger, where it was raining nothing but paving stones.' Upon the terrible din of the explosions were superimposed the splintering crashes of rending wood as the great 210 millimetre shells lopped off branches, or uprooted the trees themselves. Barely had the tree trunks fallen than they were spewed up into the air again by fresh eruptions. From his own position, still relatively immune to the shelling, Stephane watched its methodical progress with a certain macabre fascination. It was like a garden hose, he thought. First it swept *Grande Garde* 1,[1] up at the front of the wood, then it ascended the ravine

1. Under Driant's defensive scheme, there was no continuous line of trenches in the Bois des Caures. On the outskirts of the wood was a chain of small outposts, and behind them the *Grandes Gardes*, each an inde-

to *Grande Gardes* 2, 3, and 4, across to the concrete redoubt
of R.2 and the cross-roads, and back again to *Grande Garde* 1,
repeating itself every quarter of an hour.

At last, after about two hours that felt like the proverbial
eternity, the bombardment crept towards Stephane's little world
at Company Headquarters. In quick succession, four heavy
shells hit the nearby stretcher-bearers' shelter, of which First-
Aid Man Scholeck had been so proud – 'four metres under the
virgin earth, a metre for each man.' To Stephane's amaze-
ment, all four emerged by some miracle, clothes torn and
covered with earth, but unharmed. Soon afterwards, another
shell landed squarely on Stephane's own dugout, reducing it to
shambles. Barely reflecting on his own extraordinary good
fortune, Stephane's immediate thought was how aggravating
to lose the balaclava helmet Madame Stephane had so patiently
knitted for him.

All morning the devastating bombardment continued. Then,
about midday there was a sudden pause. Suspecting that the
attack was now imminent, the shaken survivors in the Bois des
Caures emerged from their cover. It was just what the Germans
had hoped for, all part of the plan (though neither Stephane
nor his commander, Driant, could know this). Now the German artillery observers could see which strong-points, which
sections of trench in the French first line appeared to have
withstood the terrible 210s. It became the turn of the precise,
short-range heavy mortars to administer the *coup-de-grâce*
with their huge packets of explosive, while the 210s lifted the
new targets further back.

At 6 o'clock [1] that morning, Driant had left his permanent
H.Q. at Mormont in the second line for the Battle Command
Post in the Bois des Caures. Before leaving he handed his wed-
ding ring and various personal objects into the safe-keeping of
his soldier servant. He had been at his Command Post several
minutes already when the first shells howled down. Quietly
and composedly he finished giving his orders, then went down

pendent stronghold containing a platoon or more of men. Further back
came the support, or 'S', line; and at the rear the 'R' line of concrete
redoubts, in which lay Driant's own Command Post.

1. 6 a.m. French time=7 a.m. German time. Henceforth all times
given are French.

into the shelter, where the chaplain, Père de Martimprey, Rector of Beirut University in pre-war days, gave him absolution. Meanwhile, from 72 Div. H.Q. a Captain Pujo and another staff officer from XXX Corps had just arrived in the Bois des Caures by car and were leisurely inspecting German lines through binoculars, before calling in on Driant. But no sooner had the bombardment started than the two staff officers rapidly changed their minds and took the quickest route back to Div. H.Q. without stopping to see Driant.

That morning, too, General Bapst himself had ridden forth on horseback from Bras, with the intention of examining the front-line at Brabant. He had got to Samogneux, half-way, when the curtain of fire descended. He rattled out some verbal orders to Lt-Col. Bernard, commanding the 351st Regiment, with instructions to alert units at Brabant, and then returned at a full trot to Bras. Every point in the Verdun sector seemed to be receiving the same terrible pounding as the Bois de Caures, all the way from Malancourt on the Left Bank down to the Éparges well south of Verdun. In the Bois de Ville, on 51 Div.'s front, the heavy shells were falling at a frequency of forty a minute. On the Vosges front, nearly a hundred miles away a French general who was to play an important role in the finale at Verdun heard the steady rumbling and wondered what was happening. In Verdun itself the deadly work of the long-range naval guns had already seriously upset the unloading of munition trains.

By 8 o'clock, after less than an hour's bombardment, almost all telephone communications to the front were cut off, from brigade level downwards. One of the Brigade Commanders of 51 Div. organized an impromptu system of relay runners, each covering – if he lived that long – 300 yards. It was a form of martyrdom that was to become one of the hallmarks of the battle in later months, but under the initial deluge of steel the tenuous human linkage could hardly survive long. Nor could troop reinforcements penetrate the barrage; two companies sent by Bapst to bolster the line at Brabant only arrived, with cruel losses, when the bombardment had ended. It had taken them nearly eight hours to struggle forward some two miles. Effective command no longer existed. The German 'boxing fire' had succeeded even better than expected.

Behind the line, the French gunners – those that had not already been knocked out by the intense gas barrage on their positions – helplessly watched the blasting of the infantry positions. Little could be done in the way of counter-battery work, because observation was useless. The few French spotter planes to penetrate the German aerial barrage reported that so many batteries were firing it was impossible to identify them; the woods hiding the German guns were said to be belching forth in one uninterrupted sheet of flame. Nevertheless some of the long range French guns nearly did better than they knew. At Billy, well behind the lines, their first shots blew up the Paymaster of the 24th Brandenburg Regiment, with his cash-box. At Vittarville, still further off, General von Knobelsdorf was in the midst of reporting to the Crown Prince on the effectiveness of the German bombardment, and on how feeble the French retaliation had been, when suddenly heavy shells began to fall around the Hohenzollern heir. In great haste, Fifth Army H.Q. withdrew to Stenay, where it remained for the rest of the battle. But apart from these two isolated minor coups, French artillery intervention was indeed practically negligible. By midday, General Beeg, the Crown Prince's chief gunner, could report that only single guns were still functioning in most of the French batteries.

To the German storm troops in the front line, the spectacle of the whole French defensive position disappearing in the vaulting columns of smoke had an effect like champagne. In the long wait in the *Stollen*, the damp had begun to rust the men as it had rusted their rifles, but now the miseries, fatigue, and anguish of the past weeks were replaced by an intoxicated elation and optimism. During the afternoon, a young Hessian of the 8th Fusilier Regiment scribbled off a last note to his mother, exclaiming, 'There's going to be a battle here, the likes of which the world has not yet seen.' German aviators returning from reconnaissance over the French lines gave vivid accounts of the terrible destruction they had seen; one told his commanding officer, 'It's done, we can pass, there's nothing living there any more.'

In the *Stollen* the infantry made their last preparations. The men unscrewed the spikes from their helmets, to avoid the risk of becoming entangled in the dense undergrowth of the

French woods, and put on white brassards, so as to recognize each other. The officers turned their caps back to front, so they should *not* be recognized by French sharpshooters. No detail had been overlooked; every man had a large-scale sketch of the French defences opposite him, and squads of machine-gunners without their weapons were waiting to go in with the assault teams, to return to service at once any captured French weapon. At 3 p.m. the German bombardment rose to drum-fire pitch; by 3.40 it had reached a crescendo, and company commanders eyed their watches. At 4 p.m. there was a cry of '*Los!*' all along the line and the grey forms surged forward. On the left of the line a regiment of Brandenburgers went in singing *Preussens Gloria*.

In sharp contrast to the British infantrymen who in less than five months' time would be advancing in straight, suicidally dense lines on the Somme, the German patrols moved in small packets, making skilful use of the ground. For under the Fifth Army's final orders – influenced by the cautious Falkenhayn in his desire that the battle should not proceed too rapidly – infantry action on the first day was to be limited to powerful fighting patrols. Acting like a dentist's probe, these patrols would feel out the areas of maximum decay in the French defences that the bombardment had caused. Only on the 22nd would the main weight of the attack go in to enlarge the holes. Two out of the three German corps adhered rigidly to this order; but rugged General von Zwehl, conqueror of Maubeuge, taking full advantage of that latitude peculiar to the German Army (and which had brought disaster to it on the Marne), decided to send in the first wave of storm-troops hard on the heels of his patrols.

*

Opposite the Westphalians of von Zwehl's VII Reserve Corps lay the Bois d'Haumont, an irregular-shaped wood to the left of and slightly forward from the Bois des Caures, of which it guarded a vital flank. It had taken a dreadful pounding; by the late afternoon many of its defenders had fallen asleep in sheer exhaustion, and the remainder were in a partly stunned and shell-shocked condition. Suddenly, a soldier in a trench to the west of the wood lifted his head and noticed a line of *Feldgrau* troops less than a hundred yards away. The alarm was given, and rapidly organized French fire stopped the Germans in their tracks. At the other end of the wood, however, closest the Bois des Caures, the French 165th Regiment were instantly faced with a grave situation. Many of their trenches had been completely levelled by the shelling; their rifle barrels filled with dirt and useless, boxes of hand grenades and cartridges buried under the debris. A sector of front nearly half a mile wide was held by two platoons exhausted from digging out their comrades. When these spotted the first German patrols, they were but ten yards away, already infiltrating through untenanted parts of the line. Two posts were occupied almost without resistance, and the whole of the first line of trenches in the Bois d'Haumont fell rapidly thereafter. Up rushed the attending German machine-gun teams to man the captured weapons, and the crews with oxyacetylene torches to cut through the remaining French barbed wire. As dusk fell, the Germans had gained a first and vital footing in the French defences. Captain Delaplace, the C.O. of the battalion defending the Bois d'Haumont, sent a frantic message to his Brigade Commander, Colonel Vaulet, asking, 'What am I to do?'

At the moment when the Westphalians occupied the first trenches in the Bois d'Haumont, the defenders in the Bois des Caures were taking stock of the situation. As the survivors came out of their holes during the second lull in the bombardment that day, they peered through the settling dust with astonishment and horror. The wood presented an appalling sight. Nothing about it was any longer recognizable. It looked as if a huge sledge-hammer had pounded every inch of the ground over and over again.[1] Most of the fine oaks and beeches had been reduced to jagged stumps a few feet high. To one soldier, they resembled a Brobdingnagian asparagus bed. From the few branches that remained hung the usual horrible testimony of a heavy bombardment in the woods; the shredded uniforms, dangling gravid with some unnamable human remnant still within; sometimes just the entrails of a man, product of a direct hit. It seemed impossible that any

1. Later it was estimated that 80,000 heavy shells had fallen in a rectangle 500 by 1,000 yards.

human being could have survived in the methodically worked-over, thrashed, and ploughed-up wood. Yet some had. Like a colony of ants in sandy soil, stamped on repeatedly by an enraged child, they had been buried and reburied, yet always some – like Stephane and Scholeck – had miraculously struggled to the surface again. Undoubtedly many owed their lives to Driant's brilliant lay-out of the wood's defences, which, broken up into redoubts and small strongholds, had avoided anything resembling the continuous line of trenches familiar to the rest of the Western Front.

Nevertheless, the losses had been severe. Concrete machine-gun posts had been blown to pieces like matchwood. Two huge shelters, R.4 and R.5, had been smashed by direct hits, a whole platoon wiped out in each. One end of Driant's own bunker, R.2, had been hit, a lieutenant killed, and nine men seriously wounded. One of them when dug out ran off screaming with mad laughter, crazed by the bombardment. Most of the Chasseurs' dugouts had caved in, and those that had not been buried under them emerged badly concussed. Of Driant's 1,300 men, perhaps less than half had escaped injury; one corporal estimated that 'in five *poilus*, two have been buried alive under their shelter, two are wounded to some extent or other, and the fifth is waiting. . . .'

Three minutes after the German guns had lifted, a Chasseur ran up to Driant with a cry of '*Voilà les Boches!*' The colonel grabbed a rifle himself and rushed out of his Command Post to rally his battered troops. 'We are here,' he is said to have shouted, 'this is our place, they shall not move us out of it.' At the same time, he sent a runner back to send up his reserve battalion. A short while later, '*Gran'père*' Stephane arrived at Driant's Command Post with a message from his company commander, Lieutenant Robin, reporting that his first positions had already been carried by the Germans, and begging for artillery support. 'I'm afraid you've lost your leave,' Driant remarked dryly to Stephane, adding that he himself had been asking in vain for a barrage of 75s over the past hour. 'Frankly, Corporal, I think we shall have to count largely on ourselves.'

A veteran already at twenty-three, Robin had shown great courage in the early days of the war rallying a regiment routed by a surprise German night attack. Now, holding the most northerly point of the Bois des Caures, he had ordered his company up on to what remained of the parapets the moment the bombardment lifted. But a patrol of Germans about 150 strong had infiltrated, unseen in the chaos of the shattered wood, between his and Captain Séguin's company on the left. Creeping up a communication trench, they had suddenly appeared at the rear of support position S.7, well behind the first line of trenches. One huge Hessian was actually aiming a revolver at Robin when shot down by his platoon Sergeant, who then proceeded to despatch another six. Robin pulled back his men to S.6 – in remarkable order, considering the surprise – where a savage hand-to-hand fight took place, with grenades and bayonets; here Robin himself was wounded with a grenade splinter in the foot. In front, the attacking Germans were held, but once again outflanking patrols appeared to right and left. As night was falling, Robin was forced to fall back a second time to the next line of support pill-boxes, his company now numbering no more than eighty.

To his left a worse situation had developed. The right flank of Captain Séguin's company was anchored by two machine guns, one operated by Sergeant Léger and the other by Corporal Pot. The good corporal had a section of five rather bolshie old soldiers with whom he was engaged in a heated discussion as to who was to bale out their flooded emplacement, when, less than fifty yards away, there appeared a line of about 200 Germans. It was too late for the bickering Chasseurs to get the gun into action, so Pot and his men fell back – in some miraculous fashion unseen by the enemy – to blockhouse S.9 in the support line. S.9 was tenanted by a platoon under the command of Sergeant-Major Dandauw, who had been badly shaken by the bombardment. At the very moment that Pot's machine-gunners arrived with alarm written all over their faces, there appeared from the opposite direction a small group of men wearing white brassards. At first Dandauw thought they were French stretcher-bearers and ordered his platoon to hold its fire. Suddenly he realized they were Germans. Losing his head he ordered the retreat, and the whole platoon retired at speed down a communication trench.

The trench led past Driant's Command Post at R.2, and there further flight was blocked by the Colonel himself. With a calm

worthy of Joffre himself, and without administering any reproof, Driant told Dandauw: 'Get your men under shelter;
rest them, and before dawn you will retake your post.' Meanwhile, what might have led to a disastrous breakthrough was
checked by the heroism of Sergeant Léger and his men. A
more experienced N.C.O. than Pot, he had carefully removed
his machine gun under cover during the bombardment, re-
mounting it at the critical moment so that the first German
patrols were met with a deadly fire. Still the enemy infiltrated
around him. Encircled, his ammunition exhausted, Léger
smashed his machine gun and continued the fight with hand-
grenades; until, almost the sole survivor of his detachment of
twelve men, he was severely wounded and collapsed unconscious.

To the east of the embattled Chasseurs, similarly confused
fighting was in progress in the Bois d'Herbebois, on 51 Division
front. For days Sergeant-Major Quintin had been peering at
Soumazzannes Farm opposite his platoon, wondering what
might be going on behind it. Now he saw the grey figures
emerge from it, like mice out of their holes, he thought. Soon
his trench was under rifle fire, and three shaken survivors of a
section that had been buried under the bombardment crawled
up to tell him that there was a large gap with not a single man
alive to his left. In characteristic fashion, as soon as Quintin's
remaining men (twelve out of about forty) opened fire, the
German patrols halted like the sea reaching a rock and then
began to flow round into the breaches. In the gathering twilight,
Quintin fell back to a new position, unimpeded by the enemy.
Through the gap to his left the grey tide trickled until it came
up against an almost intact and well-defended position, held by
a platoon under a young Officer Cadet,[1] *Aspirant* Berthon.
There was a pause and a brief conference among the enemy.
Before Berthon's men could find an effective target to fire on,
a column of searing fire enveloped them. Three days earlier
Berthon's Company Commander had observed a mysterious
huge sheet of flame and black smoke rising up behind Soumazzannes Farm. He could not explain it, but nevertheless called

1. In the French Army, cadets in the last stage of training were sent
to command a detachment at the front before actually being awarded
their commission.

for an artillery bombardment. Now Berthon's platoon were to be the human guinea-pigs for this dreadful new weapon the Germans were trying out for the first time. Soon the flame-thrower had set fire to even the wattling revetment of the trenches. The defenders, howling in agony, their clothes and hair aflame, fled in disorder. Swiftly the Germans occupied the smouldering position, establishing a machine gun to fire into the backs of the panic-stricken French.

Meanwhile, in the Bois des Caures, Lieutenant Robin had given the Hessians a sharp jolt. Though wounded, he had launched a hastily organized bayonet attack in the dark which retook two of the captured support positions. So successful was this counter-attack, that Robin then went on to recapture a section of the French front-line trench, where the over-confident German patrols had already gone to sleep. Completely surprised, the Germans fell back in disorder; several prisoners were taken, including one who revealed that this had been only a patrol action, that the main attack would not be coming until midday on the morrow. Reporting back to Driant, Robin asked, 'What am I to do against this with my eighty men?' He was told: 'My poor Robin, the order is to stay where we are.'

*

Night brought an end to the fighting, but once again the terrible bombardment began. A Situation Report sent by runner from Driant to General Bapst said, 'We shall hold against the Boche although their bombardment is infernal.' Everywhere the French feverishly repaired their battered defences and tried to do their best for the wounded. Commanders preparing their own ripostes for the dawn waited anxiously for reinforcements that, more often than not, would never arrive. From all stretches of the front desperate messages poured into divisional headquarters, like Major Bodot's from Herbebois:

I am looking for two companies of the 233rd that left the Bois des Fosses and were to join me at the Coupure, but I have had no news of them.

Throughout the line the first day of battle had been for the French one of minor disasters alternating with countless, unrecorded small Thermopylaes. Wherever the German flame-throwers made their hideous début, panic had occurred; in the Bois d'Haumont, an officer and thirty-six men had surrendered to one flame-thrower detachment alone. But, for the most part, the Thermopylaes had the day. The line had held.

In fact, for the Germans the day's fighting had provided the prelude to many disappointments at Verdun. First of all, the fantastic bombardment had not worked nearly as well as expected. Assured by their officers that they would find nothing but corpses in the French first line, the fire that had greeted them as soon as they moved into the open had come as a nasty shock. By midnight, the small numbers committed had already suffered 600 casualties. Nevertheless, initial successes were such that patrol leaders all along the line had urged that the main attack scheduled for the 22nd be sent in right away to exploit the French disarray. Apparently taken by surprise himself, Knobelsdorf had reacted quickly enough on receiving news of von Zwehl's rapid progress in the Bois d'Haumont, and ordered the other two army corps to 'push forward as far as possible.' But by the time his order could reach subordinate commanders over the cumbersome communications network, darkness was closing in. It was too late. The main body of XVIII Corps, its patrols pinned down by a mere handful of concussed Chasseurs in the Bois des Caures, had simply not moved from its *Stollen*. Only General von Zwehl's VII Reserve Corps, through his partial disobedience, had made a material contribution by seizing the whole of the Bois d'Haumont in five hours; thereby prising open the first crack in the French front. A valuable opportunity had been lost, and Falkenhayn's cautiousness had caused the Germans their first battle setback. As a further discouragement, the meteorologists had erred, and once again biting snow squalls swirled around the exposed German patrols during the night.

L'artillerie fait aujourd'hui la véritable destinée des armées et des peuples – NAPOLEON I

Delivering his orders for the 22nd, Knobelsdorf now placed no limits on Corps objectives. In person he telephoned the Chief of Staff of XVIII Corps, ordering him to get a move on and conquer the Bois des Caures that day at all costs. The bombardment of the previous morning was to be repeated, until the defenders were truly 'softened up'; and the storm-troops would attack during the afternoon. But, as dawn rose, the initiative lay momentarily with the French. At several points along the line small counter-blows of a battalion, or a single company, struck out. These were as typical in the spirited dash in which they were executed as they were representative of the 1914 indoctrination of the French Army, that all lost ground must be retaken by an immediate riposte; a revival of the *furia francese* that in past centuries had been the wonder and terror of Europe. Alas, as so often was the case, the small results gained by these penny-packet, hasty attacks were also out of all proportion to their heavy cost. Most were broken as rapidly as they were launched; either in the annihilating curtain of the new German bombardment, or by the machine guns brought up during the night by the entrenched enemy patrols, or by running headlong into greatly superior German attacks. In the Bois des Caures, the dawn attack in which the disgraced Sergeant-Major Dandauw was to retrieve his name collapsed almost at once. It was hardly aided through being shelled by the first effective French bombardment of the battle that fell promiscuously among the enemy and the attacking Chasseurs. In Herbebois, the same befell the remnants of Major Bodot's missing companies, which had finally been found and were now preparing to retake the bunker that had fallen to the German flame-thrower.

To the left of the Bois des Caures, worse confusion had

upset the biggest counter-attack planned by the French, which was aimed at retaking the lost Bois d'Haumont. The local commander, Lt-Col. Bonviolle, had tried to scrape together an *ad hoc* battalion for the attack, but half of it simply failed to materialize. Nevertheless, by 5 a.m. he had mustered enough strength to assault the south-west corner of the wood. But an hour before his attack was due to begin, a bedraggled courier arrived with an order from General Bapst. Despatched at 11 p.m. the previous night, he had taken five hours to span the intervening four miles. The order put additional troops at Bonviolle's disposal, telling him to plan an attack for 6 *a.m.* against the whole wood. By now the telephone to 72 Div. H.Q. had just been restored, somewhat shakily, and a heated discussion took place between the Colonel and the General. At least, said Bonviolle, his project was already prepared and had prospects of success. But Bapst insisted. After much misunderstanding on the bad line, a disastrous compromise was agreed upon whereby the full-scale attack demanded by Bapst would take place, but postponed until 8.30 a.m. By this time it would be full daylight.

At 7.20 a.m. Major Bertrand commanding a battalion of the 165th in reserve at Hill 344, about two miles behind the Bois d'Haumont, received orders to move up to join in the counter-attack. It was the first he had heard of it, and all he could see to his front were the huge spouts of the renewed German barrage. He decided it would be impossible to move, and sent a courier for further orders; meanwhile sitting where he was. Soon, in the broadening daylight, it was too late for any movement. German aircraft spotted his assembling reinforcements and almost instantaneously brought down a deluge of fire, wreaking carnage.

Nor had the German infantry stood idly by, waiting for the French reaction. Once again von Zwehl had jumped the gun, without bothering too much about the prolonged softening-up bombardment that had started deluging the rest of the front soon after dawn. To the west of the Bois d'Haumont, and close to the Meuse flank of the French 72nd Division, was the Bois de Consenvoye. It was defended by a Territorial regiment, composed largely of quadragenarians and the flat-footed, which should never have been in the line at all. At the

very moment when Bonviolle's counter-attack was due to un-
fold, von Zwehl's Jäger troops (the equivalent of the French
Chasseurs) now hit these Territorials with tremendous force.
Once again flame-throwers had been brought up, and this time
an entire company broke and fled without stopping until it
reached Samogneux on the Meuse. A battalion of a regular
regiment, the 351st, that tried to stem the onrush was almost
wiped out. By the afternoon, 450 prisoners, including nine
officers, were in German hands. A big hole had been rent in
the French first line, and, with all available reserves despatched
to join in Bonviolle's counter-attack, there were no troops immediately available to plug it. Samogneux was seriously threatened.

Near Haumont village, Lt-Col. Bonviolle in the last anxious
minutes before the attack observed thick masses of German
infantry advancing out of the Bois d'Haumont, behind a heavy
barrage. The German guns began to pound furiously at the
village itself. It was at once obvious to the French commander
that his project was far too late. There could be no question
now of retaking the Bois. All his assembled forces would be
needed to hang on to Haumont village. Shortly before 8.30
a.m., he gave the order calling off the attack. One young company commander, Lieutenant Derome of the 165th, never received the order. At zero-hour he charged into the German
barrage, brandishing his sabre; one depleted French company
against one of von Zwehl's crack divisions. Badly wounded, he
and fifty of his men were taken prisoners, sole survivors of
the company.

Meanwhile, Major Bertrand, still at Hill 344, watched
through binoculars the collapse of Bonviolle's attack, and
continued to stay where he was -- waiting for new orders.

The Balaclava charge of Lieutenant Derome had not been
entirely futile. It had astonished the Germans, and decided
even von Zwehl's troops to advance a little more prudently.
Thus Bonviolle was now granted a momentary respite to
detach a battalion for shoring up the sagging defences between
the Bois de Consenvoye and Samogneux. But everywhere there
were holes, and not enough material to plug them all. Closer
and closer the grey mass crept towards Haumont village. Twice
machine-gun fire from somewhere in its ruins made the storm-

troops fall back until the bombardment could be renewed. Two of the monster 420s joined their voices to the fugue of destruction, and shells and heavy mortar bombs rained down on this small village, which in pre-war days had had a population of less than a hundred, at a rate of twenty a minute. Each moment its appearance was transformed. One concrete bunker collapsed under a direct hit from a 420, burying eighty men and two machine guns. By 3 p.m. Bonviolle had less than 500 effectives defending the village; most of his officers were either dead or wounded. At 4 p.m. the Germans moved in on three sides to deliver the final blow. Still they were mowed down by French machine guns firing from the cellars of shattered houses. Up came the Pioneers with their flame-throwers, and the last brave defenders were consumed in their remorseless fire. Bonviolle himself had a miraculous escape. A flame-thrower had already poked its nozzle into the vent of the cellar he was using as his Command Post and emitted its fiery blast before he and his staff decided to leave. Somehow he got out of the village, clothes singed and torn by bullets, but otherwise unscathed. He and five officers and some sixty men were all that remained of his regiment. Casualties had totalled 1,800 men. In capturing Haumont, von Zwehl's Corps had captured the first village in the offensive; and a dangerous wedge had been driven into the French front. On one side it opened up a strategically important ravine leading directly to Samogneux; on the other, it exposed a flank of the Bois des Caures. In justifiable elation, the tired Westphalians celebrated this first notable conquest with French Army brandy that they had retrieved from the ruins of Haumont.

•

It could have been reckoned from its key position that the Bois des Caures would be the focus of German attention for the 22nd. Von Knobelsdorf had followed up his 'rocket' to XVIII Corps with instructions to both the other corps to lend their weight to this attack. Thus an overwhelming concentration of force was to be brought against the two reduced battalions of Chasseurs. Starting again at 7 a.m. the mass of the German artillery poured its fire into the wood. Aerial torpedoes from the heavy mine-throwers blasted holes in the French barbed wire twenty yards wide. Chasseurs, driven from dug-outs caved in by the shelling, scurried about frantically looking for new shelters. One such frenzied figure ran to the edge of Lieutenant Robin's post, babbling '*Mon Lieutenant,* the dugout ...' Disappearing in a blast of flame, he never finished the words. This time casualties were heavier than during the bombardment of the preceding day. The first line trenches were obliterated.

At midday, the precise moment forecast by Robin's prisoner of the previous night, the bombardment lifted, and the whole weight of the German XVIII corps moved forward against the remnants of Driant's two battalions in waves 500 yards apart. On either flank, developments rendered the Chasseurs' position extremely precarious. The capture of Bois d'Haumont had been particularly disastrous. Moving along the side of it, the German storm-troops slipped with dangerous ease through a gap in the defences left unfortified by the 165th Regiment. Their patrols had uncovered one of the Achilles Heels in the French system about which Driant had warned the Army Commission, in the letter that had so outraged Joffre. In the unfair way of war it was Driant, not Joffre, who was now to foot the bill for French neglect. To the right of the Chasseurs the Brandenburg III Corps, marching into battle behind regimental bands, had made a rapid conquest of the Bois de Ville through similar unprotected gaps, enabling the Hessians to swing round against Driant's rear. From this new direction, a mass of some 5,000 Germans now appeared, plainly visible from Driant's command post. Rocket after rocket was sent up to produce a 75 barrage. There was no response, but somehow the determined fire of the surviving French machine guns brought a halt to the advance from this flank. Again and again Driant's skilfully sited defence works caught the Germans in a withering cross-fire, inflicting heavy causualties. In the chaos of the devastated wood, the Germans found the going far tougher than expected. Platoons became separated from their companies, platoon commanders lost sight of their sections, which then strayed and became entangled with the next on-coming assault wave. Soon the attackers were reduced to fighting in small isolated groups, fired on everywhere by invisible

Frenchmen. The assault lost much of its impetus, but the odds
were too great. . . .

Up in the exposed northern pinnacle of the wood, the front-
line companies were being wiped out piecemeal. A bitter
grenade exchange took place. When the grenades ran out, the
Chasseurs resorted to stones and rifle butts. Captain Séguin's
Company was reduced to forty, then to ten men, with only six
serviceable rifles. A small shell blew off the Captain's right
arm, and while the Company Sergeant-Major was using his
bootlace as a tourniquet they were overrun. For the fate of
Lieutenant Robin, who had fought so valiantly during the first
twenty-four hours, there are two versions. Grasset, who,
though a Lieutenant with another company, is otherwise impeccable in his account of the battle, described him – having
burnt his papers – as being captured by a German patrol, rifle
in hand. Corporal Stephane, however, who was with Robin at
the time, is less romantic. Robin's bunker, he says, was suddenly surrounded almost immediately the bombardment
stopped. 'Shoot, for God's sake shoot!' cried Robin. 'It's impossible,' shouted back a Chasseur, 'They're there, hundreds
of them, six metres away.' 'Never mind, fire!' 'It's mad, Lieutenant, they're there, I tell you, more than a hundred have
encircled the post!' Stephane then claims that the young
officer broke down in tears and asked, 'What are we going to
do then?' While he was still making up his mind, Stephane
heard a voice call out in good French, 'Is anybody inside
there?' Almost immediately there appeared a man with a
spiked helmet, gold-rimmed glasses, and a pale face.

As Stephane was led back through the German lines his
immediate reaction on emerging from the dust and debris of
the Bois des Caures was to notice – for the first time in two
days – that the sun was shining brightly. To his horror he also
noticed German pioneers methodically cleaning out with their
flame-throwers a trench still occupied by his company. Further
back he passed new German assault waves, formed up with the
precision of peace-time manoeuvres and driven on by the
raucous shouts of their *Feldwebel*. The fine blond young men,
'all glittering with health and cleanliness . . . visibly the *élite* of
the German Army', were well shaven, wore clean new uniforms, and many puffed casually at cigars. If one had to be

taken prisoner, perhaps these were worthy captors. Along the road Stephane's eyes were further widened by the huge stacks of shells. A battery of the sinister 420s was in action, and it was curious, he thought, to be able to see the black spot visible in the air long after the piece had fired. Later an officer interrogated Stephane, remarking that it was a miracle anyone could have come out of the Bois des Caures alive, as an estimated 10,000 tons of shells had been dropped on it. But, he said, 'We shall nevertheless have taken Verdun by Sunday.'

From his command post at R.2 in the heart of the Bois des Caures Colonel Driant had observed with affliction the fire of the flame-throwers flickering over his forward companies. Soon the enemy were closing in on the 'R-line', the line of concrete redoubts that contained R.2. Eight hundred yards to the right, R.1 had been taken from the rear by the Germans debouching out of the Bois de Ville, and at 1 p.m. they tried to rush R.2 itself. Rifle in hand, Driant took up an exposed position outside the redoubt, coolly directing and observing the fire of the Chasseurs around him. The air was thick with bullets, and when his men beseeched him to take cover he still stood there, remonstrating, 'You know very well they've never hit me yet!' The German attack was driven off, leaving behind several prisoners. Employing their usual infiltration tactics, enemy detachments now crept in between R.2 and R.3 (to the left of R.2), and opened fire from the rear. Again the attackers were repulsed, but this time a whole German regiment appeared through the Bois d'Haumont gap and attacked R.3 frontally. By 4.30 the captain in charge of R.3 was forced to abandon it, leaving R.2 and Driant isolated.

The remnants of about eight platoons, numbering little more than eighty Chasseurs, were now concentrated around their Colonel. Yet a third attack on R.2, this time in about battalion strength, was repulsed. But suddenly rapid gun-fire began to rake the position from the rear. At first the defenders cursed, assuming the shells came from their own artillery, firing at last in response to Driant's rockets. In fact, an enterprising German field-battery commander, Captain von Wienskowski, had man-handled two of his 77s up the road from Ville and was shooting into R.2 over open sights. When he realized the source of the shelling, Driant at once ordered a lieutenant to set up a machine gun and take on the two field pieces. Barely had it opened fire than a direct hit from one of Wienskowski's pieces wiped out both weapon and crew. According to the German account, the crew of a second machine gun was then seen abandoning its post. The waiting infantry of the 87th Hessians, a regiment that had won battle honours at Sedan forty-six years earlier, now charged forward, cheering.

It was clear that R.2 was no longer tenable. In a matter of minutes the sole escape route of its survivors would be cut. In the same calm manner that he had maintained throughout the battle, Driant now told his two battalion commanders, Renouard and Vincent: 'I think it might be more prudent if we withdrew to a position further back.' The Colonel burned his papers, and a thoughtful Chasseur punctured the R.Q.M.S.'s rum barrel. Divided into three groups, the survivors were instructed to break out of the rear of the Bois des Caures towards the village of Beaumont. But as they emerged into open ground, a deadly enfilading fire from three German regiments met them. Vincent was hit twice. Leading the second group, Driant paused in a shell-hole to give first-aid to a wounded Chasseur. As he rose to move on again, a Pioneer Sergeant saw him throw up his arms and cry, '*Oh! Là, mon Dieu!*' and fall to the ground. When the Sergeant reached him he was already dead, shot through the temple. A few minutes later, Major Renouard, the second of Driant's battalion Commanders, also fell mortally wounded.

Driant and his Chasseurs had paid part of the bill for the neglect of the French General Staff. Of the two battalions, 1,200 strong, a handful of officers and about 500 men, many of them wounded, were all that eventually straggled back to the French lines. But the sacrifice was far from being in vain. The attackers had suffered heavily; in the course of the day, the two regiments in the first wave lost over 440 men, one company of the 87th alone reporting eighty casualties. The losses were the heaviest the Germans had experienced in the battle so far. Confidence was shaken. But, most important of all for France, Driant's gallant stand had held up the Crown Prince's offensive for one vital day; XVIII Corps could no longer attain its objectives set for the 22nd. On his death, Driant deservedly became one of France's legendary heroes of the First War, and his defence of the Bois des Caures was acclaimed even on the other side of the Rhine. Though, in the growing bitterness of the war, chivalrous gestures between the combatants had become rare, a German Baroness whose husband had found Driant's body sent his personal belongings back to Madame Driant, via Switzerland, together with a letter of sympathy.

*

It was now approaching 5 p.m. on the 22nd. Up on Hill 344, Major Bertrand, with the only force that could have given help to Driant, was still waiting for his orders. Meanwhile, a courier despatched from R.2 at 4 p.m. bearing a last desperate plea for relief was not to arrive at Colonel Vaulet's Brigade H.Q. till 2 a.m. that night. All along the front the French had been battered back. By nightfall, except for Herbebois and Brabant, the anchor position on the Meuse, virtually the whole of the first line was in German hands. In Herbebois, where the only effective French artillery barrage of the day had disrupted the main attack, bitter fighting was still continuing. Shrilly the bugles sounded through the woods for yet another effort by the Prussians. But once again III Corps was pulled back to await a third softening-up bombardment the following morning, before the next systematic step forward. Accustomed to ill-equipped Serbs breaking at the first hammer blow, the day's failure struck sorely at the prestige of the haughty Brandenburgers. Once again, only von Zwehl's Westphalian reservists had achieved their objectives. The Germans' overall losses for the day had totalled 2,350, quite moderate by First War standards, but they were nearly all inflicted upon the hard-to-replace, *élite* storm-troops. The defenders' losses had been far more serious, a notable departure from previous experiences on the Western Front. After two days fighting, Colonel Grasset says of 72 Division:

A half company of Chasseurs, two-and-a-half battalions of the 165th Regiment, a battalion and a half of the 351st, with two-and-a-half companies of the 44th Territorials, this was all that remained.

The French gunners had suffered little less than the infantry. Theirs had been a thoroughly frustrating day. Telephone communications had long been severed, and in the smoke of the German bombardment few of the infantry's supplicating rockets had been seen; fewer still of the runners had come through. Observation planes and balloons had been swept from the sky by the German fighters. Firing blind, batteries had for the most part contented themselves by shelling old and identified targets, little aiding the hard-pressed infantry. Meanwhile their guns were being demolished one by one by the German 150s. German observers noted a steady *diminuendo* in the French fire. Batteries lucky enough to have horses still alive were beginning to pull back their pieces; but many had to be abandoned to the advancing enemy. Typical of the devotion with which gunners defended their immobilized pieces was the episode of a young naval officer in Herbebois. Ensign Pieri had been detached to command a long-barrelled 160 mm. gun, which in a battle of David and Goliath had been taking on at ten miles' range one of the huge 380s shelling Verdun. On the 21st, a salvo of four enormous shells had virtually uprooted Pieri's gun from its rock emplacement, but he had got it back into service, and had operated it until the German infantry approached. Forced to evacuate, they blew up their ammunition and then took up a position in a nearby trench. Unfortunately the 1874 model rifles the Navy provided (for ceremonial occasions) fired black powder cartridges which gave away their location, and forced them to withdraw once again. Somehow in the confusion of battle Pieri was at one point able to regain the gun itself. Twice he tried to blow it up, but his fuses were damp. Incredibly enough, with the Germans already occupying one corner of the emplacement and busily setting up a machine gun there, he then managed to remove the breech block, which survivors of his crew broke up with a pick in a neighbouring trench.

On the night of the 22nd, severe frost once again brought only an interlude of misery to the exhausted attackers and defenders alike; it was worse still for the many wounded lying untended between the lines.

8   Breakthrough

The Will to Conquer sweeps all before it.
MARSHAL FOCH

Behind the French lines, confusion and alarm were steadily mounting at the various H.Q.s. Since his ride had been interrupted by the German shelling early on the 21st, General Bapst had had a particularly trying time. Though still a vigorous, composed personality, Bapst was over 60; an advanced age for a divisional commander. Most of his service life had been passed in the peaceful confines of artillery depots, and his H.Q. in the little schoolhouse at Bras had been organized very much on peacetime lines. For the General and all his staff, only one shelter, four yards square, had been dug. But at least he was well organized there. Then, at lunchtime on the 21st, orders had come from XXX Corps that he was to move up to Vacherauville. Hastily packing up his staff, he waited till cover of night to move. At the new H.Q., Bapst installed himself as best as he could amid scenes of excitement and confusion. There was no room to hang operational maps; the only light came from the flickering candles, frequently blown out by German shells. After complaining to General Chrétien of the difficulties of exercising command under these conditions, Bapst was granted permission to move back again to Bras. At 10 a.m. on the 22nd he set forth along a road heavily shelled and crowded with troop movements. Meanwhile, once again, 72 Division had been virtually without command during several vital hours. In some disarray he reached Bras, only to find the little school had now become a refuge for a motley of all arms, cooks, clerks, and wounded. These were duly chased out, not without awkwardness, but by now the strain had begun to tell on Bapst.

Into this atmosphere of disorganization and fatigue, there came, during the afternoon of the 22nd, menacing news from Bapst's left flank. With the German breakthrough in the Bois de Consenvoye and the capture of Haumont, the anchor position of Brabant on the Meuse was now threatened with encirclement. If the garrison there should be cut off, Bapst knew that he would have no troops to cover the equally important village of Samogneux, further up the river towards Verdun. Recalling his strict orders of 'no retreat', he hastily sent Captain Pujo off to Chrétien's H.Q. at Fort Souville, to obtain formal permission for the abandonment of Brabant. Pujo reached Souville by 5.30 and was at once received by the Corps Commander. General Chrétien was a tough veteran of wars in Indo-China made doubly fierce-looking by a scar that distorted his mouth. Yet beneath this exterior he seems to have been an indecisive man. At first his response to Bapst's pleas was an immediate and categoric *no*; it was unthinkable that a French officer could voluntarily yield any ground. It was a matter of honour. Then he began to waver and for two hours kept Pujo waiting for a definite order. Finally, Pujo was sent off with the highly unsatisfactory verdict that General Bapst, being on the spot, should make up his own mind.

Meanwhile, bad news reaching Bras was hourly being succeeded by still worse news; the enemy were reaching ever closer to the Meuse behind Brabant, and of the units pinned in at Brabant itself a captain and 60 men of the 44th Territorials had hoisted the white flag. From the rest of the front reports were either non-existent, or highly confused; Lt.-Col. Bonviolle had reached Samogneux with a handful of survivors from Haumont; Driant in the Bois de Caures was ominously silent. The strain was becoming unbearable. At last, at 12.45 a.m. Pujo returned from Souville. At last, some orders! The Corps Commander had given what seemed to be a *carte blanche*. Immediately Bapst drafted an order to evacuate Brabant. Shortly afterwards his already uncomfortable H.Q. was rendered uninhabitable by a large shell which exploded a store of hand grenades. News of his order reached Fort Souville at 3 a.m. Since Pujo had left Chrétien, promises of fresh reinforcements had reached him, and he had begun to change his mind. Brabant now seemed to assume strategic importance. For another three and a half hours he hesitated. Finally the de Grandmaison doctrine triumphed and he sent a peremptory order to Bapst: 'The Brabant position should not have been evacuated without the permission of the superior command . . . the General commanding the 72nd Division will take measures to reoccupy Brabant.'

Half an hour later, he followed it with another order, telling Bapst not to use too many men in the operation. It all revealed how sadly out of touch XXX Corps was with events at the front.

Under the fortuitous cover of a heavy Meuse mist, Brabant had already been evacuated with light losses. But Bapst, obedient soldier that he was, promptly ordered its retaking; though he must have realized how impossible this was. Word came back to Bapst that there was not a single man available for a counter-attack. The order was counter-manded, and at midday von Zwehl's men entered Brabant.

The abandonment of Brabant was hailed by French military writers as the first of the major tactical blunders in the defence of Verdun. Bapst was made a scapegoat, the first of many. Narrowly escaping a court martial, he never again held an active command. In fact his decision had clearly been right, the only possible one in the circumstances. A last-ditch defence of Brabant could only have resulted in the slaughter of what remained of two French regiments, to be followed almost certainly by an even speedier advance by von Zwehl.

The orders and counter-orders issued on the morning of the 23rd led to the inevitable disorder. The 72nd Division was nearing the end of its tether. Terrible stories brought back from the front by wounded stragglers began to spread demoralization among the few reserves that were still uncommitted. Yet still the suicidally heroic penny-packet counter-attacks were being thrown in all along the line, now often reduced to half-platoon level. One of the largest had been that of Major Bertrand's battalion, which had at last received its orders; which were to attack at dawn the Bois des Caures, now occupied by the best part of the German XVIII Corps. Through surprise at the sheer audacity of such a gesture, Bertrand had achieved some success; at the usual heavy cost. But the neighbouring force that Colonel Vaulet had ordered to join in the dawn attack did not receive its orders until midday; they had been ten hours in transit over a distance of little more than a mile. Though it was now hopelessly late, Vaulet's orders were still carried out. But hardly had the attack begun to move forward than it ran headlong into a whole German regiment, marching with rifles at the slope, singing lustily. The French were simply swept aside.

Such were the fate of these impromptu, uncoordinated, suicidal ripostes. But, once again, their ferocity had the effect of persuading the Germans to greater prudence. Though the German assault had been assumed with full force along the whole of XXX Corps' front, preceded by the usual annihilating bombardment, the third day of the battle was still to bring no breakthrough, no rout of the vastly outnumbered French defenders. On the right, 51 Division, though it had borne less of the weight of the German onslaught than the 72nd, was nonetheless fighting with equal heroism. It still clung tenaciously to Herbebois, the only portion of the first line remaining in French hands. Here the German flame-throwers had begun to lose some of their initial terror, French sharpshooters having discovered how easy it was to pick off the heavily laden German pioneers before they came within range. The huge Austrian 305 mm. mortars were now brought to bear on the wood. Finally, at 4.30 p.m. divisional H.Q. gave the order to withdraw from Herbebois; but an hour and a half later Sergeant-Major Quintin was still holding out with the remnants of his platoon, until surrounded and captured.

At the village of Beaumont, situated on a strategic rise, and to which Driant had tried to withdraw the previous day, elements of several French regiments fought to the end against repeated attacks. So costly were these to the Germans that the official history compares Beaumont to St Privat, one of the bloodiest actions in the Franco-Prussian war. As the Hessians of XVIII Corps closed in on the village they were scythed down by suicide machine guns firing out of concealed cellar apertures, that were only silenced when the houses had been brought down on top of them. To the French defenders it seemed as if the dense German formations were coming in with such rapidity that they were being physically swept forward into the French machine guns, by succeeding waves pressing from behind. Casualties among them were enormous. When Beaumont finally succumbed to this impetus on the 24th, a German lieutenant had to intervene to save the life of the captured French commander from his men, enraged by the casualties they had suffered. In the adjacent Bois de Wavrille, heavy losses had also been inflicted on the Hessians by the combined shelling of Chrétien's heavy guns now concentrated on the wood, and by their own barrage falling too short. Something akin to panic broke out, during which two regiments, the 115th and the 117th, became badly entangled with each other. When at last they were sorted out, it was too late to renew the attack that day. For the first time, expressions like 'desperate situation' and 'day of horror' make their appearance in the official German account.

The spirited and prolonged defence of Herbebois and Beaumont provided the 72nd Division an invaluable anchor, which enabled them to hold the line Beaumont–Samogneux during most of the 23rd. This resistance resulted in yet another check to the German advance, and this time it was von Zwehl's Corps that was held up. To his considerable surprise, von Zwehl found himself confronted by a defence line lying between the known first and second French positions that was recorded on none of the carefully prepared German maps. Consequently it had received relatively little attention during the preliminary bombardment. The obstacle was in fact the hastily dug 'Intermediary Line' ordered by General de Castelnau on his January visit; not the last contribution he would make towards the defence of Verdun. The few hours' delay in the ever-accelerating German advance now afforded an invaluable respite, during which Chrétien was able to push up units of a new division, the 37th African Division, behind the tottering 72nd.

But what remained of 72 Division was deteriorating rapidly. More and more runners were failing to reach their destinations, and when they did they brought such desperate messages as the following:

Lieutenant commanding 3rd Battalion of the 60th to 143 Brigade. The C.O. and all company commanders have been killed. My battalion is reduced to approximately 180 men. I have neither ammunition nor food. What am I to do?

At 10 a.m. on the 23rd, impatient at being cut off from all effective control of his brigade, Colonel Vaulet decided to move closer to the front. Vaulet was typical of the toughness of the French Army of 1914. Aged 57, he had risen from the ranks, and as a lieutenant-colonel in 1914 he had been seriously wounded in the abdomen during the 'Battle of the Frontiers'. Captured by the Germans, he escaped a fortnight later, his wound still open. He took refuge in a French gaol, where he was equipped with civilian clothes and the false papers of a vagrant about to be released. He was again caught by the Germans, tried as a spy, but acquitted and sent to a P.O.W. camp in Germany. Four months later, in very ill-health and suffering from his wound, Vaulet was repatriated via Switzerland as unfit for military service. In March 1915 he was back in the army. Since the battle began on 21 February, the tough old colonel – who had been Driant's immediate superior – had played perhaps the most distinguished role among the French Brigade Commanders. With his litany of 'counter-attack; again counter-attack; always counter-attack', he had been the very embodiment of 72 Division's will to resist. Now, as he left his shelter to move up towards the cracking front, he was seen to disappear in a burst of flame.

One by one the leaders were falling. Vaulet, Driant, and Renouard were dead; Bertrand and several other battalion commanders were wounded. Worse still, whole units were beginning to vanish. A sinister indication of the state of morale was an order received by Lieutenant-Colonel Bernard at Samogneux, telling him to keep in reserve a machine gun detachment: 'to enforce obedience upon those who might forget their duty.' But the nightmare was nearly over, it seemed. The Algerians and Moroccans, tough Zouaves and Tirailleurs, of 37 Division were close at hand. Shortly before midnight General Chrétien ordered Bapst to pull out and reconstitute the remnants of his division on the two ridges called Talou and 'Pepper Hill'.

There remained one ordeal still ahead of the division; Samogneux. The orders for Samogneux were the usual, simple – '*tenir coûte que coûte.*' In the village, where fires were raging and the bombardment was constantly growing in intensity, was the equivalent of a battalion under command of Lieutenant-Colonel Bernard. Hemmed in on two sides by von Zwehl's advancing troops, on the third side its back was to the Meuse. A battalion commanded by Major Duffet had been sent up to reinforce Bernard, but half a mile from Samogneux it had come under observation from German guns on the far side of the river. A terrible wall of shellfire interposed itself between Bernard and the relieving column, which, with heavy losses, was stopped in its tracks. Meanwhile, panic-stricken soldiers, their officers long since killed, were straggling out of Samogneux, spreading stories – in their own defence – that the village had fallen, that they were its garrison's sole survivors. The rumours reached Bapst's H.Q., and a message was immediately dispatched to Bernard demanding confirmation. Back came a piqued response from Bernard, flaying the 'cowards and panic-mongers'. The situation, he said,

is not brilliant; nevertheless I am holding at Samogneux ... all the horses have been killed, bicycles smashed, runners wounded or scattered along all the routes. I shall be doing the impossible if I keep you informed of events.

Then silence. Rumours of collapse continued to flow out of Samogneux. At 10 o'clock that evening, Chrétien's Deputy Chief of Staff, Major Becker, was passed by a courier on horseback at a full gallop, shouting 'the Boche is at Samogneux.' 'I wanted to stop him and ask him from whom had he received this information, and what was his mission,' recounted Becker. 'But despite my injunction, he merely galloped off, and I fired two shots from my revolver after him without result.'

Now a disastrous thing happened. Bapst had become convinced that Samogneux had indeed fallen, and issued the routine order for its recapture. At the same time back in Verdun, General Herr ordered the powerful French artillery now assembling on the Left Bank of the Meuse behind Fort Vacherauville to bring down all its weight on the conquered position. At 0.15 hours that night, just as Bernard was sending off a report that he was still holding, the first 155 salvos hit the French positions. The fire was unusually accurate. Within a matter of seconds the machine guns guarding the left flank had been wiped out. Frenziedly the defenders fired off green 'Cease Fire' rockets. But in vain. For two hours the French barrage did its terrible work. It killed the attacking German commander, but it also broke the back of the French defenders. The waiting Germans were quick to take advantage of the situation, and by 3 a.m. all was over at Samogneux. Out of one cave, collapsed under the bombardment, passing Germans heard a pathetic plea of: *'Pour mes enfants, sauvez-moi!'* They stopped to try to dig the man out, unsuccessfully; then were ordered forward to continue the attack. Bernard, captured, was ushered into the august presence of the Kaiser, who – feeling that Verdun was about to topple and wishing to be in at the kill – had moved close to the front to watch the action through a well-protected periscope. 'You will never enter Verdun,' the French colonel assured him defiantly.[1]

With the final tragedy of Samogneux, the 72nd Division now passes from the Verdun scene. In the words of Grasset, it no longer existed. After four days of fighting, the division had lost 192 officers and 9,636 men; its brother-in-arms, the 51st, 140 officers and 6,256 men; for both divisions a combined total of 16,224 out of an establishment of 26,523. With Driant and Vaulet dead, Bernard, Robin, Stephane, and Quintin in captivity, and Bapst in disgrace, a new *personae dramatis* enters the Verdun stage – they in their turn to disappear too and be replaced with depressing speed – and even the scenery begins to shift with a rapidity seldom experienced on the Western Front.

In the German camp, exultation was growing. Some ten thousand French prisoners, 65 guns, and 75 machine guns had been taken; moreover the initial victories had, said the *Reichsarchiv* – resorting to a rare piece of Teutonic nonsense – afforded 'renewed proof of the ascendancy of German manliness'.

*

The twenty-fourth of February 1916 was the day the dam burst. Once the Germans had broken through the 'de Castelnau Line between Beaumont and Samogneux, the whole of the French second position, inadequately prepared and pounded for four days by the most brutal bombardment, fell in a matter

1. Through faulty communications and poor artillery liaison disasters such as Samogneux occurred with dismal regularity throughout the First War. One French expert, General Percin (*Le Massacre de Notre Infanterie*) estimates that 75,000 French troops alone were 'mown down' by their own artillery in the course of the war.

of three hours. During that disastrous day alone, enemy gains equalled those of the first three days put together. By the evening, for the first time since the Marne, the war had once again become one of movement. No trenches, no more barbed wire, no deadly machine-gun emplacements. The *'rase campagne'* fighting that Foch, Joffre, and Haig had so ardently sought for in their attempts at a *percée* during the past eighteen months of sterility seemed at last to have arrived. Only its manner of coming was not quite what the Allied Commanders desired.

To plug the holes rent in the 51st and 72nd, a new division the 37th African, had been flung in by Chrétien piecemeal – like clay shovelled into the cracks of a dyke. Haig, on first receiving an account of the Verdun fighting of the 24th, recorded in his diary in that superior tone he generally adopted when writing about his Allies: 'I gather that this Division had run away much in the same way as the "Tirailleurs Marocains" used to do on my right on the Aisne.' Alas, Haig's entry was only a mild exaggeration. The 37th African Division was reputedly one of the crack units of the French Army; its Zouave regiments were comprised largely of tough *colons*, seasoned in the incessant 'pacification' campaigns of North Africa, its Tirailleurs ferocious tribesmen from Morocco and Algeria, fathers of today's *Fellagha*. These French Colonial troops had established a terrifying reputation (they were averse to taking prisoners) with the enemy, and Germans moving into a new sector always inquired nervously 'Are there any Africans opposite?' Brilliant, brave to the point of fanaticism on the attack, the North Africans – in common with soldiers of most fiery southern races – were, however, strongly subject to temperament and less consistent fighters than the more dogged northerners. When it reached the Verdun battle area on the 23rd, muffled to the ears like medieval Saracens, everything had been against the proud North African division. Split up into packets, it found itself under the command of strange officers – and the regular French Army tended to regard the Colonial troops all too frequently as mere cannon fodder. At the front, the men of the 37th learned they were expected to hold a line devoid of any prepared positions. All shelters, either against the weather or the bombardment, had been razed by the German shelling. The bitter cold gnawed into the bones of the wretched, unacclimatized North Africans, and a night of exposure had reduced their morale to a low ebb. Meanwhile, through their lines had flowed the steady, demoralizing debris of defeat; the aimlessly wandering wounded and shell-shocked, with their staring eyes; the shattered remnants of regiments with appalling tales of horror, pouring back in their search for safety, propelled by an impetus that nothing short of a bullet could check.

The incessant, all-pulverizing bombardment – catching the North Africans with none of the cover that had protected Driant's Chasseurs during the first two days of the battle – had come as the final straw. Nothing like this had ever been experienced. When the German infantry had appeared like a great, grey carpet unrolling over the countryside, a section of Tirailleurs had lost its nerve; then a platoon, a company, and finally a whole battalion wavered and broke. The Germans surged forward with gathering speed. Louvemont, on the vital Pepper Hill and key to the French third position, appeared to be lost. At the right of the front, a similar disaster had overtaken the Zouaves. After the capture of Herbebois and Beaumont, the Brandenburgers of III Corps had thrust through in the direction of Fort Douaumont. To stem the advance, General Chrétien had thrown in his very last reserves, the 3rd Zouaves, with the usual exhortation to resist to the last man. But they had, it seems, dissolved like the early morning mist. In the Ravin de la Vauche, the Germans captured a group of French heavy guns and four batteries of 75s, without encountering any infantry opposition. An escaped gunner officer reported that between the ravine and Souville he had not seen a single French infantryman. What happened to the Zouaves still remains something of a mystery; the French official history is uncommunicative. Becker, the Deputy Chief-of-Staff to Chrétien, may provide a clue in relating that that morning one battalion of Zouaves broke when its commanding officer had fallen. A captain had then taken command and in vain attempted to form a line. His shouts were disregarded; finally, 'a section of machine guns fired at the backs of the fleeing men, who fell like flies.' [1]

1. Demoralization among the North Africans is largely corroborated by German intelligence reports on the French prisoners taken; 'The

Disaster and shame were to some extent redeemed that day
by one of those small incidents of self-sacrificing gallantry that
periodically illuminate the pages of French military history. At
Louvemont, a Tirailleur battalion commander found himself
besieged with nothing to defend the village but a defeated,
panicky rabble and his Headquarters Company. The burden of
its defence fell to a platoon of young 'trainee corporals' attached to H.Q. Company. The platoon was so newly arrived
that, in the urgency of the moment, there had been no time to
allocate the new corporals to companies. Of fifty-eight of them,
only nine survived that day. But Louvemont was saved, for the
time being.

By the night of the 24th, French morale was crumbling
seriously. It seemed that almost anything might happen now.
The French artillery had become ominously silent, which
always had a depressing effect on the infantry. In the retreat
from their first positions, the French batteries had had to set
up again wherever they could. There was no time to dig emplacements. One by one the German barrage had smothered
them in their vulnerable positions. For no very clear reason,
the two biggest guns at Verdun, the naval 240s at Cumières and
Vaux had been blown up by their jittery crews; as had most of
the other long-range naval pieces in the area. Horrible doubts
grew in the minds of the infantry; were the guns pulling out on
them? Next to the disappearance of the supporting artillery
little affects a soldier's morale in battle more than the sight of
hundreds, thousands of untended wounded. Now the misery of
the men at the clearing stations (never the strongest point of the
French) almost surpassed description. Pierre-Alexis Muenier,
an ambulance driver in the first days at Verdun, tells of the
wretched men arriving for treatment, their wounds often frozen
by the intense cold. Despite the din of the bombardment, those
that still could, spoke in low voices for fear of being overheard
by the invisible enemy. 'Joffre who nibbles at them, eh!' they
muttered. Men hideously mutilated by the huge German shells
seemed utterly baffled by never once having seen the enemy

Zouaves and Turkos particularly give one an impression of complete
breakdown. The prisoners complain loudly and without moderation of
their officers and senior commanders, and spit at the captured officers of
other French regiments' (von Klüfer, p. 73).

(though this was a phenomenon that was to become one of the standard characteristics of Verdun). Outside the clearing station at Bras, the seriously wounded lay in their hundreds awaiting evacuation, exposed to the incessant shelling. It was impossible to get more than a fraction out at a time. One ambulance of Muenier's section took twelve hours to remove only five casualties from the inferno. Everywhere roads had become impassable. Motor ambulances became stuck in shell holes; horses frenzied by the shell-fire overturned their drays, scattering the badly wounded along the road. At the base hospitals in Verdun the situation was little better. The German 380s, firing with 'diabolical precision', had cut the main railway between Verdun and the rest of France, and it was taking the all-too-few motor ambulances ten hours to cover twenty miles.

General Chrétien's Corps was finished. Not a single company remained in reserve. Although Chrétien had intended before the battle opened always to have in hand the equivalent of a brigade capable of carrying out a strong counter-attack, events had forced him to squander his reserves unit by unit. On the 21st, three out of his fourteen reserve battalions had been doled out to his divisional commanders, Bapst and Boullangé; the next day nine, leaving him with only two in hand. On the 23rd, the 37th Division had arrived, but had been dismembered almost immediately and thrown in piecemeal. Thirty-six hours later it had lost over 4,700 of 12,300 complement; and with the vanishing of the 3rd Zouaves, Chrétien's last reserves had vanished, too. None of his batteries could mount more than three guns apiece; many were left with only one, scorched black with powder. At 10 o'clock that night, Chrétien was relieved by General Balfourier. But Balfourier was a commander virtually without a command. His Corps, otherwise known as the 'Iron Corps', had once been Foch's, had saved Nancy in 1914, and probably had the finest reputation in the whole army; but it was still *en route* for Verdun in a desperate forced march. The vanguard of two regiments that had arrived soon after Balfourier had received no food during the past twelve hours, had left most of its machine guns behind, and possessed only 120 rounds of ammunition per man. Ambulance driver Muenier described the arrival of these 'fresh', *élite* troops; 'a mass of men and mules envelops us ... Officers and N.C.O.s command with a high voice, brief, clear, as at manoeuvres. Movements are carried out with precision.' But the only thought of the tired, hungry men was 'if only they could have a few beds'. Reminiscent of some Verezhagin scene of the Grand Army in Russia, machine-gunners leaned against each other for protection against the bitter cold, 15 degrees below freezing. At once Chrétien wanted to throw these reinforcements into the battle, but their Brigadiers protested that the men were incapable of further effort. Chrétien insisted, remarking that at the Marne the troops had also been exhausted, 'but they were no longer so when their leaders ordered them to about-turn and march towards the enemy'. It seemed doubtful, however, whether even this latest sacrifice would gain time enough for the remainder of XX Corps to reach the front before the whole Right Bank position was lost, and with it Verdun. Had the Germans only realized it, as a French historian wrote after the war; '... on the dark evening of 24 February the way to Verdun was open to the enemy ...'

But if the Germans that night, distracted as they were by certain problems of their own, did not realize just how desperate was the French position, they certainly could not guess that they stood on the threshold of their greatest *coup* of the campaign. One of the most extraordinary episodes of the war was now about to take place.

9   Fort Douaumont

No unit of the German Army was more strongly imbued with regimental pride than the 24th Brandenburgers of General von Lochow's III Corps. With intense pride the regiment recalled Blücher's tribute from the Napoleonic Wars: 'That regiment has only one fault; it's too brave.' From the moment of joining the 24th, young ensigns had that drilled into them, plus a dictum of Frederick the Great which had become a regimental motto: 'Do more than your duty.' In 1914, the 24th had romped through Belgium, hit the British Expeditionary Force hard at Mons, then marched on to the Marne. As it goose-stepped through France, swigging 'liberated' Champagne and lustily singing '*Siegreich woll'n wir Frankreich schlagen*', there seemed no limit to the regiment's successes. Great had been its indignation when the order came to turn about on the Marne. In February 1916, the 24th had just returned from a victorious campaign in the Balkans where it had helped hurl the Serbs out of Serbia. Now, at Verdun, things had not gone brilliantly so far for the regiment. Stubborn French resistance in Herbebois had led to shaming delays, and administered a bloody nose to the 3rd Battalion, which, to a regiment accustomed to success, seemed to be almost a disgrace; especially when at the other end of the line there were reports of how well the Westphalian reservists, mere farmers in uniform, had done. As the French line bent and cracked before them, the Brandenburgers strained at the leash after fresh laurels with which to redeem the setback. Ahead there now loomed ever closer the greatest laurel of all; Fort Douaumont. Ever since they had been in the line at

Verdun they had had an eye on its great tortoise hump. You
could not escape from it. Like a small rodent under the un-
blinking gaze of a hawk, it made you feel quite naked and
unprotected. At the same time, it beckoned with an irresistible
magnetism.

Then, to the 24th's intense fury, just when the great fort
seemed only a couple of day's fighting away, Corps H.Q. placed
it within the boundary of advance of the neighbouring regiment, the 12th Grenadiers. In their marching orders for
25 February, the Brandenburgers were to halt on an objective
about half-a-mile short of the fort, eventually leaving it on
their right for their bitter rivals. It was unspeakably unfair.

From whatever angle you approached Fort Douaumont it
stood out imposingly, menacingly. Hardly a square yard of
terrain lay in dead ground to its guns. To the tottering French,
it gave the comfortable feeling of having a mighty, indestructible buttress at one's back. It was, as Marshal Pétain later
described it, the corner-stone of the whole Verdun defensive
system. It was also the strongest fort in the world at that time –
on paper. Started in 1885 as part of the 'de Rivière Line',
Douaumont had been modernized and strengthened in 1887, in
1889, and again as recently as 1913. The huge mass was constructed in the traditional polygon shape favoured by Vauban,
and measured some quarter of a mile across. The outer edge
of the fort was protected by two fields of barbed wire thirty
yards deep. Behind them came a line of stout spiked railings,
eight feet high. Below stretched a wide ditch, or dry moat,
twenty-four feet deep, girdling the fort. At the northern corners
were sited concrete galleries, facing into the moat, and at the
apex was a double gallery, shaped like a flattened letter 'M'.
These three were (supposedly) armed with light cannons or
pom-poms, machine guns and searchlights, so that any enemy
climbing down into the moat would be caught by a deadly
enfilading fire from two corners. Each gallery was connected
to the centre of the fort by a long underground passage, enabling it to be reinforced regardless of enemy fire. Next, on the
north side, came the gradually sloping glacis, itself swept by
the fort's machine gun turrets – should the flanking galleries
somehow have been knocked out. Even if an enemy survived
the traversing of the glacis and penetrated to the Rue de Rem-

part that ran from East to West across the middle of the fort, he could still be taken from the rear by the garrison emerging out of shelters deep below ground.

At the southern under-belly of the fort, the entrance was protected by an independent blockhouse, also with double flanking galleries. The south-western approach was masked by a bunker, called a '*Casemate de Bourges*', out of which fired two

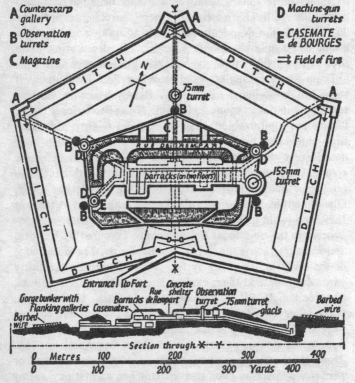

75 mm. field guns. Meanwhile, the whole of this side of Douaumont also came under cover of the guns of Fort Vaux and other neighbouring fortifications.

Inside, the fort was a veritable subterranean city, connected by a labyrinth of corridors that would take a week to explore. There was accommodation for the best part of a battalion of troops, housed in barracks on two floors below ground level. The barrack rooms had rifle embrasures in the thick concrete of the exposed, southern side, so that each could put up a spirited defence as an independent pill-box; if ever the enemy got that far. As a reminder to the garrisons of their duty, there was painted up in large lettering in the central corridor: RATHER BE BURIED UNDER THE RUINS OF THE FORT THAN SURRENDER. But the real teeth of the fort lay in the guns mounted in its retracting turrets. There was a heavy, stubby-barrelled 155 that could spew out three rounds a minute; twin short 75s in another turret mounted in the escarpment to the north; three machine-gun turrets, and four heavily armoured observation domes. For their epoch, the gun turrets were extraordinarily ingenious; their mechanism adopted, with little alteration, for the Maginot Line thirty to forty years later. Forty-eight-ton counterweights raised them a foot or two into the firing position; but the moment the enemy's heavy shells came unpleasantly close, the whole turret popped down flush with the concrete. Only a direct hit of the heaviest calibre on their carapace of two-and-a-half-foot thick steel could knock them out, and until they were knocked out they could exact a murderous toll on an approaching enemy. Though, under Joffre's purge of the forts in 1915, the guns in the flanking galleries and the *Casemate de Bourges* had been removed, these powerful turret guns were still in operation.

The whole fort lay under the protective slab of reinforced concrete nearly eight feet thick, which in turn was covered with several feet of earth. Unlike the great forts of Belgium that had caved in beneath the blows of the German 420s, the concrete roof of Douaumont had been constructed like a sandwich, with a four-foot filling of sand in between the layers of concrete. The sand acted as a cushion, with remarkable effectiveness. Exactly a year before the Verdun offensive began, in February 1915, the Crown Prince had brought up a battery of 420s to try their hand at Douaumont. Sixty-two shots in all were fired, and German artillery officers noted with satisfaction 'a column of smoke and dust like a great tree growing from the *glacis* of Douaumont'. The fort guns remained silent, so the Germans assumed that Krupp's 'Big Bertha' had once again done its stuff. In fact, though the reverberations and concussion within the fort had been extremely unpleasant, the bombardment achieved little other than knocking away half

the inscription, DOUAUMONT, over the main gate. (Why the
fort's 155 never returned the fire was quite simple; its maximum range was just over 6,000 yards, which would not have
carried as far as the French front lines.) In the bombardments
of February 1916, again the German 420s had caused negligible
damage. Thus, it seemed – contrary to the pessimism of Joffre
and G.Q.G. – that Douaumont was virtually impregnable.

By 25 February 1916 the attacking Germans had reason to
assume that Fort Douaumont had been badly knocked about,
but was still likely to prove a stubborn and prickly obstacle.
Never could they have guessed that it was both undamaged
and – through an almost unbelievable series of French errors –
to all intents and purposes undefended!

•

The 24th Brandenburg Regiment's orders for 25 February
were to capture Hassoule Wood, then halt on a line about 750
yards to the north-east of Douaumont. The usual annihilating
bombardment had started at 9 a.m. and was to lift to the fort
itself, when the attack would begin. The line-up was as follows:
2nd Battalion on the right, 3rd on the left, with the 1st in
reserve. On the right flank the 12th Grenadiers (in whose line
of march the fort now lay, but who were also to halt short of
it), and on the left the 20th Regiment, were to advance simultaneously. But in one of those last minute upsets that occurred
so frequently in the First War when runners and word-of-
mouth took the place of 'Walkie-Talkie', neither regiment received its orders in time. So at zero hour as the barrage lifted,
the 24th found itself advancing unsupported. Rather typically,
it paid no attention and thrust forward with its usual impet-
uousness. As luck would have it, instead of finding itself in a
nasty trap, the 24th burst into a vacuum left by the Zouaves
that had melted away the previous day. The few remaining
French in the Brandenburger's path scattered rapidly, in some
disarray. Two hundred prisoners were taken, and then followed
a wild pursuit after a fleeing enemy. Within less than twenty-five
minutes, advanced detachments from the 2nd Battalion of the
24th had reached the objective, having progressed over three-
quarters of a mile. It was just about a record for that war.

On the extreme left of the 2nd Battalion was a section of Pioneers, commanded by a Sergeant Kunze. Kunze at twenty-four was a regular soldier of Thuringian peasant stock; from his photograph one gets the impression of heavy hands and limited intelligence; from his subsequent action, one gets an impression of complete fearlessness, but perhaps of that variety of boldness that often reflects lack of imagination. Men like Kunze were the backbone of any German Army; they would go forwards in execution of what they held to be their orders, unquestioningly and unthinkingly, until at last a bullet dropped them. In the usual practice of the German Army, Kunze's section had been detailed to accompany the first wave of storm troops, to clear any wire or other obstacle that might hold them up. Aided by the land contours, it was on the objective well to the fore. Kunze himself had already had an eventful afternoon. In a captured machine-gun post he had stopped and given first-aid to a wounded French N.C.O., but the ungrateful gunner had somehow regained his weapon and reopened fire. Kunze hastily returned and dispatched the man with little compunction. At another enemy position, a few minutes later, Kunze saw a Frenchman raise his rifle, but he shot first. When at last he reached the objective his blood was thoroughly up; after the day's brief action he was, in that favourite but quite untranslatable German Army expression, *unternehmungslustig*. As he paused to recover his breath, he saw the great dome of Douaumont looming ahead, incredibly close to him, terrifying but at the same time irresistibly enticing. French machine guns were chattering away busily to the right, but the Fort seemed silent. Kunze now reconsidered the orders he had received that morning; to eliminate all obstacles in front of the advancing infantry. And here, just in front of him, was the biggest obstacle of all! Ignoring in the excitement of the moment the other order – not to go beyond the prescribed objective – and with little thought as to what he would do when (or if) he got there, he set off in the direction of the Fort. His section followed obediently. Ten men against the world's most powerful fortress! It seemed an act of the most grotesque lunacy.

Within a matter of minutes Kunze and his section reached the wire of the Fort glacis. Encouragingly enough, nobody had fired at them, but Kunze had noticed the 155 in the Fort shooting over their heads at some distant target. He also noticed troops on the right flank of the 24th being given a bad time by a French machine gun cunningly placed aloft the church spire in the village of Douaumont. Much of the heavy barbed wire had been torn up by the German bombardment, and – with the aid of their pioneer wire-cutters – the section soon made a way through the two entanglements. They reached the spiked railings some fifty yards east of the northern apex of the fort. It was now shortly after 3.30. There was absolutely no way of getting through or over the obstacle. Kunze now followed the railings, moving leftwards; his choice apparently dictated by the machine gun over to his right. He turned the north-east corner and there, just round it, to his delight was a gap about four feet wide that a shell had blasted in the railing. While contemplating how to get down into the twenty-four-foot abyss of the moat, Divine Providence made up Kunze's mind for him, in the shape of a near-miss that wafted him over the edge. Temporarily stunned, but otherwise unhurt, Kunze now urged the rest of his section to join him. A corporal, convinced by now that the section leader was out of his mind, announced that he was pulling back, but – possibly persuaded by their own heavy shells which were still falling thickly on the exposed superstructure of the fort – the remainder lowered each other down to where Kunze was standing.

The moat was deserted. Near the breach in the railings were what looked like some small windows and a closed steel door (they were in fact the orifices of the north-east Gallery), set high up in the face of the wall. The barrel of a small cannon could be seen protruding from one, so Kunze and his men rapidly took cover as best they could among the debris lying about in the moat. But there was no sign of life here either. Once again, without pausing to consider the possible hazards, Kunze set about getting into the gallery. The steel door, however, was stoutly barred, and the gun embrasures were over twelve feet from the bottom of the moat. Then Kunze suddenly remembered something from the tedious PT exercises of pre-war days. Quickly he ordered his men to form a human pyramid. Several times it collapsed in a tangle of limbs, but eventually Kunze was able to squeeze his body through an embrasure, pushing aside the unmanned revolver-cannon that stood there. The gallery was quite empty. After several efforts, he prised open the steel door, and exhorted his men to climb up into it. Faced though with this gaping, tenebrous mouth in the fort exterior, and all the terrible unknown perils that might lie beyond it, Kunze's little troop now began to lose its nerve. Death under one's own shells was infinitely preferable! All but two melted away, abandoning the sergeant in his folly.

Still never hesitating, Kunze set forth down a long, inky-dark tunnel. After the ear-splitting din of the bombardment outside, the silence was oppressively eerie. On and on plunged Kunze. The tunnel seemed endless. Where was it leading them? And where was the French garrison? At last came some stairs. Kunze climbed them, then found at the top that the passage branched. He could now hear what sounded like the dull boom of a heavy gun firing close at hand. Leaving his two companions to cover one passage, he followed the other towards the sound of the firing. Soon he was close enough to hear the clatter of ejected cartridge cases. Pistol in hand, the intrepid sergeant flung open a door, bellowing '*Händehoch!*' Four French gunners, faces blackened with powder, stood there in utter astonishment. Before they could collect their wits, they had been roughly hustled out of the turret. Single-handed Kunze had stopped the fire of the 155 mm. gun, the biggest in the fort.

In the midst of this grim battle an interlude of almost Marx Brothers comedy now began. On emerging from the turret, Kunze must have taken the wrong turning in the Douaumont rabbit warren; he was unable to re-discover his two companions keeping watch in the passage. Instead, marching the four Frenchmen before him, Kunze saw daylight glimmering ahead and once again heard the noise of the bombardment. Soon they came out into the open (the south courtyard of the fort), and suddenly the prisoners bolted. Quick as lightning they turned back into another opening in the fort. Kunze followed, and was about to fire when they disappeared into a doorway to the left. Kunze caught a rapid glimpse of a barrackroom where an elderly N.C.O. appeared to be giving a lecture to a group of about twenty men. Once again Kunze shouted '*Händehoch!*' but at that instant a heavy shell exploding above blew out the candles inside the room. In the ensuing confusion, Kunze's immediate thought was, 'Now they will rush me.' Quickly he slammed the heavy door, and, as luck would have it, was able to lock it from the outside. For a while Kunze kept watch outside the barrackroom, but no new candidates for his bag appeared. Time began to grow heavy on his hands, and he resumed his reconnaissance in search of further exploits. Soon he ran into another unarmed French soldier, who in utter terror kept calling him '*mon Capitaine*'. Though not speaking a word of French, Kunze somehow made it plain that he wanted to know where the fort's officers were. Accordingly, his latest trembling captive led him into another barrackroom, evidently belonging to the officers' mess. The room was empty, but upon a table stood a large basket full of eggs, wine, and other provisions. It was something Kunze had not seen for many a month. He had not had a square meal since the battle began, and only iron rations during the miserable weeks of waiting in the *Stollen*. Suddenly he felt ravenously hungry. In his simple peasant mind the instinct to eat and drink now overruled all other considerations. The prisoners locked up in the barrackroom, his presence alone in a hostile fort surrounded by the enemy, the very war itself, all was forgotten. Before the astounded eyes of his latest captive Kunze sat down and began to gorge himself.

But where, one might well ask, was the main garrison of this mighty bastion during all these events?

At the beginning of the war, Douaumont had a permanent garrison of some 500 infantrymen. Then, in 1915, Joffre's order de-rating the forts had sent the garrison out into the line, leaving only the artillerymen manning the remaining turret guns (by a twist of Fate, Douaumont's first wartime garrison had been decimated fighting near the Bois des Caures in the first days of the battle, its commander severely wounded). Under the statutes governing French fortresses, those at Verdun came directly under the Governor of Verdun – now General Herr. The Corps Commander in whose sector they lay had no control over them. Thus' when General Chrétien had paid a visit to Douaumont on first taking up his command, he had received an extraordinary rebuff. At the drawbridge he had been turned away by the elderly *Gardien de Batterie*, a mere Warrant Officer called Chenot, with the words: 'the fort opens only to the Governor of Verdun. I cannot allow anybody to enter without his order. I wasn't warned of your visit. I should have you arrested as a spy!' Thus after this humiliating episode Chrétien worried no more about the fort, assuming perhaps that if it could keep out a three-star General it had little to fear from the enemy; in any case, it was not *his* responsibility. When the battle began the occupants of Douaumont in fact consisted only of Sergeant-Major Chenot and his fifty-six Territorial gunners manning the 155 and 75 turrets that alone had kept their weapons after the Joffre purge. On the desperate day of the 24th, General Herr had actually dictated that all the Verdun forts be prepared for demolition; Douaumont's tenants had accordingly been increased by one Sapper sergeant, but the officer sent from Verdun to organize the mining disappeared *en route*. The mining was never carried out.

Meanwhile, the first two brigades of XX Corps had arrived on the scene and at Souville Chrétien was about to hand over his command to General Balfourier. Shortly before this took place, he had been rung up from Verdun by a frantic Herr and told to re-occupy 'the line of the forts' and 'defend them to the last'. As one of his last acts, Chrétien had detailed his staff to pass this order on to the divisional commanders. On his arrival, Balfourier, exhausted from the long forced march, accepted without query Chrétien's assurance that the garrisoning of the forts was in hand, that there was nothing to worry about there. General Deligny, the commander of the two new brigades that were up in position on both sides of Douaumont, asked Chrétien whether he should not set up his H.Q. in the Fort. No, said Chrétien, the fort is taken care of, you can take over my H.Q. here when I pull out tomorrow.

Under the stress of sustained battle, the best-regulated staffs sometimes break down. Errors that would otherwise be inconceivable arise. Such a one occurred now. Somebody on Chrétiens staff, perhaps a humble corporal-signaller, forgot to transmit the vital order for the re-occupation of the forts. Deligny, separated from Chrétien's H.Q. by just a partition, swears he never heard of the order until it was already too late the next day. Up at the front the two brigadiers concerned – comfortably assuming that Fort Douaumont lay between them as a solidly defended bulwark, while recalling the dreadful reputation forts had for attracting shell-fire – ordered the regiments under them to give it the widest possible berth.

While Kunze was sating his appetite within the fort, from the wings without three officers of the 24th were preparing their various appearances. Their names were Radtke, Haupt, and von Brandis. In short succession, but quite independently of each other from their different points on the battlefield, they too had been seized by the intoxicating magnetism of Douaumont. Radtke was a twenty-four-year-old lieutenant in 6 Company, a reservist who with his rimless glasses and sloping shoulders reminds one more of a bank clerk or petty official than a Prussian officer. With his platoon he had followed more or less the same course as Kunze through the objective, and then on to the edge of the fort's wire, creeping up under cover of a defile called Strawberry Ravine. When he emerged into the open again at the wire he was surprised not to find himself fired upon by the French in Douaumont village. His two worries were the heavy German bombardment coming down around him and the fact that there appeared to be no sign of the 12th Grenadiers on the right. Radtke fired off all his Very cartridges to get the guns to lift their barrage, but as often happened they were not noticed by the artillery. The nerves of some of his men were beginning to crack under the intense shelling, but Radtke urged them on. Like Kunze he easily found a way through the wire, and reached the fort near the northern apex, but somewhat to the right of Kunze. To his great good fortune a heavy shell had in the meantime blown a new, and much larger gap in the railing near the apex. It had also blasted a hole in the edge, leaving a pile of debris in the moat immediately below, so that the actual drop was considerably reduced. Followed by about twenty men, Radtke clambered down into the moat, the first German officer to enter Fort Douaumont.

To some extent, Radtke's leap into the Douaumont moat must have required more real courage than Kunze's. About half an hour behind, he could not have seen Kunze enter the moat unchallenged, and as an officer he knew enough about fortifications to expect to be met by a murderous fire from the flanking galleries. As soon as he realized that these were in fact unmanned, he set up some heavy timber, discovered in the moat, against the breach to facilitate the entry of succeeding groups. Instead of breaking into a gallery like Kunze, Radtke and his men now moved forward up over the glacis, creeping on all fours because of the German shelling. Having reached the Rue de Rempart, they soon found an opening leading into the upper floor of the barracks. Here the corridors were lit by dimly flickering kerosene lamps. There was a sound of footsteps, the Germans crouched back in the shadows, and Radtke made his first bag of three unarmed and terrified Frenchmen. To his astonishment, they told him there were only about sixty men in the fort, and then promptly led him to another group of five in a barrackroom.

On the floor below, Kunze had now finished his meal and decided it was time to resume duty. Marching his single prisoner down the corridor, he propelled him into the room where he had incarcerated his other prisoners. But, *du lieber Gott*, the room was now empty! At this very moment they were probably alerting the whole garrison. The full significance of his dereliction began to dawn on Kunze. How could he explain matters to his officer? As a final touch of comedy, a relief crew of four French gunners had meanwhile reached the 155 turret, utterly dumbfounded at finding no trace of the crew they were to relieve. Nevertheless, with a Gallic shrug of the shoulders, they took their posts and after an interruption of about half an hour the gun once again started firing aimlessly into the distance.

Captain Haupt now makes his appearance. Aged nearly forty, a modest officer of long service, Haupt was the commander of the 7th Company. Gathering as many of his company as he could, Haupt moved towards the fort five minutes after Radtke. It was now snowing heavily. When one of his subalterns objected that they had already gone far beyond the halt line, Haupt replied, 'We are going to storm the fort.' Approaching from a little further to the right, Haupt's group came under heavy fire from the machine guns in the spire of Douaumont Church, and a subaltern was mortally wounded. Haupt pressed on, to find the north breach in the railings and Radtke's conveniently placed timbers. Still the German heavy shells rained down on the fort, and with commendable bravery one of Haupt's men now stood upright on the top of the fort to wave a large artillery flag, in hopes of stopping the fire. Entering the upper floor of the barracks in much the same way as Radtke, Haupt almost immediately ran into a French gunner, who, it transpired, had found Kunze's twenty-six captives, and released them, some quarter-of-an-hour earlier. Demoralized by this encounter with a fresh set of Germans, he quickly led them to the white-bearded Chenot himself, evidently taking refuge from the bombardment on the lower level of the fort. The poor man was almost overcome with distress when he realized that the fort had been invaded by only a handful of Germans.

Gradually, all the threads became knitted together. Radtke met up with Haupt; Kunze was re-discovered by his officer, Lieutenant Voigt, who had reached the fort with Haupt, and to whom Kunze now gave only the most blurred account of his recent activities. Assuming command as the most senior officer present, Haupt quickly organized the defence of the fort against a possible French counter-attack, and sent Radtke to winkle out the remnants of the garrison. Their extraordinary success made the Germans suspicious that a hidden time bomb would now blow the fort and themselves to smithereens, so for double security the unhappy Chenot and his fellow captives were lodged in a room right above the magazines.

The arrival of Haupt and his capture of Chenot form the point at which Fort Douaumont passed from French to German hands. The whole day's fighting had cost the Brandenburg Regiment only thirty-two dead; not a shot had been fired in defence of the world's greatest bastion, the loss of which, in the estimation of one French divisional commander at Verdun, was to cost France a hundred thousand men.

It was now about 4.30, three-quarters of an hour after Kunze had landed in the moat.

There remains von Brandis and his somewhat equivocal role in the capture of Douaumont. Brandis was a twenty-seven-year-old regular *Oberleutnant* (the nearest equivalent rank in the British Army would be Captain) commanding 8 Company. Through his own writings he betrays some of the less attractive Prussian characteristics; bombast and contempt of the *Übermensch* for the lesser European breeds. On marching to the Marne in 1914, he had noted scornfully the rustic untidiness of French farms, deducing that this was a true indication of the decadence of the race. War, in von Brandis's eyes, was a succession of demoralized Frenchmen, hands above their heads, murmuring *'Pardon, Camarades!'* On 25 February, Brandis's company had been on the extreme right of the battalion. Undoubtedly it had had the worst time that day. The non-appearance of the 12th Grenadiers and heavy machine-gun fire from Douaumont village had both slowed down his advance and caused him more casualties than any other company. Thus at 4.30 he was well behind Haupt's and Radtke's companies, and still out in the open. According to Brandis's story, at the moment when he, too, was seized with the impulse to move on the fort he had no idea that anyone else had got there first. But a remark made to the Battalion Adjutant at this time reveals that he *had* in fact seen Haupt's group reach the fort, and it seems unlikely that at least someone in his company should not have noticed the large German artillery flag when it was waved from the top of the fort at so short a distance away. In a swirling snowstorm, he reached the north breach, strangely enough not fired upon by the French in the village, to whom he was of course closer than either Haupt or Radtke had been. He and his men clambered down the timbers that stood under the breach, without – supposedly – pausing to wonder who might so conveniently have placed them there, and without noticing the tracks made by the fifty-odd men who had reached the fort before him. Traversing the glacis, he entered the fort interior through an opening at the east end, and descended to the lower floor, where behind a closed door French voices were heard. A soldier who had once been a waiter in France shouted out *'vous êtes prisonniers'*, and a lively debate ensued, with the French within querying how they would be treated. When told 'as soldiers', twenty-six territorial gunners came out (Brandis claimed 'between fifty and sixty'). All the French in the fort had been rounded up, without a shot being fired. There were now just over ninety Germans on the scene. Shortly before 5, Brandis met Haupt, and as second in seniority was put in charge of external defence. A quarter-of-an-hour later, in the gathering dusk, Brandis's men repulsed a weak French patrol approaching the fort, the only attempt to retake it that day. At 5.25, Haupt sent Brandis back to report to the C.O. and bring up the rest of the battalion. This was the full extent of Brandis's part in the capture, though it was not the last that would be heard of Brandis.

Before leaving the actual seizure of Douaumont, two puzzling questions about the French defence need to be answered. Why had Chenot not seen the Germans approaching, and why had he not brought his twin 75s to bear on them? Why had the French troops on either side of the fort apparently done so little to stop them?

The answer to the first question is a simple, and human one. Though none of the 420 shells had penetrated the fort's concrete, the effect of the last three day's bombardment on the occupants had been demoralizing. Each time a heavy shell landed above, lamps blew out, corridors were filled with dust and asphyxiating fumes, and the reverberations underground imparted a sensation of being inside an immense drum. Well might the elderly Territorials have feared that any moment the fort would collapse about their ears. Consequently, Chenot and all the gunners not actually manning the 155 gun turret had taken refuge as far below the surface as possible; on the cellar floor. After his capture, Chenot claimed in self-defence that the observation domes were destroyed. This was not so; they were simply unmanned. Isolated from the rest of the world, out of touch with the course of the battle, Chenot had no idea that the Germans had advanced at such fantastic speed during the past twenty-four hours. Therefore, he had seen no need to man the observation domes. The crew of the 155, encased in their turret, had merely been firing blind on computed positions; on targets which had long since moved on. Some warning that the Germans were nearer than anticipated had apparently reached Chenot about half an hour before his capture. He had still not ascended from the cellars to verify this himself, but had sent a crew to man the 75s for the first time. It was too late, Radtke was already in the fort and apprehended the gunners *en route*.

The answer to the second lies in the last of the series of tragic French errors. It will be recalled that the two brigades on either side of Fort Douaumont, the first arrivals of Balfourier's 'Iron Corps', had been told that the fort could look after itself. On the 25th, the 95th Regiment was solidly occupying the village of Douaumont, with excellent observation to the northern approaches of the fort. In the haste and confusion of its arrival, all it knew of neighbouring friendly forces was that somewhere on its right (i.e. covering the fort to the North) was a regiment of Zouaves. During the afternoon, the machine guns in the church spire had kept up a brisk fire on the attacking Brandenburgers, about half a mile away. It was snowing hard and visibility was worsening rapidly. Suddenly a group of men appeared, well in advance of where the Germans had last been spotted, heading up the glacis of the fort, and within a couple of hundred yards of the flanking French company. This company at once opened fire, but the supposed enemy neither returned the compliment, nor was fired upon from the fort; moreover it was marching straight into its own heavy barrage. Straining his eyes in the grey of the blizzard, the French company commander now gave the order to cease fire; it was painfully clear to him that his company had been firing on their own side. He swore that he could now even distinguish their *Chéchias*, the characteristic headgear worn by Zouaves. Thus the detachment of Haupt and Brandis had been allowed to progress the last vital yards up the glacis and into the fort virtually unchallenged by the French 95th. (Kunze and Radtke, it will be remembered, approached the fort in covered ground, along a defile to the east.) What the French had mistaken for *Chéchias* must have been the German helmets with their spikes removed to facilitate passage through the dense Verdun thickets. Pericard and Durassié, the principal French witnesses to this event, incredulous that Douaumont could have been taken without recourse to some kind of Trojan Horse guile, insist to this day that the Germans were clad in captured Zouave uniforms. Alas, no sufficient evidence to corroborate the thesis of the 'false Zouaves' has ever come forward. Certainly none of the men Chenot saw that afternoon was dressed in anything but *Feldgrau*.

In Germany, scenes of great jubilation acclaimed the capture of Douaumont. It was, as a British war correspondent noted later, 'the highwater mark of German efforts on the Western Front', the most notable triumph there since the breakthrough to the Marne. Church bells were rung all over the country, and schoolchildren were given a special holiday. One German newspaper reported the evacuation of Bar-le-Duc and Ste Ménéhould, twenty-five miles behind Verdun; another declared VICTORY OF VERDUN ... THE COLLAPSE OF FRANCE ... Even hardened 'Easterners' on the General Staff began grudgingly to admit that maybe Falkenhayn had been right in his decision to attack in the West. At the Crown Prince's Stenay headquarters, the All-Highest arrived to express in person his appreciation of the Brandenburgers' feat.

To the victor, the spoils. Once the Germans had assured their tenancy within the fort it remained only to hand out the medals for this outstanding exploit. To the reader it should be fairly evident who among the Brandenburgers were most deserving of reward. But often in the course of war the ribbon merited by one in fact goes to another. So it happened at Douaumont. It was *Oberleutnant* von Brandis who had been detailed by Haupt to carry the news of the capture of Douaumont back to Battalion H.Q. Having given his account of it to the C.O., Major von Klüfer, Brandis then requested permission to convey the news back to Regimental H.Q. On the basis of Brandis's account alone, the staff at Brigade that night recorded in the war diary that Douaumont had been '... stormed by 7 and 8 Companies of the 24th, led by Captain Haupt and *Oberleutnant* von Brandis. Both officers most conspicuously distinguished.' And so, in this form, the citation passed back along the line until it lay on the desk of the Crown Prince himself. Meanwhile, the next morning – before he could give an account of his part in the action – Radtke was seriously wounded in a French counter-attack. For over a week he lay in a torpor in the fort sick-bay, then was transported to hospital in Germany. There he heard that Haupt and von Brandis had been awarded the *Pour le Mérite*, Germany's highest decoration, and he had received nothing (nor, for that matter, had Kunze). In vain Major von Klüfer tried subsequently to set the record straight, but the heir to the Hohenzollerns could admit no mistake. Besides, von Brandis, with the 'flashing eyes' the Crown Prince so admired in his legions, was manifestly more of the stuff that heroes are made of than the faintly un-military Radtke; the fact that he was a *von* and Radtke was not may also have had its influence.

The modest Haupt, thoroughly deserving of his high award, soon slipped back into anonymity. Not so Brandis. Rapidly he assumed the position of favourite with the Crown Prince; was given a gold cigarette case inscribed 'Wilhelm', photographed with him in his staff car, or with arms linked in the company of other heroes, like the great air ace, Oswald Boelcke. His book, *The Stormers of Douaumont*, which appeared the following year, full of bombast and relegating even Haupt to a lesser role, was an instant best-seller. Letters of hero-worship flooded in by the hundred from Germany, even offers of marriage. After the war, a village in Prussia was named after Brandis, whose inspiring lectures to schools on the capture of Fort Douaumont are recalled to this day by a later generation of Germans. For ten years von Brandis's role remained undisputed. Then the official *Reichsarchiv* appeared, establishing for the first time that, second only to Haupt, Radtke had played the most important part in the capture. Next Radtke himself published his own account of the action. At last, Sergeant Kunze, now a police constable, provoked by this reopening of the discussion and evidently feeling that after the passage of so much time it might now not be too imprudent to admit the dereliction of nearly twenty years ago, contacted his old C.O., Major von Klüfer, and told him his whole story. On the eve of the Second World War when interest in who took Douaumont had all but disappeared, Klüfer's meticulously compiled account, representing years of research, appeared. Radtke's claim was confirmed and for the first time it was revealed that a Pioneer Sergeant, not a Prussian officer, had been the first to penetrate the fort. Kunze was rewarded with accelerated promotion to Inspector; in belated compensation, Radtke received a signed photograph from the Crown Prince.

If in their exaltation at the capture of Douaumont the Germans had exaggerated a trifle, it was nothing by comparison to French efforts to play down the disaster. The propagandists of G.Q.G., abetted by 'Anastasie' the ugly old lady with the scissors who personified French censorship, rose nobly to the occasion. The first communiqué on the 26th was a masterpiece:

A fierce struggle took place round Fort Douaumont which is an advanced work of the old defences of Verdun. The position carried by the enemy this morning, after several fruitless assaults which involved them in very heavy losses, has since been reached and passed by our troops, all the enemy's endeavours having failed to drive them back.

Then, when it was realized there was no hope of its recapture, communiqués concentrated on the desperate German losses; one report thus inspired spoke lyrically of a 'whole autumn of green-grey leaves fallen on the snow'. Finally it was allowed to 'leak out' that the fort had in fact been demolished by the prescient French sometime previously, and the Germans had merely occupied a useless ruin. To important neutral countries like the U.S.A., it was pointed out somewhat mysteriously that the French Army was employing a 'new system of war, for which Verdun was fully prepared', in which forts played no part. At the Elysée, the G.Q.G. attaché, 'April Smiles' Pénélon, blandly assured President Poincaré that the French bombardment would not allow the Germans to remain in Douaumont long; then told him that it had in fact been recaptured. But the world could not be deceived for long. When the truth became apparent, Poincaré, in his mild fashion, notes that there was 'excitability' in the Chamber of Deputies that day. In fact, the shock experienced by all Frenchmen was as devastating as the impact in Britain of the fall of Tobruk in 1942; with the difference that Fort Douaumont was but 150 miles from the Arc de Triomphe.

On the battlefield itself, the impact of the fall of Douaumont was immediate and grave. The commander of the 37th African Division, the last of the units of XXX Corps still in the line, now did a disastrous thing. The battle had gone extremely badly for de Bonneval. On arriving at Verdun, he had seen his fine division promptly dismembered and fed piecemeal to the 51st and 72nd Divisions. Worse still, he had seen its crack colonial units falter and break, one after another, in an unheard of fashion. Though described by contemporaries as having 'the bearing of a great commander', by the afternoon of the 25th de Bonneval was thoroughly depressed. Suddenly from his command post on Froideterre Ridge he had spotted the German rockets fired from Fort Douaumont to halt the bombardment. A disastrous breakthrough must have taken place on the right! His battered division, now holding the vital spurs of Talou and Pepper Hill, would be trapped in a pincer movement with its back up against the flooded Meuse. Though he had not been attacked at all that day, he at once gave orders to withdraw in stages, first to Froideterre, then right back to Belleville Ridge. The important bridge at Bras was also blown up. Belleville was the last of the transverse Meuse spurs before Verdun,

looking down into the very city itself, and within machine-gun
fire of it. Retreat to Belleville Ridge meant the yielding of all
the forts and entrenchments on the Right Bank; within a short
space of time, it must inevitably mean the loss of Verdun too.

The Germans had been quick to capitalize on their triumph
by scattering leaflets from planes over the French lines, announcing, 'Douaumont has fallen. All will soon be over now.
Don't let yourselves be killed for nothing.' Something alarmingly like mass panic began to sweep through Verdun. At the
front, Sergeant Dubrulle of the 8th Regiment, one of the new
units hurled precipitately into the battle, noted in his journal
'the beginning of incoherent sentiments which pave the way to
defeat. We are lost! They have thrown us into the furnace,
without rations, almost without ammunition. We were the last
resources; they have sacrificed us ... our sacrifice will be in
vain.' A melée of guns, wounded, and deserters was pouring
back along all the roads. A Zouave overheard a general remark,
'Even if I were Napoleon, I couldn't stop the defeat of this
shower.' Battle-shocked remnants of the 51st Division took
refuge in the barracks where they had been lodged, and refused to budge. But even in barracks out of the line, terror
pursued the French troops. Down upon Marceau Barracks
where Dubrulle and his regiment were quartered, on being
relieved from the line, there suddenly rained a deluge of German long-range shells. A sickening carnage was executed on
the horses tethered outside. Then the roof of one of the buildings crumpled, crushing some hundred or more men. Survivors
rushed out into the night, only to be blown to pieces among the
crazed and pitifully wounded horses. Eventually, the exhausted,
demoralized troops were marched out of the death trap of the
barracks back towards the front again, and ordered to dig
trenches for themselves.

Human endurance had reached its limits. In Verdun itself a
Lieutenant was arrested for running through the streets, shouting *'Sauve qui peut!'* Seeing the Meuse bridges prepared for
demolition and all the other signs of impending withdrawal,
the civil populace began to abandon its houses. Shortly afterwards, an order was issued that all civilians were to evacuate
Verdun, within a matter of hours. The pathetic flotsam of war
that was to become so familiar a sight on French roads a gen-

eration later – the hopeless columns of refugees, painfully pushing mattresses and belongings in prams before them – now added to the chaos on the roads leading from the city. In their haste, some of the citizens of Verdun had left even the food out on the table; others had found time to drag barrels up from the cellars and puncture them in the streets. The gutters ran red with wine. A food depot near the Citadel was thrown open, and soldiers told to take what they could carry. Elsewhere in the city that invariable companion of military rout, pillage, took place. Frightened troops who had taken refuge in the cellars of evacuated houses got drunk on their contents, then looted the other floors. There were reports of gendarmes being strung up by drunk looters when they attempted to intervene.

The twenty-fifth of February was, in the view of one foremost French authority, General Palat, 'perhaps the darkest of the whole assault on Verdun'. That night nothing seemed to stand between the victorious Crown Prince and the conquest of France's mightiest bulwark. It was no exaggeration to say, as he later wrote in his memoirs 'We were, in fact, within a stone's throw of victory!' Would he deny Falkenhayn the opportunity of trying out his 'bleeding white' experiment? There did indeed seem a possibility that the victim would die of shock before that sinister process could do its work.

Postscript. When writing about the capture of Fort Douaumont, I was led to believe that Eugen Radtke was already dead. Several years after the German translation appeared, however, I was agreeably surprised to receive a long letter from him in Berlin, kindly commending me on the accuracy of my reconstruction, with the words: 'I am amazed, Mr Horne, where you gained this detailed knowledge of the assault. Only we who were in the first wave could have had this knowledge . . .'

Later I met Radtke, then in his seventies, in Paris (his first visit to France since the Battle of Verdun fifty years previously) in a confrontation with the French veteran, Durassié (see page 131). When it came to the issue of the 'false Zouaves', the two old soldiers embarked on a violent dispute, that threatened to end in a resumption of the Great War.

10   De Castelnau Decides

When one has the misfortune to make war in the interior of one's own country, pure strategy cannot always have the last word – LT-COL. DE THOMASSON, *Les Préliminaires de Verdun*

At Chantilly, news of the first two days' fighting had not particularly upset General Joffre. The placid, *petit bourgeois* routine of life had continued as ever. In the *Illustrated London News* a correspondent declared that Joffre had 'been seen ... literally rubbing his hands over the attack'. On the 23rd, however, even after percolating the softening filters of G.Q.G. the reports sounded so bad that Joffre was persuaded to dispatch his Assistant Chief of Staff, Colonel Claudel, to Verdun to make an on-the-spot report. Claudel seems to have possessed an abundance of the talents (notably optimism) required by his post. The following afternoon – i.e. the day the Germans made their most menacing gains – he telephoned that the attack had 'slowed down and it looked as though we would be able to hold out and even make a counter-attack.' That evening, Joffre's supper was interrupted by a telephone call from General de Langle de Cary (as Commander of Army Group Centre, the immediate senior to General Herr) with a much gloomier account. He asked permission to evacuate the whole of the Woevre Plain, now menaced by the rapid German advance on the Meuse Highlands. To a French general, conscious that in the usual manner of things there must soon be a hunt after scapegoats for the Verdun disaster, Joffre's calmly non-committal response of 'It's up to you' can hardly have been comforting. The Generalissimo returned to his meal. An hour later, Joffre's second-in-command, General de Castelnau, arrived with three other generals to impress upon him the urgency of the situation at Verdun. De Castelnau recommended that the entire Second Army, currently in reserve, should at once be transferred to Verdun, to defend the Left Bank. Its commander was a General Philippe Pétain.

Joffre agreed. At 11 o'clock de Castelnau, by now in receipt of further intelligence which seemed to presage the total collapse of the defence on the Right Bank, was back in Joffre's office. But, in accordance with inflexible routine, the great man had already retired for the night. One version of what then ensued caused an uproar in France when it was published, a few months later, in *Le Matin* – through the evident complicity of a coterie of officers ardently desiring to install de Castelnau on Joffre's throne. This account had it that de Castelnau was first turned away by the orderly officer, saying that on no account was the Commander-in-Chief to be disturbed. De Castelnau, however, persisted, and went to the Villa Poiret in person. There he sent in an A.D.C. to awake Joffre, who, unbarring the double-locked door, then appeared in his night shirt. Telling Joffre how serious the situation had now become, de Castelnau requested authorization to go to Verdun himself, armed with plenipotentiary powers, to take whatever measures he felt necessary. According to *Le Matin*, Joffre (responding in much the same way as he had to General de Langle earlier), said 'let him do what he wants' and then went back to sleep. Joffre firmly denied the episode; the Editor of *Le Matin* was killed at Verdun. Whatever really happened, two facts are certain: de Castelnau had his request granted, and Joffre completed his night's rest. In Joffre's own words, that night 'I wished more than at any time of my life that I had the gift of omnipresence.' But to have gone himself to Verdun at this hour would have demolished at a stroke the legend of imperturbability, upon which so much had been built, and the crash would have been deafening. Besides – and in the way the French Army of those days functioned it is hard to believe such considerations did not pass through Joffre's mind – if things went badly wrong henceforth at Verdun, the Generalissimo's responsibility would now be shared by another.

De Castelnau's position at G.Q.G. was a curious one. Following the disasters of 1915, pressure from above (principally from Galliéni, the gifted but ailing Minister of War) had forced a purge of the G.Q.G. upon Joffre. Foremost among the changes had been the appointment in December of de Castelnau to be Chief-of-Staff, as a sort of *éminence grise* at Joffre's side. It was hardly a secret that Galliéni, no admirer of Joffre (who, among other things, had stolen much of the honour due to Galliéni for the victory of the Marne), wanted eventually to pull him back to Paris in the largely administrative capacity of a C.I.G.S., while placing the executive command of the armies in the field under de Castelnau. Although the latter once jocularly remarked to Briand, the Premier, that in his relationship with Joffre 'apart from sleeping together, we couldn't do anything more to show our intimacy,' and although every afternoon – as part of the Chantilly ritual – he accompanied the Commander-in-Chief on his post-prandial stroll, Joffre and his coterie were as jealous as Turks of the brother-general placed so dangerously near the throne.

Noël Marie Joseph Edouard, Vicomte de Currières de Castelnau, to give him his full title, was a warm-blooded Pyrenean like Foch and Joffre, but he was also a nobleman and the scion of a long line of fighting generals. There were few French wars in which the de Castelnau clan had not distinguished itself; there had been a General de Castelnau under the great Napoleon, and another had been selected by Louis Napoleon to accompany him into exile after the dismal capitulation at Sedan. Now sixty-five, the present head of the clan had also fought in the Franco-Prussian War. Partly, perhaps, because of the impact of this degrading defeat, partly because of heritage, he had become the 'High Priest' of the de Grandmaison sect of *'Attaque à outrance'*. It was he who in 1913 had told the Military Governor of Lille, General Lebas, that he would have 'nothing to do' with fortified strongholds. But, unlike most of the other apostles of this sect among the French General Staff, de Castelnau was a man of outstanding intellect, quick-witted and flexible. No force had taken a worse drubbing in the first mad onrush of Plan XVII than the Second Army that had then been under his command; yet, in the moment of defeat, he had made an astonishing turnabout. By a brilliant defence based on a clever choice of terrain that would have been beyond most of the other French generals at that time, de Castelnau saved the vital city of Nancy. In the defence of Verdun, it will be recalled, de Castelnau had already rendered an invaluable service in the 'Intermediary Line', hastily constructed as a result of his *coup d'oeil* in January, and – had there been time for the completion of the Third Position that he had also prescribed then – there seems a chance that the German break-through on the 24th might have been prevented altogether. Witness to de Castelnau's very real ability was the fact that he had managed to rise so high in the French Army. For in Republican France, still on the rebound from the Dreyfus Affair, both his heredity and his religion told strongly against him. Known throughout the army as '*le Capucin Botté*' (the Fighting Friar), in his entourage de Castelnau was always accompanied by his own private chaplain, a Rabelaisian Jesuit who also happened to be his nephew. It is held that, although he lived until the end of the Second World War, his clericalism and conservatism alone deprived him of his Marshal's baton.

Jean de Pierrefeu, who wrote a vivid and often caustic chron-icle of the G.Q.G., describes de Castelnau as follows:

A jovial, dapper little man, of quick and kindly speech, he was, with his martial bearing and white moustache, the typical French cavalry officer. He was absolutely worshipped by all disinterested persons at G.Q.G. When he entered the hotel,[1] tapping the floor with his stick and looking about him with the mischievous and bright glances of a boy, every one came up to him instinctively, only too pleased to see him. He had the art of lighting up the faces of those he met by a single kindly word, and so making them his admirers in a flash. This little man, so alert and cheerful, radiated honesty and trustworthiness.

It was not only the sophisticated staff officers at Chantilly who fell to the de Castelnau spell; soldiers at the front were equally susceptible. In some magical way, the sight of the dumpy figure in the long black cloak could rekindle the fight-ing spirit in utterly battle-weary troops.

For all that de Castelnau had learned since 1914, he was still very much a 'fighting general' of the Foch school. Indeed, according to Poincaré, when Foch himself expressed doubts about an Allied offensive in 1916, de Castelnau 'exploded' with impatience. During the worst weeks of the Verdun fighting, de Castelnau impressed Colonel Repington (the heavyweight *Times* correspondent who, in between the purveyance of social tittle-tattle from one dining table to another, was a fairly astute military critic) on his way to dine at the Ritz, with the words: 'Rather than accept slavery at German hands the French race

1. Where G.Q.G. was lodged.

would die upon the battlefield.' To tradition and instinct, de Castelnau could add personal reasons for wanting to hit hard at the enemy; three of his sons had already laid down their lives for France.

Such was the man who departed post-haste for Verdun shortly after midnight on 24–5 February. Brief as his role was to be in the battle, it was one of quite exceptional importance.

De Castelnau paused at Avize to quell the pessimism at de Langle's H.Q. and to telephone ahead a warning to poor Herr not to yield any more ground, or 'the consequences would be most grave for him [Herr]'. At breakfast time on the 25th, he reached Verdun. There he found General Herr 'depressed', and 'a little tired'; though this was hardly surprising. Despite his sleepless night, de Castelnau at once went on to the Right Bank and plunged into the work of re-animating the defence. While, at the front, the rout had still to reach its climax, behind the scenes, in the various headquarters, a transformation took place that was, by all accounts, miraculous. That day 'wherever he went, decision and order followed him.' As his eyes roved over the terrain, speedily the agile mind made its appreciation. At 3.30 on the 25th, almost the precise moment when Sergeant Kunze was leaping into the moat of Fort Douaumont, de Castelnau was telephoning his conclusions to G.Q.G. Verdun could be saved. An effective defence could be maintained on the remaining cross-ridges of the Right Bank. There must be no retreat to the Left Bank. Pétain, he recommended, should now be put in command not only of the Left Bank, but of the Right Bank as well; the 'fatigued' General Herr should be kept on for a while as Pétain's adviser, then quietly *'limogé'*. (He would not be among strangers; among those preceding him at that limbo for disgraced generals were the unfortunate Bapst, de Bonneval, and Chrétien.) Making use of his plenipotentiary powers, de Castelnau then dispatched the necessary order to Pétain, without awaiting Joffre's sanction.

De Castelnau's snap decision was one that in its fateful implications would affect not merely the course of the Battle of Verdun, or even of the war itself, but also the whole stream of subsequent French history. Although, later, as the salvation of Verdun seemed assured, the Joffre coterie claimed the honours, there is nothing to suggest that, at the moment of de

Castelnau's departure from Chantilly, Joffre had definitely made up his mind not to retreat to the Left Bank. (One also has to recall Joffre's preoccupation during the six months preceding the German attack with the establishment of a line of withdrawal *behind* Verdun, on the Left Bank.) So there seems little doubt that the vital decision was de Castelnau's, and his alone. The little cavalryman, embodiment of all the ancient martial instincts and *panache* of the race, had taken up the German gauntlet. France had done exactly what Falkenhayn had expected (and hoped) she would do. At least in his judgement of French national psychology, Falkenhayn's appreciation had been accurate. Now the 'bleeding white' could begin.

After the passage of nearly half a century, how easy it is to criticize the decision taken by a general in the midst of a most desperate battle. Why did he not do this instead? Why could he not have foreseen what we see now? Already since the Second World War critics have arisen to castigate Montgomery for not pressing home with sufficient zeal the pursuit of the defeated Afrika Corps after Alamein. Perhaps they are right. But the stresses and strains of the moment, the all-important moral factors, tend to be submerged by time. In the vision of the military critic writing *ex post facto*, the uncertain temper of the men of Britain's Eighth Army after years of consistent defeat becomes obliterated behind the imposing shapes of tactical and material considerations. So at Verdun. In the light of what we in our omniscience now know of Falkenhayn's intentions, and of the hideous tragedy that was to ensue at Verdun, we may say that France should not have decided to hold the city at all costs. Winston Churchill, with extraordinary perspicacity, wrote at the time:

Meeting an artillery attack is like catching a cricket ball. Shock is dissipated by drawing back the hands. A little 'give', a little suppleness, and the violence of the impact is vastly reduced.

Instead of standing stubbornly and heroically on the Right Bank, the French could have drawn back their hands from Verdun, which, since the dismantling of its forts, was in any case no longer such an indispensable defensive pinion. Behind Verdun on the Left Bank the undulating hill and wooded country continues for some twenty-five miles, as far as Ste Ménéhould. Here a fighting withdrawal could have been staged, with the German advance checked by successive lines of defence on each feature. With the means then available, a German breakthrough to the flat open country around Châlons-sur-Marne would have been virtually impossible. Instead a terrible toll of the Crown Prince's manpower would have been exacted by the French 75s and machine guns in their prepared emplacements, at relatively little cost to the defenders. The attack would have petered out, leaving the Germans exhausted and weakened to meet the Allied sledge-hammer blow on the Somme.

This is what *could* have happened. Had Pétain, the man who was to carry out Castelnau's decision, been in de Castelnau's place it is probably what would have happened. But a withdrawal, however fighting, was not in keeping with French military indoctrination of the First War; it was also not in keeping with the character of de Castelnau. Above all, in formulating his decision, de Castelnau was influenced by psychological imponderables. As Colonel de Thomasson, one of the more level-headed French writers on Verdun, remarks: 'Sometimes sentiment provokes a courage which could not be otherwise inspired by cold reason.' The army at Verdun was in a state of demoralization bordering on rout. Eighteen months of unremitted, bloody, disheartening failures lay behind it. Who knew whether it could now be called upon to fight a steady fighting withdrawal? Who could tell whether the rout might not merely be accelerated, turning into a complete collapse and unbarring the most direct approach to Paris? In the Franco-Prussian War in which de Castelnau had fought as a young officer he could recall all too vividly how, once it had started retreating, the French Army had never ceased until it was rounded up piecemeal. He knew his French soldier. With more spirit and *élan* on the attack than the dogged Britisher, he was also much more impressionable in adversity, altogether less capable of the kind of orderly, defensive retreat such as Britain's soldiers have been accustomed to during so much of her military history. Moreover, these were French peasants fighting on French soil, every inch of it hallowed. In these circumstances, as de Thomasson remarks, 'pure strategy cannot always have the last word.'

Finally, could the nation morally survive the shock of losing Verdun, with all its legendary mystique? De Castelnau was committed; and so too was the man appointed to carry out de Castelnau's decision.

11 Pétain

> There had emerged a leader who taught his army to distinguish the real from the imaginary and the possible from the impossible. On the day when a choice had to be made between ruin and reason, Pétain received promotion.... – COLONEL CHARLES DE GAULLE, *France and her Army* (1938)

> Marshal Pétain has traced in our history pages some of which remain luminous while others give rise to interpretations that still conflict and arouse lively passions. We must celebrate the first. We cannot ignore the second – ANDRÉ FRANÇOIS-PONCET (1953)[1]

Six weeks before the assault on Verdun, the French Second Army had been relieved by the rapidly expanding British Army, and was pulled back out of the line to form a general reserve. After the hard autumn fighting in the Champagne the rest was felt to be well deserved. For the Army Commander, ensconced at Noailles, life had become extremely leisurely, consisting of daily rides in the beautiful forest. In fact, limited as are the distractions in any French provincial town, it was really almost too quiet.

When the first order announcing Pétain's appointment was received by his staff, there was consternation at Noailles. It was after 10 p.m. and the General was to report to Joffre in Chantilly at 8 the next morning. But the General was not in his office; he was not in his quarters; he could be found nowhere. Alarm! France in her hour of need called for her saviour, but the saviour-designate was missing. Fortunately for her, however, Pétain's Staff-Captain, Serrigny, knew – as a good A.D.C. – something of the elderly bachelor's habits. Ordering a staff car, he drove at top speed through the night to Paris. As he wrote years later in his long unpublished memoirs, 'hazard or Providence made me knock on the door of the Hôtel Terminus of the Gare du Nord.' It was now 3 a.m. The proprietress at first

1. *Éloge* to the *Académie Française* on his election to the seat left vacant by the death of Marshal Pétain.

energetically – and no doubt with the liverishness customary to Parisian *hôteliers* roused at this hour – denied that Pétain had visited her hotel that evening. Serrigny played on her finer feelings, insisting that it was 'a matter of life or death for France'. Eventually the proprietress admitted that the General was in the hotel, and somewhat hesitantly led Serrigny upstairs. Outside a bedroom door stood 'the great commander's yellowish boots with the long leggings, which, however, on that evening were agreeably accompanied by some charming little *molière* slippers, utterly feminine.' Undeterred, Serrigny knocks at the door. Wearing 'the scantiest of costumes', the General emerges. There, in the dingy station-hotel corridor, ensues a brief conference; in its historic connotations – though perhaps rather different circumstances – a little evocative of Drake at Plymouth. Serrigny relays the summons from Joffre. Sobs from within the unlit bedroom. Pétain, impassive, decisive, tells Serrigny he must find a bed in the hotel. In the morning they will journey together to G.Q.G. Meanwhile the night imposes its own duties. To these Pétain now returns.

What manner of man was this amorous general who was soon to earn from his countrymen so much honour and love, that would later be replaced by so much hatred and dishonour? At the time of which we write, Pétain was a bachelor of sixty, with commendable vigour for his age. After the war, a doctor who gave him a check-up (incredibly enough not recognizing him) remarked: 'One can see that you weren't in the war.' (Alas, but for his robustness, the final degradation might have been spared him.) With the commanding posture that was the unmistakable and indelible mark of St Cyr, and clad in the uniform of 'horizon blue', there was no more impressive sight on a French parade ground. To have seen him and de Castelnau together, one might well have assumed that Pétain was the born aristocrat, the squat and rather swarthy general the peasant; though in fact it was the reverse. The cynical, observant Pierrefeu writes of Pétain on his advent to G.Q.G.:

I had the impression of a marble statue, of a Roman senator in a museum. Big, vigorous, of imposing figure, impassive face, and pale complexion, with a direct and thoughtful glance. . . .

And François-Poncet, on succeeding him at the Académie:

... a majestic carriage, naturally noble ... his blue eyes contained a certain mystery. One would think they were made of ice ... from his whole personality emanated an air of sovereignty ... Wherever he appears, he imposes ... Whoever once saw this figure, will never forget it.

Certainly women never did. His easy success often led him into precarious adventures; in 1917 the French intercepted a cable from the German Ambassador in Madrid reporting to Berlin that he had found a mistress for the new Commander-in-Chief, for the modest fee of 12,000 pesetas a month.

Many of Pétain's peasant characteristics remained with him throughout his life. One was his simplicity – which he shared in some measure with Joffre. That was about all they had in common. He was early to rise and late to bed. In rare moments of leisure he liked to potter around the garden, and always said he would take up farming when he retired. His favourite pastime of an evening was to leaf through historical albums, studying portraits of the men who had made their mark on Europe during the past half-century. He seldom went to bed before midnight, and then often read the plays of Corneille till 2 a.m. In contrast to Foch always ready to adopt the conqueror's pose, one foot before the other, Pétain so hated being photographed that the only portrait Repington could find in 1918 for *The Times* was one of him characteristically glaring at the camera. At his trial in 1945, he himself insisted on wearing the very simplest uniform of a Marshal of France, his only decoration the *Médaille Militaire*.

Not entirely unrelated to this dislike of show and publicity was Pétain's chronic contempt for all forms of intrigue, and especially for politics and politicians. Already as a subaltern, when most of his contemporaries, mindful of where lay the springs of promotion in the Third Republic, were assiduously sucking up to the politicians, Pétain had the audacity to place a reservist Deputy under arrest for some minor military infringement. In his well-known '*boutades*' against politicians, Pétain appeared to fear no one; to Poincaré he once remarked acidly that 'nobody was better placed than the President himself to be aware that France was neither led nor governed.' In 1939, Pétain refused to be a candidate for the Presidency, recalling that he had once described it as only 'suitable for

defeated marshals'. In 1917 Pétain threw a share of the blame
for the mutinies upon the frequent visits of Deputies to the
front. The distrust had become mutual; about the same time,
Abel Ferry, one of the more impressive French Deputies of the
epoch, wrote in his diary:

Pétain is a *bastard*. He has command, but he is closed to everything which is not exclusively pertaining to military order. He sees
only the defects of parliamentary collaboration.

The sourness in Pétain's relations with parliamentarians may
partly have been due to a curiously unexpected timidity in his
make-up, derived from the insecurity of his humble background. Instead of 'rolling himself into a ball' like Joffre when
'got at' by politicians, Pétain retreated behind a barrier of
wounding, cold irony. Whatever the explanation, the facts remain, and the antipathy was an unfortunate one. The slight to
Poincaré alone was never forgotten, and would later prove
both detrimental to Pétain's career and – more disastrously –
to the conduct of the war.

In many ways Pétain appears as the odd-man-out in the
French military hierarchy of the First War. Where Joffre, Foch,
and de Castelnau were Pyreneans, Pétain came from a peasant
family in the Pas-de-Calais and had all the characteristics of a
northerner. The Pétains had never boasted of a military tradition. Aged fifteen when the Franco-Prussian War ended, Pétain,
unlike Joffre and de Castelnau, had been too young to partici-
pate. His choice of the army seems to have been inspired by the
anecdotes of a nonagenarian great-uncle who had been a
veteran of the Grand Army. Having worked his way through
the Spartan mill of St Cyr, he opted to join the newly formed
Chasseurs Alpins. Five years' rigorous service with them no
doubt accounted in part for his splendid physique. He then
transferred to the infantry at Besançon, where he became friends
with a Lieutenant Herr. Pétain was extremely industrious, yet
advancement went slowly for him; unusually so even by peacetime standards; five years a *sous-lieutenant*, seven years a lieutenant, and ten a captain. He was forty-four before he got his
battalion. The outbreak of war found him a colonel of fifty-
eight, who had never served abroad. Imminent retirement lay
ahead after a career of almost sub-average distinction, in an-

ticipation of which he had already bought a small house on the edge of St Omer. Then, in the space of eighteen months, from commanding a regiment of a few thousand men he was to rise to be an Army Commander with over half-a-million at his behest.

Confession had not been a factor in the slowness of Pétain's promotion in the way that it had checked the career of Foch, de Castelnau, and other ardent Catholics; indeed, Pétain could boast that he had not been to Mass for thirty years, so on this score alone he should have been earmarked, as things stood, for rapid advancement. But in an age where friends-at-court were vital to a military career, Pétain the peasant from St Omer had no influence. Nor, it might be said, had Joffre, the cooper's son, but he had been quick to cultivate what he lacked, whereas Pétain never made an effort to conceal the contempt of the Third Republic that he had acquired early in his career. In sharp contrast to most of his contemporaries, Pétain seemed unambitious almost to the point of self-extinction; when offered the post of Commandant of the Rifle School, he refused because it would have meant his promotion over the heads of more senior majors. What told most against Pétain, however, was that while Joffre, Foch, and de Castelnau all swam vigorously with the current, he alone stood against the prevailing tide of the de Grandmaison movement. While the others seemed still obsessed with the catastrophe of 1870, Pétain was assiduously and pragmatically studying more recent campaigns such as the Boer War and the Russo-Japanese War of 1905, where the defence had given so good an account of itself. The potential-ities of the new weapons that the Grandmaisonites contemptu-ously dismissed from their armoury, the machine gun and the heavy howitzer, and even of the humble rifle in its modern form (he was himself a remarkably good shot) did not escape Pétain. The nucleus of Pétain's discoveries was that 'firepower kills'. Carried to their logical conclusion his theories meant that (if he were right) the *attaque à outrance* could be broken by a well-organized defence long before it reached the enemy.

It was sheer heresy. For a long time, the way ahead barred, Pétain found no opening for preaching his gospel. It was not till 1906 that a post as instructor at the École de Guerre gave him an opportunity. There, with the de Grandmaison wave at its peak, his lectures seemed singularly unglamorous alongside those of the fiery Foch and Colonel de Maud'huy, the Chief of the Infantry Course, who was alleged to make his sons pray each evening to become as 'brave as Bayard'. Pétain's students nicknamed him *'Précis-le-sec'*. But he had his converts, too. One of them was a thoughtful, gangly young man called Charles de Gaulle, who, so impressed was he by Pétain's teachings, applied on leaving St Cyr to join the regiment then under his command, the 33rd. To Pétain, for whom the future seemed to hold nothing but the obscurity of a colonel in retirement, the war and the dramatic failure of Plan XVII brought an unexpected opportunity to prove his ideas. Joffre's ruthless *limogeage* of inept generals resulted in rapid promotions for those who had shone, and Pétain was foremost among these. The stonewall defence, the deadly concentrated firepower of his troops in the retreat from the frontiers, and then at the Marne, impressed friend and foe alike. At the end of August 1914 he was promoted to Brigadier on the field; so suddenly that an elderly spinster had to furnish him with stars unsewn from her father's uniform. His rise to Divisional, then Corps Commander followed in rapid succession. In the abortive Artois offensive of May 1915, the attack by Pétain's Corps at Vimy Ridge was so well prepared that for a moment it seemed as if the whole German front might collapse. In the autumn, in Champagne, Pétain had one of his few failures. The intense preliminary bombardment, so characteristic of Pétain, was just too prolonged and sacrificed the vital element of surprise. But at least Pétain, unlike most of the other First War Commanders – and in opposition to de Castelnau, then his immediate superior – knew when to stop, instead of trying to redeem failure fruitlessly, and at terrible cost in lives.

All the time, Pétain was learning with a rapidity almost unique among his fellows, and with an adaptability rare for his age. Says Spears, 'at every stage of the war he was just a little ahead of practice, theory, and thought of the moment.' In an age when infantrymen and gunners almost prided themselves in their ignorance of each other's function, Pétain, the St Cyrien, had learnt more about the use of artillery than many gunners would ever know. During the Artois offensive, it was said that Pétain laid every gun himself. Even Haig was agreeably impressed by his first encounters with him: 'I found him business-like, knowledgeable, and brief in speech. The latter is, I find, a rare quality in Frenchmen!'

By the end of 1915 – now an Army Commander widely respected by the army élite, though still little known to the public – Pétain had developed his theories on firepower into a series of pithy axioms and coherent formulae. 'The offensive is the fire which advances; the defensive the fire which stops,' said Pétain; 'Cannon conquers, infantry occupies' (a conclusion he had reached well before Falkenhayn composed his Verdun Memorandum). In explaining the suspension of his corps' operations during the spring Artois offensive, Pétain coldly and sardonically assaulted the most sacred litany of the French Army:

> It is always prejudicial to cede ground to the enemy. But these inconveniences cannot be related to those which could result at a given moment from the capture by the enemy of three or four battalions, with a loss, by consequence, of several thousands of men.

After the failed offensives of the autumn, Pétain wrote a report which conveyed a barely disguised criticism of Joffre's bull-headed striving for a *percée*. Because of the Allies' inadequate resources of heavy artillery, he declared, it was impossible to

> carry with the same *élan* the successive positions of the enemy ... one does not seek, in fact, to produce a breakthrough. In this first offensive act, what one wants is to inflict such casualties on the enemy that it will be possible later on to attack in depth, at certain chosen points, with superiority.

Pétain was also a disciple of attrition, but in an entirely different sense from Joffre and Haig with their inhumanly simple calculations that the Germans could be beaten in the long run through losing man for man, by virtue of the Allied superiority in cannon fodder. 'One does not fight with men against *materiel*', was one of Pétain's favourite maxims; attrition had to be performed by guns, not infantrymen. In his belief in a series of minutely planned, economical offensives with limited objectives – each adding to the total exhaustion of the enemy until the moment for the 'definitive effort' arrived, instead of the one 'Big Push' – Pétain bore some resemblance to the great

Turenne. He might also be likened to Montgomery, in that he
judged this 'definitive effort' could not take place until there
was certainty of success; until the attacking force had three-to
one superiority. Another of his favourite maxims was: 'audacity is the art of knowing how not to be too audacious.' It was
a tenet that lay at the roots of his later reputation as the
over-cautious general, later still as a pessimist, and finally, a
defeatist.

But this caution, this frugal husbanding of manpower, was
not founded purely on cold reasoning. To those close to him in
rank – and particularly to visiting politicians and journalists –
Pétain gave an impression of regal, almost inhuman chilliness,
accentuated by the statuesque majesty of his figure. After dining
with Pétain in 1918 (where he had clearly not enjoyed his
wonted social success), Colonel Repington noted in his diary:
'Freezing formality as usual. Pétain inspires terror except
among a few of his old hands. He reminds me of the average
royal personage, who is one person in company and another
when alone. ... As usual no one addressed Pétain unless he
first addressed them, and only one person spoke at a time.' A
violently hostile book written in 1943 tells of Pétain's icy formality when taking over the 33rd Regiment as a colonel. A
lieutenant-colonel, who had evidently been a close friend in his
class at St Cyr, greeting the new C.O. had addressed him as *tu*,
only to receive a shrivelling rebuff: 'Colonel, I must request
you to keep your distance. I shall require you to salute me, to
speak to me only as *vous*, and, when you must address me, I
should prefer to be called *mon colonel*.' Even allowing for the
passions of the moment, the story is probably true; it is
thoroughly in keeping with Pétain's character (and the 33rd
was suffering from lack of discipline when he took it over).
But for all Pétain's coldness to his near-equals, the reputation
he enjoyed with the *poilus* was legendary, and unique among
French commanders. He was the paternal figure, the leader
who really cared for his men, who suffered what they suffered.
Word had quickly got round that at the Marne, in contrast to
the generals of the Plaza-Toro breed, who led attacks from the
various Châteaux of France, Pétain had moved up into the
front line when the infantry quailed under the German shells.
Later, inspecting a decimated regiment, he said:

You went into the assault singing the *Marseillaise*; it was magnificent. But next time you will not need to sing the *Marseillaise*. There will be a sufficient number of guns to ensure your attack's a success.

He kept his word. After the 1915 offensives, the troops had come to believe that if Pétain called for an attack there must be some point to it, that it would not be a senseless sacrifice of lives in the way of those over-ambitious generals, out to gain recognition from the conquest at any price of a few yards of enemy trench.

Those long years in junior command had given him an intimacy with the *poilu* denied to most of the other French chiefs, and because of his low rank in 1914 he knew – unlike Haig and Joffre – very well what wounded men looked like. In his rapid rise to stardom he still retained a measure of the paternalism of the good C.O. He knew how much apparently little things mattered to the fighting soldier. Neglect of them could throw him into a searing rage; as when he discovered that a rest camp for troops out of the line had been placed within sound of the guns. 'What an idiot!' cried Pétain, on learning at Verdun that a battalion commander, having received the order of alert just as the rations arrived, had ordered his men to depart forthwith on empty stomachs; 'He doesn't deserve to be a corporal.'

Like a Napoleon or a Montgomery, in fact like any truly great captain, Pétain enhanced his magnetic influence over rank-and-file by frequent surprise visits to the front, presenting medals in person immediately after an attack, inquiring about the wounded. The northern, pale-blue eyes seemed to be everywhere, and he was reputed to have a remarkable instinct for knowing whom to praise and whom to blame. Though he was apparently deeply affected by his visits to hospitals, Pétain refused to allow squeamishness to deter him from his duty. On one such occasion he was so moved by meeting a hopelessly wounded eighteen-year-old that he arranged, at his own expense, for the young soldier to see his mother.

Many years later, at the nadir of tragedy, when Pétain, in his dotage, was being pressed to closer collaboration with the Nazis, the faithful Serrigny remarked to him: 'You think too much about the French and not enough about France.' Perhaps it was true. Certainly Pétain's love for the French soldier in 1916 seems to have been entirely naïve and genuine, remarkably free (whatever may have been written more recently) of bogus popularity seeking; in any case, soldiers the world over are phenomenally quick to distinguish the genuine from the phony. As Pierrefeu says of him, after his appointment to the Supreme Command:

Never did Pétain cease to be himself in the presence of the troops. No familiarity, no fatherly affection, no display of sentiment; for such do not deceive the soldier for a moment. He remained calm and imposing, a true Commander-in-Chief wielding sovereign authority. He spoke as man to men, dominating them with his prestige, without trying to put himself on a lower level, as do those who form a false picture of the people. But there was such sincerity and seriousness in his tone, he seemed so absolutely honest, just, and human, that nobody doubted his word. The General derived all his strength, in fact, from his humanity.

As has been seen, the choice of Pétain to command at Verdun was made less because of his qualities than because he happened to be available at the moment. Yet obviously his two great assets – his understanding of the defensive and the devotion he inspired among the troops – ideally suited him to the task there. It was the tragic irony of Fate that, because of the terms of reference to which de Castelnau had committed him in advance, this uniquely humanitarian general would be called upon to subject the men under his command to what was shortly to become the most inhuman conflict of the whole war.

12   The Take-over

À la Guerre, les hommes ne sont rien; c'est un seul homme qui est tout – NAPOLEON I

On reporting to Chantilly on the morning of 25 February, Pétain and Serrigny found that 'the panic was at its peak'. The fall of Verdun was expected momentarily, 'and everybody was saying that General Herr should be shot'. Somehow it leaked out that Pétain had come from Paris, not Noailles, and the word was quickly passed round by those veterans of intrigue that he had first been to see the Minister of War, Galliéni, the implacable foe of G.Q.G. Doubtless the rumour helped augment the alarm in the air. Only Joffre himself, true to form, seemed unaffected by it all. Greeting him with the words '*Eh bien!* Pétain, you know that things really aren't bad at all,' he gave a laconic resumé of the situation, then sent the new Commander on his way, remarking cryptically, 'Now you are easy in your mind.'

The party set forth on the road for Verdun. At Châlons-sur-Marne, Pétain stopped to lunch with General Gouraud, the one-armed hero.[1] By now Pétain appeared to have sunk into a kind of gloom (and no doubt fatigue), as betrayed by a nervous tic of the right eyelid. Always the perfect aide, Serrigny tried to distract him with Rabelaisian reminiscences from army life of twenty years ago. In the course of the conversation, it was revealed that Nini, the garrison belle of Amiens, with whom Gouraud had been passionately enamoured as a Captain, had in fact bestowed her favours on all three officers in the course of time. Gouraud's manifest disconcertion delighted Pétain, and – according to Serrigny – he 'left Châlons in complete serenity'. But his earlier mood soon returned. Deep snow-drifts and sheet ice slowed down the party's progress, and beyond Bar-le-Duc it was reduced to an average of two miles an hour, on running into the chaotic rear of the Verdun army. All the unmistakable

1. His son, also General Gouraud, was among the army leaders imprisoned for their part in the 1961 Algerian revolt.

signs of defeat greeted Pétain's eyes in his first glimpse of the
men he was to command. Every few yards the narrow road was
blocked with an indescribable mêlée. Convoys of reinforcements intermingled with men from the depots of Verdun,
civilian refugees and shattered regiments all streaming back
to the rear. Disorder was accentuated by the terrible conditions.
Horses drawing guns slithered helplessly on the icy road, ambulances full of wounded skidded into ditches. The spectacle,
especially of the broken infantrymen, strongly affected Pétain.
A lieutenant filing past with seventy-five mud-stained survivors
of the decimated 2nd Zouaves noted that the new general was
unable to hold back his tears; it was a detail he remembered
all his life.

Reaching Herr's headquarters at Dugny, Serrigny recalls he
'had the impression very clearly that we had entered a lunatic
asylum. . . . Everybody was talking and gesticulating at the same
time.' Herr, on the verge of breakdown, made little sense. His
Chief of Staff (Ops) did not even seem to know what were the
boundaries of the various corps under command; there was no
map of troop positions, and no one could state just what orders
had been issued. All they could tell Pétain with certainty at
Dugny was the dreadful news that Douaumont had fallen.
Quickly taking stock of the atmosphere, Pétain remarked icily
to Serrigny: 'In these circumstances we shall install ourselves
at Souilly, where I hope we may find a little more calm.' Re-
tracing his footsteps to the little village of Souilly that lay
astride the main Bar-le-Duc–Verdun road, Pétain was met by
de Castelnau, to whom he relayed the dire tidings about Douaumont. Tearing out a sheet from his notebook, de Castelnau
scribbled down his historic order that Verdun must be defended
at all costs on the Right Bank, and handed it to Pétain. The
command of all forces at Verdun was to be taken over at midnight. It was already 11 p.m. and at first Pétain demurred on
the grounds that he was not yet *au fait* with the situation. But
de Castelnau was adamant, having already promulgated (unknown to Pétain) this second order.

The ebullient little general now disappears from the picture,
his dramatic role at Verdun completed.

At midnight Pétain in his first act of command telephoned
General Balfourier, the commander of XX Corps:

'*Allo! C'est moi, général Pétain.* I have taken over command. Tell your troops. Hold fast. I have confidence in you.'

Balfourier replied:

'*C'est vous, mon général? C'est bien!* Now everything is going to be all right.'

A similar call was made to General de Bazelaire, now commanding units on the Left Bank. In his memoirs Pétain recorded tersely:

'*La liaison morale, du chef aux exécutants, était assurée.*'

By now Colonel de Barescut, his Chief-of-Staff, had arrived, and with a thick charcoal Pétain traced out the front to be held by his command. All that could be done that day had been done. It now remained to find the general somewhere to lay his head for the night. There was barely room for a primitive headquarters in the tiny Mairie at Souilly, let alone anywhere to sleep. Eventually Serrigny found a small house belonging to the local solicitor. Attempts to light a fire in the glacial dining-room had to be abandoned when it smoked out the house. After a meagre supper of beans left over from the orderlies' meal, Pétain slept, huddled in an armchair. The next morning the inevitable occurred. For an elderly man, even with the robust constitution of Pétain, the long chase through snow and night, the unheated house – added to the exertions of the previous night – proved too much. Pétain awoke with a high fever, and a doctor diagnosed double pneumonia. In the days before M and B, there was no forty-eight-hour wonder cure; the general would be confined to his bed for at least five or six days. The disease might even be fatal. Was there no limit to the disasters besetting France?

The doctor was pledged to secrecy, and an iron curtain of security was rung down on the headquarters lest news of the new commander's prostration further demoralize the men with their backs to the Meuse. De Barescut and Serrigny were dispatched again and again to the front as Pétain's eyes, and – like Saxe on his litter at Fontenoy – over the next days he directed the battle, shaking with fever, from his sickbed. Somehow the secret was remarkably well kept.

With astonishing rapidity the sick man gathered the threads of the battle into his hands. Order began to replace chaos. He quickly realized that, tactically, the situation at Verdun was not quite as desperate as it had seemed at first sight. Only one bastion of prime importance to the city's defence had been lost so far: Douaumont. In his opinion, 'the fact that Verdun still remained in our hands on 25 February constituted a real success.' Balfourier's 'Iron' XX Corps had now reached the front in its entirety; two further corps were on their way, and a third standing by; Haig, with rather ill grace, had agreed to take over a further sector of the line from the French, so an adequate supply of reinforcements seemed assured. If only Verdun could hold out another two or three days, it would be safe, Pétain thought. But, 'Our façade, so rudely shaken, could crumble from one moment to another.' There was no room for any more deadly mistakes. Methodically, Pétain set about ensuring there would be none. De Castelnau, true to form, had dictated the immediate recapture of Fort Douaumont, but after one suicidal failure Pétain immediately rescinded the order. 'Conserve your strength,' he told his commanders; 'the counter-offensive will follow.' Instead, a '*position de barrage*', a well-organized defensive wall was to be erected along the 'Line of Resistance' that Pétain had traced out the night he took over command. The backbone of this line would be formed by the neglected and despised forts. Orders were sent out to rearm them, to neutralize the demolition mines, and infantry garrisons were dispatched complete with fourteen days' rations and solemn instructions never to capitulate. (At the same time, though its existence was naturally concealed from the rank-and-file, a 'Line of Panic' was also drawn up on the inner circle of forts, Belleville, Souville, Tavannes, and Moulainville. If all went awry and there was to be a last ditch fight for the city, this is where it would take place.)

No component of the French forces at Verdun was more conscious of the influence of the new commander than his ancient passion, the artillery. Pétain himself virtually took over control of the artillery, asking his commanders each morning: 'What have your batteries been doing? Leave the other details till later.' Again and again he insisted that the artillery 'give the infantry the impression that it is supporting them and that it is not dominated.' While the infantry was still too weak to wrest the initiative from the enemy, carefully prepared artillery 'offensives' were directed by Pétain, to cause maximum loss to the enemy at minimum cost to himself. For the first time in the battle the French guns ceased their uncoordinated, spasmodic flea-biting and became welded into one concentrated, fearsome weapon. Nothing quite like it had been seen on the Allied side hitherto. The impact on the Germans was immediate; from this moment, said the *Reichsarchiv*, 'began the flanking fire on the ravines and roads north of Douaumont that was to cause us such severe casualties.'

Though, in the last desperate days of February, it may hardly have seemed the most dramatic, undoubtedly the gravest problem confronting Pétain was one of communications. Only the most precarious of lifelines now connected Verdun with the rest of France. Before 1916, G.Q.G. had stolidly resisted the Army Commission's recommendations to establish new railway lines to Verdun. Now the main line up the Meuse was severed by the enemy astride it at St Mihiel. The second, to Paris via Ste Ménéhould, was under steady bombardment by the Crown Prince's naval guns. Already its dislocation had forced the Verdun artillery to cut its ammunition expenditure sharply. There remained only a narrow-gauge track, reminiscent of an Emmett railway and called the *Meusien*, that was designed to supply the wants of a peacetime garrison, and the second-class road that ran alongside it for some fifty miles from Bar-le-Duc. This road represented the sole act of prescience displayed by the French High Command at Verdun prior to the German attack. In 1915 it had been widened to seven yards, just large enough for an up- and down-column of trucks. But for this Verdun would have been doomed to die of slow strangulation. As it was, to Pétain, mindful of the chaos he had witnessed on the icy road the day of his arrival, there was room for every possible doubt. Soon the Verdun army would total half a million men and 170,000 animals; Pétain's ravenous guns would be demanding twice and treble their previous flow of shells. Could this huge array be supplied without straining to breaking-point the thin lifeline? Certainly no army of this size had ever been maintained by road before.

Pétain's organizing genius was ably supplemented by the engineer responsible for transportation to Verdun: Major Richard. Together they laid down strict rules to keep the vital traffic moving. The road was divided up into six cantonments, each with its own crews of pioneers and vast workshops to service the primitive vehicles. It was to be reserved exclusively for motor transport, all marching columns to keep to the field on either side; any truck breaking down was at once to be heaved into the ditch. There could be no hold-ups. At the same time ten battalions of Territorials were set to work building a new broad-gauge railway to Revigny. But were there enough motor vehicles in the French Army to sustain the flow? The new invention had been badly neglected in the French Army before the war, like most others. In 1914 there were only 170 vehicles in the whole army, and throughout the war the officer in charge of the French Service Corps never held a higher rank than lieutenant-colonel. Fortunately the brilliant improvisation of the Marne aroused G.Q.G. to the possibilities of motor transport. At the time of the German attack, the combined resources of the R.F.V.[1] and the neighbouring Third Army could raise 700 trucks, representing a daily capacity of 1,250 tons. But it was estimated that the forces at Verdun would require at least 2,000 tons a day, plus another 100 for every additional division brought up. Major Richard and his men scoured France for transport. Once again the miracle of the taxis of the Marne was repeated; this time in Paris the price of vegetables doubled as one by one the civilian *camions* disappeared off the streets. Even by the time Pétain took over, Richard had somehow assembled 3,500 assorted vehicles. It was an astonishing feat for a mere major. But still there was a chronic shortage of trained crews. After fifty, sometimes seventy-five hours without a break, drivers began to collapse at their wheels, and another precious vehicle would be written off. Senegalese brought into the service depots at first ate the grease supplied to lubricate the strange monsters. Lack of skill combined with the sheer unreliability of the primitive mechanisms kept Richard's workshops constantly overflowing.

The antics of the vehicles with their solid, treadless tyres on the icy roads reminded an American observer of the irregular march of young elephants: 'Many of them slid over the edge, turning upside down, and others caught fire.' But still the traffic kept flowing. Seen from a distance at night, the dimly lit vehicles resembled 'the folds of some gigantic and luminous

1. *R.F.V.* = *Région Fortifiée du Verdun.*

serpent which never stopped and never ended.' On either side of the road their headlamps lit up the bowed backs of the endless columns of marching men. It seemed as if all the vitality of France were flowing up this narrow artery. Then, on 28 February, disaster struck. There was a drastic thaw, and in a matter of hours the unmetalled road turned to liquid mud. At places it was sinking up to eighteen inches. The young elephants threatened to flounder to a halt, and with them the flow of life-blood to Verdun. Delegated complete powers by Pétain, Richard in desperation summoned up all available Territorials. Almost shoulder to shoulder they were lined along the road, hurling gravel non-stop under the wheels of the passing trucks. An anxious Pétain telephoned Richard:

'Will the road hold?'

'The road will hold.'

'Good. Otherwise I was going to give the order to evacuate the Right Bank.'

The road held. During the critical week beginning 28 February, over 25,000 tons of supplies and 190,000 men were brought in over it to Verdun. At its peak, in June, when 12,000 vehicles were employed, one passed along it every fourteen seconds, and it was estimated that the mileage accrued each week along its short fifty miles added up to twenty-five times the earth's circumference. To ensure that the crisis of February could never be repeated, Pétain employed the equivalent of more than a whole division of men permanently mending the road. All the colourful components of France's Colonial Empire were to be found at work keeping the Verdun lifeline open; powerful Senegalese, with their chants of '*cassa-le-caillou*', wielded picks next to industrious little Annamites, clad in yellow uniforms. During the ten months the siege was to last, Richard's road gangs were said to have shovelled nearly three-quarters of a million tons of metal on to the road. Aptly compared by one historian to General Grant's Chattanooga railway of 1863, it established military history. With something like two-thirds of the whole French Army to pass along it bound for the dreadful Calvary of Verdun, the title Maurice Barrès coined for it was hardly a profanity: the *Voie Sacrée*.

At the front the news 'Pétain is in control' had an instant and magical effect. 'France has her eyes on you,' he had told them in his first Order of the Day, and the troops had their eyes on Pétain; even though for the best part of a week they were not actually to see the new commander in person. What the appearance of de Castelnau had done to raise morale at the various H.Q.s, the mere name of Pétain did among the ordinary soldiers. The sagging line stiffened, and finally froze. The 27th of February, the *Reichsarchiv* recorded as being 'the first day of the Battle for Verdun that, despite the heroic fighting of the troops and despite great and bloody sacrifices, brought German arms no success anywhere.' The *élite* XX Corps was now fully entrenched on the Right Bank, and, as already noted, other big reinforcements were on their way to Verdun. Even the gaping hole left by de Bonneval's precipitate retreat on Belleville Ridge had been plugged before the over-cautious Germans could exploit it – although it had been left open for twelve hours. A hastily assembled group of the famous 75s had been pushed forward on to Froideterre, and its lethal barrage had given one of the fresh divisions of XX Corps just enough time to move up through the ebbing debris of de Bonneval's 37th African Division and establish a firm line from Bras to Haudromont.

It was around Douaumont Village that the main fury of the fighting raged. For the best part of a week it continued. Three times the Germans attacked in vain. Under cover of the machine-gun turrets in the fort (operated by von Brandis) the 24th Brandenburgers were thrown into the fray again, still flushed with their triumph. But this time they suffered their heaviest casualties since the battle began. A new regiment of Saxons made its appearance, only to be massacred by its own heavy guns. On the 27th, a Jäger battalion lost 413 killed. Several times the village actually changed hands. The 420s were then deployed to flail its ruins with their one-ton projectiles. A French lieutenant holding a bunker in the village noted that under the bombardment 'this vast block, 30 metres square, oscillated, at times actually rising up, like a ship.' Yet still the suicide machine-gun nests stayed behind in the pulverized debris and mowed down the German assault waves. The grey carpet that lined the slopes leading up to Douaumont grew thicker. The French 95th Regiment which had held the village

on the disastrous day of 25 February was withdrawn, decimated, from the battle. Other regiments followed. At last, by a
strange quirk of irony, Pétain's own, the 33rd, took its turn at
Douaumont. On the way to the line, an officer of the 33rd wrote
to his parents with premonition, 'Is this farewell?' For many
it was. Within three days word came back to Pétain that one
whole battalion of his old regiment had been virtually wiped
out, and one of its companies reduced to nineteen men. On the
list of officer casualties appeared the name of a young company commander who Pétain recalled had been particularly
eager to join his regiment, and had seemed to have quite a
promising future. Now, badly wounded, he had been taken
prisoner. His name was Captain Charles de Gaulle.

Early on the morning of 4 March, the remnants of the 33rd
were mopped up and the fragmented stones that had once been
Douaumont village fell to the Germans. Still the local commander attempted to retake it by one of those spontaneous
counter-attacks, but Pétain now intervened, crying hold,
enough. With the fall of the village the first phase of the battle
ended, and an even grimmer one began.

13   Reappraisals

On 27 February, Franz Marc, the artist, wrote home in an awed tone from the Verdun front; '... the whole French line is broken through. No man who has not experienced it can have an idea of the fantastic rage and force of the German attack ...' adding, with a characteristic note of compassion, 'the poor horses!' A letter dated 2 March already betrays some misgiving through its protestation: 'I don't for one minute doubt about the fall of Verdun.' 3 March, pure gloom; 'For days I have seen nothing but the most terrible things that can be painted from a human mind.' The next day a French shell put an end to the correspondence, and to a great talent.

One of the things that makes war so fascinating to its students and so frustrating to its participants is that in a moment of supreme crisis it is rarely given for one side, obsessed by its own difficulties, to see just how bad things are in the enemy camp. Though the hard-pressed French could not see it at the time, something had in fact gone dramatically wrong with the meticulous German plans; that is, with the *Crown Prince's plans*. For all its terrifying initial impetus, by the end of February the attack had bogged down, and to a large extent of its own accord. In one most important sense, the bogging down was quite literal. Pursuant to Falkenhayn's scheme of grinding the French Army to pieces by sheer weight of artillery, the Fifth Army's guns had orders to move up to new positions as soon as the enemy first line had been overrun. The timetable for leapfrogging them forward had been a masterpiece of staff work, but – as not infrequently occurs to the end products of the thorough German military mind – one small omission arose to defeat it. No allowance had been made for the physical difficulty of getting heavy guns over a battlefield where all roads had been obliterated and every inch of ground thrown up into huge mounds and craters by the attackers' own bombardment.[1] The thaw which had so earnestly menaced France's lifeline to Verdun became, on balance, more her ally than her foe; it turned the pulverized earth into a glutinous quagmire that sucked off the close-fitting knee-boots of the German infantry; the eight-ton howitzers sank up to their axles in it, and the Germans' new motor tractors were too few and too underpowered to extract them. There remained only the horses and human muscle. With brute strength (it took at least ten horses to shift even one medium field gun), the Germans eventually moved their guns forward but the delays involved meant that many of the deadly 210s, so essential a part of the German offensive technique, were *hors de combat* over long periods of the battle during its most critical phase.

Caught out in the open, the German guns had a heavy toll exacted by the long-range French 155s, now arriving in ever-increasing quantities. A splinter killed the commander of III Corps Field Artillery, brave old General Lotterer who had seldom been far from his forward guns during the first phase of the battle. Particularly terrible was the suffering of Franz Marc's horses; in one day alone, 7,000 died, and 97 were killed by a single shot from a French naval gun. The mere wear-and-tear of the prolonged firing contributed to German losses; after superhuman efforts, one of the monster 420s had been moved up to the Bois des Fosses in order to knock out Fort Souville, but on the third shot a shell exploded in the worn barrel, killing almost the entire crew. When at last the guns were in position, utter exhaustion on the part of the gunners sorely reduced both the rapidity and accuracy of their fire. Finally, over the devas-

1. But at least the Germans learned, which could all too rarely be said of the Allied commanders; much of their success in the 1918 breakthrough was due to Ludendorff's provision of portable ramps and heavy duck-boards so that the artillery could be rushed forward over the shell ground.

tated battlefield and the approach roads – the latter rendered quite chaotic by the even more viscous mud of the Woevre, and clogged with the moving gun-teams – it was impossible to bring up enough ammunition to sustain anything like the rate of fire of the first four days. Supplies became so critical that by 3 March several batteries of howitzers had to be withdrawn altogether.

The effect of this decline in German firepower at a moment when the French artillery, reorganized by Pétain, was beginning to be effective, was immediate and lethal. More and more frequently the assaulting infantry discovered that French machine-gun nests had been left untouched by the artillery. It was all becoming depressingly similar to the mournful experiences of every Allied offensive on the Western Front. What, now, of Falkenhayn's promise that the infantry would just walk into Verdun once the artillery had done its stuff? The casualty lists were growing longer and longer. In the period 21–6 February, the French losses amounted to 25,000 men, and, although during that time the ratio of French and German casualties was reliably estimated at three to one, by the 29th German losses had already passed the 25,000 mark. On 1 March a French listening post overheard a German remark on the telephone: 'if it goes on like this we shan't have a man left after the war.' In III Corps, one battalion of the Prussian Leib Grenadiers had been reduced to 196 strong in the fighting for Douaumont village, and another regiment of the same brigade had, by the second day of March, lost 38 officers and 1,151 men. In XVIII Corps, the three Hessian regiments of the brigade that had overwhelmed Driant in the Bois des Caures had also lost over a thousand men each. Both Corps had to be pulled out of the line, exhausted, on 12 March; by which time the XVIIIth alone had lost 10,309 men and 295 officers.

But perhaps the most punishing – and undeserved – losses had been suffered by von Zwehl's VII Reserve Corps, which had done so brilliantly in the first days of the battle. In its rapid advance up the right bank of the Meuse, it had increasingly exposed its flank to the French on the hills the other side of the river. By 27 February Pétain had amassed a powerful array of heavy batteries there. Even though, forged before the introduction of recoil mechanism, they bounced back and had

to be relaid after each shot just like cannon of the Napoleonic
era, the elderly French 155s cracked and thundered with remarkable accuracy. Firing visually into the dense grey packs
moving across their front on the slopes opposite, only a few
thousand yards off, gunners can seldom have had so superb a
target. One particularly exposed ravine running down to the
Meuse was nicknamed the 'Bowling Alley' by the Germans,
and indeed the image was an apt one. With extremely heavy
losses, the advance of the 77th Brigade over Talou Ridge was
stopped in its tracks. The usury paid merely to hold the conquered ground became daily more prohibitive. Nowhere
seemed to be safe from the searching French guns; during the
first days of March one regiment lost more men while behind
the lines in reserve than during its assault on Haumont Wood
the first day of the offensive. Worse, the Germans seemed helpless to stop the slaughter. Every available battery was brought
to bear on the French guns, but many of these had taken up
position behind the parapets of the forts clustered on the Bois
Bourrus ridge and were consequently most difficult to hit.

To General von Zwehl the slaughter of his triumphant corps
was particularly galling. On three separate occasions before the
war he had taken part in manoeuvres dedicated to the capture
of Verdun, and each had ended with the conclusion that the
attack would have to be made simultaneously on both banks to
obviate the danger of flanking fire. Before the offensive began
he had tried in vain to impress this upon his superiors. Now it
was his men that were paying the penalty. In desperation he
attempted at dawn on the 27th to throw a force across the
Meuse at Samogneux, but the attackers were caught up on wire
entanglements hidden beneath the flooded river. Almost all of
them were either drowned or captured. Von Zwehl now dispatched his Chief of Staff to the Crown Prince to urge once
again, and in no uncertain terms, that a full-scale attack be
launched on the Left Bank.

As the German losses mounted, an eye-witness tells of a
battle-shocked captain, summoned to his Battalion Commander, exclaiming: 'What! . . . Battalion? Is there still such a
thing?' Elsewhere a General described the spectacle of
wounded men that streamed back uncontrollably past his H.Q.
as being 'like a vision of hell'. Each commander began to be-

seech his immediate superior for reinforcements. But, by 25 February, the day when the way to Verdun was wide open, the whole Fifth Army had only one fresh regiment left in reserve. The Crown Prince telephoned Falkenhayn urgently for the reinforcements he had been promised. They were not, and would not be, forthcoming. Battalions that had lost four hundred men received half that number of replacements, in driblets. Meanwhile, the two promised divisions, which, had they been available at the right moment, would almost certainly have presented Verdun to the Germans, were still firmly held at Metz, two days' march away. And Falkenhayn had no intention of releasing his grip on them until the bulk of the French Army had been lured into his trap. The remainder of the German reserves on the Western Front were sitting uselessly opposite the British, awaiting the relief offensive that Haig manifestly had neither the will nor the wherewithal to make. Thus Falkenhayn through his pusillanimity, his passion for half-measures, and his obsession with the 'bleeding white' experiment, on 25–6 February lost the opportunity of bringing off one of the greatest triumphs of the war. It was one that would never recur. Little did he know then, but he had thrown away probably the last good chance that Germany had of winning the war.

Among the German miscalculations that on various historical occasions have seemed Heaven-sent to save the Allies, Falkenhayn's denial of reserves to the Crown Prince reminds one of Hitler halting his Panzers before they closed in on the B.E.F. at Dunkirk, different though the motives may have been. But whatever blame for the German failure in the first week at Verdun may attach to Falkenhayn (and in his Memoirs the Crown Prince heaps all of it on him), the Fifth Army Command was not entirely beyond reproach. It is felt by responsible military critics, French and German, that the Crown Prince could still have taken Verdun on the initial thrust *without* the reserves withheld by Falkenhayn. Certainly, in its execution of the attack the Fifth Army had displayed a cumbersomeness and excess of caution that would never have been countenanced by most of Hitler's captains. By limiting itself to cautious probing on the 21st (all except for the disobedient von Zwehl who had registered the day's only success), it had lost a valuable day.

1 The Kaiser at the Crown Prince's Headquarters at Stenay

2 German 305 mm. Mortar

3 Pioneer Sergeant Kunze
4 Lieutenant Radtke

5 French N.C.O. in a Verdun dugout

6 General Erich von Falkenhayn

7 General Nivelle

8 General Mangin in his Battle Command Post at Verdun

9 Lieutenant-Colonel Driant at his command post in the Bois des Caures, January 1916

10 Lieutenant Rackow: the first
German Officer on Fort Vaux

11 General Pétain

12 Inside Fort Vaux ; wounded and stretcher bearers in the First Aid Post

13 French troops ' de-bussing ' on the Voie Sacrée, April 1916

14 French runners entering Fort Vaux

15 The glacis of Fort Vaux in 1917. (Note the dome of the shattered 75 mm. turret and, behind, a fragment of the heavy turret ring)

16 North of Fort Douaumont ; Christmas Eve, 1916

17 General Joffre (centre) and General de Castelnau (left)

18 The Crown Prince visiting men of the Fifth Army at the front

As late as the 24th, when it was obvious the whole French front was collapsing, the German storm troops still waited for a renewed artillery preparation, and then moved circumspectly, as if half-expecting to walk into some kind of trap. It seemed as if, after eighteen months of complete stalemate on the Western Front, with neither side able to make a breakthrough, the subordinate German commanders at Verdun had lost confidence to succeed where so many others had failed.

On the last day of February a conference took place between the Crown Prince and his staff, and General von Falkenhayn. What was the Fifth Army to do next? The atmosphere was hardly warm. All Falkenhayn could set against the Fifth Army's disappointment at Verdun was the news that the simultaneous U-boat campaign (as ordained in his Memorandum to the Kaiser) had already had outstanding success. As he dwelt particularly on the menace of the French positions on the Left Bank, the Heir to the Throne must have had some difficulty hiding a note of 'I-told-you-so'. For Falkenhayn, in his insistence on limiting the attack to one bank only, had stood in an isolation that was hardly splendid. General de Rivière, the creator of Verdun fortress, had warned that its Achilles Heel lay on the Left Bank. There was the lesson of the pre-war German manoeuvres, and the fact that all Falkenhayn's artillery advisers had stressed the necessity of attacking on both sides of the Meuse. And even Crown Prince Rupprecht, far removed from Verdun, had warned him days before the offensive began that the advance would be halted by flanking fire from the Left Bank. But the cold, aloof Commander-in-Chief had asked no one for advice, and had taken none. In his Memoirs he claims feebly he had foreseen the dangers, but believed that with the limited forces available an attack on the Left Bank would have been stopped by the 'well-constructed' enemy position. (In fact, the French lines there on 21 February were no better prepared than they had been on the Right Bank, and the rejoinder that if he had not had adequate forces he should *not* have undertaken the offensive in the first place is almost too obvious.)

Asked for his views on the future of the offensive, the Crown Prince said, however, that he thought it should continue. Undoubtedly progress would henceforth be more difficult now surprise had been lost, but the prospects of a 'considerable moral and material victory' were still immensely enticing. He insisted on three conditions. Firstly, the offensive must be spread at once to the Left Bank; not, now, because this might represent the best way to Verdun, but 'rather on the tactical necessity of relieving our main attack.' Secondly, he must be 'absolutely assured that the High Command was in a position to furnish us with the necessary men and material for the continuance of the offensive, and that not by driblets, but on a large scale.' Thirdly, the campaign should be halted the moment 'we ourselves were losing more heavily and becoming exhausted more rapidly than the enemy.'

Falkenhayn's precise reply has not been recorded, but it appears to have satisfied the Crown Prince and General von Knobelsdorf. Preparations were set in hand for a major effort on the Left Bank on 6 March, for which a new Army Corps, the VI Reserve, was earmarked (representing, in terms of manpower, an outlay of rather more than the reserves Falkenhayn had withheld in February). Conjointly, a second attack was to be launched the following day on the Right Bank to capture Fort Vaux, whose enfilading guns had also stopped the Fifth Army on its other flank. Until these two menaces were eradicated the centre, anchored on Fort Douaumont, would stand still. The so-called 'Battle of the Wings' was about to begin. Like a fast-growing tumour, Falkenhayn's 'limited' offensive had already doubled in size.

At his headquarters behind the Somme, the astute Prince Rupprecht of Bavaria noted down in his diary: 'I hear that at Verdun the Left Bank of the Meuse is to be attacked now, too. It should have been done at once; now the moment of surprise is lost.'

Geographically, the two banks of the Meuse stand in appreciable contrast to each other. The one is broken by frequent, sudden gullies and steep ridges thickly clad with woods; ideal, as it had proved, for the practice of German infiltration techniques. The other, the Left Bank, is open rolling country where sheep graze prosperously on the broad grassy slopes; valleys are wide, hills less crowded, the cover sparse, and views extensive. It is, in fact, not unlike Salisbury Plain. Of the features between Verdun and the front line, the chief objective designated by the German command was a long, bare barrow running at right angles to the river, and topped with twin hillocks. It was called *le Mort Homme*. Though its elevation was some three hundred feet lower than Fort Douaumont, the field of vision in every direction from it was remarkable. Capture of the Mort Homme would eliminate the most injurious of the French field gun batteries that were crouched behind it, and would effectively dominate the next ridge towards Verdun, the vital Bois Bourrus where the French heavies were concentrated. Just two miles from the German forward positions, the Mort Homme seemed hardly beyond the scope of a determined thrust – especially when it was recalled that the Fifth Army had advanced three times as far during the first four days alone on the Right Bank. But in fact the Mort Homme, with its sinister name acquired from some long-forgotten tragedy of another age, was to be the centre of the most bitter, see-saw fighting for the best part of the next three months.

When, each morning of that first anxious week, Colonel de Barescut attended the sickbed at Souilly to report on the events of the previous night, he had been asked the same question: 'What's new on the Left Bank?' As still the expected attack did not materialize – despite constant intelligence warnings of long columns of troop transports, of construction of the now familiar *Stollen* on the Left Bank – Pétain was heard to remark, 'They don't know their business.' This time France would not, at least, be caught by surprise. Defences were feverishly reinforced, and unremitting artillery fire forced even the Crown Prince to admit that 'our preparations for the attack were considerably interrupted.' By the morning of the 6th, when the thunderous German bombardment began to roll over the French positions, General de Bazelaire had four divisions up in the line on the Left Bank and a fifth in reserve. It was the nearest thing to a coherent defence system yet seen at Verdun.

Nevertheless, the new German onslaught at once chalked up some depressingly easy successes. With an intensity comparable to the devastating bombardment of 21 February, the heavy German shells rained down on a French division of mediocre calibre, the 67th, whose experience of this kind of thing had so far been limited to second-hand accounts from across the river.

Within half an hour, all telephone lines to the rear were, as usual, severed. Morale was shaken. Then, with less delay this time, the German infantry attacked. In a driving snowstorm, the German 77th Brigade crossed the flooded Meuse at Brabant and Champneuville, redeeming its earlier failure. Ingeniously General von Zwehl had smuggled up an armoured train whose well-protected guns gave the infantry close support across the river. The watchful French gunners behind Bois Bourrus soon pin-pointed the train by the tell-tale smoke from its engine, and it was forced to retire, a little ignominiously. But the damage was done; von Zwehl's men were established on the Left Bank, well behind the French first line. Now a quite un-expected calamity overtook the French; the Bois Bourrus gunners rained down a murderous hail on the advancing Ger-mans but in the soft swampy ground bordering the Meuse many of the shell fuses failed to explode. Dismay spread among the defenders. Moving speedily up the Left Bank of the river, General Riemann's 22nd Reserve Division joined up with von Zwehl's men, to effect a neat pincer on the French hemmed within the bend of the river at Regneville. The defence was feeble. By nightfall the Germans had taken the villages of Forges and Regneville and the important Height 265 on Goose Ridge (Côte de I'Oie). At its western extremity this ridge merged into the Bois des Corbeaux that flanked the Mort Homme directly from the northeast. Already, the swift-moving German vanguard was groping its way into the Bois des Corbeaux; the only wood near the Mort Homme, where those well-tried in-filtration tactics could be used to excellent advantage.

However the frontal, main attack towards the Mort Homme had barely moved from its point of departure; stopped by a veritable wall of gunfire from the French artillery that had been anticipating attack from this direction for many days. Repeatedly the hoarse-voiced Feldwebels tried to rally their men forward in one more supreme effort, but the result was always the same. Already an established feature in the fighting of Verdun, success or otherwise of the opposing artillery en-tirely predetermined the fortunes of the infantry.

On the French side, consternation. The 67th Division had given ground too readily. By the end of the second day's fight-ing, over 3,000 of its men had surrendered; more than 1,200 from the 211th Regiment alone. The customary draconian edict was dispatched from General de Bazelaire's H.Q. (alas, also to fall into German hands); the commander at Forges had failed in his duty and would be court-martialled; artillery and machine guns would be turned upon any unit retreating further. It was easy to divine German intentions, and how menacing they suddenly seemed. The crucial Mort Homme was to be taken by a flanking attack from the north-east, via the Bois des Corbeaux. By the afternoon of the 7th, to the accompaniment of barrages enveloping the whole sector that seemed to reach a crescendo of fury, the Germans captured the whole of the Bois des Corbeaux; including the wounded Colonel of the 211th, saved no doubt from savage disgrace himself by a spirited last-ditch defence.

At all costs the Bois had to be retaken. With a crack regiment drawn from the other end of his line, de Bazelaire decided to throw in at dawn on the 8th one of those swift counter-attacks.

Selected to lead this desperate attack was the elegant Lieutenant-Colonel Macker, whose upswept moustachios seem to epitomize all the pride, spartanism, tradition, and fanatical courage that constituted the St Cyrien of pre-1914 France. His action reads more like a page from Austerlitz or Borodino than from the grey annals of the First World War. Aroused by his orderly before dawn, *le beau Colonel*, under a tumultuous bombardment, composedly and meticulously groomed himself for the fray, washing his moustachios in *pinard*, in the absence of water. Like a Napoleonic formation, the regiment lined up shoulder to shoulder in three tight echelons, the colonel at its head brandishing his cane and calmly smoking a cigar. At a steady walk the regiment began to cover the 400 yards to the wood. Great holes were torn in it by the German machine guns and shrapnel, but with a discipline that would have honoured the Old Guard, it closed ranks. At one hundred yards, Macker's men fixed bayonets and charged. Inside the wood the somewhat precarious salient formed by the German advance had been inadequately reinforced. Thoroughly taken aback by the superb *élan* of the French attack coming at them with steel glinting grey in the snowy twilight, and further unnerved by the early death of their commander, the German force now fell back.

By 7.20 a.m. virtually the whole of the Bois des Corbeaux was again in French hands.

News of its loss disjointed German overall plans on the Left Bank at a most critical moment. A bombardment of the Mort Homme that was to prelude an all-out final attack was abruptly called off, and all efforts switched to holding the territory conquered on the 6th against fresh French sallies. Seldom had an impromptu French counter-attack succeeded so well. By 9 March when the Germans were ready to make a renewed attempt on the Mort Homme, via Bethincourt to the north-west, the French were well-consolidated after their initial setback; the *Reichsarchiv* chronicled the 'tragedy of the first utterly collapsed assault on the Left Bank'. But *le beau Colonel*, alas, was barely to outlive his triumph. In yet a second, spirited dawn attack on the 10th, his regiment had pushed the Germans out of another small wood adjacent to the Bois des Corbeaux. Afterwards Macker moved forward to congratulate one of his battalion commanders. Both were struck dead by a German machine-gunner. At this very moment, the Germans attacked again and, as so often happens on the death of an inspired leader, Macker's men lost heart. Once more the Bois des Corbeaux changed hands, but German losses were so high (one Silesian battalion was reduced to 300 men) that they could advance no further. For the next month the front on this approach to the Mort Homme barely shifted.

*

Meanwhile, on the Right Bank the renewed German endeavour had met with even less success. Up to the last minute the enormous problems of ammunition supply to the guns had not been overcome. Even the tough German infantrymen had been used as human mules, lugging the heavy shells up on their backs. But the gas shells to be used in the big trench mortars had displayed a nasty unreliability and troops were not unnaturally reluctant to carry them. In the end the attack had had to be postponed forty-eight hours, so that, once again, the advantage of a synchronized effort on both sides of the Meuse was lost. The impetus of the initial onslaught carried it into the outskirts of Vaux village and to the very edge of the fort.

But there it petered out in a welter of bloody, confused fighting. Amid the confusion (Vaux village is said to have changed hands thirteen times during the March fighting), word came back to the German Divisional Commander, bearing the imaginative name of von Guretzky-Cornitz, that the fort had actually been taken. Without bothering to confirm the report, Guretzky-Cornitz passed it on to Army H.Q., embellished with a few boastful addenda of his own. Again without a query, the news was triumphantly relayed all over the world, with the simultaneous announcement that the Kaiser had bestowed the *Pour le Mérite* upon Guretzky-Cornitz. German troops marched off in column of four, without reconnaissance, to take over the fort. Like tin soldiers they fell; for none of their nation had yet set foot in Fort Vaux. At G.Q.G. the propagandists – still deflated from their bludgeoning over Douaumont – seized on the German blunder and ensuing attempts at justification with shrieks of joy. Joffre himself was jubilant at the news of the German attacks being held all along the line, proclaiming victory and standing by to take most of the credit himself. To the men of the Second Army he declared in a vibrant Order of the Day: 'You will be those of whom it will be said – "they barred the way to Verdun!"' To the National Defence Council he asserted that of course there had never been any intention of abandoning the Right Bank. To an annoyed Pétain he began talking about an early major counter-offensive at Verdun.

14 The Mort Homme

The enemy can renew his endeavours.... France, reassured and confident, knows that the barricades with which the army will oppose them will not be thrown over – GENERAL GALLIÉNI

Neither Pétain nor any of the French commanders at Verdun entirely shared Joffre's optimism. For the Crown Prince was far from having shot his second bolt. The promised reserves were flowing more freely this time, and on 14 March – the first radiant day of spring sunshine – a new all-out attack was launched frontally on the Mort Homme with no less than six divisions. Day after day it continued. To the French it seemed as if there were no limit to the amount of men and shells the enemy was prepared to expend in order to gain possession of this one desolate hill. A monotonous, deadly pattern was established that continued on this one tiny sector of the battlefield almost without let-up for the next two months. After hours of saturating bombardment, the German assault troops would surge forward to carry what remained of the French front line. One could not speak of trenches; they no longer existed. What the advancing Germans occupied were for the most part clusters of shell-holes, where isolated groups of men lived and slept and died defending their 'position' with grenade and pick-helve. For once the Germans were no better off; there were no materials with which to build their beloved *Stollen*, even had the French artillery provided a respite. When once the German impetus had exhausted itself, ground down by the lethal barrages from the Bois Bourrus guns, the inevitable French riposte would – within twenty-four hours – push the survivors back again. But always, always the movement was like that of the incoming tide; each wave in its flow and ebb brought the sea of *Feldgrau* a little further forward.

At what cost! In the fury of the battle casualties on either side were mounting appallingly. A contemporary cartoon in London's *Land and Water*, entitled 'Verdun. Storming Le Mort

Homme', depicted the Kaiser and the Crown Prince flogging German soldiers on into the arms of Death. By the end of March the totals had reached 81,607 Germans to 89,000 French. Compressed as the battle arena had become, losses suffered among the senior commanders were every bit as grievous as among the rank-and-file; in one French division, three out of four full colonels were killed during the mid-March fighting.

On the Left Bank the Germans began to find themselves at an increasing tactical disadvantage. Gone were the woods and broken country where their infiltration methods could excel. The terrifying flame-throwers had now largely become suicide weapons, an immediate target the moment they appeared in the open. In horrible fascination French troops watched as the fuel cannisters, punctured by a grenade or shell, turned their bearers into writhing torches; or when, wounded, the German Pioneers spun round to hose their own companions with the hellish liquid. But worst of all these tactical disabilities was the flanking fire that was crippling their frontal assaults the moment they debouched into open ground. The Fifth Army had spread its attack across the Meuse to eliminate the guns that were gnawing its right flank. Now, in turn, that secondary attack was being eviscerated by French guns that had set up to its right, on a ridge that was the western twin of the Mort Homme, called simply Côte 304. As the Allies had discovered in all their abortive offensives, however wide the front might be there would always be a devilish machine gun on a flank that could hold up a whole division; broaden the front to eliminate that machine gun, and inevitably there would be yet another on the new flank. Like a surgeon treating galloping cancer, the knife is enticed even further from the original point of application. Thus now the Germans, after the costly failure of their first series of attacks on the Mort Homme, decided they could proceed no further until Côte 304 was theirs.

As before, their first effort was crowned with an unattended disaster for the French. In their initial – and nearly successful – attempt on the Mort Homme the Germans had sought to outflank it from the north-east, and now they tried a similar movement on Côte 304 from the west. The point they selected was the western extremity of the Verdun salient, between the villages of Malancourt and Avocourt, where the front swung south through the tip of the Forest of Hesse. Here, in the Bois d'Avocourt, was a dangerous re-entrant in the French lines, but recognized as such and heavily fortified. Well-concealed redoubts were guarded by a triple barrier of barbed wire, fifty yards deep. It was probably the strongest section of the French line on the Left Bank. To the Germans, however, it presented the key to Côte 304, which was the key to Mort Homme, which in turn was the key that would unlock the Right Bank, *und so weiter*.

The task fell to the 11th Bavarian Division, a unit that had recently distinguished itself under von Mackensen in the Serbian and Galician campaigns. Its commander, von Kneussl, had won the *Pour le Mérite* for the capture of the Russian fortress of Przemysl. For a long time the industrious Bavarians had been preparing for such an attack. The usual deep *Stollen* had been dug, and sappers had run several mineshafts beneath the French defences. None of this had escaped French notice, and some of the heaviest mortars they could muster had been brought up; resulting in the burying alive of many of the Bavarians underneath their *Stollen*. Moreover, at the critical moment at least one of the mines failed to go off. However, none of these preparations was necessary; success was presented to the Bavarians in quite another way. The French 29th Division holding the Bois d'Avocourt had been just too long in the trenches. Many of its men came from the soft and dreamy *Midi*. Morale was low and desertion was high. From deserters von Kneussl's intelligence officers gained very precise information on the passages through the enemy wire; even the French themselves afterwards claimed that 'doubtful elements' had entered into parleys with the Germans, and actually shown them the way. Whichever the true cause (and the mystery has never been entirely solved, the German official history still preferring to attribute the success to the sheer 'force' of the Bavarian attack), within four hours on the morning of 20 March the entire position fell, with negligible losses to the attackers. A whole French brigade was surrounded and compelled to surrender; the total bag amounting to 2,825 troops, twenty-five machine guns, and twelve assorted cannon, and a box full of brand new *Croix-de-Guerres* – a discovery which delighted German war correspondents. Among the fifty-eight French officers captured were the Brigadier and two Regimental Commanders, the former taken in his dugout before he had heard a shot fired.

To those in the know in France, the disaster at Avocourt was a stunning blow. President Poincaré wrote gloomily in his diary: *'Encore une défaillance!'*, revealing that this was not the first news he had received of a lapse of morale at Verdun. In the opinion of General Palat this episode was 'perhaps the most deplorable to occur on our side during the Great War'. The disgrace, coupled with the new grave menace it presented, roused the Left Bank defenders to a new fury, and the French 155s made tenancy of the Bois d'Avocourt as disagreeable as possible for the Bavarians. On the 22nd, a major German attempt to capitalize on the Avocourt success was caught by brilliantly sited French machine guns, firing at them from three sides. Rain had turned the battlefield to a swamp, and it proved impossible to move up heavy mortars to knock them out. The French machine-gunners fired until whole battalions were slaughtered, almost to a man. The *Reichsarchiv* speaks of the day's fighting being 'one of the most heroic' of the entire battle, an adjective not infrequently used by First World War official-dom when casualties had been particularly hideous. In fact, the losses of the comparatively few German battalions engaged in this small corner of the Verdun front that day alone exceeded 2,400, little less than the total British casualties on D-Day in 1944. The gain was nil.

On 29 March, the French tried to replug the menacing hole in their lines at Bois d'Avocourt. The attack was led by a distinguished French military writer, Lieutenant-Colonel de Malleray. He retook part of the wood, but, as so often happened, was mortally wounded soon afterwards, with both his legs severed. The story has it that young de Malleray, a second-lieutenant in the same regiment, having heard the first news but not the sequel, was himself on the way up to the line that evening, and encountered his father's Colonel. 'Are you pleased with my father, *mon Colonel*?' the son asked proudly. *'Ah! mon pauvre petit!'* was all he could reply.

Signs of exhaustion were growing among the attackers. One lieutenant-colonel in his prime died of a heart attack, and the

German M.O.s began expressing serious concern about the physical state of the troops. For the first time there were reports of German units refusing to 'go over the top', or surrendering too easily. Increasingly familiar became the tone of letters home like the following: 'Of my section, which consisted of nineteen men, only three are left ... Those who got away with a *Heimatschuss* (a "blighty wound") say they were lucky.' Part of the trouble lay in the German command's ruthless system of keeping divisions in the line over lengthy periods, constantly topping up the losses with new replacements. As the leavening of hardened veterans became sparser and sparser, so the pathetic eighteen-year-olds fresh from the parade grounds in the Fatherland showed themselves less and less capable of standing up to the remorseless demands of the Verdun fighting. Their faltering affected the hitting power of whole regiments. In his usual cold manner, Falkenhayn summed up the March results as follows: 'owing to the peculiar conformation we could not use these successes to bring our artillery far enough forward, and consequently the preparatory work here had to be continued.' Despite the omens of stress and the disappointing results, the Germans kept up their 'preparations', doggedly battering away on the Left Bank, regardless of cost. Steadily the grey tide inched forward. On 31 March, Malancourt fell; on 5 April, Haucourt, and 8 April, Bethincourt. For the French, thought the German commanders, circumstances must be so much worse, casualties so much higher; how much more could they stand? On 1 April, the Kaiser – publicly exposing the German hand for the first time – declared: 'The decision of the War of 1870 took place in Paris. This war will end at Verdun.'

Again the Germans changed their tactics. Now, on 9 April, they decided to mount a full-scale offensive along the whole Verdun front, on both banks of the Meuse; doing what should have been done on 21 February. Côte 304 and the Mort Homme were both to be assaulted simultaneously. The Fifth Army command had been streamlined, with General von Mudra placed in command of the whole Right Bank, and General von Gallwitz brought back from the Balkans to command the Left Bank sector. Von Gallwitz was a talented artillerist, having been the Inspector General of the Field Artillery just before the war, and more recently had added to his lustre in leading the Eleventh Army to victory in Serbia. With him came a young staff officer destined to become one of Germany's greatest commanders in the Second World War; Erich von Manstein. But hardly had General von Gallwitz arrived at Verdun before he was forcibly impressed by the potency of the French artillery: it had just blown to pieces one of his divisional commanders in his car. Gloomily he confided to his diary, 'too great a task, undertaken with inadequate reserves.'

For the actual conquest of the elusive Mort Homme, none other than the elder brother of the Commander-in-Chief had been selected; General of the Cavalry, Eugene von Falkenhayn, commander of the XXII Reserve Corps, and childhood tutor to the Crown Prince. He seems to have had his full share of the family cautiousness; complaining of his methodical slowness, von Gallwitz remarked sarcastically: 'We shall be in Verdun at the earliest by 1920.' Under the relentless pressure all along the front, French commanders of every sector were desperately appealing for reserves; which often were simply not there. Yet, for all the massive support on either side of him, all the elder Falkenhayn could achieve was to push the line up on to the north crest of the Mort Homme. Great was the rejoicing, briefly, in the German camp; for their maps marked this crest as the Mort Homme itself. The rejoicing was not shared by the weary infantrymen who had just fought their way on to it. Beyond, a few hundred yards distant, lay yet another summit, 100 feet higher, the true Mort Homme, which was still firmly held by the French. Few mountaineers can ever have experienced more bitter frustration.

For this latest effort, the greatest since 21 February, the Germans had expended seventeen trainloads of ammunition and many thousands more men. One of the elder Falkenhayn's divisions alone left 2,200 men on the blood-soaked northern slopes of the Mort Homme. But everywhere, with a minor dent here and there, the French line had held. Once again, much of the German casualty list had been caused by those infuriating guns behind Côte 304. In a rare note of optimism Pétain issued an Order of the Day, beginning, 'The 9th of April was a glorious day for our forces,' and ended with a famous paraphrase of Joan of Arc:[1] *'Courage, on les aura!'*

After 9 April it was often difficult to tell to whom the Mort Homme, smoking like a volcano from the concentrated fire of both artilleries, actually belonged. Back and forth between its two summits, Points 265 and 295, swayed the opposing forces, locked together in a crescendo of desperation that typified the worst of the months of ceaseless combat on the Left Bank.

General von Gallwitz now told von Knobelsdorf, the Crown Prince's Chief-of-Staff, with some force, that it would be pointless pursuing the attacks on the Mort Homme until Côte 304 was finally conquered. With characteristic ingenuity, the Germans set to boring two mile-long tunnels – appropriately called 'Gallwitz' and 'Crown Prince' – in order to bring troops right up to the northern base of the Mort Homme in safety. Meanwhile, persistent French counter-attacks during April retook the whole crest of the Mort Homme, wiping out virtually all the German gains of 9 April, and the Côte 304 guns continued to reap their heavy toll.

For twelve days after the 9 April attack, it rained solidly, suspending all operations. The misery of the troops of both sides, clinging to their wretched holes in the corpse-reeking mud, multiplied. The *Reichsarchiv* recorded:

Water in the trenches came above the knees. The men had not a dry thread on their bodies; there was not a dugout that could provide dry accommodation. The numbers of sick rose alarmingly. ...

But at least the enforced postponement saved the Germans from setting off yet another attack at half-cock. To Gallwitz, the gunnery expert, the new attempt on Côte 304 would be a pure artillery exercise; it would literally blast the French off the hill; moreover, it would succeed. Never before – not even on 21 February – would such a concentration of firepower have been seen.

On 3 May, a day of oppressive heat, over 500 heavy German cannon opened fire along a front of little over a mile. For two days and a night the bombardment continued, until French

1. The original: *'Nos ennemis, fussent-ils pendus aux nuages, nous les aurons! Et nous les bouterons hors de France.'*

aviators reported columns of smoke rising to an altitude of two-and-a-half-thousand feet. To the men on the ground it seemed 'as if to finish things off the Germans had decided to point one cannon at each one of us.' Casualties among the French, badly deficient of deep shelters after the weeks of heavy shelling, were appalling. One French officer describes how he was buried three times that day in his trench, and dug out each time by his men. Others were less fortunate. Of one battalion, only three men were said to have survived; many of the remainder were simply buried alive by the shells. One by one the French machine guns were destroyed. For over two days no food or supplies could be got through to the defenders, nor any wounded evacuated. Reinforcements fortunate enough to arrive got lost in the chaos atop the ridge, wandering all night to find their new positions. One company commander who survived the attack recalled that 'nobody knew exactly the location of the mixed-up regiments ... it was impossible to move. Orders had pushed up men on top of men and set up a living wall against the monstrous German avalanche.' Finally, under the obscurity of dust and smoke the Germans managed to get a foothold on the summit, but it took three more days of bitter close combat before the vital Côte 304 was finally theirs.

One of the first demands of the conquering Germans was for a double ration of tobacco – to mask the intolerable odour of corpses. When the balance sheet was finally totted up after the war, it was estimated that 10,000 Frenchmen alone had laid down their lives on this one small corner of France.

The capture of Côte 304 represented the first breach in the 'Line of Resistance' that Pétain had prescribed on taking up his command, and with it the stage was set for the final German attack on the Mort Homme, with the elder Falkenhayn once again in command. This time he could afford to make no mistake; his former pupil, the Crown Prince, was there at his elbow, watching every move. Never since 1914, said the Crown Prince in glee,

have I been able to see a fight so clearly. ... The intense barrage fire of our artillery sweeping the whole slope of the hill was at once a magnificent and awe-inspiring sight; the Mort Homme flamed like a volcano, and the air and the earth alike trembled at the shock of thousands of bursting shells. As zero hour was reached, and punctually to the very minute our barrage lifted, through my glasses I could clearly observe our skirmishers leave their trenches and move steadily forward; here and there I could even distinguish the smoke puffs of bursting bombs. Close behind followed reserves, carrying-parties, and entrenching companies. How were things going? Then from the French trenches were to be seen streaming back to our lines, first a few prisoners here and there, then more and more, and at last whole columns of them; I breathed freely once more! There followed a perceptible pause. My Chief-of-Staff, who had been following the progress of the attack from a more distant position in Consenvoye Wood on the eastern bank, telephoned to me that the attack had failed and that everywhere our men could be seen falling back. I was able to correct him; what he had seen were the crowds of prisoners!

By the end of May, the Germans had taken the whole of the Mort Homme, as well as to its east the important village of Cumières. At one time the tide, before it was checked, had reached the railway station at Chattancourt and was lapping around the very foot of the Bois Bourrus ridge. It was the end of the German offensive on the Left Bank. The Crown Prince had achieved what he set out to do in March; though his small auxiliary clearing action had taken him nearly three months and cost as many lives as the whole of the rest of the fighting to date. Worse still, by the end of May there were indications that for the first time German losses might be exceeding those of the French; within a week one completely new brigade had been as good as wiped out. But the margin of retreat for the French had become very narrow indeed, and now the full weight of the Germans in the West could be thrown against Pétain's men on the Right Bank of the Meuse.

15   Widening Horizons

A Dieu! que la guerre est jolie
Avec ses chants ses longs loisirs.
GUILLAUME APOLLINAIRE, *L'Adieu du cavalier*

. . . The best thing of all has been the chance of taking part
in this war. . . . Every day one goes on learning, every day
one's horizon widens – from *German Students' War Letters*
(ed. Philip Witkop)

Although from March to the end of May the main German
effort took place on the Left Bank of the Meuse, this did not
mean that the Right Bank had become a 'quiet sector'. Far
from it! Frequent vicious little attacks undertaken by both
sides to make a minor tactical gain here and there regularly
supplemented the long casualty lists caused by the relentless
pounding of the rival artilleries. Within the first month of the
battle the effect of this non-stop bombardment, by so mighty
an assemblage of cannon, their fire concentrated within an area
little larger than Richmond Park, had already established an
environment common to both sides of the Meuse that charac-
terized the whole battle of Verdun. The horrors of trench warfare and of the slaughter without limits of the First War are
by now so familiar to the modern reader that further recounting merely benumbs the mind. The Battle of Verdun,
however, through its very intensity – and, later, its length –
added a new dimension of horror. Even this would not in itself
warrant lengthy description were it not for the fact that Verdun's peculiarly sinister environment came to leave an imprint
on men's memories that stood apart from other battles of the
First War; and predominantly so in France where the nightmares it inspired lingered perniciously long years after the
Armistice.

To a French aviator, flying sublimely over it all, the Verdun
front after a rainfall resembled disgustingly the 'humid skin
of a monstrous toad'. Another flyer, James McConnell, (an

American, later killed with the Lafayette Squadron) noted after
passing over 'red-roofed Verdun' – which had 'spots in it where
no red shows and you know what has happened there' – that
abruptly

there is only that sinister brown belt, a strip of murdered nature.
It seems to belong to another world. Every sign of humanity has
been swept away. The woods and roads have vanished like chalk
wiped from a blackboard; of the villages nothing remains but grey
smears. ... During heavy bombardments and attacks I have seen
shells falling like rain. Countless towers of smoke remind one of
Gustave Doré's picture of the fiery tombs of the arch-heretics in
Dante's 'Hell'. ... Now and then monster projectiles hurtling
through the air close by leave one's plane rocking violently in their
wake. Aeroplanes have been cut in two by them.

With the noise of the battle drowned out by his aircraft's
motor, 'it is a weird combination of stillness and havoc . . .'.

The first sounds heard by ground troops approaching Verdun
reminded them of 'a gigantic forge that ceased neither day nor
night'. At once they noted, and were acutely depressed by, the
sombre monotones of the battle area. To some it was 'yellow
and flayed, without a patch of green'; to others a compound of
brown, grey, and black, where the only forms were shell holes.
On the few stumps that remained of Verdun's noble forests
on the Right Bank, the bark either hung down in strips, or else
had long since been consumed by half-starved pack-horses. As
spring came, with the supreme optimism of Nature, the shattered trees pushed out a new leaf here and there, but soon these
too dropped sick and wilting in the poisonous atmosphere. At
night, the Verdun sky resembled a 'stupendous *Aurora Bore-
alis*', but by day the only splashes of colour that one French
soldier-artist could find were the rose tints displayed by the
frightful wounds of the horses lying scattered about the
approach routes, lips pulled back over jaws in the hideousness
of death. Heightening this achromatic gloom was the pall of
smoke over Verdun most of the time, which turned the light
filtering through it to an ashy grey. A French general, several
times in the line at Verdun, recalled to the author that while
marching through the devastated zone his soldiers never sang;
'and you know French soldiers sing a lot'. When they came out
of it they often grew crazily rapturous simply at returning to

'a world of colour, meadows and flowers and woods . . . where rain on the roofs sounds like a harmonic music'.

A mile or two from the front line, troops entered the first communication trenches; though to call them this was generally both an exaggeration and an anachronism. Parapets gradually grew lower and lower until the trench became little deeper than a roadside ditch. Shells now began to fall with increasing regularity among closely packed men. In the darkness (for obvious reasons, approach marches were usually made at night) the columns trampled over the howling wounded that lay underfoot. Suddenly the trench became 'nothing more than a track hardly traced out amid the shell holes'. In the mud, which the shelling had now turned to a consistency of sticky butter, troops stumbled and fell repeatedly; cursing in low undertones, as if fearful of being overhead by the enemy who relentlessly pursued them with his shells at every step. Sometimes there were duckboards around the lips of the huge shell craters. But more often there were not, and heavily laden men falling into the water-filled holes remained there until they drowned, unable to crawl up the greasy sides. If a comrade paused to lend a hand, it often meant that two would drown instead of one. In the chaos of the battlefield, where all reference points had long since been obliterated, relieving detachments often got lost and wandered hopelessly all night; only to be massacred by an enemy machine-gunner as dawn betrayed them. It was not unusual for reliefs to reach the front with only half the numbers that set out, nor for this nightmare approach march to last ten hours or longer.

One of the first things that struck troops fresh to the Verdun battlefield was the fearful stench of putrefaction; 'so disgusting that it almost gives a certain charm to the odour of gas shells.' The British never thought their Allies were as tidy about burying their dead as they might be, but under the non-stop shelling at Verdun an attempt at burial not infrequently resulted in two more corpses to dispose of. It was safer to wrap the dead up in a canvas and simply roll them over the parapet into the largest shell-hole in the vicinity. There were few of these in which did not float some ghastly, stinking fragment of humanity. On the Right Bank several gullies were dubbed, with good cause, '*La Ravine de la Mort*' by the French. Such a one, though most of

it in French hands, was enfiladed by a German machine gun
at each end, which exacted a steady toll. Day after day the
German heavies pounded the corpses in this gully, until they
were quartered, and re-quartered; to one eye-witness it seemed
as if it were filled with dismembered limbs that no one could
or would bury. Even when buried,

shells disinter the bodies, then reinter them, chop them to pieces,
play with them as a cat plays with a mouse.

As the weather grew warmer and the numbers of dead multiplied, the horror reached new peaks. The compressed area of
the battlefield became an open cemetery in which every square
foot contained some decomposed piece of flesh:

You found the dead embedded in the walls of the trenches, heads,
legs, and half-bodies, just as they had been shovelled out of the
way by the picks and shovels of the working party.

Once up in the front line, troops found that life had been
reduced, in the words of a Beaux Arts professor serving with
the Territorials, 'to a struggle between the artillerymen and
the navvy, between the cannon and the mound of earth.' All
day long the enemy guns worked at levelling the holes laboriously scraped out the previous night. At night, no question of
sleep for the men worn out by the day's shelling (it was not
unknown for men in the line to go without sleep for eleven
days). As soon as darkness fell, an officer would lay out a white
tape over the shell ground, and the 'navvies' began to dig;
feverishly, exposed, hoping not to be picked up by enemy flares
and machine guns. By dawn the trench would probably be little
more than eighteen inches deep, but it had to be occupied all
day, while the enemy gunners resumed their work of levelling.
No question of latrines under these conditions; men relieved
themselves where they lay, as best they could. Dysentery became regarded as a norm of life at Verdun. Lice, made much
of by combatants on other fronts, receive little mention. With
luck, by the second morning the trench might have reached a
depth of barely three feet.

Over and again eye-witnesses at Verdun testify to the curious
sensation of having been in the line twice, three times, without
ever having seen an enemy infantryman. On going into the line

for the first time, one second-lieutenant who was later killed
at Verdun, twenty-six-year-old Raymond Jubert, recalled his
Colonel giving the regiment instructions that must have been
repeated a thousand times at Verdun:

You have a mission of sacrifice; here is a post of honour where
they want to attack. Every day you will have casualties, because
they will disturb your work. On the day they want to, they will
massacre you to the last man, and it is your duty to fall.

Battalion after battalion decimated solely by the bombardment would be replaced in the line by others, until these too
had all effectiveness as a fighting unit crushed out of them by
the murderous shelling.[1] After nights of being drenched by icy
rain in a shell-hole under non-stop shelling, a twenty-year-old
French corporal wrote:

Oh, the people who were sleeping in a bed and who tomorrow,
reading their newspaper, would say joyously – 'they are still holding!' Could they imagine what that simple word 'hold' meant?

The sensation provoked by being under prolonged bombardment by heavy guns is something essentially personal and sub-
jective; first-hand accounts cover a wide range of experience.
To Paul Dubrulle, a thirty-four-year-old French Jesuit serving
as an infantry sergeant at Verdun, whose journals are outstanding for their un-embellished realism, it seemed as follows:

When one heard the whistle in the distance, one's whole body
contracted to resist the too excessively potent vibrations of the
explosion, and at each repetition it was a new attack, a new fatigue,
a new suffering. Under this régime, the most solid nerves cannot
resist for long; the moment arrives where the blood mounts to the
head; where fever burns the body and where the nerves, exhausted,
become incapable of reacting. Perhaps the best comparison is that
of seasickness ... finally one abandons one's self to it, one has no

1. To us this kind of futile sacrifice symbolizes the First War mentality.
Yet one must always remember the dilemma facing the French at Verdun,
once de Castelnau had picked up the German gauntlet. By 1916 both
sides had already experimented successfully with 'thinning out' the forward areas to reduce shell-fire casualties. But in the cramped space at
Verdun where the loss of a hundred yards might lead to the loss of the
city the risk of any such thinning out could not be taken by the French.
Similarly the Germans, always attacking, could not avoid a permanent
concentration of men in the forward lines.

longer even the strength to cover oneself with one's pack as protection against splinters, and one scarcely still has left the strength to pray to God. . . . To die from a bullet seems to be nothing; parts of our being remain intact; but to be dismembered, torn to pieces, reduced to pulp, this is a fear that flesh cannot support and which is fundamentally the great suffering of the bombardment. . . .

Dubrulle survived Verdun, but was killed in the Nivelle Offensive of the following year.

More than anything else, it was the apparently infinite duration of the Verdun bombardments that reduced even the strongest nerves. Sergeant-Major César Méléra, a tough adventurer, who had sailed around the world in peacetime and who appeared little affected by the horrors of war, describes his experience of Verdun shell-fire initially with an unemotional economy of words: 'Filthy night, shells.' Three days later he was confiding to his diary that the night bombardment made him 'think of that nightmare room of Edgar Allan Poe, in which the walls closed in one after the other.' The following day: 'Oh how I envy those who can charge with a bayonet instead of waiting to be buried by a shell,' and, finally, the admission:

Verdun is terrible . . . because man is fighting against material, with the sensation of striking out at empty air. . . .

Méléra survived Verdun and the rest of the war, to be killed a fortnight before the Armistice.

With the steadily increasing power of the French artillery, experiences of the infantryman on both sides became more and more similar. In June a soldier of the German 50th Division before Fort Vaux declared that 'the torture of having to lie powerless and defenceless in the middle of an artillery battle' was 'something for which there is nothing comparable on earth.' Through this common denominator of suffering, a curious mutual compassion began to develop between the opposing infantries, with hatred reserved for the artillery in general. To Captain Cochin on the Mort Homme, it seemed as if the two artilleries were playing some idiotic game with each other, to see which could cause the most damage to the two unhappy lines of infantrymen.

What the P.B.I. felt about their own gunners may be gauged

from a French estimate that out of ten shells falling on a Verdun trench, 'on an average two were provided by the friendly artillery'. Sergeant Élie Tardivel tells how in June seven men from a neighbouring platoon had just been killed by a single French 155 shell:

I met the company commander; I told him I had brought up some grenades and barbed-wire; I asked where I was to put them. He replied: 'Wherever you wish. For two hours our own guns have been bombarding us, and if it goes on I shall take my company and bombard the gunner with these grenades!'

Emotions between the infantry and gunners resembled those sometimes held towards the heavy-bomber crews of World War II,[1] whom the ground troops viewed as sumptuously quartered well away from the enemy, making brief sorties to spray their bombs indiscriminately over both lines. A French company commander, Charles Delvert, describes passing two naval batteries en route for Verdun:

Not a single man on foot. Everybody in motors. The officers had a comfortable little car to themselves. . . . I looked at my poor troopers. They straggled lamentably along the road, bent in two by the weight of their packs, streaming with water, and all this to go and become mashed to pulp in muddy trenches.

Other infantrymen were irked by the impersonal casualness with which the heavy gunners crews emerged from their comfortable shelters to fire at targets they could not see, 'appearing to be much less concerned than about the soup or the bucket of wine which had just been brought.'

This picture is to some extent endorsed by the artillery themselves. Staff-Sergeant Fonsagrive, serving with a 105 mm. battery wrote in his journal during the peak of the March battle on the Right Bank; 'the fine weather continues, the days lengthen; it is a pleasure to get up in the morning. . . .' Watching the planes dog-fighting overhead, there was plenty of leisure time for day-dreaming about wives and families. Later, Fonsagrive notes with some vexation:

One day when, quietly sitting underneath an apple tree, I was

1. Though emotions were more violent, with members of the two arms coming to blows when they met on leave.

writing a letter, a 130 mm. shell landed forty metres behind me, causing me a disagreeable surprise.

Major Henches, another artilleryman (killed on the Somme that autumn) found time to write to his wife during the May fighting at Verdun:

Tell the children we have a poor refugee dog which suffers from a terrible fear and displeases me because he is dirty and snores at night. Two swallows have made their nest near us. . . .

Not all French gunners, however, were as fortunate as Sergeant Fonsagrive. When death came from the long-range German counter-battery guns, it came with frightening suddenness. A gunner sipping his soup astraddle his cannon, a group of N.C.O.s playing cards would be expunged by an unheralded salvo. In action, the field artillery particularly had even less cover than the infantry; often reduced still further by officers of the old school of that notably proud French arm, '*La Reine des Batailles*', who believed (and there were still many like them) that to take cover under fire was almost cowardice. Casualties among some batteries were in fact often at least as high as among the infantry. Captain Humbert, a St Cyrien of the 97th Infantry Regiment, testifies to the effect of the German artillery's systematic sweeping of the back areas, knowing that the French field batteries must all be there:

Nobody escapes; if the guns were spared today, they will catch it tomorrow. . . . Whole batteries lie here demolished, . . .

Lieutenant Gaston Pastre, though also a heavy gunner, provides a very different picture to Fonsagrive. Arriving at Verdun in May, he found the unit he was relieving had lost forty per cent of its effectives; 'If you stay here a month, which is normal,' they warned him, 'you will lose half of yours too.' The reverse slopes up to Fort St Michel on the Right Bank, where Pastre's battery was sited, were crammed with every calibre of gun; it was 'nothing more than one immense battery, there are perhaps 500 pieces there.' A wonderful target for German saturation fire – anything that falls between Fort Michel and the road is good.' There were generally only two periods of calm in the day; between 4 and 6 a.m. and between 4 and 7 p.m. when, like subhuman troglodytes, the French gunners emerged from the ground to repair the damage. For the rest of the time, to move from one shelter to another – a distance of about twenty yards – required considerable courage. By night the solitary road from Verdun came under constant fire from the German gunners, certain that French munition columns must be coming up it nose to tail. It presented 'a spectacle worthy of Hell', in which men not killed outright were often hurled off their gun carriages by shell blast, to be run over and crushed by their own caissons in the dark.

Next to the incessant bombardment, the stink of putrefaction, and the utter desolation of the battlefield, Verdun combatants testify again and again to the terrifying isolation, seldom experienced to the same degree in other sectors. Verdun was the epitome of a 'soldier's battle'. Within an hour or less of the launching of each organized attack or counter-attack, leadership over the lower echelons ceased to play any significant role. Company commanders would lose all but the most spasmodic and tenuous contact with their platoons, often for days at a time. The situation where one French machine-gun section found itself holding a hole in the front two hundred yards wide with its two machine guns for several days in complete detachment from the rest of the army, was by no means unique. To add to this demoralizing sense of isolation, the tenacious curtain of smoke from the bombardment meant that the front line frequently could not see the supporting troops behind; nor, worse still, could their rockets of supplication asking for the artillery to bring down a barrage, or cease shelling their own positions, be seen at the rear. Countless were the true heroes of Verdun, fighting small Thermopylaes in the shell-holes, who remained unsung and undecorated because no one witnessed their deeds.

After twenty months of fighting, where twenty times I should have died [Raymond Jubert admitted] I have not yet seen war as I imagined it. No; none of those grand tragic tableaux, with sweeping strokes and vivid colours, where death would be a stroke, but these small painful scenes, in obscure corners, of small compass where one cannot possibly distinguish if the mud were flesh or the flesh were mud.

Of all the participants qualifying for the title of hero at Verdun, probably none deserved it more than three of the most humble categories: the runners, the ration parties, and the stretcher-bearers. As a regular lieutenant in charge of the divisional runners at Souville stated, simply: 'The bravery of the man isolated in the midst of danger is the true form of courage.' With telephone lines no sooner laid than torn up by shell-fire, and the runner become the sole means of communication at Verdun, the most frequently heard order at any H.Q. was 'send two runners'. From the relative protection of their holes, the infantry watched in silent admiration at the blue caps of the runners bobbing and dodging among the plumes of exploding T.N.T. It was an almost suicidal occupation. Few paths were not sign-posted by their crumpled remains, and on the Mort Homme one regiment lost twenty-one runners in three hours.

Perhaps demanding even more courage, though, was the role of the *cuistot*, *ravitailleur*, or *homme-soupe*, as the ration parties were variously called, in that it was played out in the solitariness of night.

Under danger, in the dark, one feels a kind of particular horror at finding oneself alone. Courage requires to be seen [noted Jubert]. To be alone, to have nothing to think about except oneself ... to have nothing more to do than to die without a supreme approbation! The soul abdicates quickly and the flesh abandons itself to shudders.

On account of the shelling, motor transport could approach no closer than a cross-roads nicknamed 'Le Tourniquet' at the end of the *Voie Sacrée*. The massacre of the horses, unable to take cover upon the warning whistle of a shell, had become prohibitive. Thus all rations for the men at the front had to come up on the backs of other men. The *cuistots*, three or four to a company, were generally selected from among the elderly, the poor shots, and the poor soldiers. One of the most moving pictures printed in *L'Illustration* during the war was of one of these unhappy *cuistots* crawling on his stomach to the front at Verdun, with flasks of wine lashed to his belt. Each carried a dozen of the heavy flasks, and a score of loaves of bread strung together by string, worn like a bandolier. They often made a round trip of twelve miles every night; even though, bent under their loads, at times they could barely crawl, let alone walk, in the glutinous mud. They arrived, collapsing from fatigue, only to be cursed by comrades, desperate from hunger and thirst, on finding that the flasks of precious *pinard* had been punctured by shell fragments, the bread caked with filth. Frequently they never arrived. Fixed enemy guns fired a shell every two or three minutes on each of the few well-known routes with the accuracy of long practice. Crossing the worst danger zones was like some horrible game of 'Last Across'; they told you that forty *cuistots* had got across safely since the last casualty; you waited for the explosion, then staggered frantically over the open space, knowing that if you were No. 41 the next shell probably had your name on it.

For all the gallantry and self-sacrifice of the *cuistots*, hunger and thirst became regular features at Verdun, adding to the sum of misery to be endured there. Twenty-two-year-old Second-Lieutenant Campana notes how he dispatched a ration party of eight men one night in March. The following morning five came back – without rations. That night another eight set out. None returned. The next night some hundred men from all companies set forth, but were literally massacred by violent gunfire. After three days without food, Campana's men were reduced to scavenging any remnants they could find upon the bodies lying near their position. Many had been decomposing for several weeks. The experience was more the rule than the exception; so too, as winter sufferings gave way to a torrid summer, was this spectacle:

> I saw a man drinking avidly from a green scum-covered marsh, where lay, his black face downward in the water, a dead man lying on his stomach and swollen as if he had not stopped filling himself with water for days ...

Worst of all was the lot of the stretcher-bearers, which usually fell – until the supply was used up – to the regimental musicians. The two-wheeled carts that comprised the principal means of transporting the wounded on other French sectors proved quite useless over the pock-ridden terrain at Verdun; the dogs used to sniff out the wounded went rabid under the shelling. Unlike the runners or the *cuistots*, when carrying a wounded man the unhappy *musiciens–brancardiers* could not fling themselves to the ground each time a shell screamed overhead. Often the demands simply exceeded what human flesh could obey. Response to pleas for volunteers to carry the wounded was usually poor, and the troops at Verdun came to recognize that their chances of being picked up, let alone brought to medical succour, were extremely slim.

During the Second World War, there were cases when the morale of even veteran British Guardsmen suffered if, in the course of an action, they were aware that surgical attention might not be forthcoming for at least five hours. On most Western battlefields, it was normally a matter of an hour or two. Surgical teams and nursing sisters, copiously provided with blood plasma, sulfa-drugs, and penicillin, worked well forward in the battle area, so that a badly wounded man could be given emergency treatment without having to be removed along a bumpy road to hospital. For the more serious cases, there was air transport direct to base hospital, possibly hundreds of miles to the rear. In contrast, at Verdun a casualty – even once picked up – could reckon himself highly fortunate if he received any treatment within twenty-four hours. During the desperate days of July, the wounded lingered in the foul, dark, excrement-ridden vaults of Fort Souville for over six days before they could be evacuated.

Poorly organized as were the French medical services, demand far outstripped supply almost throughout the war, but several times at Verdun the system threatened to break down altogether. There were never enough surgeons, never enough ambulances, of course no 'wonder drugs', and often no chloroform with which to perform the endless amputations of smashed limbs. If a casualty reached the clearing station, his ordeals were by no means over. Georges Duhamel, a doctor at Verdun and later a member of the Academy, vividly describes the chaos in one of these primitive charnel houses in '*La Vie des Martyrs*'. Arriving during the early stages of the battle, he noted in despair, 'there is work here for a month.' The station was overflowing with badly wounded who had already been waiting for treatment for several days. In tears they beseeched to be evacuated; their one terror to be labelled 'untransportable'. These, not merely the hopelessly wounded, but those whose wounds were just too complicated for the frantic surgeons to waste time probing, or who looked as if they would be little use to the army again, were laid outside in the bitter cold. It was not long before German shells landed among this helpless pile, but at least this reduced the doctors' work. Inside, the surgeons, surrounded by dustbins filled with lopped-off limbs, did the best they could to patch up the ghastly wounds caused by the huge shell splinters.

Later Duhamel and his team were visited by an immaculate Inspector-General who told them they really ought to plant a few flowers around the gloomy station. As he left, Duhamel noticed that someone had traced *'Vache'* in the dust on the brass-hat's car.

At the clearing stations the backlog of even the partially repaired mounted alarmingly as, with the constant demand of the *Voie Sacrée* supply route, all too few vehicles could be spared for use as ambulances. British Red Cross sections appeared on the front (among them the poet Laurence Binyon), and later American volunteers. Though the crews drove twenty-four hours at a stretch, unable to wear gasmasks because they fogged up, still there seemed to be more wounded than the ambulances could hold. Meanwhile in the overcrowded, squalid base hospitals, those who had survived so far were dying like flies, their beds immediately refilled. Clyde Balsley, an American very badly wounded with the 'Lafayette Squadron', noted in contrast that

the miracles of science after the forced butchery at Verdun ... made a whole year and a half at the American Hospital pass more quickly than six weeks in the [French] hospital at Verdun.

The wounded in these hospitals lived in terror of the periodical decoration parades; because it had become a recognized custom to reward a man about to die with the *Croix de Guerre*. Of slight compensation were the visits of the 'professional' visitors, such as the patriotic, exquisite, 'Lady in Green', described by Duhamel, who spoke inspiredly to the *grands mutilés* of

the enthusiastic ardour of combat! The superb anguish of bounding ahead, bayonet glittering in the sun. ...

Equipment in these hospitals was hopelessly inadequate, but at Verdun the situation was exacerbated still further by the poisonous environment, virulently contaminated by the thousands of putrefying corpses. Even the medically more advanced Germans noted the frequency of quite minor wounds becoming fatal. Gas gangrene, for which an effective cure was not discovered till a few weeks before the Armistice, claimed an ever-increasing toll; during the April fighting on the Right Bank, one French regiment had thirty-two officers wounded of whom no fewer than nineteen died subsequently, mostly from gas gangrene. In an attempt to reduce infection of head wounds, Joffre issued an order banning beards; the *poilus* complained bitterly, and still the wounded died. After the war, it was estimated that, between 21 February and the end of June, 23,000 French alone had died in hospitals as a result of wounds received at Verdun. How many more died before ever reaching hospital can only be conjectured.

So much for the physical; and what of the spiritual effects of this piling of horror upon horror at Verdun? Many were affected like the young German student, highly religious and torn with doubts about the morality of war, who wrote home shortly before being killed at Verdun on 1 June:

Here we have war, war in its most appalling form, and in our distress we realize the nearness of God.

As in every war men confronted with death who had forgotten, or never knew how, began to pray fervidly. Sergeant Dubrulle, the Jesuit priest, was revolted above all by the hideous indignities he had seen T.N.T. perpetrate upon the bodies God had created. After one terrible shelling early in the battle when human entrails were to be seen dangling in the branches of a tree and a 'torso, without head, without arms, without legs, stuck to the trunk of a tree, flattened and opened', Dubrulle recalls 'how I implored God to put an end to these indignities. Never have I prayed with so much heart.' But, as day after day, month after month, such entreaties remained unanswered, a growing agnosticism appears in the letters from the men at Verdun. Later, on the Somme, even Dubrulle is found expressing singularly non-Catholic sentiments:

Having despaired of living amid such horror, we begged God not to have us killed – the transition is too atrocious – but just to let us be dead. We had but one desire; the end!

At least this part of Dubrulle's prayer was answered the following year.

For every soldier whose mind dwelt on exalted thoughts, possibly three agreed with Sergeant Marc Boasson, a Jewish convert to Catholicism, killed in 1918, who noted that at Verdun 'the atrocious environment corrupts the spirits, obsesses it, dissolves it'.

Corruption revealed itself in the guise of brutalization. As twenty-one-year-old Lieutenant Derville (killed on the Aisne, 1918) predicted at Verdun well before the battle even started:

> Perhaps we shall soon all reach the degree of brutishness and indifference of the soldiers of the First Empire.

It was indeed not very exalting to watch wounded comrades-in-arms die where they lay because they could not be removed. One Divisional Chaplain, Abbé Thellier de Poncheville, recalls the spectacle of a horse, still harnessed to its wagon, struggling in the mud of a huge crater. 'He had been there for two nights, sinking deeper and deeper', but the troops, obsessed by their own suffering, passed by without so much as casting a glance at the wretched beast. The fact was that the daily inoculation of horror had begun to make men immune to sensation. Duhamel explains:

> A short time ago death was the cruel stranger, the visitor with the flannel footsteps ... today, it is the mad dog in the house ... One eats, one drinks beside the dead, one sleeps in the midst of the dying, one laughs and one sings in the company of corpses ... The frequentation of death which makes life so precious also finishes, sometimes, by giving one a distaste for it, and more often, lassitude.

A period of conditioning on the Verdun battlefield manufactured a callousness towards one's own wounded, and an apathetic, morbid acceptance of mutilation that seem to us – in our comfy isolation – almost bestial. Captain Delvert, one of the more honest and unpretentious of the French war-writers, describes his shock on approaching the Verdun front for the first time, when his company filed past a man lying with his leg shattered by a shell:

> Nobody came to his assistance. One felt that men had become

brutalized by the preoccupation of not leaving their company and also not delaying in a place where death was raining down.

In sharp contrast to the revolted and tortured Dubrulle, young Second-Lieutenant Campana recounts how, at the end of his third spell in the line at Verdun, he cold-bloodedly photographed the body of one of his men killed by a shell that hit his own dugout,

laid open from the shoulders to the haunches like a quartered carcass of meat in a butcher's window.

He sent a copy of the photograph to a friend as a token of what a lucky escape he had had.

Returning from the Mort Homme, Raymond Jubert introspectively posed himself three questions:

What sublime emotion inspires you at the moment of assault?
I thought of nothing other than dragging my feet out of the mud encasing them.
What did you feel after surviving the attack?
I grumbled because I would have to remain several days more without *Pinard*.
Is not one's first act to kneel down and thank God?
No. One relieves oneself.

This kind of moral torpor was perhaps the commonest effect of a spell at Verdun, with even the more sensitive – like Jubert – who resisted the brutalizing tendency admitting to a congelation of all normal reactions. Jubert also recalls the man in his regiment who, returning from the front, was overjoyed to find his house on the outskirts of Verdun still intact; but, on discovering that all its contents had been methodically plundered, he simply burst into laughter.

To troops who had not yet been through the mill at Verdun, passing men whom they were about to relieve was an unnerving experience; they seemed like beings from another world. Lieutenant Georges Gaudy described watching his own regiment return from the May fighting near Douaumont:

First came the skeletons of companies occasionally led by a wounded officer, leaning on a stick. All marched, or rather advanced in small steps, zigzagging as if intoxicated ... It was hard to tell the colour of their faces from that of their tunics. Mud had covered everything, dried off, and then another layer had been re-applied ... They said nothing. They had even lost the strength to complain ... It seemed as if these mute faces were crying something terrible, the unbelievable horror of their martyrdom. Some Territorials who were standing near me became pensive. They had that air of sadness that comes over one when a funeral passes by, and I overheard one say: 'It's no longer an army! These are corpses!' Two of the Territorials wept in silence, like women.

Most of the above accounts come from the French sources. For, compressed in their hemmed-in salient and hammered by an artillery that was always superior, maintained and succoured by organization that was always inferior, things were almost invariably just that much worse for the French. But, as time went on, the gap between the suffering of the opposing armies became narrower and narrower, until it was barely perceptible. By mid April German soldiers were complaining in letters home of the high casualties suffered by their ration parties; 'many would rather endure hunger than make these dangerous expeditions for food'. General von Zwehl, whose corps was to stay at Verdun, without relief, during the whole ten months the battle lasted, speaks of a special 'kind of psychosis' that infected his men there. Lastly, even the blustering von Brandis, the acclaimed conqueror of Douaumont for whom war previously seems to have held nothing but raptures, is to be found eventually expressing a note of horror; nowhere, he declares, not even on the Somme, was there anything to be found worse than the 'death ravines of Verdun'.

16   In Another Country

. . . We agreed that we should be considered rather callous to go on with our usual life when we were reading of 3,000 to 4,000 casualties a day. . . – COLONEL REPINGTON, *The First World War*

They are different men here, men I cannot properly understand, whom I envy and despise. I must think of Kat and Albert and Muller and Tjaden, what will they be doing? . . . Soon they will have to go up to the front-line again – ERICH MARIA REMARQUE, *All Quiet on the Western Front*

One of the characters in Barbusse's great war novel, *Le Feu*, comments bitterly while on leave; 'We are divided into two foreign countries. The front, over there, where there is too much misery, and the rear, here, where there is too much contentment.' It was a sentiment shared in full measure by combatants of both sides at Verdun. After a spell in the line the men felt as if they belonged to some exclusive monastic order whose grim rites were simply beyond the comprehension of the laymen at the rear.

More and more the soldiers felt a certain indefinable malaise during their brief periods of leave at home. Many young Germans, with that strong national instinct for *cameraderie*, regarded their periods of recuperation at rest camps, set amid the glorious woods and hills of Alsace and spent in the company of those with whom they had shared the common experience of Verdun, as among the more idyllic moments of the war. Home leave in the *Vaterland*, austere and grey under the privations of war, all too often presented a sad contrast. Returning soldiers found the civil population too obsessed with their own hardships to try to understand what they were being subjected to at Verdun. Of all the major belligerents, Germany by 1916 was feeling the pinch of war most. There was no mistaking the deadly effectiveness of the British blockade. Everywhere there were shortages. Deprived of the fertilizers so essential to the poor soil, German farms were beginning to conform to the law of diminishing returns. In 1915 the first major demonstration of the war had taken place in Berlin, when five hundred housewives protested before the *Reichstag* that the quality of whipped cream was not up to pre-1914 standards. The following year they protested no longer, as there was no cream at all and butter had become very scarce. Coffee was a nauseous substance concocted from acorns; bread had already been rationed by the beginning of 1915 to about two lb. a week, and goodness knows what was added to the flour to make it so grey and gritty! Things were steadily getting worse, until the following winter would become known as 'the turnip winter'. Most of the copper roofs had disappeared off public buildings, to make driving bands for the shells being so voraciously expended at Verdun, and the park railings were about to follow the roofs. In the streets, vehicles clattered along on tyreless wheels, with the day not so far off when even at the front the airforce would be forced to encase plane wheels in wooden clogs when being wheeled from the hangar, just to save precious rubber. An acute shortage of cotton had already reduced the civil hospitals to using bandages made of paper, and it was hardly surprising that there was also a human shortage in the country, so that soon after the Somme conscription of labour was decreed for the ages of seventeen to sixty.

Far removed from this Spartan scene reigned the Kaiser, in an environment that to some of his disquieted advisers seemed rapidly to be regaining the splendour of pre-war days in inverse proportion to the hardships that were mounting in the rest of the country. Since the first disappointments at Verdun, the All-Highest had withdrawn still further into his fairy-tale world, a world whose contact with reality relied principally upon those improbable 'trench anecdotes' that were imported from the front for his insatiable consumption; or often simply invented. The hunting expeditions had become more numerous; more and more time was spent in the isolated, leisurely magnificence of Schloss Pless in Upper Silesia, or with the Kaiserin and her entourage taking the waters at Bad Homburg. The evenings were whiled away in endless games of *skat* (which the Kaiser seldom appeared to win) with the bored but acquiescent courtiers. At Berlin and G.H.Q. Charleville-Mézières, the Kaiser's appearances were becoming so infrequent that even his senior counsel-

lors were openly expressing disapproval at his aloofness from
the war. Nevertheless, the authoritarian structure of Imperial
Germany, censorship, and the natural self-discipline of the Germans were such that disenchantment remained largely confined
to the upper echelons. Liebknecht's attempt to hold an anti-war
rally in the Potsdamer Platz on 1 May 1916 was not yet anything
more than a flash in the pan. The solid bulk of the nation was
as dedicated as ever to the war, phlegmatic and unquestioning,
turning a closed mind and a deaf ear to the tales men brought
back from Verdun, in much the same way as when, to the succeeding generation, rumours began to filter out from the concentration camps.

On reaching the City of Verdun itself, French troops just out
of the line experienced a sensation not altogether different from
the delight of the Germans transported to Alsace's Elysian
Fields. In one of the city's music halls, the little Green Rooms
still bore the traces of the wistful decorum of peacetime garrison life, in the form of notices decreeing:

By Order of the Police, artistes are forbidden to receive in their
rooms during the show.

But the artistes had all long since departed, and smashed-up
mechanical pianos cluttered the abandoned music-hall. Already
by early March, Verdun had become a ghost town. The civil
population had been summarily evacuated; a few enterprising
and courageous camp-followers, evading the grasp of the gendarmes, had clung on to the last, but eventually all that remained were three elderly townsmen permitted to run a canteen
for the troops. Much of the centre of the city had been destroyed by the German 380 mm. long-range guns. On every
deserted street gutted houses sagged open, their contents in-
decently exposed to view. In one house pulverized by a shell
all that remained was a bust of Napoleon, arms folded and
facing north as if defying the Germans with its stony glare. But,
melancholy as the deserted and shattered city might seem to a
casual visitor, to men out of the line it spelled life. In the subterranean catacombs deep below Vauban's Citadel, there was
safety, a hot meal, a bunk, possibly even a bath; but above all
a respite from the German shells.

In contrast to the Germans, the French civil population

suffered relatively little from commodity shortages. (The exception was, of course, in the occupied areas of the north-east;
but even there life on the whole was considerably more bear-
able than it was in Occupied France under the Nazis.) The
worst scarcity was in coal, some forty per cent of French pro-
duction having been lost owing to the German invasion of the
Lille area, and the population shuddered at the approach of
each winter. For all the agricultural losses, food rationing had
never become a serious matter; in 1914, the fabrication of
croissants was banned, but permitted again after only five
months. In the autumn of 1915 the Government had assumed
powers to requisition at fixed prices all cereal products; in 1916
these powers were extended to sugar, milk, and eggs, but only
limited use was made of them. As in post-Pearl Harbour U.S.A.,
a meatless day each week was decreed, but little effort was made
to enforce it. It was not until 1917, when the U-boat campaign
had reached its zenith, that a Ministry of Food was created;
which then ordered the butchers to close their doors two days
a week, forbade the bakers to sell fancy cakes, and at last
reluctantly began issuing ration cards. Meanwhile, the gastro-
nomic-minded citizens grumbled, but made shift with the aid
of the black-market, so that throughout 1916 the food scarcity
was still barely noticeable.

On his infrequent leaves, the *permissionaire* from Verdun
naturally gravitated towards Paris. Though a mere 150 miles
away, it was indeed like entering another country, another
world. Sometimes he wondered whether the Capital knew about
the War at all. The natural effervescence of Paris can never be
suppressed for long, and it had begun to burst forth from the
restraint of the early days so that, by mid 1916, it presented to
the war-weary world a façade of miraculous brilliance; to the
men from Verdun it was an Arabian Night Baghdad. Mistin-
guett was drawing huge crowds at the Folies-Bergères; the great
Bernhardt, though aged and ailing, was still as seductive as
ever, dividing her time between the theatre and her hospital for
the wounded at the Odéon; at the Opéra Comique *Manon* was
all the rage, and in May, when the Germans were hammering
their way on to Côte 304, there was a glittering film première
of *Salammbô* and once again the Spring Flower Show was
reinstated in all its pre-war glory. Already the ranks of the

creative arts had been woefully thinned; Braque badly wounded, Léger gassed, Derain unscathed but reduced to decorating shell cases; Péguy and Alain-Fournier had been killed, and Apollinaire wounded in the head. Yet somehow the galleries were open again and doing a brisk trade, and publishers could not remember when they had sold so many books.

The men from Verdun viewed this dazzling scene with mixed feelings. Captain Delvert, appraising in April 1916 the crowds of gorgeous well-dressed women who promenaded in the Bois de Boulogne on the arms of their escorts, was reminded of

a national holiday or Longchamp Races ... It appears [he added sourly] that the nation is suffering and that all energies are being strained towards the goal of ultimate victory; however this effort does not diminish the number of promenaders.

And elsewhere during his leave he comments with uncharacteristic bitterness:

Life is good ... one can understand these people behind the lines resigning themselves to the war. ... What is consoling is that one may be perfectly sure that if one perishes in the barbed wire, they will not be too much affected by the loss.

It was with almost a certain sense of relief that Delvert returned to his regiment.

Beyond the sparkling bravado of Paris, in the country at large the inevitable distortions and corruptions that war breeds were readily detectable. By 1916 these were beginning to rankle sorely with the men at the front. There were the *embusqués*, who had somehow dodged the war, and the profiteers who had already amassed sizeable fortunes (from which they were rapidly enriching the restaurateurs and the jewellers, who had never known business to be better). Even the humblest worker in a war plant was earning 100 *sous* a day, compared to the *poilu*'s five. As a result, inflation was gaining speed; by the beginning of 1916, the cost-of-living index had reached 120 (July 1914 = 100), and at the end of the year it would be 135. There was a vigorous black-market, and from time to time the authorities had to cajole citizens to cease hoarding gold. There had been bad and costly muddles in the early days of the war; agriculture had been disrupted by the number of peasants called to the colours, and eventually some had had to be returned to the fields; the great Renault motor works was closed down, all but for a small shop making stretchers – motor vehicles evidently being considered a luxury with little application to the war effort. (What would have happened at Verdun had Renault remained out of business can readily be deduced from what has already been said about the *Voie Sacrée*.) But somehow the economy functioned, often inexplicably, under what was derisively known as the '*système D*' (a derivation from the verb '*se débrouiller*', meaning literally 'to muddle through').

The periodic convulsions that resulted under '*système D*' usually came of good intentions. Less innocent were the scandals such as that exposed in 1916 of Hospital 27, where a crooked doctor had been providing bogus discharges from the army at several thousand francs a time. The offenders got off with unduly light sentences, and ugly rumours persisted that there had been some urgent covering-up by Deputies, and even Ministers, who had been embroiled. Still more sinister were the activities of the defeatists, ranged around the *Bonnet Rouge* newspaper and headed by Malvy, a former Minister of the Interior, and of the downright traitors who earned millions of francs from German sources for their work of demoralization. It was not until well into 1917 that the reckoning came; Malvy was sentenced to five years' banishment, Bolo Pasha and Mata Hari shot, and Almeyreda found strangled in his cell. But, more than the muddlers, the *embusqués*, the profiteers, and the defeatists, of all the excrescences growing at the rear, the fighting men probably resented most of all the so-called *bourreurs de crâne*. These were the writers and newspapermen, paid hacks of the propaganda machine and tools of 'Anastasie', the censor, who from their comfortable offices in Paris wrote of the nobility of war in the terms of Déroulède; of the brave boys dying beautifully *pour la Patrie*; who described the piling up of 'mounds of German dead' at each attack at Verdun, to the accompaniment of 'negligible' French losses; and who published photographs of the *grands mutilés* with such captions as 'A Soldier Who Has Lost Both Feet, Yet Walks Fairly Well With Clever Substitutes', or 'Who Has Lost Both Hands, Yet Can Handle a Cigarette and Salute as Before'.[1] Nothing en-

1. On the other side, the Germans also suffered (though, because of the greater imaginativeness of the French writers, perhaps not quite to

raged the men submitted to the inferno of Verdun more than
nauseous effusions like these, and their officers often went to
extraordinary lengths to obtain copies of *Le Journal de Genève*,
for a reasonably accurate rapportage of the war.

If the gaiety of Paris was only skin-deep, so the various
scandals of inefficiency and corruption were infections that had
as yet penetrated but little further. Beneath, the flesh and organs
of France were still sound, healthy enough to resist worse
privations, and to withstand more savage slashes of the surgeon's knife. True, in a body wearied and weakened by sacrifices
at Verdun, these diseases were to display a certain malignance
the following year,[1] but the time had not yet come. Despite her
losses and suffering, France – like Germany – still displayed a
remarkable solidarity towards the pursuance of the war. Prop-
ping up this solidarity were predominantly two staunch
columns: *Union Sacrée* and the women of France. For a nation
of radicals and independents such as France, the creation of the
Union Sacrée whereby men of all political hues, even the left-
wing pacifists, submerged their feuds in the interests of national
unity, was a miracle such as has not been seen in France since
Napoleon I (and was not to be seen again in the Third, Fourth,
or even Fifth Republics). Its spirit was reminiscent of that
which (temporarily) demolished the social barricades in Britain
during the Blitz. There was that staunch anti-militarist, socialist,
and crypto-anarchist, Anatole France (having attempted to en-
list, aged seventy), resuming his seat among the Conservatives
of the *Académie* which he had abandoned shortly after the
Affair. There was that eater of clerics, Clemenceau, observed
kissing an Abbé on both cheeks. What was even more surprising
was that this *Union*, so unnatural to France, should still endure
after nearly two years of war and reverses. It was significant
that when the International Revolutionary Socialists had held
their conference of April 1916 in Switzerland, barely any of
the French Socialists voiced support for their resolutions call-

---

the same extent); typical of German '*bourrage de crâne*' were the reports
at the beginning of the war that French shells did not explode and their
bullets tended to go clean through one without causing excessive damage!

1. Whereas on the home front in 1914–15 strikes had been negligible,
in 1916 there were 314 (most of them in the last quarter of the year), and
in 1917, the year of the Army mutinies, 696.

ing for an immediate peace. Almost the sole exception was a
young Deputy called Pierre Laval.

To the women of France, the war had brought an emancipa-
tory revolution. Never had they been so great a power in the
country. At the outbreak of war, to a woman they had rushed
off to become nurses, fill the administrative gaps left by the
men, work in the munitions factories. The soldiers grumbled
on returning home to find their wives turned yellow by picric
acid, but they had little redress. Initially, the women were
doubtless drawn by the glamour of the nurse's uniform and by
a sense of adventure; later, as the French women who had not
lost a husband, lover, or brother became fewer and fewer, the
more frivolous motives became replaced by a formidable
dedication. Most of them had become *marraines* to one or
more soldiers, according them benefits ranging merely from
encouraging letters to parcels of food and woollies to the
highest a woman can offer a man. All of them in their letters
exhorted their adopted soldier to '*tenir coûte que coûte*' and
their influence was mighty. No other section of the French
community was boosting the will to war more substantially
than the women; and it was certainly no accident that, as a
source of inspiration, *La Madelon* had almost replaced *La
Marseillaise*. Perhaps symbolic of the whole spirit of 1916 was
the divine Sarah Bernhardt, one leg amputated, but still stump-
ing the boards with a wooden leg. Here was France herself,
mutilated but undaunted.

And so, as the fighting at Verdun was reaching a climax of
frightfulness, the continuance of both the war and the battle
was assured by a firmness on the home fronts of the adversaries
that would not be seen again.

17 The Crown Prince

During the months of March, April, and May, while at Verdun the Germans were painfully inching forward towards the summits of Le Mort Homme and Côte 304, in the world outside there was little enough the belligerents could find of positive comfort. For the first time in British history, and after a long struggle, conscription had become law; but in Dublin the 'Easter Rising' had set the spark to Ireland, and in Mesopotamia General Townshend had surrendered to the Turks at Kut. The Russians had taken Trebizond from the Turks, but had suffered bloodily in the Narocz marshes after a noble response to Joffre's plea for a diversionary offensive to relieve Verdun. On the seas, the packet-steamer *Sussex* had been torpedoed with several Americans aboard, bringing a sharp ultimatum from President Wilson; and both sides were shortly to claim victory in the Battle of Jutland. In Berlin's Potsdamer Platz, Liebknecht had tried to hold an anti-war rally, leading to Germany's first war-time strikes. In Switzerland, Socialists from all over the world had met to condemn the war and prophesy mutual exhaustion. The war went on. At the other end of the world, Shackleton had reached South Georgia Island after two years' isolation in Antarctica:

'Tell me, when was the war over?' I asked.
'The war is not over,' he answered. 'Millions are being killed. Europe is mad. The world is mad.'

At Verdun, the three months represented the period when the least progress was made by either side, for the highest cost. We have already seen how, on the Left Bank, with a fearful expenditure of lives, the German all-out offensive had bought possession of two hills of secondary importance. On the Right Bank the fighting surged back and forth within a small area, well named the 'Deadly Quadrilateral', at the southerly approaches to Fort Douaumont. In a series of sharp, local attacks, the initiative lay alternately with either side. During most of April, von Zwehl's VII Reserve Corps found itself preoccupied in a see-saw battle for one small feature, the stone quarries at Haudromont. Over the whole period, the front on the Right Bank never shifted as much as 1,000 yards; for the Germans, a bitter contrast to the five miles they had advanced in the first four days of the offensive. Meanwhile, never for a second was there any lifting in the murderous artillery blanket laid down by the cannon of the opposing sides, now nearly 4,000 strong.

Have so many ever died for so little gain? Between 1 April and 1 May, the casualty totals had mounted from 81,607 Germans and 89,000 French to 120,000 and 133,000 respectively; by the end of the month, French losses alone had reached approximately 185,000 (roughly equal to the overall German losses in the Battle of Stalingrad).

As the casualty lists mounted, so signs of strain began to appear within the higher commands on both sides, almost simultaneously. At the end of March, the Crown Prince and his Chief-of-Staff, von Knobelsdorf, were still dedicated to the capture of Verdun, come what may; equally, Falkenhayn was still true (in his indecisive fashion) to his aim of bleeding the French Army to death at Verdun, regardless of whether or not the city fell in the process. But gradually a change in positions becomes apparent.

On 29 February, it will be recalled that Falkenhayn had agreed to a spreading of the offensive, to 'clear' the Left Bank, and had allocated some of his jealously guarded reserves for the purpose. Now, after the Fifth Army's first abortive assaults on the Mort Homme, Falkenhayn wrote on 30 March to the Crown Prince, noting that 'the employment of four fresh divisions ... had led to no successes', and asking for information as to his future intent and expectations. A reply framed by Knobelsdorf on the following day, still full of optimism, declared that the offensive had already forced the French to bring 'by far and away the largest part of their reserves to Verdun'. (Falkenhayn wrote caustically in the margin: 'unfortunately not!') Because of their losses at Verdun, continued Knobelsdorf, the French were capable of carrying out local attacks, but no major operation. (Falkenhayn: 'Wrong; be-

cause there are also fourteen British divisions available!')
Summing up, Knobelsdorf said, 'I therefore incline unreservedly
towards the view that the fate of the French Army will be
decided at Verdun.' He urged a continuation of the offensive,
recommending that the thrust be resumed on the Right Bank
as well, with the object of pushing forward to the line *Ouvrage
de Thiaumont* – Fleury – Fort Souville – Fort Tavannes. But,
said Knobelsdorf, the new attacks would demand the 'same
replacements as before'. (Falkenhayn's marginal note: 'That
is impossible!')

Four days later, the Fifth Army leaders received a cold and
curiously revealing reply from Falkenhayn. Their appreciation
of 31 March was, he said, 'not correct in certain essential
points'. He criticized them for being 'too optimistic as to what
is and what is not possible to us', and also for under-estimating
the enemy's ability to launch a major offensive.[1] He went on
to chide the Fifth Army:

> The hypothesis that we are in a position to keep up a constant
> supply of fresh and highly-trained troops to replace those exhausted
> in battle, and also of the necessary supplies and ammunition, is
> erroneous. Even with the best will in the world, we could not do it.

With this *caveat*, he endorsed the Fifth Army proposal for
resuming the offensive on the Right Bank. Then, in a remarkable display of vacillation, he proceeded to pour cold water on
Knobelsdorf's assertion that 'the fate of the French Army will
be decided at Verdun', though this had been the very founda-
tion of his own Memorandum of less than four months earlier.
As soon as it becomes clear that the new attacks would not
achieve their objectives within a reasonable period, then we
must abandon them and 'seek a decision elsewhere', said Falkenhayn half-heartedly, adding:

> Our chances of ending the war quickly would certainly be greatly
> increased if the battle were won; but if we failed to win it, even

---

1. That Falkenhayn was equally prey to excessive optimism is revealed
by the fact that he considered the French had already lost 200,000 men
by the beginning of April; and even up to the publishing of his memoirs
in 1919, he still deluded himself that, during the March fighting 'for two
Germans put out of action, five Frenchmen had to shed their blood,' a
ratio that the previously cited casualty returns show to have been complete
delusion.

after what had already been achieved, our victory would merely be postponed and not rendered impossible, especially if we resolved in good time not to persist with our useless efforts at Verdun, but to take the initiative of attack elsewhere.

To an Army Commander, plunged up to the hilt by his superior in the most desperate battle of the war, this last can have provided little of encouragement or inspiration. Nevertheless, says the Crown Prince, 'I agreed absolutely with his proposal that the question as to whether the offensive should be continued or broken off should be settled by the result of the partial attack on the East [Right] Bank.' It was the last time he and Falkenhayn would be in such agreement.

Now it is clear that Falkenhayn was already beginning to lose interest in the 'bleeding white' experiment. On 6 April, unbeknown to the Hohenzollern Crown Prince, he was asking Crown Prince Rupprecht whether his Sixth Army might not be able to carry out a swift blow at Arras, against the British Army, whose anticipated (by Falkenhayn) relief attack had not yet materialized. This latest change of mind must have thoroughly exasperated Rupprecht. On 21 March, a dispatch from Falkenhayn admitted that Rupprecht had been right about the British not being able to take the offensive, and at the same time it ordered the withdrawal of three of his divisions for the general reserve. Ten days later, Falkenhayn was on the telephone himself, expressing the fear that the British were after all about to attempt a relief operation, 'and probably a landing attempt'. It was hardly surprising that on 17 April Rupprecht – irritated and not keen to be involved in another of Falkenhayn's half-measure offensives that he deplored – coolly declined his invitation to attack the British, pointing to the strong reinforcements now in the line. Reluctantly, Falkenhayn was forced to switch his gaze back to Verdun.

Meanwhile, a blow that would add still further to Falkenhayn's disillusion was about to fall from a totally different direction. The 'second pillar' of his Memorandum had been the launching of unrestricted submarine warfare, to cut off supplies bound for the French front. Initially, the new campaign had shown great promise, but the sinking of the *Sussex* provoked an unexpectedly violent reaction from President Wilson. This alarmed the Kaiser and his Chancellor, Falkenhayn's arch-enemy.[1] 'the Good Theobold' Bethmann-Hollweg, who from the beginning had opposed unleashing the U-boats. In a walk around the garden of G.H.Q. on 30 April, Falkenhayn, with that sure touch of his, managed to reassure his master, who then declared to Bethmann: 'Now you have the choice between America and Verdun!' But the next day a conversation with Gerard, the American Ambassador, convinced the Kaiser that the United States would indeed sever diplomatic relations if the sinkings continued, and, abruptly changing his mind, he promised an immediate ban on unrestricted submarine warfare. Piqued, Falkenhayn tendered his resignation to the Kaiser, but it was rejected.

*

Following Falkenhayn's letter of 4 April, the Fifth Army energetically began preparations for its offensive towards Fort Souville on the Right Bank. But April passed, and then May, without it materializing. Three factors combined to cause repeated postponement; firstly, bad weather throughout most of April impeded the digging of jumping-off trenches; secondly, the French – under a new local commander on the Right Bank – had taken to launching a series of costly, but annoying, counter-attacks; but thirdly, and most important, the attack along the Left Bank had fallen far behind schedule, and before those deadly flanking batteries could be mastered there was little prospect of an advance on the Right Bank. Instead, General von Mudra, the commander on the Right Bank, recommended a system of local advances on a small scale. However, after the spirited French defence of 9–11 April, even von Mudra admitted that this new technique was not likely to succeed. A sharp row flared between himself and Knobelsdorf, with von Mudra – one of the ablest German Corps Commanders – expressing pessimism as to the whole future of the Verdun offensive. On 21 April, he was sent back to his corps in the Argonne by Knobelsdorf, but before departing he gave vent to his doubts in a memo to the Crown Prince.

The twenty-first of April was a red-letter date for the German

1. Bethmann-Hollweg had from the beginning been the focus of opposition to Falkenhayn within the German ruling clique. It was he who had forced Falkenhayn to surrender, in 1915, his post as Minister of War.

Command at Verdun. It was the day the Crown Prince, swayed by von Mudra, came to the irrevocable conclusion that 'Operation GERICHT' had failed, and should be called off altogether. He writes:

I was now convinced, after the stubborn to-and-fro contest for every foot of ground which had continued throughout the whole of April, that although we had more than once changed our methods of attack, a decisive success at Verdun could only be assured at the price of heavy sacrifices, out of all proportion to the desired gains. I naturally came to this conclusion only with the greatest reluctance; it was no easy matter for me, the responsible commander, to abandon my dreams of hope and victory!

The Crown Prince could recall how, the previous year, when Hindenburg and Ludendorff had stood seemingly on the very brink of a Russian collapse, Falkenhayn had terminated the immensely successful Gorlice offensive. More recently, it was impossible to forget how he personally had been let down over the reserves pledged for the first phase at Verdun. On top of Falkenhayn's natural indecisiveness, the Crown Prince now knew enough of what lay behind his frequent references to 'bleeding the French white' to suspect that, even once a critical point had been reached in the battle, the C-in-C could not be relied upon to provide replenishments for 'heavy sacrifices' involved. Thus all the Fifth Army's efforts would end in a futile waste.

With one exception, says the Crown Prince, his views were supported by the Operations Staff of the Fifth Army; 'that exception was my Chief-of-Staff.' That same day, Knobelsdorf replaced the pessimistic von Mudra by General von Lochow, the commander of the Prussian III Corps, who in his views on warfare was roughly equivalent to the more ardent disciples of the *'attaque à outrance'* in France. His role was to 'introduce a quicker tempo' in the Verdun offensive. Also that day, to the Crown Prince's surprise and considerable annoyance, Knobelsdorf engineered – without consulting him – the transfer of his own personal staff officer, Lieutenant-Colonel von Heymann, who was evidently the only officer in the Crown Prince's entourage who could stand up to the iron will of Knobelsdorf. War was now declared between the Hohenzollern heir and his Chief-of-Staff.

On 8 May, the Crown Prince's resolve was strengthened by a dreadful disaster that occurred inside Fort Douaumont. Repeatedly the Fort's Artillery Officer had warned, in vain, against the danger of an accidental explosion. Though no eye-witness survived, there is reason to believe that it all began with some Bavarian soldiers brewing up coffee – in a delightfully careless South German way – on upturned cordite cases, using explosive scooped out of hand grenades as fuel! A small explosion resulted which detonated a store of hand grenades, which in turn set off a number of flame-thrower fuel containers. In a matter of minutes, the flaming liquid was flowing through the corridors of the fort. Before any action could be taken, it had reached a magazine full of 155 mm. shells. It exploded. Those of the fort's garrison who were not instantly blown to pieces had their lungs burst by the blast waves travelling along the corridors. Further away, others that survived the explosion became asphyxiated by its fumes. All lights were extinguished, and panic broke out. An even more tragic fate befell many who, amid the crazed stampede, were able to get out of the fort. As they emerged through the smoke and chaos, with uniforms shredded and faces blackened, they were taken by their countrymen defending the fort outside to be that most feared of enemies – French African troops – and were relentlessly mown down. Six hundred and fifty Germans, including the whole Regimental Staff of the 12th Grenadiers, perished. To this day most of them lie walled-up in one of Douaumont's casemates that were devastated by the explosion.

Five days after the disaster at Douaumont, on 13 May, the third major conference of the campaign took place at the Crown Prince's headquarters. Lt-Col. Hoffman von Waldau, the Chief-of-Staff of X Corps, which now formed the spearhead on the Right Bank, opened with a thoroughly gloomy report. Front-line troops were being used up quicker than units pulled out into reserve could recover; moreover, they were demoralized by what had happened inside Douaumont. The centre division of his corps, the 5th, was incapable of any further effort. But, poorly placed as X Corps was for any new attack, its position on either side of Fort Douaumont was so untenable that just by sitting still it was losing 230 men a day to French shellfire. Therefore, on balance he thought, reluc-

tantly, it would be better to push forward on to the high ground
on the line Thiaumont–Fleury. The other Chief-of-Staff from
the Right Bank, Major Wetzell, was no more confident, making
the old familiar complaint of the lack of forces available.
Whereupon, the Crown Prince hastily intervened to say that
'we were only bound to attack if leaders and troops were fully
confident of success.' Obviously they were not, so he recommended that once again the 'great offensive' on the Right Bank
be postponed. Surprisingly enough, Knobelsdorf agreed. Furthermore, he went so far as to express readiness to try to gain
approval from Falkenhayn for the termination of all operations
at Verdun. The Crown Prince was delighted.

But, on arriving at Charleville-Mézières, Knobelsdorf in fact
took quite the opposite line with Falkenhayn. Pointing out that
on the Left Bank, Côte 304 and most of the Mort Homme had
now been captured, he urged the irresolute Commander-in-
Chief that all could yet be won at Verdun, if only the offensive
were continued on the Right Bank. Falkenhayn wavered, finally gave his permission for the new attack, and even allocated
a fresh division for it.

When news of the new decision reached Stenay, the Crown
Prince was thrown into 'despair':

I exclaimed: 'Your Excellency tells me one thing today and
another tomorrow! I refuse to order the attack! If Main Headquarters order it, I must obey, but I will not do it on my own responsibility!' And, indeed, Main Headquarters shortly afterwards
issued instructions for the continuance of the attack on Verdun!

Three days later, Falkenhayn himself arrived at Stenay. The
Crown Prince writes, utterly disenchanted:

I now became quite clear in my own mind as to the agreement
between him and General von Knobelsdorf. The attack now pro-
jected, with the aid of the promised reinforcements, was to be only
a prelude to a further offensive on a great scale.

Of the three German principals, the Crown Prince was now
all for ending the whole Verdun offensive; Falkenhayn had
lost interest and could be wafted either way by the prevailing
wind; there remained only Knobelsdorf, the most subordinate
of the three, who in his conversion to Falkenhayn's 'bleeding
white' dogma had become more Catholic than the Pope, and

who supported continuation at all costs. Konstantin Schmidt von Knobelsdorf was undoubtedly a most forceful personality. His contemporaries described him as being 'oak-hard', and in his photographs the bullet-head, the upswept moustaches, and rather pig-like eyes remind one more of a typical Prussian *Feldwebel*, with all its connotations of brutal, unimaginative single-mindedness. No elegant, indecisive Falkenhayn this! Well can one imagine Knobelsdorf, swept along by ambition, seeing himself as the organizer of victory at Verdun, exalted to become the Ludendorff of the Western Front. Over both his superiors to some small extent he wielded a moral advantage; on the Army List, he was Falkenhayn's senior and had been his immediate predecessor in command of the 4th Guard Regiment; and just before the war he had been the Crown Prince's mentor in tactics and strategy. But, for all the toughness of Knobelsdorf, one may well ask why the Crown Prince, with his unique access to the ear of the All-Highest, could not prevail over the views of his Chief-of-Staff? In the Sixth Army an order seldom went out without the full support of Crown Prince Rupprecht of Bavaria; why, then, was the influencce upon policy by the heir to the throne of all Germany not still greater? The truth lies in the Crown Prince's own background.

'Little Willy', as he had come to be nicknamed in Britain, was probably one of the most maligned figures of the whole war. The leptic, unfinished-looking figure, with the narrow, sloping shoulders and almost deformed Modigliani neck in its high collar, and the elongated features of an amiable greyhound, was a boon to the caricaturists. The two whippets that accompanied him even at the front and the outsize shako of the Death's Head Hussars he usually wore rounded out the picture. He looked an ineffectual fool, and in some ways he was both ineffectual and foolish. But this was not entirely his fault.

The Crown Prince was just six years old when his father came to the Imperial Throne, and from that moment on all communication – even the most personal – between himself and the Kaiser took place through the formal intermediary of the Chief of the Military Cabinet. His education was placed in the hands of a series of military tutors, and before the pathetic little boy was seven he had been appointed the youngest cor-

poral in the Prussian Army and made to congratulate his father
on his thirtieth birthday in full uniform. It was perhaps no
wonder that he reacted against the spartan, puritanical environment of Potsdam. Initially his reaction took the form, from
an early age, of a series of not always well-chosen amorous
adventures. All his long life the taste never abandoned him.
On a pre-war state visit to India, he outraged officialdom by
cutting a banquet to slip away to a pretty Burmese princess
he had met at the Middlesex Regiment Ball. During the war,
his entourage was frequently scandalized by his affairs with
Frenchwomen in occupied France, and when, in 1923, he was
secretly smuggled back to Germany from exile in Holland, his
friends hustled him through breakfast out of fear that he might
fall in love with some hotel chambermaid and thus jeopardize
the whole plot.

In many ways the Crown Prince's relationship to his stern
father bears a passing resemblance to that of the Prince of
Wales and King George V. Like his cousin, he was intensely
bored by pomp and ceremony; after an official visit to Königs-
berg, he dispatched a typical wire to the Kaiser, reporting
'seventy-five speeches, four and a half hours' duration, and the
usual horrible banquet'. On another occasion, he was actually
placed under house arrest by the Kaiser for skipping a state
function. He loved sport (from which his crippled father was
of course precluded), and in 1909 shocked the Court by flying
with Orville Wright. He had an eclectic, and democratic circle
of acquaintances, and was in touch with social and political
trends in Germany that to many seemed dangerously *avant
garde*. Many were the times when he had his knuckles rapped
sharply for meddling in politics or foreign policy. He had a
genuine interest in the stage and opera (his longest-lived passion
was the American singer, Geraldine Farrar). Most evenings
after dinner there was music at his Headquarters in Stenay,
with the Crown Prince himself sometimes playing the violin,
at which he was a fair performer. Of all his kinsmen, it was
hardly surprising that his favourite had been gay, great-uncle
Edward – his father's *bête noire*.

As the war approached, the Crown Prince had become closely
identified with the warmongering, Pan-German faction. At the
time of the Agadir crisis, he had declared bombastically that

it was 'high time this insolent clique in Paris should be made once more to feel what a Pomeranian Grenadier can do.' He edited a book for children, entitled 'Germany in Arms', glorifying war, and was fond of speaking to German youth about the forthcoming 'happy – cheerful war', whatever that meant. At dinner, he once shocked the wife of an Allied ambassador by saying that it was 'his cherished dream to make war and lead a charge at the head of his regiment.' America's ambassador in Berlin, James W. Gerard remarks that the Crown Prince

surrounded by his remarkable collection of relics and reminders of Napoleon, dreamed only of taking the lead in a successful war of conquest, . . . said that he hoped war would occur while his father was alive; but, if not, he would start a war the moment he came to the throne. However [adds Gerard] I cannot subscribe to the general opinion of the Crown Prince. I found him a most agreeable man, a sharp observer, and the possessor of intellectual attainments of no mean order.

For those bombastic outbursts, Gerard shrewdly blamed 'the effect of his infernal military education, commencing when he was a child', and here indeed, when one recalls the poses being struck throughout pre-war Europe, the Crown Prince appears as little more than a child of the age.

What was remarkable, and commendable, was that once the tragedy had begun, quicker than anybody else in Germany, the Crown Prince realized where it would lead. Impetuous, irresponsible playboy that he may have been, the Crown Prince was endowed beneath it all with an insight, a basic common sense that was certainly deficient in his father. (Had he been permitted to use these qualities, who can tell how different the fate of Germany, and all Europe, might have been?) Long afterwards, giving evidence at the Nuremberg Trials in 1947, the Crown Prince made this interesting remark:

My father said that the Crown Prince has a woman's instinct in political matters. I wished my father had listened more to me. When something unpleasant was about to happen, I always had a cold feeling – purely physical. I also had it in the World War. And if I had this cold feeling, the operation in most cases failed too.

At the time of the Marne, the Crown Prince had communicated his concern to the Kaiser about the difficulties von

Kluck's right wing had run into – only to receive the patronizing rebuff: 'My dear boy! Your fears are quite groundless.' After the Marne, the Crown Prince astonished an American correspondent by stating openly at Stenay, 'We have lost the war. It will go on for a long time but lost it is already.' In December 1915, at the very time Falkenhayn was submitting his Memorandum, he was writing to his father about the possibility of a separate peace with England or Russia, 'if we do not want our fatherland to keep on fighting until complete exhaustion.' At the end of April 1916, he is reputed to have expressed to General Gallwitz his readiness to come to terms with France, and even to hand back Metz.

That this playboy prince-cum-amateur-soldier should have seen the writing on the wall before the professionals hardly enhances one's admiration of the First War military mind. And amateur he was indeed. A corporal at seven, captain at twenty-three, and major at twenty-five, his advancement had been deleteriously rapid. In 1911, aged twenty-nine, the Crown Prince was sent off to Danzig to command a Hussar Regiment (it was a fairly transparent form of exile to preserve him from the temptations of political and amorous indiscretion in Berlin), but he showed himself singularly adept at escaping from the tedium of regimental duties. *Simplizissimus* lampooned him as clad in tennis clothes and remarking: 'Danzig, Danzig! I've heard that name somewhere before!' Thus, when promoted general (aged thirty-two) on the outbreak of war, he was manifestly Germany's most inexperienced commander. Herein lay one main source of the weakness of his position vis-à-vis Knobelsdorf.

Upon mobilization, the Duke of Wurtemberg and the Crown Prince of Bavaria promptly received the command of an army each. It was dynastically imperative that the Prussian heir should be placed at the head of an army, too. But, unlike him, the other two were serious professional soldiers and were entitled to their commands on their own merits. The Kaiser left his son in no doubt about this fact. At the same time he appointed the Crown Prince's former mentor, von Knobelsdorf, to be his Chief-of-Staff, with the injunction: 'Whatever he advises you, you must do.' And the Kaiser did everything he could to ensure that his son should be no more than a figurehead in the army given under his command. At a parade a few years before the war, when the Crown Prince was a major rising thirty, the Kaiser had shown him up before all his men by calling out to the Brigadier, 'teach the boy how to ride!', and now their relationship was as distant and difficult as ever. Although the war had had, in the words of Winston Churchill, 'a sobering and concentrating effect upon a hitherto careless mind', he was still rigidly refused direct access to his father. To Ludendorff, the Crown Prince complained:

If I want to talk personally with my father about something and am admitted to him, he talks for an hour about something or other and then the time of the talk is over and I have not been able to say what I had wanted to say. If I present my ideas in writing, my father marks them for the appropriate offices. . . .

In 1915, Grand Admiral von Tirpitz confided to his diary: 'The Kaiser does not give him a chance.'

Thus, just at the moment when the Battle of Verdun was about to enter its grimmest phase, the one man on the German side who could have put an end to the butchery was impotent to do so. And a similar state of affairs had meanwhile come about on the other side of the lines.

18 The Triumvirate

We have the formula.
GENERAL ROBERT NIVELLE

Douaumont! Douaumont! Ce n'est le nom d'un village, c'est le cri de détresse de la Douleur immense – CHARLES LAQUIÈZE

On 24 March, President Poincaré, clad in that para-military uniform of his own design that somehow contrived to make him look like an elderly chauffeur, and accompanied by Joffre and Prince Alexander of Serbia, made his first visit to Verdun since the battle began. Climbing up to a fort, he noted that Joffre had put on a lot of weight and was badly out of breath; in contrast, 'Pétain has in his eyes a nervous tic, which betrays a certain fatigue.' In fact, Pétain's 'tic' betrayed more than that. Already the battle had made a deep emotional impression upon him. As he stood on the steps of his H.Q. in the *Mairie* at Souilly, watching the coming and going along the *Voie Sacrée*, he had deduced as clearly as through the eyes of a combatant the full horror of the fighting before Verdun. In a passage that reveals a compassion to be found virtually nowhere else in the writings of the other great French commanders, he says:

My heart leapt as I saw our youths of twenty going into the furnace of Verdun, reflecting that with the light-heartedness of their age they would pass too rapidly from the enthusiasm of the first engagement to the lassitude provoked by suffering. ... Jolted about in their uncomfortable trucks, or bowed by the weight of their fighting equipment, they encouraged one another to feign indifference by their songs or by their badinage. ... But how depressing it was when they returned, whether singly as wounded or footsore stragglers, or in the ranks of companies impoverished by their losses! Their expressions, indescribably, seemed frozen by a vision of terror; their gait and their postures betrayed a total dejection; they sagged beneath the weight of horrifying memories; when I spoke to them, they could hardly reply, and even the jocular words of the old soldiers awoke no echo from their troubled minds.

A grim quandary had faced Pétain from the start. There is little doubt that, tactically, in accordance with his ideals of firepower on the defensive and of limiting losses, had it been left to him he would have evacuated the murderous salient on the Right Bank, abandoned Verdun, and 'bled white' the Crown Prince's army as it advanced through a series of carefully prepared lines. Soon after taking up his command he had prepared highly secret plans for just such a withdrawal, and put them under lock and key. After the war, Joffre claimed that on at least two occasions Pétain had to be prevented from evacuating the Right Bank; the claim should perhaps be taken with a judicious amount of salt, but at least it infers that the thought was never far from Pétain's mind. But, whatever he might have liked to do out of good, tactical common sense, it was brutally apparent to him that on the first move towards evacuation he would instantly be sacked by Joffre and de Castelnau; almost certainly to be replaced by an *attaque à outrance* general with none of Pétain's concern about husbanding lives. Thus, to a very real extent, his hands were tied. Nevertheless, in compensation for fighting a battle he disliked, he was at least able to mitigate conditions firstly by placing the strictest permissible limits on French offensive action at Verdun, and partly through getting Joffre to agree to a system of rapid replacements, known as the '*Noria*'.

Pétain, from his own combat experience augmented by what he saw daily from the *Mairie* at Souilly, had at once sensed the rapid decline in the fighting value of troops that had been too long in the line at Verdun. Under the *Noria* system, divisions were pulled out after a matter of days, before their numbers were decimated and morale was impaired, and sent to rest far from the front where they could peacefully regain their strength and assimiliate replacements. In contrast, the Germans (perhaps banking on the national ability to accept horror more phlegmatically than their opponents) kept units in the line until they were literally ground to powder, constantly topping up levels with replacements fresh from the depots. The weaknesses of this system have already been commented on. By 1 May, forty French divisions had passed through Verdun, to twenty-six German. The discrepancy had two important effects upon the Germans: firstly, it tended to demoralize the men in the field, who asked themselves repeatedly 'where do the French get all these fresh men from?'; secondly, it deceived the German Intelligence into assuming that French losses were far heavier than they in fact were – thus further encouraging Knobelsdorf to continue the offensive. (To the French, it also meant that more men of that generation would have the memory of Verdun engraved on their memory than any other First War battle.)

Back at Chantilly, Joffre was becoming increasingly restive at Pétain's conduct of the battle. Admittedly the territorial losses had been minute, but since his appointment Pétain seemed to have done nothing but surrender ground, and by the beginning of April he was still refusing to contemplate a major counter-stroke. It was strictly against the book! Moreover – with their miraculous arithmetical process, described by Pierrefeu as simply adding 'a hundred thousand or thereabouts' every fortnight – the *Deuxième Bureau* placed German casualties by 1 April at 200,000 to only 65,000 French. (Strangely enough, the magical figure of 200,000 was also the figure selected by Falkenhayn as representing French losses up to that date; as has already been noted, the true totals were in fact 81,607 Germans to 89,000 French.) Deceived by these estimates, Joffre could not believe the enemy would be able to maintain his effort much longer; goaded on by the Young Turks of G.Q.G., Pétain's tic worsened, but he stood firm. At Chantilly, it was noted that for the first time in his career as Generalissimo, the mighty Joffre found his authority thwarted. Worse still, the needs of Pétain's *Noria* were draining the reserves that Joffre had been hoarding for the great Anglo-French 'push' on the Somme that summer, upon which he had staked his all. In his Memoirs, Joffre claims that if he had yielded to all Pétain's demands for reinforcements 'the whole French Army would have been absorbed in this battle. .... It would have meant accepting the imposition of the enemy's will.' In fact, by 'accepting' Falkenhayn's challenge at Verdun in the first place, the French High Command had obviously done just that; and, with the hand de Castelnau had dealt Pétain in February, it looked to the man on the spot as if the securing of Verdun would indeed require 'the whole French Army'.

Thus began the rift between Joffre and Pétain. Joffre was

determined not to abandon the Somme offensive, determined
to give it first priority in men and material; but, at the same
time, he also wanted Pétain to strike an offensive attitude at
Verdun. Pétain, growing ever more aggrieved at G.Q.G.'s lack
of sympathy, was convinced that – if Verdun were to be held –
the major French effort for 1916 must be devoted to it; eventually moving to the extreme position that the Somme should
be left entirely to the British. He also left Joffre in no doubt
that he thought that a breakthrough would not be achieved on
the Somme with the means available. As a general, Pétain certainly had his limitations. He had none of the broad strategic
grasp of Foch or de Castelnau; with his gaze concentrated
upon his immediate front (as so often happens to field commanders), he lacked the overall vision of the war that was
accessible to Joffre. All this is true. But, though Pétain may
have seen Verdun as everything, what he saw there in terms
of human intangibles the French Army mutinies of spring 1917
proved he saw with far greater clairvoyance than Joffre, Foch,
or de Castelnau.

Within a matter of weeks of Pétain's appointment, Joffre
was thoroughly regretting it and already contemplating ways
of removing him. But Pétain, regarded as the 'saviour of Verdun', was already the idol of France, while Joffre's own popularity – following the stories that had begun to creep out about
Verdun's unpreparedness – was at its lowest ebb since the first
disastrous month of the war. Those inveterate intriguers at
Chantilly counselled that it would be professional suicide to
sack Pétain now. Suddenly, the advent of a new star at Verdun
presented Joffre with a ready-made solution.

General Robert Nivelle, fifty-eight at the time of Verdun,
came from an old military family and had a mixture of Italian
and English blood. Though he afterwards chose to become a
gunner, he had passed through the famous cavalry school of
Saumur, and still retained all the *panache* of a French cavalryman. At the Marne, Nivelle had been a colonel in command
of an artillery regiment. When the French infantry in front of
him broke, Nivelle drove his field-guns through the retreating
rabble and engaged von Kluck's troops at close range with such
speed and precision that they too broke and ran. In October
1914, Nivelle was promoted brigadier; a divisional commander

three months later, and by December 1915 he had been put in command of III Corps. Meteor-like, his orbit was swift and brilliant; also like a meteor, he was to disappear without a trace. In the rapidity of his early promotion he resembled Pétain, but no further. He was an out-and-out Grandmaisonite, and like Foch he believed that victory was purely a matter of moral force. His ambition was as boundless as his self-confidence. When it came to casualty lists among the infantry he commanded, he combined the blind eye of an artilleryman with the unshakable belief that so long as the end was success the means mattered not. But, in complete antithesis to both Pétain and Joffre, the supreme attribute of Nivelle – cultured, courteous, suave, and eloquent – was his ability to handle the politicians. His allure seems to have been almost hypnotic. Abel Ferry, the youngest and most critical member of the parliamentary Army Commission, gives a typical description of the impact of Nivelle:

Good impression; clear eyes which look you in the face, neat and precise thoughts, no bluff in his speech, good sense dominates everything.

Poincaré was utterly captivated; even Pierrefeu, the cynical chronicler of G.Q.G., fell at first sight, and Lloyd George, for all his generic, instinctive distrust of generals, was seduced into endorsing the disastrous offensive that bore Nivelle's name, in 1917. With an English mother, Nivelle's perfect English may have played its part here, but it was his irradiating self-confidence that really swept people away. His square shoulders gave a potent impression of strength and audacity. His face burned with ruthless determination, and when he expressed an intent his audience was somehow made to feel that it was already *fait accompli*. It was he, not Pétain as is sometimes thought, who gave birth to the immortalized challenge at Verdun:

'Ils ne passeront pas!'

But Nivelle was in reality a triumvirate. His left hand was his Chief-of-Staff, a sombre and sinister character called Major d'Alenson. Immensely tall and bony, with a cavernous face and arresting eyes:

Always badly dressed, with untidy hair and beard, he walked about the corridors with his hand in the belt of his breeches, seeing no one, lost in thought with the air of a melancholy Quixote ... [says Pierrefeu].

One of the most brilliant officers that ever passed through Staff College, d'Alenson was Nivelle's *éminence grise*. He was also dying of consumption, but only he knew it. Feverish, inflamed, sometimes apparently verging on insanity, he believed it was his mission to save France before he died. 'Victory must be won before I die,' he remarked later, 'and I have but a short time to live.' To one under sentence of death himself, the lives of others cannot have assumed undue importance. On and on he drove the hardly unwilling Nivelle into the attack. It was he, more than anyone, who was to fire his commander's imagination with the fatal 1917 offensive on the Chemin des Dames which broke the French Army. A few weeks later he was dead.

Nivelle's right hand, his chief executive, his hatchet-man, was the toughest general in the whole French Army; Charles Mangin, sometimes known to his troops as 'the butcher' or 'eater of men'. At the time of his entry into this account, Mangin was commanding the 5th Division in Nivelle's III Corps, aged forty-nine. Born in the 'Lost Territories', Mangin was the French colonial soldier *par excellence*. Two-thirds of his peacetime career had been spent in the colonies; much of the time engaged in 'pacification', during which he had been wounded three times. In 1898, as a lieutenant he had led the advanced guard of Marchand's remarkable expedition across Africa to Fashoda, which had so nearly brought France to blows with Britain. When he returned to France to lead a brigade to war, he still slept whenever possible in a desert tent – regardless of the obvious dangers. He was a staunch admirer of the qualities of African troops; though this admiration often inflicted terrible massacres upon the wretched colonials thrown into his offensives.

Mangin was a killer, and he looked the part. His face was burnt and eroded by the Sahara; his square jaw seemed permanently set, like a terrier with its teeth clamped into a rat that it was vigorously worrying to death. His mouth was wide, thin-lipped, and cruel; his jet-black hair stood up fiercely *en brosse.* He walked with a quick, nervous gait, and had a Napoleonic habit of standing with his hands behind his back, his head thrust forward. An American correspondent (who whole-heartedly approved of Mangin) remarked that 'his whole appearance gave the impression of an eagle searching for prey'. Seeing him again at the Victory Parade, the same correspondent noted that as Mangin approached the Arc de Triomphe, characteristically 'his sword rises and sweeps back in the most splendid salute ever seen'. The only unexpected thing about this savage-looking soldier was his surprisingly high-pitched voice and great charm.

Whatever else might be said about Mangin, he was one of the technically most competent generals in the French Army. Precise to a fault, nobody was better at coordinating an attack and geting his troops over the top at zero hour. Every bit as self-confident as Nivelle, he assured his men that he possessed '*Baraka*' (an Arab expression for heaven-endowed good fortune). They believed it, and sacrificed themselves again and again for him – even after 1917. Teddy Roosevelt, too, was apparently swept away by Mangin's infectious vigour (perhaps the excitement at meeting so kindred a spirit proved too much for him) in the spring of 1914, and cancelled his visit to Berlin, deciding to stake his money on France – so the story goes. Mangin's motto was: 'concentrate all at one point; but then, right to the limit!' The trouble was he knew no limit. Fear and death meant nothing to him. A real front-line general, more than once he had been wounded during the war while taking grotesque risks. After his disgrace in 1917 there was no doubting his sincerity when he expressed the wish to re-engage as a simple soldier; nor is there any doubt that, had he been allowed to do so, he would have given his life as carelessly as he had required the men under his command to give up theirs. Winston Churchill sums him up brilliantly:

... reckless of all lives and of none more than his own, charging at the head of his troops, fighting rifle in hand when he could escape from his headquarters, thundering down the telephone implacable orders to his subordinates and when necessary defiance to his superiors, Mangin beaten or triumphant, Mangin the Hero or Mangin the Butcher as he was alternately regarded, became on the anvil of Verdun the fiercest warrior-figure of France.

As Mangin's erstwhile chief in Morocco, the great Lyautey remarked of him,

there is no man more capable of getting you into a mess ... and there's no one more capable of getting you out of it!

But could France, in 1916, afford the cost of extrication in terms of the so precious blood of her youth?

Shortly before the Battle of Verdun began, Nivelle had saved Mangin from disgrace when Territorials under his command (apparently pressed too hard) broke badly. From that moment until the end of Nivelle's brief meteoric career, the two were inseparable. At the end of March, III Corps, commanded by the Nivelle triumvirate, was transferred to Verdun and allocated the sector opposite Douaumont on the Right Bank. On the very day Mangin arrived, 2 April, news reached him that a surprise German attack had taken the important Bois de la Caillette. Immediately he threw the only regiment at his disposal into the counter-attack. The wood was retaken three days later. The attack heralded a new French posture on the Right Bank. Few days now went by without some vigorous small-scale attack being launched by Nivelle–Mangin. Were they worth the cost? The Crown Prince admits they contributed to dislocating German plans for resuming the offensive that side of the Meuse; but they were probably less effective than the stubborn defensive battle ordained by Pétain on the Left Bank or the German's own internal difficulties. Meanwhile Pétain fretted at their costliness and did his best to restrain Nivelle. But matters were soon to be placed beyond his control. On 10 April, Joffre visited Nivelle's sector and

was so agreeably impressed by the results obtained that I asked Pétain to give General Nivelle the means of pursuing his advantage on the right and left of Douaumont. But Pétain's demands became more and more pressing. ...

Joffre now had his opportunity. Instead of sacking the obdurate Pétain, he would promote him.

On 19 April, de Castelnau telephoned Pétain from Chantilly. The Commander-in-Chief, he said, had decided to *limoger* de Langle de Cary, Commander of Army Group Centre; Pétain was to move into his shoes; and Nivelle would take over the

Second Army at Verdun. Pétain would still be in indirect control of the battle, insofar as the Second Army lay in his group, but henceforth he would exercise this control from the distance of Bar-le-Duc, while Nivelle would be the man on the spot. It was an admirably neat solution. Joffre explained it to posterity as a

means of withdrawing General Pétain from the battlefield of Verdun, hoping that by giving him a more distant perspective ... he would take in the general situation with a clearer view. ... He was not pleased.

It was a mild understatement. Bitter, frustrated, and thoroughly pessimistic at what he sensed lay ahead for 'his' troops at Verdun, Pétain packed up his simple one-room H.Q. at Souilly. On 1 May, Nivelle arrived. As he mounted the steps of the Mairie, the departing Serrigny heard him declare to d'Alenson, evidently for the consumption of the world at large: 'We have the formula!' Within a few days of Pétain's withdrawal, Joffre followed up by renouncing the Noria system; henceforth whatever miracles it might be required to perform, the army at Verdun could expect no more regular supplies of battle-fresh troops.

*

When Mangin (then in another part of the front) heard of the German capture of Fort Douaumont, he told his officers: 'the retaking of the fort by our troops would be a feat of arms that would excite the imagination of the Universe.' Now, as he peered out from his new H.Q. in Fort Souville at Douaumont's great dome just two miles away, he fell prey to the same irresistible magnetism that had acted upon Haupt and his Brandenburgers. He could think of nothing else but its recapture. The fort was indeed a crippling thorn in the French side. Most of the Nivelle–Mangin counter-attacks had collapsed bloodily, owing to the mere fact of German occupancy of Fort Douaumont. Though its turret guns were no longer functional, the Germans had burrowed several new entries to the north and used it as a gigantic *Stollen*, from which fresh and rested troops could sally the moment there was a French threat. Every night, an average of a thousand men passed through the fort in each direction. But above all it provided the finest observation point on the whole front. One of Mangin's machine-gunners, Robert Desaubliaux, describes its impact on the April–May fighting:

They dominate us from Fort Douaumont; we cannot now take anything without their knowing it, nor dig any trench without their artillery spotting it and immediately bombarding it.

Mangin had already made one attempt on the fort, on 22 April. Then, with remarkable *élan*, his men had actually reached the superstructure but had been driven off by the fort's machine guns. On 8 May he had seen the huge plume of smoke billow out from Douaumont, and gradually the full significance of the disaster within seeped through to his H.Q. Would there ever be a more propitious moment to carry the fort than now when its defenders were still in disarray? Mangin proposed to attack with two regiments on a front of just one kilometre. Nivelle's blessing was immediate. Pétain – who would have preferred to wait until sufficient troops were available to attack on a much wider front, thereby ensuring greater promise of success – was reluctant. However, great was the pressure from Joffre; the Douaumont explosion argued cogently; and finally the suave persuasiveness of Nivelle tipped the balance.

On 13 May, the same day that Knobelsdorf had pushed Falkenhayn into granting a resumption of the German Right Bank offensive, the first orders for the attack (scheduled for 22 May) left Nivelle's H.Q. Within forty-eight hours the Germans knew every detail. All their offensive projects were immediately suspended and work began urgently on patching up Douaumont's defences. Security was never one of Nivelle's strongest points, as was to become tragically apparent the following year.

One day shortly before the attack Mangin paid a visit to Fort Moulainville, the almost exact twin to Douaumont. Standing outside, apparently oblivious to the constant heavy shelling, he interrogated the Commandant as to what was the best way of taking a fort. What kind of guns are you going to use, he was asked? Some brand-new 370 mm. mortars, replied Mangin. '*Mon Général,*' said the Commandant, whose fort had been under steady bombardment by German 420s for the past ten weeks and had not decisively suffered, 'that's quite inadequate.' Mangin stumped away.

For the preliminary bombardment Mangin mustered some three hundred guns, including four of the 370 mm. mortars he set so much store in. It was the most powerful French concentration yet seen at Verdun. Daily for five days preceding the attack (thereby sacrificing what element of surprise there still remained) a thousand tons of shells rained down on the quarter of a square mile of mud that constituted the objective. Spotting conditions were excellent as the French had by now won mastery of the air over Verdun, and aerial photographs of the damage taken at zero hours minus forty were in the hands of Mangin's intelligence officers before the attack went in. All the omens seemed favourable, and one of the battalion commanders was assured by Mangin that

the artillery preparation would permit us to reach the fort with our rifles slung, as it would be completely flattened.

Among the German troops out in the open the French bombardment levied the usual grim toll, and one of the first heavy shells smashed the principal new entry into Douaumont from the North. From all sides the streams of whimpering wounded poured into the fort until its field hospital could take no more. The signal station on top of the fort was wiped out, together with its operators, and by 22 May all the observation turrets had been knocked out. Dust and fumes from the exploding shells made the air inside almost unbreathable. Some elusive leaks in the exhaust of the donkey engine that had just been installed to supply the fort with electric light made matters still worse. When this was remedied, a blast brought a whole sandbag barricade down on top of the engine. With the fort now plunged into darkness inside, its eyes on the outside world blinded, an unpleasant atmosphere of apprehension grew in the fort. For some the strain was too much; three men had to hold down a company commander who had roamed through the pitch-black corridors, shrieking wildly that he wanted to shoot his C.O. A direct hit which opened up the south-west flanking turret forced its abandonment. The breach thus caused was to play a most important role during the French attack, but apart from this not even a crack was made in the main body of the fort by Mangin's mortars. The Commandant of Moulainville had been right.

In the French jumping-off trenches, Guy Hallé, a twenty-three-year-old sergeant of the 74th Infantry Regiment, was experiencing that familiar knotting of the stomach. All his faculties were concentrated on a single thought, he wrote later;

to be able to comport oneself correctly in face of death. It's not very difficult to say this little phrase; but, My God, what a terrible effort it demands! What a hideous thing; to say to oneself, at this moment, I am myself, I am completely whole in myself; my blood circulates and pulses in my arteries; I have my eyes, all my skin is intact, I do not bleed! . . . Oh to be able to sleep thinking that it is finished, that I shall live, that I shall have raptures, pains, grief, pleasures; that I shall not be killed!

Thirty-five minutes before zero hour two solitary German shells fell on the French trenches. Old hands like Hallé shuddered, knowing full well that this meant the Germans had their range and were just waiting for the attackers to show their heads. Despite the fact that early that morning French aircraft firing a new type of rocket had destroyed five out of the six German observation balloons in the sector, the German gunners had had such an ample warning in which to sight their pieces that observation was hardly necessary, and as the first French soldier went over the top a murderously accurate counter-barrage swept the whole line. In a matter of minutes, the 129th Regiment, earmarked for the actual taking of the fort, found its companies reduced to an average of forty-five effectives; one had no more than a lieutenant and twenty-seven men left. A battalion of the 74th, commanded by fifty-year-old Major Lefebvre-Dibon, that had been appointed to the right wing of the attack, reached its objective to find that there was no sign of the battalion on its left which was to have seized the eastern side of Fort Douaumont. It had simply been wiped out; and the battalion of the 74th, that should have been supporting Lefebvre-Dibon to his right, never left the trenches, pinned down by German fire. On top of Fort Souville, Mangin, watching the course of the attack – as usual out in the open – had a lucky escape when a shell severely wounded the four staff officers with him.

Nevertheless, charging fearlessly and magnificently through

the hail of shot and shell, what remained of the 129th reached the fort in eleven minutes flat. It was an incomparable display of the *Furia Francese*. Within half an hour, three-quarters of the fort superstructure, bounded by a line running from the northern apex to the south-east corner, was in French hands. From a distance, *Oberleutnant* Brandis looked on in utter dismay as the *horizon bleu* figures swarmed across 'his' Douaumont. The Crown Prince himself admitted afterwards, it indeed 'seemed likely at one time that the work itself must be lost.' Inside the fort the shaking reverberations of heavy shellfire had meanwhile been replaced by a sharper sound. Hand grenades! At once there was a cry of 'the French are here!'

A small group of French under Sergeant Piau had penetrated into the fort through the breach in the *Casemate de Bourges* at the south-west. Unchallenged, they reached the main East–West passage, the very heart of the fort. For a few tense minutes it seemed as if Douaumont might change hands again. Then a German *Jäger* detachment arrived on the scene. Three of Sergeant Piau's men were killed, the rest thrown back, and a machine gun was set up to ward off future intrusions. For the rest of the day fighting continued in the outer tunnels, but gradually the French were pressed back.

Outside, the French 129th Regiment had taken charge of the semi-wrecked *Casemate de Bourges* and installed a well-protected machine-gun nest on its roof. The position completely dominated the whole superstructure of the fort. Repeatedly, with courage but quite incredible stupidity, the German fort garrison sallied forth to take the machine-gun post frontally. Fifty men of the 20th Regiment charged it; thirty-three of them were mown down. Seventy *Jägers* tried their hand, and fifteen returned; of forty *Leibgrenadiers*, only a couple crawled back into the fort. Yet another assault was broken up with heavy casualties by the German's own field artillery. Attempts to smoke out the machine-gun post failed, and all through the night of the 22nd and the following day it continued to control the fort superstructure.

On the evening of the 22nd, reports came back on both sides that the French were in possession of the fort. Mangin arrived at Nivelle's H.Q. followed by a staff officer carrying a huge satchel full of the dossiers of officers to be recommended for decoration, and pronounced, 'Douaumont is ours!' But the dice were heavily loaded against the attackers. The German ripostes now began in earnest. Under their blows, the French units holding the left flank of the advance melted away in the morning mists of the 23rd, and the two battalions left on the fort found themselves in a narrow salient caught by fire from three sides. On the right flank, Lefebvre-Dibon reported back to his colonel that he had by now lost over forty per cent of his men, and that it was becoming impossible to hold his front without reinforcements. But fresh units ruthlessly hurled forward by Mangin either arrived decimated or not at all. Company-Commander Charles Delvert who watched the whole action from a neighbouring position provides a description typical of these relief attempts:

Two companies of the 124th carried the German trenches by assault. They penetrated there without firing a shot. But they were insufficiently supplied with hand-grenades. ... The Boche counter-attacked with grenades. The two companies, defenceless, were annihilated. The 3rd Battalion, coming to their aid, was smashed up by barrage fire in the approach trenches. Altogether nearly 500 killed or wounded. ... The dead were piled up as high as the parapet. ...

Serving with the 124th was twenty-one-year-old Second-Lieutenant Alfred Joubaire, who had marched to Verdun a few days previously behind the regimental band gaily playing 'Tipperary'. For the past fifteen months he had kept a diary which was largely restricted to matter-of-fact, almost flippant observations of life at the front. His entry for 23 May (one of the last before a shell killed him) ends on a remarkably different note:

Humanity is mad! It must be mad to do what it is doing. What a massacre! What scenes of horror and carnage! I cannot find words to translate my impressions. Hell cannot be so terrible. Men are mad!

By late afternoon of the 23rd Lefebvre-Dibon's battalion to the right of the fort was encircled and forced to fly the white flag; over seventy-two per cent of its effectives were either dead or wounded. On top of the fort, the 129th was now also cut off. Still its machine-gun post at the south-west turret hammered away stubbornly. But ammunition was running out. Worse still, because the French had never occupied the whole superstructure, the Germans were able to push reinforcements into the fort underground, through a tunnel at the north-east corner. By this means they smuggled up a heavy mine-thrower on the night of the 23rd. As the sun rose through the Meuse haze, the weapon had been built into an emplacement less than eighty yards from the French machine-gunners, but impervious to their direct fire. In rapid succession it lobbed eight aerial torpedoes, each containing a huge charge of explosive, at the south-west turret. Before the smoke from the last shattering blast cleared away, three German companies leapt out of the fort on to the stunned survivors.

It was the end. That night a few remnants of the French spearhead crept back to their lines in ones and twos. Heavy as the defenders' losses had been those of the French were incomparably higher, with a thousand prisoners alone left in enemy hands. Mangin's 5th Division had not as much as a single company in reserve, and for a time there was a dangerous hole in the front 500 yards wide. Mangin himself was abruptly withdrawn from the sector by his Corps Commander, Lebrun, passing – for neither the first nor last time – into temporary disgrace. The whole episode was a tragic case of too little, too soon. Had the forces been available to attack on a broader front – as Pétain had wanted – the fort might possibly have been retaken. But since they were not, the attack should clearly not have taken place when it did. Pétain assumed full responsibility for the débâcle, and the fact that his account of the battle contains no single breath of reproach for Nivelle or Mangin reveals a magnanimity rare among the *ex post facto* writings of war leaders.

But, at the front, the failure brought about a noticeable decline in morale. Ominously, cases of 'indiscipline' were reported from Verdun towards the end of May. In Paris, the news of Douaumont threw Galliéni of the Marne, already weakened by an operation, into a profound depression. Two days later he was dead.

19 'May Cup'

Of all man's miseries the bitterest is this: to know so much
and to have control over nothing – HERODOTUS

. . . I cannot too often repeat, the battle was no longer an
episode that spent itself in blood and fire; it was a conditioned
thing that dug itself in remorselessly week after week. . .
– ERNST JÜNGER, *The Sorm of Steel*

As May gave way to a torrid June at Verdun, the three-and-
a-half-month-old battle entered its deadliest phase. It was not
merely the purely military aspects that made it so. In all man's
affairs no situation is more lethal than when an issue assumes
the status of a symbol. Here all reason, all sense of value, ab-
dicate. Verdun had by now become a transcendent symbol for
both sides; worst of all, it had by now become a symbol of
honour. *L'honneur de France!* That magical phrase, still
capable today of rousing medieval passions, bound France in-
extricably to the holding of Verdun's Citadel. To the Germans,
its seizure had become an equally inseparable part of national
destiny. On a plane far above the mere warlords conducting
operations, both nations had long been too far gone to be
affected by the strategic insignificance of that Citadel. In their
determination to possess this symbol, this challenge-cup of
national supremacy, the two nations flailed at each other with
all the stored-up rage of a thousand years of Teuton–Gaul
rivalry. Paul Valéry, in his eulogy welcoming Marshal Pétain
to the Académie, referred to the Battle of Verdun as a form 'of
single combat . . . where you were the champion of France face
to face with the Crown Prince'. As in the single combats of
legend, it was more than simply the honour, it was the virility
of two peoples that was at stake. Like two stags battling to the
death, antlers locked, neither would nor could give until the
virility of one or the other finally triumphed.

Confined to the most sublime plane, Valéry's metaphor was
a noble and apt one. But, to the men actually engaged in it, a

less noble form of symbolism was apparent. In the last days of peace, there had seemed to come a point where the collective will of Europe's leaders had abdicated and was usurped by some evil, superhuman Will from Stygian regions that wrested control out of their feeble hands. Seized by this terrible force, nations were swept along at ever-mounting speed towards the abyss. And once the fighting had started, one also senses repeatedly the presence of that Evil Being, marshalling events to its own pattern; whereas in the Second World War somehow the situation never seemed entirely to escape human manipulation – perhaps because the warlords, Churchill and Roosevelt, Hitler and Stalin, were titans when contrasted with the diminutive statures of the Asquiths, the Briands, and the Bethmann-Hollwegs. So now, as the Battle of Verdun moved into June, its conduct had in fact been placed beyond the direct control of the two 'champions', Pétain and Crown Prince Wilhelm. With the ascendancy of Nivelle and Knobelsdorf, each pledged to the continuance of the battle regardless of cost, the fighting had reached a higher peak of brutality and desperation. The battle seemed to have somehow rid itself of all human direction and now continued through its own impetus. There could be no end to it, thought one German writer,

until the last German and the last French hobbled out of the trenches on crutches to exterminate each other with pocket knives or teeth and finger nails.

In the diaries and journals of the time, on both sides, mention of the vileness of the enemy becomes more and more infrequent; even the infantryman's hatred for the murderous artillery grows less pronounced. The battle itself had become the abhorred enemy. It had assumed its own existence, its own personality; and its purpose nothing less than the impartial ruin of the human race. In the summer of 1916, its chroniclers accord it with increasing regularity the personifications of 'ogre', 'monster', 'Moloch', and 'Minotaur', indicative of the creature's insatiable need for its daily ration of lives, regardless of nationality. All other emotions, such as simple, nationalist, warlike feelings, had become dwarfed in the united loathing of the incubus; at the same time it was accompanied by a sense of hopeless resignation that would leave an indelible mark on a generation of French and Germans.

Abroad, beyond the general admiration for France's heroism at Verdun, there was widespread unanimity in the kind of
symbol it evoked among the cartoonists. In the United States,
The Baltimore American printed an adaptation from Millet,
with the Kaiser sowing skulls at Verdun: In an Italian cartoon
Death says to the Crown Prince, 'I am weary of work – don't
send me any more victims;' a British cartoon of the period
shows Death sitting on top of the world – 'The only ruler whose
new conquests are undisputed.' From Germany, a grisly armed

The Sower

As ye sow, so shall ye reap.

—From The Baltimore American.

knight pours blood over the earth out of a copious 'Horn of
Plenty', and in a propaganda medallion – dedicated with an
ironic twist of things, to Pétain – Death is portrayed as a
skeleton pumping blood out of the world. Looking back from
the autumn of 1916, the New York Times summarized the
diseased, *Totentanz* imagery which Verdun had sparked off
with a monstrous Mars surveying three-and-a-half million
crosses; 'The end of a perfect year'.

*

When the Chief-of-Staff of the German Third Army visited
Supreme Headquarters during the French counter-attack on
Douaumont, he had found the normally insusceptible Falkenhayn rubbing his hands with glee, declaring that this was 'the
stupidest thing they could do'. Far from disrupting new German offensive plans as Nivelle might have hoped, the French
failure temporarily halted Falkenhayn's wavering and threw
his full support behind Knobelsdorf. Preparations for the new
assault, bearing the delectable code name of 'MAY CUP',
now went ahead at top speed, with reinforcements in men and
material promised by Falkenhayn. The prospects seemed
rosier than they had for some time; the French line on the
Right Bank had been seriously weakened by the losses suffered in the Douaumont venture;[1] there were also indications
of a decline in morale. On the Left Bank, both the commanding hills of Mort Homme and Côte 304 had been taken at last,
and from them German guns could place a deadly restraint on
the French heavy artillery massed behind Bois Bourrus ridge.
Despite all Pétain's efforts, by the end of May the Germans
still had an appreciable superiority in artillery at Verdun, with
2,200 pieces against 1,777. Everywhere the French margin of
retreat had become exceedingly slim. Once again the German
Press was encouraged to declare bombastically:

'Assuredly we are proposing to take Verdun. ...'

'MAY CUP', the most massive assault on the Right Bank
since the initial onslaught in February, was to be launched with
three army corps, I Bavarian, X Reserve, and XV Corps, attacking with a total of five divisions. The weight of the attack
was nearly equal to that of 21 February, but this time it was
concentrated along a front only five, instead of twelve kilometres, wide; or roughly one man for every metre of front.
This time there would be no surprise, no provision for manoeuvre; the attack would punch a hole through the French
lines by sheer brute force alone. Its objective was to gain
'bases of departure' for the final thrust on Verdun. These comprised, reading from west to east, the Thiaumont stronghold,

1. During the last fortnight in May, French casualties were in fact
considerably higher than for any other period since the initial German
onslaught, and 9 out of 17 divisions in the line had to be relieved.

the Fleury ridge, and Fort Souville; but, first and foremost, Fort Vaux, the bastion on which was anchored the north-eastern extremity of the French line.

It will be recalled that premature claims to the capture of Fort Vaux had brought much ridicule upon the Germans in early March. There had been subsequent vain attempts to take the fort in April and May; with Falkenhayn arriving in person to attend its delivery on the last occasion. After each failure, the German infantry had been pulled back while the 420 mm. 'Big Berthas' resumed the siege.

Verdun marked the final eclipse of this 'terror weapon' which had brought the Germans such cheap and unattended successes at the beginning of the war. From February onwards the 420s had kept the Verdun forts under steady bombardment from their one ton projectiles. After the fall of Douaumont, Fort Moulainville – Douaumont's 'twin' to the east of Verdun – had become their principal target. Perhaps because its concrete carapace was less efficiently cushioned than Douaumont, Moulainville had suffered the most structural damage of any Verdun fort. One (fortunately unexploded) 420 shell was dis-covered to have penetrated six feet of earth, ten feet of con-crete, and finally a wall thirty inches thick. In several places the shells burst inside the fort, with terrible effects. Casualties were high, with many simply asphyxiated by the deadly T.N.T. gases trapped inside the fort. The Commandant at once ordered the removal of all the covers that the garrison – with typical French horror of '*courants d'air*' – had placed over the fort's ventilators; but the moment his back was turned they were replaced! The terrifying noise of the descending shell (described as like 'an express rushing over a metal viaduct'), followed by the atrocious concussion that was felt throughout the fort – to say nothing of the sheer suspense of waiting for the daily bombardment to begin – drove many of the occupants out of their wits. After one bad shelling, the Commandant find-ing himself confronted with a minor mutiny by shell-shocked 'lunatics', was forced to round them up at pistol point and lock them up in a casemate. Then the fort M.O. himself went mad and ran out of the fort into the neighbouring woods, where he was later discovered sitting on a tree stump, in a state of com-plete amnesia. But gradually the garrison became acclimatized to the bombardment. A nineteen-year-old Sergeant noted that from an observation post on top of the fort he could see the flash of the 'Big Bertha' firing from behind the Jumelles d'Ornes, seven miles away, and that thereafter he had a whole 63 seconds to warn the fort, and take cover himself. The knowledge that the giant projectiles would not plunge down on the fort unawares seemed to ease nerves; at last, when the shelling was at its worst, the Commandant took the simple expedient of evacuating the whole garrison during the day, into trenches outside.

The Germans made a serious tactical error in concentrating the 420s on Moulainville. They had primarily been persuaded by the need to knock out its 155 mm. turret which had caused much annoyance. But in fact the fort – never in the front line – was only of secondary importance. Much more promising candidates for the undivided attention of the 'Big Berthas' would have been Forts Vaux and Souville. Though neither mounted guns, Souville was the vital nerve centre of the whole French defence on the Right Bank – as well as being its chief observatory – and its thinner protection might well have caused it to succumb. Equally an all-out bombardment might have rendered Fort Vaux uninhabitable. But two other factors had further impaired the efficacy of the 420s. By June they had all fired far more shots than the maximum allowed for by Krupp. Barrels were badly worn so that shells had a habit of 'keyholing', sometimes turning end over end in flight, which seriously reduced penetrating power. More than one gun had actually blown up, with nasty consequences for their crews.

The immobile 420s had also suffered heavily from French counter-battery fire, in which French artillerists excelled. Minutes after the 'dud' 420 shell had embedded itself in Fort Moulainville, experts arrived to compute from its position the angle of its trajectory, and thereby pinpointed the gun that fired it. An endless battle of David and Goliath went on, the French opposing the 420 mm. giants with light, but long-barrelled pieces of 155 mm. or less. One of the high-precision naval batteries brought to Verdun specially for this purpose was commanded by Lieutenant – later Admiral – Darlan. The odds were against the Goliaths, which were exceedingly vulnerable because of their immobility, the hugeness of their ammunition stockpiles, and their short range that forced them to come perilously close to the front. One by one they were knocked out, and one vast dump containing 450,000 heavy shells in the Forest of Spincourt was sent skyhigh by the French naval gunners early in the battle. To support its attack on Fort Vaux in June, the Fifth Army possessed only four worn-out 'Big Berthas' out of the original thirteen of the previous February.

*

The first of June was a glorious summer day; it was also, in the view of the *Reichsarchiv*, 'one of the very few days of German victories not clouded over by some failure.' On each previous occasion attacks on Fort Vaux had been stopped dead before even approaching the fort by enfilading fire from the denuded slopes of la Caillette and Fumin woods. These lay between Vaux and Douaumont and were still in French hands. With startling rapidity, the massed storm troops of the 1st and 7th German divisions now swept down la Caillette, across the Vaux Ravine, and up again on to the Fumin promontory that abutted Fort Vaux; a distance of about 800–1,000 yards. By the evening the French sector commander, General Lebrun, was forced to admit to Nivelle the 'total disappearance' of the units holding the lost ground. He got back the inevitable order to counter-attack immediately. But it was already too late; with one leap the Germans had eliminated the flanking fire that covered the approaches to Fort Vaux. Although the German plans envisaged no attack on the fort itself until four days later, at 6 p.m. that evening the commander of XV Corps, General von Deimling, called his staff together and told them that the day's successes had been so encouraging that he intended now to rush Fort Vaux with a surprise attack at 3 a.m. the very next morning. Taken aback, his Chief-of-Staff complained that there simply was not enough time to make preparations. But the General insisted.

The only success registered that day by the French was the maintenance of a position called R.1.[1] Bois Fumin was defended by three concrete entrenchments running along it from

1. 'R' stands for *'Retranchement'*.

north-west to south-east, respectively R.3, R.2, and R.1; the last lying only 400 yards from Fort Vaux. R.3 and R.2 fell within a matter of hours, but R.1, occupied by a company of the 101 Regiment under command of Captain Charles Delvert, was to hold out against enormous odds for a full week. Delvert's own account of its defence ranks among the most realistic of the whole battle. His company had arrived at the front just before the Douaumont attack, for which he had had a grandstand seat. As he moved up towards Vaux, the communication trench crowded with soldiers, twilight glinting upon their helmets made him think of being

on the ramparts of Elsinore and among sentinels being relieved during the night. But the sentinels here were not being relieved.

At the Regimental Command Post, chaos. The Colonel could spare no men to provide Delvert with a guide, so for two hours his company wandered lost in the dark, among exploding shells and howling wounded men who blocked what remained of the communication trenches. When he finally reached R.1, it was, he discovered, little more now than a chain of shell holes; his own Company H.Q. 'a niche under a slab of reinforced concrete torn up by a 380 shell'. The soil in the Bois Fumin itself 'had been so churned up by the shells that the earth had become as fluid as sand and the shell holes now resembled sand dunes'. The unit relieved by Delvert told him that fifteen of its men had been killed by their own 75s during the past four days; it was 'very encouraging'.

As soon as the German bombardment had lifted on the morning of 1 June, Delvert saw the German infantry swarm out of their trenches, 'like ants when one has kicked an antheap'. Out of range, there was nothing he could do but watch, once again, 'as if from a balcony'. Soon he could see the enemy jumping into the French front-line trenches on the Caillette slopes; 'puffs 'of white smoke showed us that a hand-to-hand grenade battle was taking place. Then silence returned. ...' Then the blue-clad figures were falling back 'in disorder', down into the valley below the Bois Fumin, with shells bursting in their midst. Next, there was a thin line of the same blue-clad figures sixty to eighty strong moving in the opposite direction, without weapons. Prisoners! A short time later, coal-scuttle

helmets were seen bobbing up and down in the trench immediately to Delvert's front, little more than twenty-five yards
distant. A spirited exchange of fire – 'the kind of fighting that
excites everyone' – took place. At Delvert's side a nineteen-
year-old soldier collapsed with a hole in his forehead. Then
suddenly there was a shout that the enemy had reached R.2,
200 yards away, on Delvert's left flank; 'a lively fusilade. They
are resisting! At last!'

By 2.30 that afternoon, R.2 had been overwhelmed too.
'Almost immediately, the conquering Germans were observed
beginning to dig sap-heads towards us. Now the ravine alone
separates us from them. Are we going to be trapped here like
mice?'

For the rest of that day Delvert's machine guns managed to
keep the enemy on two sides at a respectful distance, while in
the afternoon heat a nauseating plague of bloated bluebottles
descended on the dead in the trench.

Friday 2 June. A night of anxiety and constant alerts ... No
rations reached us yesterday. Thirst is particularly troublesome.
Biscuits are foul ...

Abruptly Delvert's writing was interrupted by a violent concussion and he was covered with earth. A French 75 shell had
landed in the next dugout, blowing to pieces his quartermaster-
sergeant. The rest of the day passed in an exchange of rifle
fire. That evening the Germans opposite made their first attack:

I issued grenades all round, because at such close range rifles are
useless.

The enemy was repulsed. Suddenly, flame and smoke bil-
lowed out behind Delvert. It must be an enemy flame-thrower!
'Even the boxes of grenades began to catch fire!' (Actually, as
it transpired later, Delvert's absent-minded runner, Champion,
ordered to send up a red rocket appealing for an artillery barrage, had set it off between his legs and ignited the rest of the
rockets.) At 10 o'clock that night an *homme soupe* arrived with
five water bottles – one of which was empty – for the whole
company. That meant two gallons between sixty-eight men and
three officers – and it 'smelt of corpses'.

But there was worse to come for the men inside Fort Vaux.

20 Fort Vaux

Verdun has brought war back into honour, the sort of war in which the individual man and personal courage are given their full chances of values – H. H. VON MELLENTHIN, The *New York Times Monthly Magazine* (June 1916)

Fort Vaux was the smallest in the whole Verdun system, covering less than one-quarter the area of Douaumont. It had no 155 mm. turret, only one bearing a single 75. But this had been completely destroyed when a German 420 detonated a three-quarters of a ton demolition charge laid there in the panic following the fall of Douaumont. As Vaux too had had all its flanking 75s removed by Joffre, by June 1916 it possessed no armament bigger than a machine gun. None of these was mounted in an armoured turret. Apart from the shattering of the 75 turret, one of the underground corridors had been opened by a shell, and was now blocked with sandbags; most of the outlying galleries had been damaged in some degree, and an enormous crack ran disquietingly along the length of the underground barracks. Otherwise the fort had withstood the bombardment well. Less satisfactory was the work carried out (or rather, *not* carried out) under Pétain's orders of February to rehabilitate the forts. No deep underground approach tunnel had been dug (as the Germans had done at Douaumont) to link the fort with the rear – so that it could easily be cut off. Worse still, nothing had been done to improve the water supply, despite grave warnings. Both these shortcomings were to have serious consequences.

In command of the fort was Major Sylvain-Eugene Raynal, a tough Colonial soldier from Bordeaux, aged forty-nine, to whom promotion had not been particularly kind. Badly wounded several times in the war already, he limped on a cane and should by rights have been invalided out of the army. He had however managed to persuade his seniors to send him back to the front, on fortress duty, which was considered less arduous than the trenches. On 24 May, the day the attempt to recapture Douaumont failed, Raynal reached his new post at Vaux. His first impression of the fort was of soldiers crowded together.

in such numbers that it is extremely difficult to move, and I took a very long time to reach my command post. ... If an attack materialized all the occupants would be captured before they could defend themselves.

Apart from its regular garrison, the fort was filled with stray stretcher-bearers, signallers, and the debris of regiments that

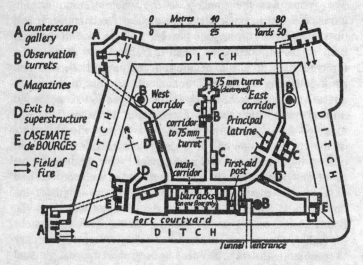

had lost contact with their units in the chaos of the German onslaught and had come to seek refuge. Raynal at once tried to chase these fugitives out, but still more arrived and soon it became impossible for troops to leave the fort. Thus when the siege began, instead of the maximum complement of 250 for which it was designed, Raynal found himself with over 600 troops in his charge, many of them wounded. In addition, Vaux's garrison numbered four carrier pigeons and a cocker-spaniel brought in by the survivors of a signal unit.

On 1 June, Raynal had watched helplessly through binoculars as the Germans advanced across the Bois de la Caillette a mile and a half away. If only he had had one 75 in the fort! Nevertheless, two machine guns set up on the superstructure, firing at extreme range, achieved miraculous results. Baffled by the mysterious, invisible weapon that was tearing holes in their ranks, the German Grenadiers kept on coming until Raynal could see a whole trench choked with grey bodies. Then the attackers disappeared out of sight into the valley.

To the north-east of Vaux, the land falls so rapidly towards the Woevre that the approaches right up to the fort wall lay in dead ground both to its guns and those of Delvert in R.1. Now that the protective flank of La Caillette and Fumin had been lost, it was abundantly clear to Raynal that nothing could stop the Germans reaching Fort Vaux the following morning. The night was spent frantically erecting sandbag barricades, with loopholes for throwing grenades through, at nine breaches in various parts of the fort. Meanwhile the German bombardment rose in a tremendous crescendo; at one period, according to Raynal, shells were falling on the small area of the fort at a rate of 1,500 to 2,000 an hour. Just before dawn on the 2nd the barrage abruptly ceased. The moment had come.

Waiting in trenches less than 150 yards below the lip of the fort were two battalions of the German 50th Division, under the special direction of Major-General Weber Pasha who had recently distinguished himself in organizing the defence of the Turkish forts at Gallipoli. In a matter of seconds his men were swarming into the fort moat. At once, they came under heavy machine-gun fire from the two flanking galleries, similar to those that the Brandenburgers had found untenanted in Fort Douaumont, at the north-west and north-east corners. On these the initial fighting was focused. Crouching on the roof of the north-east gallery, German pioneers first tried unsuccessfully to knock it out by lowering bundles of hand-grenades and exploding them outside the loopholes.

The French machine-gunners continued to fire at the Germans attacking the other gallery. Then the pioneers heard below the unmistakable click followed by curses as the machine gun jammed. Quickly they hurled grenades into the gallery, dispatching the gun crew. Out leaped a courageous French officer, Raynal's second-in-command, Captain Tabourot. For a while, almost single-handed, he kept the attackers away from the entrance to the gallery by hurling hand-grenades, until – his abdomen ripped open by a German grenade – he crawled back into the interior to die. Shortly afterwards, the defenders, thirty-two men and an officer, surrendered the gallery; in it the Germans found two small cannon – minus their breech-blocks.

It was now 5 a.m., and the attackers had already taken one of Vaux's two main strongpoints. Things did not go quite so easily with the larger, double gallery at the north-west. Pioneers tried first to 'smoke out' its inmates by poking over the fort wall specially elongated tubes fitted to flame-throwers. In the initial surprise, the French machine guns stopped firing, and taking advantage of this Lieutenant Rackow of the 158th Paderborn Regiment managed to slip across the moat with about thirty men. They were the first Germans to reach the superstructure of the fort itself. But almost immediately the French machine guns were back in operation, and for several agonizing hours Rackow and his small group sat isolated on the fort. In the terrible din of the Verdun bombardment their comrades only twenty yards away were unable to hear their shouts for support. The German pioneers, with considerable fortitude, now tried lowering sacks full of grenades on a rope outside the gallery, but did themselves more damage. All through the morning the struggle continued, until one after the other the French machine guns were silenced and some fifteen of the gallery's inhabitants had been wounded. Still it held out. Then at last the Germans on top of the fort discovered the sandbags with which Raynal had plugged a large breach in the corridor leading to the north-west gallery. They removed them, and began hurling grenades into the corridor. Realizing what was happening, Raynal ordered the gallery to be abandoned immediately, before its defenders could be taken from the rear.

By about 4 p.m., Raynal had lost both his exterior defences, the superstructure was solidly occupied by the enemy, and the battle was about to move underground. A little like the children and the pirates in *Peter Pan*, members of the fort garrison gazed helplessly through the slits of the observation cupolas at the young Germans sprawled out on the ground just above their heads, nonchalantly smoking pipes and occasionally making insulting gestures for their consumption. Meanwhile, during the contest for the galleries, Raynal had hastened to build sandbag barricades inside the corridors leading to them from the central fort.

As soon as both galleries had been occupied, Lieutenant Rackow, who had now assumed control of all operations on the fort, ordered a party under Lieutenant Ruberg of the Pioneers to break into the fort proper along the north-east corridor. Obediently Ruberg and a handful of men set off down a dark narrow passage, similar to the one that had confronted Sergeant Kunze in Douaumont three months earlier. A long flight of steps led down under the moat and then up again, and soon Ruberg came to a steel door barring his path. Behind it he could hear French voices whispering. Swiftly he prepared a charge out of hand-grenades (because of General von Diemling's acceleration of the attack on Vaux the Pioneers had had no time in which to prepare proper demolition charges), pulled the pin out of the last grenade, and ran.

Behind the steel door was Raynal himself, inspecting a hastily erected barricade which was not entirely to his liking. From the noises made by Ruberg, he realized what was afoot and quickly ordered his men back. Just in time; for the barricade 'disintegrated in a powerful explosion.' On the other side of the door, the five-and-a-half-second grenade fuse had not given Ruberg time to get clear, and he was hurled backwards by the explosion, lacerated with splinters. The force of the blast and the wounding of their chief caused the Germans to hesitate before re-entering the deadly tunnel just long enough for Raynal to rebuild his barricade and site a machine gun behind it. For the time being the French remained masters of the corridor.

That night Raynal, with all his telephone lines to the rear already severed, sent off the first of his four pigeons bearing a report of the situation.

Early on 3 June, German assault troops worked their way round to the south of the fort. Vaux was now completely cut off, even from R.1, which still maintained a tenuous link with the rest of the Second Army. The siege was on, and a curious stalemate was established with a German commander, Rackow, on top of the fort, and a French commander, Raynal, underground. All through the day the main battle continued ferociously in the two corridors leading to the heart of the fort. In each the French had built sandbag barricades several feet thick, defended by one brave grenadier. The German pioneers had meanwhile brought up more powerful explosives, so that it was only a matter of time before the French grenadier was knocked out, and his rampart demolished. But beyond was yet another barricade, from behind which a machine gun spewed death on the attackers at point-blank range, while the French were preparing yet a further series of obstacles to its rear. Yard by yard the Germans advanced, but at heavy cost.

Of all the horrors in the fighting at Verdun, it is difficult to imagine any much more appalling than the struggle that took place day after day in the underground corridors of Fort Vaux. Here the battle went on in pitch darkness, relieved only by the flash of exploding grenades, in a shaft for the most part no more than three feet wide and five feet high, in which no grown man could stand upright. Machine-gun bullets ricocheting from wall to wall inflicted wounds as terrible as any dum-dum, and in the confined space the concussion of the grenades was almost unendurable. Repeatedly men of both sides felt themselves asphyxiating in the air polluted by T.N.T. fumes and cement dust stirred up by the explosions. Added to it was the ever-worsening stink of the dead, rapidly decomposing in the June heat, for whom there was no means of burial inside the fort.

The two attacking German battalions had already suffered grave losses. Before being silenced, Vaux's gallery machine guns had cut swathes in the attackers, and by the evening of 2 June the battalion of the 53rd Regiment had only one officer left unwounded. Meanwhile, Rackow and his men on the roof of the fort were being exposed to an ever-increasing intensity of French gun-fire, to which the deadly 155 in nearby Fort Moulainville now added its voice. On the night of 3 June both battalions had to be withdrawn exhausted. But for Raynal and his six hundred there was no relief.

Out at R.1. Delvert had meanwhile successfully repulsed two more German attacks, and spent the rest of the day under heavy bombardment. He noted in his diary that he had not slept for seventy-two hours. At ten o'clock that night, Captain Delvert was overjoyed by the arrival of a subaltern, bringing a company of reinforcements. But the company numbered only eighteen men. An hour later, another subaltern appeared, claiming to have brought up a company.

'How many men have you?' asked Delvert.

'One hundred and seventy.'

Delvert counted them. There were twenty-five.

Back at Sector Headquarters, General Lebrun had received Raynal's pigeon message, and – under heavy pressure from Nivelle – prescribed an immediate counter-attack to regain the fort. Almost hysterically, Lebrun told the wretched general commanding the 124th Division that he was, if necessary, to lead the attack in person. At dawn on the 4th, the French went in in six dense waves, actually reaching the western extremity of the fort. But fresh replacements of Düsseldorf Fusiliers were already in position, and they drove off the attackers at bayonet point.

For Raynal, 4 June was to be the grimmest day so far. It nearly proved fatal. The previous night German Pioneers had managed, with a great effort, to bring up six flame-throwers on to the fort superstructure (four having been destroyed by artillery fire en route). They would smoke Vaux's heroic garrison out like rats. At a given moment, the Germans attacking below ground were withdrawn, and the nozzles of the infernal devices were inserted into apertures and breaches in the fort exterior. (Fortunately for the garrison a detachment of Germans trying to seal hermetically the fort by filling in one of the larger breaches was dispersed by the vigilant crew of the Moulainville 155.) The first warning Raynal had was a cry of 'Gas!' from all parts of the fort. Almost immediately an asphyxiating black smoke poured into the central gallery. Down the north-west corridor fled its defenders, faces blackened and burnt, their barricades abandoned. Flickers of flame began to appear in the main body of the fort, and for a moment mass panic threatened. Then the flame-throwers ceased. Reacting quickly, and with almost super-human courage, Lieutenant Girard darted back into the smoke-filled north-west corridor. He reached the abandoned machine gun there a second before the Germans. Wounded several times in the ensuing action, he held on until the situation was re-established; then fell unconscious from the toxic effects of the smoke. Meanwhile, Raynal had ordered the opening of all possible vents to clear the smoke, and to minimize the recurrence of such an attack.

A similar German attempt to rush the defenders in the north-east corridor had also failed, while an attack on the bunker at the south-west corner of the fort had ended in a minor French triumph. All the German Pioneers had been killed, and their flame-throwers captured. With this acquisition the garrison were able to keep the southern moat of the fort clear of the enemy. The net result of the new German effort had been dreadful burns for some fifteen members of the French garrison and the capture of twenty-five yards of the north-west corridor, with one of Raynal's three observation cupolas.

Shortly before midday Raynal dispatched his last pigeon with the message:

We are still holding. But ... relief is imperative. Communicate with us by Morse-blinker from Souville, which does not reply to our calls. This is my last pigeon.

Badly gassed in the recent attack, the wretched bird fluttered around half-heartedly, returning to settle on the loophole of Raynal's Command Post. After several more failures, it was finally coaxed into the air. It reached Verdun, was delivered of its message, then – like Pheidippides at Marathon – fell dead. (The only one of its species to be 'decorated' with the *Légion d'Honneur*, the noble emissary was stuffed and sits to this day in a Paris Museum.)

Reaction to the message brought by Raynal's last pigeon was speedy. Fort Souville, which suspected that Vaux had already succumbed and its signals were a German trick, now blinked out an encouraging message to Raynal, and the mounting of yet another relief attack was prepared.

Grave as had been the events of the morning, something far more menacing transpired in the fort that afternoon. Says Raynal:

A sergeant of the fort Quartermaster's Staff came to me, requesting a word in private, and said in a choking voice: '*Mon Commandant*, there is practically no water left in the cistern.'

I leaped up, I shook the sergeant, I made him repeat his words; 'But this is treachery!'

'*Non, mon Commandant*, we have distributed only the quantities you indicated, but the gauge was inaccurate.'

The agony began. I gave the order to preserve what little remained and to make no distribution today.[1]

The three-hundred odd supernumerary troops inside the fort had now become useless mouths that could endanger the whole garrison. Somehow, Raynal realized, it was imperative to evacuate them. But Vaux was encircled by the enemy. A desperate risk had to be taken. Summoning Officer Cadet Buffet, a nineteen-year-old brought up in an orphanage, he ordered him to scout a way out from the fort late that night. The bulk of the escaping troops would then follow in small, well-spaced packets.

While in the acrid darkness of the fort the garrison knew and cared little about the weather outside, Delvert in R.1 recorded that the 4th was a beautiful sunny Sunday. There were more German attacks, but in the June sunshine Delvert had time to comment lyrically on the essential beauty of the grenadiers poised to hurl their missiles, *'avec le beau geste du joueur de balle'*. Unfortunately, the day was later spoilt by a new prolonged bombardment from French guns, and by maddening thirst exacerbated by the heat. That night at 9.30, Delvert ordered his company to stand by to be relieved. The men were almost too tired to rejoice. An hour and a half later a runner arrived from regimental headquarters postponing the relief, 'because of circumstances'. Mercifully, there was rain the next day, and the company put out groundsheets to catch the water. Meanwhile, in the German trenches opposite there were signs of unprecedented activity. Communication trenches were being widened, all of which could only mean a new all-out attack on R.1. Would relief come before the remanants of Delvert's heroic company were submerged?

After dark on the 5th, the awaited relief at last arrived. But the ordeal was not yet over. With no communication trench to provide cover, Delvert's company were silhouetted targets for the machine guns installed in R.2. Then followed a dreadfully accurate artillery barrage. When the company reached safety, it numbered only thirty-seven broken men; but – on German

1. In fact, as a later inquiry showed, despite warnings as early as March about the inadequacy of Vaux's water supply, nothing had been done, and the cisterns appear to have been half-empty when Raynal assumed command. It was a piece of negligence on a par with the failure to garrison Fort Douaumont.

figures – it had inflicted over three hundred casualties. For another three days Delvert's successors continued the valiant defence; then R.1 fell to the Germans with 500 prisoners.

For Raynal and his men there could be neither relief nor rainwater to assuage their growing thirst. The fifth of June, the fourth day of the siege, had begun at dawn with a shattering explosion near the *Casemate de Bourges* on the south-west corner of the fort. A huge breach had been blown in the wall, and German Pioneers were on the spot at once with a flame-thrower. But a freak current of air blew the flame back in their faces. A grenade-thrower counter-sally, led by Lieutenant Girard, restored the situation. In the course of it, Girard was wounded again.

Through peepholes Raynal could now see the Germans, thwarted in their attacks up the corridors, digging fresh mine-shafts under other parts of the fort from the outside.

It was not a pleasant sight. He flashed a message to Souville, requesting 'hit them quick with artillery'. The reply came with gratifying alacrity; there was a muffled thud, and the watching Raynal saw 'German bodies hurled into the moat. Work above us ceased at once.'

Outside the fort, the latest failure of the flame-throwers had flung the attackers into acute depression. The infernal machines, it was felt, were causing them more casualties than the be-sieged, and they were withdrawn. Little did the Germans realize how close the flame-throwers had come to breaking Vaux's re-sistance the day before; or that its water had run out. All they could see was the heavy toll exacted by the incessant French gunfire on the fort's superstructure, and the almost negligible progress being made along the underground corridors. The fort indeed seemed impregnable. Perhaps the men inside could hold out for another month, or a year. Finally, to make things worse, the Pioneers had received an insulting message from General von Deimling, declaring that the fort had been taken, but that a few isolated groups of French were still holding out in one or two cellars. These were to be 'mopped up' forthwith.

Later that same day, Raynal suffered two new reverses. A second after the blinker operator had completed a message to Souville a shell landed on the post, killing three men, and wounding several others, while destroying the signal equipment.

In the course of the day's subterranean fighting along the north-east corridor, the enemy had taken the entrance to the last accessible latrine; an important morale factor in the already foully stinking fort. By now of the eight surviving officers under Raynal, one was gravely wounded; three had been wounded to a lesser extent (two of them at least twice), but stayed at their posts; a fourth had a bad case of fever, while Raynal himself was shivering with recurrent malaria. That evening he inspected his men,

crushed with fatigue, silent, and gloomy. If I were to ask one more effort of them, they would have been incapable. Therefore I decided to distribute to them the last drops of water. . . .

This amounted to less than a quarter of a pint per person, for men who had not had a drop the previous twenty-four hours – and it reeked vilely of corpses. There was no question of eating any of the highly salted *singe'* (of which there was a plentiful supply); Raynal noted that no food had passed his lips for two days. How much longer could the garrison keep up its strength? That night, rigging up an *ad hoc* blinker, Raynal signalled Fort Souville:

Imperative be relieved and receive water tonight. I am reaching the end of my tether. . . .

Suddenly, into this atmosphere of extreme dejection burst a mud-stained figure from another world. It was young Buffet, proudly wearing a bright new medal. The garrison crowded around him, fatigue and thirst temporarily forgotten.

He had achieved the impossible. It transpired that most of the escapers had been cut down by German machine guns, or taken prisoner, but Buffet and eight others had made it. Reaching the refuge of Fort Tavannes, he had been passed from the Brigadier to the Sector Commander, General Lebrun, and finally on to Nivelle himself, who had decorated him and told of an imminent counter-attack being prepared which would, this time, succeed. At once the nineteen-year-old Officer Cadet volunteered to creep through the German lines again to take the news back to the fort. The sergeant accompanying him was wounded and had to be abandoned on the way, but a second time Buffet got through.

Eagerly the garrison officers pressed Buffet for details of the promised relief attack. It was to begin at 2 a.m. the following morning, said Buffet, and a whole battalion would be taking part. 'I saw the faces of my officers darken,' recalls Raynal, 'and I guessed what was going on inside them, because I shared their thoughts; the operation, as conceived, seemed to be, *a priori*, inadequate.'

Shortly after midnight the fort defenders heard the characteristic scream of French 75 mm. shells. But not a single explosion. The 'softening-up' barrage was falling, quite harmlessly, well over the fort. At 2 a.m., the garrison took up positions to give support to the relief force. The barrage lifted, and anxiously the besieged searched the horizon for their deliverers. At 2.30, still no sign. Finally, towards 3 a.m., a message from the *Casemate de Bourges* reported sighting a small force, of about platoon strength, pinned down by German machine-gun fire a few yards from the fort. The observers watched in despair as the isolated French were picked off one by one and then rose from their shell-holes, hands above their heads. It was all Vaux saw of the relieving attack that Nivelle had promised Buffet. The relief force had done its best, and suffered terrible losses, with a sergeant-major taking over command of the battalion when every single officer was either killed or wounded.

Morale inside the fort fell to its lowest point. Under the strain, a young lieutenant went off his head and threatened to blow up the grenade depot. It would be impossible to hold out much longer. Raynal blinked out another message, pleading 'intervene before complete exhaustion ... *Vive la France!*' But there was no longer any response from Souville, once again convinced that the fort must have succumbed. Later that day a huge shell landing on the fort caved in part of the vault of the central gallery, and now the threat of being buried alive was added to that of asphyxiation and thirst. Still the Germans could make no headway along the underground corridors. But by evening the suffering from thirst was indescribable. Over the past three June days each of the garrison had received a total of one half-glass of foul water. In their despair, men tried to lick the moisture and slime off the fort walls. As he inspected the fort, leaning heavily on his stick, Raynal found men fainting in the corridors, others retching violently – hav-

ing drunk their own urine. Worst of all was the plight of the
ninety-odd wounded, with no drop of water to assuage their
raging fever, some atrociously burnt, and many lying in the
dark, foul lazaret without proper attention since the beginning
of June.

Fort Vaux had done its duty, Major Raynal decided. Shelled
by Big Berthas, besieged, attacked by gas and fire, cut off from
France, with nothing more imposing than machine guns for
its defence, it had held off the weight of the Crown Prince's
army for a week. Even after the Germans had actually penetrated the fort, they had been able to advance no more than
thirty or forty yards underground in five days of fighting. Only
thirst had conquered Vaux. What wonders could not mighty
Douaumont have achieved had it been commanded by a
Raynal!

Having made his decision, to Raynal late that night there
came a last flicker of hope when once again the French guns
flared up. Was Nivelle coming to save them after all? But by
midnight a strangely eerie silence fell over the whole battlefield.
There would be no new relief attempt.

At 3.30 on the morning of 7 June, sleepy observers in Fort
Souville picked up the corrupted fragment of a last blinker
message from Vaux. '... *ne quittez pas* ...' was all that could
be deciphered. A few hours later the fort surrendered amid
scenes of pre-twentieth century courtesy, an appropriate
epilogue to what was one of the most heroic isolated actions of
the war. From behind a barricade in the north-west corridor,
Lieutenant Werner Müller of the German Machine Gun Corps
saw a French officer and two men bearing a white flag. They
handed over a formal letter addressed 'To The Commander of
the German Forces Attacking Fort Vaux'. Barely able to conceal his joy, Müller fetched his captain and together they were
led to Raynal past a guard of French soldiers, standing rigidly
to attention, 'like recruits', in the dimly-lit tunnel. The terms
of surrender were formally signed, and then Raynal handed
over to the Germans the highly ornamented bronze key of the
Fort.

The evacuation of the captive garrison began. To one German war correspondent, its survivors presented 'the living
image of desolation'. Nothing was more demanding of com-

passion than the spectacle of the captured, imitating Raynal's dog and crawling on their stomachs to drink frenetically of the putrid water from the very first shellhole. As they counted heads, the Germans were as surprised by the numbers of the garrison as they were by the sight of the cocker at Raynal's heels, bedraggled, battle-worn, but still alive. The garrison had suffered about a hundred casualties, including less than a score killed. To take Fort Vaux (which, but for thirst, could almost certainly have held out longer) the four German battalions (plus their Pioneers) directly concerned had alone expended 2,678 men and sixty-four officers. It was hardly surprising that French military thinkers would soon be making some far-reaching deductions about the value of underground forts.

Next day Raynal was taken to see the Crown Prince at Stenay. He was at once agreeably surprised to note that 'he is not the monkey our caricaturists have made him out to be ... has none of that Prussian stiffness.' Speaking fluent French, the Crown Prince heaped praises on the French defenders, several times using the word '*admirable*'. He congratulated Raynal on being decorated by Joffre with one of the highest degrees of the *Légion d'Honneur*; a piece of news that had not reached him in the fort. Finally, observing that Raynal had lost his own sword, as a supreme token of military esteem he presented him with the captured sword of another French officer.

*

Though Raynal and his men were on their way to two-and-a-half years in a prisoner-of-war camp, there remained one more tragic scene to be played out at Fort Vaux. Since 2 June, Nivelle had ordered five separate attempts to be made to relieve the fort. Each, inadequate to the task, had foundered with bloody losses. Following the failure of the attack on 6 June that had broken the heart of Vaux's garrison, Nivelle had immediately ordered yet a sixth attack, this time to be carried out in brigade strength, by a special '*Brigade de Marche*' formed from crack units drawn from various parts of the Verdun front. It would be unleashed at dawn on 8 June. At a conference attended by some twenty of the generals under his command, vigorous protests were raised. Even Nivelle's evil genius, Major d'Alenson, seems to have been opposed to this new attempt. But Nivelle was adamant; his reputation was involved. When the German radio broadcast the news of the surrender of Fort Vaux the following day, he declared it to be a German hoax – just like the one in March.

The two regiments designated for the '*Brigade de Marche*' were the 2nd Zouaves and the *Régiment d'Infanterie Coloniale du Maroc*; both comprised of North African troops that were far from fresh. The commander, Colonel Savy, was told by Nivelle in person that they had been chosen

for the finest mission that any French unit can have, that of going to the aid of comrades in arms who are valiantly performing their duty under tragic circumstances.

Hastily the North Africans were pushed up to the front, under an avalanche of rain. Meanwhile, at the identical moment that they were to go in, the German 50th Division was about to capitalize on the capture of Vaux by thrusting out towards Fort Tavannes. The two attacks met head on.

Thirty-two-year-old Sergeant-Major César Méléra had been detailed – to his evident annoyance – to take up the rear of his battalion of the Régiment Colonial, and stop stragglers falling back. He describes tersely the ensuing action as viewed from the immediate rear. Leaving for the front, a man committed suicide, 'tired of the war which he neither understood nor saw'. On the approach march:

The clay is so slippery and so difficult to climb that one marches as much on one's knees as one's feet. Arrived in a sweat at Souville Plateau where the Battalion is awaiting its rearguard. Lost the Machine-Gun Company. Found them again after half an hour. . . . Have to hold on to the coat of the man in front so as not to lose oneself. Fall into a hole. Arrive in a glade. Halt; the machine-gunners lost again. Three-quarters of an hour's pause.

At 4 a.m. Méléra reached Fort Tavannes, where he spent the day of the 8th. That night,

runners bring news. The attack has miscarried . . . At the moment we were going to sortie, the Germans appeared at other points . . . the two infantries massacred by each other's artillery, obliged to return to their lines. 1st Battalion reaches Vaux. The Boche evacuate. Our own are forced to do the same. The Boche return. The 8th advances as far as the wood on the right. The Boche evacuate. Ours are again forced to do the same. As for the Zouaves, situation similar. Nothing to be gained by attacking. The German infantry has again diminished in quality. A pile of mediocre men supported by a fantastic artillery. The Vaux garrison has capitulated. Nothing is left in the attacking battalions but debris.

The Zouaves, in fact, had never left their point of departure. Caught in an annihilating barrage of 210 mm. howitzers designed to clear the way for the Germans' own attack, the C.O. and all but one of the Zouave officers were killed. The survivor, a second-lieutenant, led what remained of the battalion back to its starting position. The Moroccans alone attacked. Of the centre battalion, seven out of eight officers fell, and companies were reduced to an average of twenty-five men apiece. Inside Fort Vaux, which Colonel Savy's force had been told was still in French hands, the embrasures were tenanted by German machine-gunners. They waited until what remained of the attackers were within a few yards, then mowed them down at almost point-blank range.

In all the ten months' battle it would be difficult to find an action that was both more futile and bloody. That day Pétain, enraged at the slaughter, intervened in what was strictly his subordinate's prerogative, and ordered Nivelle to make no more attempts to retake Vaux.

> If Verdun is taken one day, what a disaster! If it is saved, how can we ever forget the price? – RAYMOND POINCARÉ, *Au Service de la France*

Fort Vaux, the Allied propagandists hastily told the world, was 'not a vital point in the Verdun defences'. But this was a view shared by neither of the forces locked together at Verdun. Vaux formed one of the principal buttresses in the 'Line of Resistance' designated by Pétain in February, and the French command now betrayed the significance of its loss by setting every available man (including Delvert and the thirty-seven half-dead survivors of his company) to digging trenches close to the city. Even Nivelle now began considering an evacuation of the whole Right Bank. On the German side, the ponderous offensive had awaited only the elimination of Fort Vaux before it could move forward again.

Von Knobelsdorf's immediate aim was to secure the flanking positions for the supreme punch through the centre that would take Fort Souville, the last effective major strongpoint between him and his goal. The new attacks were hardly aided by the weather, for since the fall of Vaux it had rained for days on end, as if the Heavens were mourning Raynal and his brave men. On the left, towards Fort Tavannes, they made disappointing headway. In terms of terrain conquered, results on the right flank were not much more encouraging. Here the objective was a fortified position called the *Ouvrage de Thiaumont*. Somewhere between a large bunker and a small fort, but mounting no artillery, the importance of the *Ouvrage* was its uniquely commanding position. It sat (close to where the monstrous *Ossuaire* is now sited) on a geographical crossroads, formed by the intersection of two ridges. One of these runs from Douaumont south-west to Froideterre, the other southeast through the village of Fleury and Fort Souville. Whoever held Thiaumont was master of the approaches to Souville, and for the next two months it was to provide virtually the focus of the Verdun fighting. On 8 June, the *Ouvrage de Thiaumont* was taken by the Germans, but almost immediately reoccupied, with heavy losses on both sides. Fourteen more times it changed hands during the course of the summer, indicative in itself of the constantly mounting frenzy of the battle; the French, with their back ever closer to the wall, the Germans seeing the long-promised triumph nearly within their grasp and feeling each time that this must be the final effort.

In the course of the initial fighting for Thiaumont there occurred an episode that was to become one of the great French legends of the First War, the *Tranchée des Baïonnettes*. Guarding the Ravine de la Dame immediately below and to the north of Thiaumont were two regiments from the Vendée, traditionally the home of France's most stubborn fighters, and among whose officers was one destined many years later to become a Marshal of France; de Lattre de Tassigny. No. 3 Company of the 137th Infantry Regiment was holding a line of trenches on the north-western slopes of the Ravine, tactically an ill-chosen position that was well observed by the German artillery. All through the night of 10 June and the succeeding day, the regiment was deluged by shells from the German 210s. At roll call on the evening of the 11th, there were only seventy men left out of 164 in 3 Company, and the bombardment continued with even greater ferocity that night – probably augmented by short-falling French 155s. By the following morning, the 137th no longer existed (its Colonel declared that all he saw of its remnants afterwards was one second-lieutenant and one man), and de Lattre's regiment was moved up hastily to close the gap. It was not until after the war that French teams exploring the battlefield provided a clue as to the fate of 3 Company. The trench it had occupied was discovered completely filled in, but from a part of it at regular intervals protruded rifles, with bayonets still fixed to their twisted and rusty muzzles. On excavation, a corpse was found beneath each rifle. From that plus the testimony of survivors from nearby units, it was deduced that 3 Company had placed its rifles on the parapet ready to repel any attack and – rather than abandon their trench – had been buried alive to a man there by the German bombardment.

When the story of the *Tranchée des Baïonnettes* was told it caught the world's imagination, and an American benefactor preserved it for posterity by encasing the trench in a sombre concrete shrine. In the light of later research, however, it seems probable that the real story was somewhat different. To begin with, it is taxing probability to extremes to believe that a whole section of trench, some thirty yards long at least, could have been filled in on top of its occupants by simultaneously exploding shells, and that not one single soldier – seeing the fate of some of his comrades – was able to escape interment. A much more plausible explanation is that the men of 3 Company indeed died at their post, but that the advancing Germans, finding the trench full of corpses, buried them where they lay, and planted a rifle above each in lieu of a cross. But whatever the truth of the *Tranchée des Baïonnettes* it detracts nothing from the gallantry of the *Vendéens*, and both in its circumstances and the fact that none survived to tell the tale, it testifies further to the new degree of intensity in the June fighting at Verdun.

With this intensification of the battle there came to Nivelle and Pétain daily more and more disquieting evidence of a slump in French morale. Because of Joffre's stubborn holding back of fresh units for the Somme offensive, both Pétain's *Noria* system and its beneficent effects were running down. During the June fighting, divisions forced to remain longer in the line were losing an average of 4,000 men each time they went into action. Many troops had now experienced the peculiar horror of Verdun for the second, and even third time.

On top of all that the men at Verdun had to endure, thirst was now superimposed as a new regular torment. Typical was the experience of a brigade holding the line at Fleury in mid June. In a first abortive attempt to get water up to them, barrels and wagons had all been blown to pieces by German artillery. During two more days of scorching heat the brigade had nothing to drink. Eventually 200 men were detailed to carry water up from La Fourche, over a mile away. When the thirst-crazed men reached the water supply, they became oblivious both to their orders and the German shelling, and a chaotic scramble ensued. After they had satisfied their own thirsts, they set off with what remained of the water in buckets for their comrades, but under the shellfire most of it slopped away en route. The brigade suffered yet another day of thirst. Physical conditions were getting to be more than human nerves could stand; added to which, the psychological effects of months of steady retreat, liberally sprinkled with disasters but not even a minor tangible triumph, were beginning to tell. No sooner had the Second Army got over the depression that followed the failure of the counter-attack on Douaumont than Fort Vaux was lost. Now the Germans were grinding ahead again, apparently supported by an even mightier artillery than ever before, and who could tell where it would end?

In Paris, President Poincaré noted that the defeatist *Bonnet Rouge* was becoming more active than ever. At the front, the feelings of the more articulate soldiers were probably accurately represented by the letter of a thirty-year-old art historian, Sergeant Marc Boasson. At the outbreak of war, Boasson – a Jewish convert to Catholicism – had joined up gaily, filled with 'the patriotism of the warrior' and a powerful hatred for the enemy. Verdun had changed all that. On 4 June from near Douaumont, Boasson wrote his wife:

One begins to ask oneself where is Victory, and whether it might not lie in any kind of a peace which would at least save the race. An artery of French blood was cut on 21 February, and it flows incessantly in large spurts. . . .

A few days later the former militarist was recounting to his wife his supreme joy on having been transferred to a non-combatant unit. (It gave him an extension of life of nearly two years.) Later he puts his finger on the psychological exhaustion felt by all the men at Verdun:

I have changed terribly. I did not want to tell you anything of the horrible lassitude which the war has engendered in me, but you force me to it. I feel myself crushed . . . I am a flattened man.

Morale was running down, and for the first time in the war manifestations of this began to show in the French Army. Reporting from his comfortable staff quarters 'certain acts of indiscipline' that had followed the Douaumont fiasco, the G.Q.G. Liaison Officer at Second Army noted that

in the 140th some fifty men refused to return to the trenches. The attitude of these soldiers has been excused by all the officers up to and including the Brigade Commander. They were brought before a Court Martial but only received sentences insignificant in relation to the offence committed.

In the 21st Division, in particular the 64th (Regt), protests were formulated against sending this unit back into the Verdun butchery.

Similarly in XII Corps rumours have been circulating about a sit-down strike. . . .

It was an alarming preview of what was to overtake the French Army on a vast scale just under a year later. To tackle this *'crise de tristesse sombre'*, as Louis Madelin so eloquently described it, Nivelle ordered all his officers to adopt the sternest measures, reiterating at the same time the well-worn exhortation: *'Ne pas se rendre, ne pas reculer d'un pouce, se faire tuer sur place.'* These measures soon had to be invoked in an arbitrary and tragic fashion.

After the fall of Vaux, the terrain to the right of the *Ouvrage de Thiaumont* was held by the 52nd Division under General Boyer. During the night of 7 June its forward regiments had been subjected to the same murderous bombardment that descended on the *Tranchée des Baïonnettes*. When the German assault waves moved in the following morning, one battalion of the 291st Regiment surrendered almost *in toto* after its C.O. had been killed. Its neighbour, the 347th, had suffered even worse under the shelling (which, as so often, had included a goodly sprinkling of French 155s), and was reduced to six officers and some 350 men before the attack even began. Still it held to its position. Later that day a Second-Lieutenant Herduin, seeing his company – now down to some thirty-five men – about to be encircled, gave the order to withdraw; thereby contravening the Nivelle mandate. His order appears to have released a chain reaction; elements of the 347th broke, and some of its men did not stop running until they reached the very suburbs of Verdun. The default of the two regiments momentarily created a dangerous gap in the centre of the line. There were questions from Nivelle, and General Boyer ordered Herduin and another young ensign, Millaud, to be shot – without trial – for cowardice. The sentence was carried out by the officers' own platoons, with tears in their eyes. The official account of the death of Herduin says that he was granted the 'favour of commanding the firing squad to fire', and that his last words allegedly were:

Soldiers! You are going to shoot me; but I am not a coward, nor is my comrade, but we did abandon our post, we should have stayed there to the end, to the death. If you find yourselves in the same situation, do not retreat ... remain to the end ... And now, aim well, right at the heart! Proceed! Fire.

Somehow it does not quite ring true.

The story of the two second-lieutenants was not released to the public until after the war, and then it raised a great outcry. Justice on this occasion seems to have been questionable; Herduin and Millaud had evidently both been noted in the regiment for their bravery under fire, on that particular occasion as well as previously, and it is possible that others bore at least as great a responsibility for the breaking of the 347th. A few days after the executions, an order from Joffre announced that the disgraced 347th and 291st Regiments were to be 'suppressed' forthwith, their colours returned to the depots. Such was France's draconian treatment of waverers as the supreme crisis approached at Verdun.

*

From a quiet sector on the Woevre, a French Company-Commander, who had fought at Verdun during March and April, watched the events of June, and concluded with extreme gloom that the city was going to fall; worse, 'the French Army had to admit itself impotent and beaten'. At Army Group H.Q. in Bar-le-Duc, still further from the battlefield, Pétain had also become infected by the depression reigning in the Second Army. With his remarkable, almost mystic and often oversensitive intuition, he sensed better than anyone just what the men at Verdun were suffering, and just how potentially explosive morale had become. In material terms, too, the situation seemed to him desperately dangerous. Because of Nivelle's costly counter-attacks of May and early June, divisions were being used up at a rate of two every three days, instead of one every two days as had been previously allowed for. Even more serious was the state of the all-important artillery. Apart from the steady losses due to enemy counter-battery fire, with the astronomic number of rounds fired guns were wearing out quicker than they could be replaced. Yet the German supply

of replacements seemed inexhaustible. In a letter to Joffre of
11 June, Pétain noted that he now had fewer heavy guns than
a month ago and that 'from the point of view of artillery we
are fighting in a proportion of one against two.' Moreover,
with each step backward the French artillery had become
critically short of observation points, one of the principal
reasons for the demoralizing frequency with which the infantry
got shelled by its own guns; with the brief appearance of
Boelcke's 'Flying Circus', there was also a serious threat that
the Germans might regain supremacy in the air.

In the position to which Joffre had cunningly elevated him,
Pétain found himself caught in a monstrous nutcracker between
Nivelle and Joffre, both sublimely self-confident and ignoring
or turning a blind eye to the desperate earnestness of the situation at Verdun. On one side, Nivelle was grinding down the
backbone of his army with his futile counter-attacks, and all
the time crying for more men. On the other side, Joffre, dedicated to the all-out push that was shortly to come on the
Somme, for over a month had been stubbornly denying Pétain
fresh replacements, and even withdrawing some of his precious
heavy guns. Relations between the two had become very
strained. Meanwhile, though in the initial stages of the battle
he had wanted to abandon the Right Bank and fight behind
Verdun, and though even Nivelle was talking of the necessity
to evacuate, Pétain, with his sure touch on the pulse of French
morale, knew that *now* it would be unthinkable to abandon
Verdun. A brave man under torture sometimes reaches a point
where, having already endured so much torment, there is no
giving in and he must go on to the end, even though he knows
that it will bring permanent mutilation, if not death. It would
have been possible for France to yield Verdun in February or
March, and even perhaps in April or May, but now too much
had been committed – too much of her own life-blood – to its
defence. The fall of Verdun in June could easily bring about
a total collapse of national morale – as Pétain wrote to Joffre,
on 11 June:

Verdun is menaced and Verdun must not fall. The capture of
this city would constitute for the Germans an inestimable success
which would greatly raise their morale and correspondingly lower
our own. A tactical success by the English, however great it might

be, would not compensate in the eyes of public sentiment for the loss of this city, and at this moment sentiment possesses an importance that it would be inexpedient to disregard.

Utterly frustrated and impotent within the Joffre–Nivelle nutcracker, Pétain was beginning to show signs of strain. That tell-tale *tic* was worse than ever, and his intimate entourage noted a marked change in his outlook dating from this period. The fatal pessimism, which a generation and a war later was to be styled defeatism, had set in. After the loss of Côte 304 in early May, Pétain had already written to Joffre expressing his fear that 'we shall end up by being beaten, if the Allies do not intervene.' A sense of deep bitterness towards France's British ally began to permeate Pétain; a bitterness that would henceforth never quite leave him. While France was bleeding to death on the altar of Verdun, the British for four months had stood by doing nothing! It was a cry echoed widely in the French Army ('*Sales gens, ces Khakis*', growled Sergeant Boasson), and of course played upon by German propaganda.[1] Again and again Pétain urged Joffre that Haig be persuaded to advance the date of the Somme.

*

In June *Simplizissimus* printed a cartoon of Joffre dangling by the seat of his pants from a tree overhanging a precipice, which tree was about to be chopped down by a German soldier, with the caption: 'The situation gives no cause for uneasiness.' But the tree supporting Joffre was now under attack from other sides as well. In Paris the parliamentarians of the Third Republic, so long muted by the almost dictatorial supremacy of Joffre and the G.Q.G., thoroughly shared Pétain's misgivings about Verdun and were now giving vigorous tongue to their dissatisfaction.

Under a truce – the '*Union Sacrée*' – that seemed almost unnatural in France, political peace had endured undisturbed

1. Neither Pétain nor his men could of course appreciate the fantastic difficulties that had faced unmilitary Britain in building up a twentieth-century war machine from virtually nothing. With an effort unparalleled in her history, she had already increased her original six B.E.F. divisions (which had been virtually annihilated during the Mons retreat in 1914) to fifty-two; but none of this was visible to the sore-tried men at Verdun.

among the various parties since the outbreak of war. On 16 June 1916 it came virtually to an end when opponents of the Government forced it to hold the first Secret Session of the war. Verdun was the subject, though even this was kept concealed from the French public by 'Anastasie', the censor. The debate was opened by ex-Sergeant Maginot, an imposing figure over six feet tall, leaning heavily on a stick as a result of wounds received at Verdun earlier in the war. Maginot knew Verdun and he had known Colonel Driant, whose constituency marched with his. Hesitantly he began, 'What might seem astonishing is that until now we have all kept quiet.'

Then he warmed to a scathing attack on the French High Command. Its optimism, claiming that twice as many Germans as French were being killed at Verdun, he debunked by quoting German revelations of actual casualties. His conclusion that French losses had been very little lower than the Germans (in fact they had been substantially higher) caused a sensation in the Chamber. Producing the Galliéni–Joffre correspondence that Driant had inspired in December 1915, Maginot went on to declare with much emphasis that Verdun was 'proof of the lack of foresight and the inadequacy of our High Command'.

Another Deputy, Viollette, cited General Gouraud as claiming that on the day of the Nivelle attack on Douaumont, because of the shortage of heavy artillery, there were sixty German batteries that were beyond the French reach on the Right Bank alone. '... above all,' he added, 'the soldier had the feeling that, for eighteen months, he has been thrown at every instant into the furnace, for nil results.'

Both General Roques, Galliéni's successor as Minister of War, and Briand, the Premier, gave only the feeblest of defences for G.Q.G.'s conduct at Verdun, with Briand stating blandly that Joffre had been taken by surprise in February because the Germans had attacked, 'as is not the rule', without digging any jumping-off trenches. When Roques mentioned that 'disciplinary action' was to be taken against some generals, there was a howl of 'names, the names!' The Chamber was restless and dissatisfied, and for a time it seemed as if the Government might be brought down. But by the close of the Secret Session on 22 June some deft political manoeuvring had assured its survival. Maginot was persuaded to withdraw his motion of censure, but insisted that it be entered into the archives. In an Order of the Day, a special homage to the C-in-C was deleted in favour of a 'collective homage' to the Army Commanders. The Chamber had hammered home the first nail in 'Papa' Joffre's coffin.

On 8 June Joffre had left Chantilly to accompany Premier Briand on a visit to London. In his absence, Pétain – thoroughly disturbed as one may imagine by the fall of Vaux, followed by the new German attacks and the disastrous implications of the breaking of the 291st and 347th Regiments – had made a telephone call to G.Q.G. which, according to Joffre afterwards, 'produced considerable emotion'. Pétain, he found, 'had once more scared everybody', and was threatening the immediate evacuation of the Right Bank before the mass of artillery there should be lost to the Germans. On Joffre's return, that devastating unshakable tranquillity speedily allayed all alarm. Pétain was exaggerating, there was really nothing at all to worry about, we are told by Joffre. But, just to confirm his own impeccable judgement:

> I thereupon decided to send General de Castelnau to Verdun the next morning so as to obtain his judgement on the situation. De Castelnau returned to G.H.Q. during the night of 13–14 June, bringing a most favourable impression of the condition of affairs at Verdun. ...

Writing smugly a long time *ex post facto*, Joffre was not being strictly honest in his *Memoirs*. To begin with, for all Pétain's prevailing pessimism, it was not true that at this junction he was seriously contemplating any panic evacuation of the Right Bank; this is abundantly clear from his letter to Joffre of 11 June, already quoted.

Moreover, he had not exaggerated that threat to Verdun, which had evidently worried even the shrewd and perceptive de Castelnau sufficiently for him to ring up both Haig and Foch and beg urgently that the Somme offensive be put forward. That Joffre too may have been rather more ruffled at the time than he would like posterity to believe is suggested by the imploring tone of his Order of the Day of 12 June:

> Soldiers of Verdun! ... I make one more appeal to your courage, your ardour, your spirit of sacrifice, your love of country. ...

The period 8–12 June was indeed, potentially the most dangerous for the French since 25 February; by the 12th, Nivelle had at hand no more than one fresh brigade in reserve, and there was no indication that the German push had yet exhausted itself. Had the Germans thrust on then, they could almost certainly have broken through to Verdun. As it was, they were within an inch of success. But, by the time de Castelnau reached Verdun to find everything so 'favourable', the German offensive had quite unaccountably petered out on the very brink of ultimate success. And, much as Joffre might like to claim credit for his prescience, the reason for this petering out had nothing to do with him, or any other French leader. Verdun's salvation this time owed itself to an event occurring far away, at the other extremity of the European battlefield; an event for which – indirectly – it was Erich von Falkenhayn the French had to thank.

Achilles: Patroclus, I'll speak with nobody.
SHAKESPEARE, *Troilus and Cressida*

Some of the errors inherent in Falkenhayn's 'bleeding-white' experiment that had cost the Crown Prince's Army victory in February have already been enumerated; the failure to attack on both banks of the Meuse simultaneously, the holding back of reserves at the crucial moment. Then had followed his endless wavering which surrounded every subsequent attempt to continue the offensive. Indecisiveness was a fatal flaw of Falkenhayn's character; so too was his arrogance and his passion for secrecy, the results of which were now – in a dramatically unexpected fashion – to rob Germany of her last chance of a victory in the West in 1916.

During his planning of 'Operation *Gericht*' at the beginning of the year, Falkenhayn had committed the exceptional error of not informing his opposite number and ally, Field Marshal Conrad von Hötzendorf, the Austrian Commander-in-Chief, of his intent to attack Verdun. One can find many contributory causes for the Central Powers' failure to win the First World War, but it would be hard to select any single factor more influential than the extraordinary lack of coordination and cooperation between Germany and Austria. There was never a 'Supremo', no Joint Council of War, and only the barest minimum of liaison between the two senior partners. To a generation with memories of the Eisenhower stewardship in World War II, this seems incomprehensible, and even by First War standards it compares unfavourably with what degree of cooperation the bickering Allies achieved under Joffre, and later – at the eleventh hour – under Foch, as Supreme Allied Generalissimo. In practice, this meant among other things that the Central Powers were rarely able to make full use of their one supreme strategic advantage over the Allies – their interior lines of communication.

It was the disastrous personal relations of Falkenhayn and Conrad that they were largely to blame. General von Kuhl describes the two together at one of their rare meetings; the former tall, stiffly erect, sartorially immaculate, every inch a Junker; Conrad,

small and elegant, almost girlish in figure. His clever face, with its white Imperial, was agitated by a nervous twitch of the mouth and eyelids. His uniform was clothing, not adornment; seldom was there an order on his jacket; indeed on ceremonial occasions he often forgot such decorations. So they stood together, the two men whose decisions set thousands in motion. The first was more of a soldier; the second the more deeply instructed soldier. Over one there remained something of the bloom of his days as a lieutenant; over the other the irritable air created by mental toil.

Theirs was the fundamental incompatibility of the Northern and the Southern German. Conrad was typical of the Austrian aristocracy of the period. He had been fourteen at the time of the Battle of Sadowa in 1866; memory of that catastrophic defeat, and the degrading subordination of the ancient Habsburg Empire to the upstart Prussians that followed, rankled as ceaselessly as did 1870 to the generation of Foch and de Castelnau. And the arrogant Falkenhayn, in his whole bearing and manner, was a constant reminder of that humiliation. It was typical of the man that Falkenhayn should once have been heard through closed doors, pounding the table and shouting at the Archduke Karl, the Habsburg heir:

What is Your Imperial Highness thinking of? Whom do you think you have in front of you? I am an experienced *Prussian* General!

One might think this was hardly the best way of getting results from a hypersensitive ally. Even Falkenhayn's own entourage warned him from time to time that he ought to adopt a more diplomatic attitude towards the Austrian commanders, but he merely replied that 'one must be tough with the Austrian if one wishes to prevail.' Worst of all, his form of 'toughness' included making no attempt to disguise his views on the current military prowess of the Austrians, whom he regarded with much the same kind of contempt that the *Wehrmacht* leaders reserved for their Italian and Rumanian allies. A few months after Falkenhayn's appointment, Conrad noted in his diary a deadly insult uttered – again in the presence of Archduke Karl – to the effect that 'our troops were disorganized . . . we achieved nothing, our troops did not march.'

There was, undeniably, a great deal of truth in Falkenhayn's remark. About Austria-Hungary's only success in the war had been the elimination of tiny, primitive Montenegro; a dubious triumph. When confronted by the Russians her miscegenate, half-hearted forces of which forty-seven per cent were Slavs – Czechs, Slovaks, Poles, Slovenes, and Croats – and eighteen per cent Magyars, disintegrated like sand castles licked by the sea. Again and again the Germans had to come to their aid on the Eastern Front. All this was particularly unbearable to Conrad – who was in fact as a general and a strategist far superior to Falkenhayn. He was one of the most outstanding on either side, the unique instance in the First War of where a commander was actually *better* than the troops he commanded (he also lasted longer than either Joffre or Falkenhayn; thirty-one months to their twenty-eight and a half and twenty-three and a half respectively). Lastly – but by no means the least consideration – long before Ludendorff indiscreetly proclaimed that Austria should by rights be 'Germany's prize of victory in this war', Conrad was well aware of Big Brother's political intentions, and as early as the seventh month of the war was referring to the Germans as 'our secret enemies'.

From his weaker position, Conrad developed his own way of striking back at Falkenhayn. At their rare meetings, he never tried to match Falkenhayn's superior power of rhetoric; instead he remained silent and sullen, giving Falkenhayn the false impression that his view had prevailed. Later, Falkenhayn would be infuriated to discover – by letter or by an action – that Conrad had not changed his mind at all. In November 1914, soon after Falkenhayn's appointment, the German and Austrian liaison staffs had tried to arrange a first meeting between their Commanders-in-Chief. But Falkenhayn, already displaying a disastrous lack of tact, insisted that Conrad come to meet him in Berlin; Conrad retorted by sending his Adjutant, a mere lieutenant-colonel. That same autumn, on purely rational administrative grounds, Conrad asked that the German Ninth Army, newly arrived on the Russian front, should be placed under Austrian command. Falkenhayn, not countenancing any diminution of his own control over that front, refused. A short time later Conrad retaliated by refusing a similarly reasonable German request to have the Austrian First Army put under Hindenburg, after the Warsaw offensive had been held up by lack of coordination between the two forces.

To us it all seems almost unbelievably petty and childish – though one only has to recall Lloyd George and Haig to realize that the relationship between Falkenhayn and Conrad was by no means the exception in the First War. With this background of personal animosity alone, it was perhaps hardly surprising that the two warlords never saw eye to eye on the conduct of hostilities. But, apart from this, their strategic philosophies were in sharp discord. Falkenhayn was essentially, as has been noted earlier, a 'Westerner', though his policy of 'security at all points' precluded a knock-out offensive anywhere. Partly influenced by his Austrian orientations, Conrad was an 'Easterner', as well as being a disciple of von Schlieffen to the extent of believing that the Central Powers could only win by concentrating on their enemies one at a time. Agreeing in principle with Hindenburg and Ludendorff, who wanted to stand on the defensive in France until Russia was smashed, at the same time he felt that successive minor blows should dispatch from the war the weaker Allies – Serbia, Montenegro, and Italy – which would then release Austria's full strength for use against Russia. Conrad's belief that the biggest plums were to be plucked in the East was substantially endorsed by the huge success of the Gorlice Offensive in May 1915. No campaign of the whole war produced greater material results than Gorlice; 1,500,000 prisoners and 2,600 guns taken, and an advance of 430 kilometres (the equivalent in five months at Verdun: 65,000 prisoners, 250 guns, and ten kilometres). And Gorlice had sprung originally from an idea of Conrad's; to his fury, when it succeeded Falkenhayn claimed it for his own.

The final, fatal rift between Falkenhayn and Conrad occurred later in 1915. Falkenhayn had agreed to lend German troops to finish off Serbia (there was a certain parallel with the Germans and Italians in Greece in 1941) where the Austrians – many of them Croats, with little desire to fight against their blood brethren – had been struggling ineptly since 1914. Characteristically, he insisted that all forces there should be placed under a German, General von Mackensen. Conrad resisted, but had to climb down when the Bulgarians supported Falkenhayn. When Conrad attempted to exert some influence over the course of the campaign (where the majority of the troops engaged were still Austrian) he was coldly informed that Mackensen could only receive orders from the German High Command.

As soon as Serbia was conquered, Conrad, true to his philosophy, announced that he was going on alone to liquidate Montenegro. In mid December, he wrote to Falkenhayn that 'now the campaign in Serbia is over, it is considered that the subordination of the Third Army under Mackensen is also ended.' On receiving this letter, Falkenhayn expostulated: 'That would tear up the agreement with the Bulgarians.' But before he could protest to Conrad, Conrad had already marched on Montenegro. Livid with rage, Falkenhayn declared that it was 'a breach of solemn promises' and broke off all personal relations with Conrad.

After he had successfully concluded the operation against Montenegro, Conrad wrote a conciliatory letter to Falkenhayn. He received no acknowledgement. About this time, he also wrote proposing a blow to knock out Italy in 1916, using sixteen Austrian divisions and four German, plus another four German divisions to relieve Austrian forces on the Russian front that would be required for the offensive. He received a cold, almost insulting, reply. In his Memoirs, Falkenhayn contemptuously dismissed the scheme on the grounds that Italy was of no military importance.[1] Meanwhile Falkenhayn was busy with his plans for Verdun. Motivated partly by his obsession for secrecy, but also without any doubt by his pique with Conrad, Falkenhayn never breathed a word of what was to be Germany's principal effort for 1916 to his chief ally.

It was incredible. When he first heard of the offensive in February, Conrad was quite understandably almost speechless with rage. If the Germans treated him this way, well then he

1. Although the merits of Conrad's proposal are of little concern to this story, at least one outstanding German military critic, General von Hoffmann, felt that Conrad was right, and that a Caporetto-style defeat in 1916, instead of 1917, might easily have brought Italy to collapse and struck a serious prestige blow at the Allies, while freeing troops for other fronts.

too would go his own way without consulting them. With a secrecy that would have commended itself to Falkenhayn, he set about planning an offensive against the Italians single-handed. Five of the best Austrian divisions were withdrawn, without replacement, from the Russian front and transferred to the Tyrol. Unfortunately for Conrad, the Alpine weather was against him; late snows caused the postponement of the offensive for the best part of a month, until 15 May, by which time the element of surprise had been lost. The Italians at Asiago suffered heavy losses, but within a month they had stopped Conrad's advance.

Suddenly one of the worst disasters of the whole war hit the Austrians. In answer to President Poincaré's desperate pleas to the Tzar for a relief offensive to loosen the Germans' teeth from Verdun, Russia's ablest commander, General Brusilov, attacked with forty divisions on 4 June. He struck the Austrians in Galicia at the weakest point in the line; just where Conrad had withdrawn his five crack divisions for the offensive in Italy. The blow fell without any warning, and the Austrian front collapsed like the walls of Jericho. Off galloped the artillery, leaving the infantry in their thousands to the mercy of the charging Cossacks; but frequently the Slavs in the hotch-potch Austro-Hungarian Army did not even wait for the guns to depart before they threw down their arms. By the time the Brusilov Offensive petered out, 400,000 prisoners had been taken. It was Russia's supreme moment, and the only success-ful campaign of that war to go down in history adorned with its author's name.

It seemed as if the whole Austro-German line in the East might cave in. On 8 June, the day the new German offensive was unleashed at Verdun, Conrad came to Falkenhayn in Berlin, pleading for German assistance. Falkenhayn, now see-ing the whole of his grand strategy falling in ruin, hardly spared him in this hour of greatest humiliation.

Just as Moltke had transferred two vital army corps to meet the Russian threat to East Prussia, thereby crippling the Ger-man lunge into France in 1914, so now Falkenhayn was forced to dispatch hastily eastwards three divisions from the Western Front. At Verdun, the Crown Prince received orders to suspend the offensive temporarily; there were unmistakable signs that the long-awaited British offensive in the West could not be very far off, and more reserves would be required to meet that. For over a week Falkenhayn hesitated. During this time, the Crown Prince seized the opportunity once again to persuade Falkenhayn to give up the Verdun offensive for good. Once again he was thwarted by his father and Knobelsdorf. His memories of this period, he wrote later, were 'amongst the most painful of the whole war . . . I was absolutely opposed to the idea of continuing the attack, yet I had to obey orders.'

But the danger from the East soon began to look less menacing; in the West the British batteries had not yet opened their ranging fire, and Falkenhayn was still Knobelsdorf's man. The resumed effort against Fort Souville was now fixed for 23 June. However, the critical moment for the French had meanwhile passed. Nivelle – thanks to Brusilov – had to some extent been able to replenish his desperately low reserves and repair his defences.

23 The Crisis

> One more effort, said the Commander, and we have it. They
> said it in March, April . . . and up to the middle of July, and
> then they said it no more – ARNOLD ZWEIG, *Education
> Before Verdun*

> In their minds there appeared a vision, pale and bloody, of the
> long procession of their dead brothers in *Feldgrau*. And they
> asked: Why? Why? And in their tormented hearts most of
> them found no answer – *Reichsarchiv*, Vol. 14

Fort Souville commanded the last of the major cross-ridges
running down to the Meuse on which the Verdun defences
had been based. Behind it lay only Belleville Ridge, with its two
secondary forts which were not reckoned capable of any serious
resistance. Otherwise from Souville it was downhill all the way
to Verdun, less than two and a half miles away, and once the
fort (which constituted part of Pétain's original 'Line of Panic')
fell into enemy hands it would be but a matter of time before
the city itself was rendered untenable. The approach to Souville
in front lay along a connecting ridge, placed like the bar in a
letter 'H', linking the Souville heights to those that ran from
Froideterre to Douaumont. The distant end of the bar was
commanded by the disputed *Ouvrage de Thiaumont*, currently
in French hands, and astride it lay the important village of
Fleury. Both these had to be captured before an assault on
Souville could be made.

For the attack, Knobelsdorf had somehow scraped together
30,000 men – including General Krafft von Dellmensingen's
recently arrived Alpine Corps, one of the most highly rated
units in the German Army. Compressed within a frontage of
attack of about three miles, the new effort represented a greater
concentration of force than even the initial thrust of February.
Despite Brusilov's interruption, von Knobelsdorf – in sharp
contrast to his Army Commander – was brimming over with
optimism. He would be in Verdun within three days. Already
he had ordered up the colours and bands of the various regi-

ments for the triumphal entry to follow, and invited the Kaiser to watch the administering of the *coup de grâce* from Fifth Army Headquarters. During the days before the attack, Colonel Bansi, commanding the German heavy guns, noted rapturously the joy of once again being able to gallop his horse from battery to battery, 'through the glorious summer weather, and fresh blooming fields. . . . That gave one heart and courage, a freer and fresher feeling.' The Germans' light-hearted confidence was not entirely braggadocio nor just wishful-thinking. Von Knobelsdorf had one last trick up his sleeve.

As the German storm-troops passed by the artillery emplacements on their way up to the line, their eyes fell upon great piles of shells all painted with bright-green crosses. There was a deliberate air of mystery and secrecy surrounding the unfamiliar markings, but it was widely sensed that it had something to with the leaders' assurances that this time they were going to break through to Verdun, and no mistake.

*

On the evening of 22 June, Lieutenant Marcel Bechu, an officer on the staff of the French 130th Division, was sitting down to supper with his general at his command post near Souville. It was a beautiful summer night without a breath of wind, spoilt only by the German bombardment that had raged all day. Abruptly all the German guns ceased. For the first time in days there was silence, total silence; a silence that seemed 'more terrible than the din of the cannonade'. The officers glanced at each other with suspicion in their eyes; for, as Bechu remarked, 'man is not afraid of fighting, but he is terrified of a trap.' The French guns went on battering away, but for once were unanswered. For minutes that seemed like hours the uncanny silence continued, while in the shelter disquiet mounted. Then there came a sound above, said Bechu poetically,

of multitudinous soft whistlings, following each other without cessation, as if thousands and thousands of birds cleaving the air in dizzy flight were fleeing over our heads to be swallowed up in swarms in the Ravine des Hospices behind. It was something novel and incomprehensible. . . .

Suddenly a sergeant burst into the shelter, without knocking or saluting, his mouth trembling with agitation.

'*Mon Général*, there are shells – thousands of shells passing overhead, that don't burst!'

'Let's go and have a look,' said the General.

Outside, Bechu could now hear the distant rumble of the German guns, but still no sound of exploding shells. Then, out of the ravine, as they stood listening, crept 'a pungent, sickening odour of putrefaction compounded with the mustiness of stale vinegar.'

Strangled voices whispered: 'Gas! It's gas!'

In the neighbouring 129th Division, Lieutenant Pierre de Mazenod heard the silent shells falling all round his battery of 75s. It was, he thought, just like 'thousands of beads falling upon a large carpet'. For a few moments of blissful delusion, his men believed that the Germans were firing duds. Then came the first strangling sensations of the vile-smelling gas. The pack-horses plunged and reared in frenzy, broke from their tethers, and ran amuck among the battery. Swiftly the gunners whipped on their gasmasks and ran to man their cannon. The masked men struggling at their guns reminded de Mazenod of 'the Carnival of Death'. The crude gasmasks of those days so constrained breathing that every action required several times the normal effort, but at least they saved one from asphyxiation. Now, however, men with their masks on still coughed and retched and tore at their throats in a desperate struggle for air. In some ghastly way the gas seemed to be getting through the masks.

It was supposed to. For months German scientists had been experimenting with a new formula. At last they had produced a gas against which they discovered that captured French gasmasks were only partially effective, and now it was being tried out for the first time. Phosgene was its name – or 'Green Cross Gas' as the German Army called it, on account of its shell markings – and it was one of the deadliest gases ever used in war. Little wonder that the Germans had such confidence in this new attack.

The 'Green Cross Gas' attacked every living thing. Leaves withered and even snails died; as one minor blessing, the flies swarming over the corpse-infested battlefield also disappeared temporarily. Horses lay, frothy-mouthed and hideously contorted, along all the tracks leading up to Souville. The chaos was indescribable; abandoned mobile soup-kitchens stood tangled up with artillery caissons and ambulances. None of the supplies of cartridges and water that the front-line infantry had been calling for frantically all the previous day could get through the gas curtain, which in the stillness of the night lingered undissipated. Its effects extended to the rear areas, and even behind Verdun. A wounded subaltern recalls being treated by a spectre-like surgeon and his team, all wearing gasmasks, while nearby a 'faceless' Chaplain gave absolution to the dying. Occasionally the medicos clutched their throats and fell.

It was the French artillery that bore the brunt of the 'Green Cross'. In de Mazenod's battery, gun crews were reduced to one or two men each, many of them 'green like corpses'. One by one the French batteries on the Right Bank fell silent. As bad luck would have it, even the immensely useful 155 mm. gun in Fort Moulainville, which had stayed in action all through the battle and had not been affected by the gas, was at last knocked out that morning by a 'Big Bertha' shell exploding inside the fort. For the first time in the titanic four-month-old artillery duel, one set of gunners had gained the upper hand over the other. By dawn on the 23rd, only a few scattered cannon were still firing. Then, as abruptly as it had begun, the 'Green Cross' shelling ended, replaced once more by the thunderous barrages of high explosive. At 5 a.m. the German infantry moved forward in the densest formations yet seen, the reserves following closely behind the first waves. Before de Mazenod could get his 75s back into action, the Germans were too close. Soon he and the survivors of his battery found themselves keeping them at bay with rifles.

*

The main German blow struck right between the French 129th and 130th divisions, both suffering acutely from thirst, short of ammunition, and badly demoralized by the lack of artillery support. French listening posts gloomily overheard German patrols reporting back that they had reached the French forward posts, and found them abandoned. A deep hole was punched with alarming rapidity right through the centre of the French line. In their first rush, the Bavarians overran the *Ouvrage de Thiaumont* and reached and momentarily encircled the Froideterre fortification. Other Bavarian units broke through to the subterranean command post on the edge of the Ravine des Vignes called *'Quatre Cheminées'*, which contained the H.Q.s of no less than four separate French units. For several days the staffs remained besieged inside, with the Germans dropping hand-grenades on them down the ventilator shafts that constituted the 'Four Chimneys'.

To the left of the Bavarians, the greatest triumph of the day was won by von Dellmensingen's Alpine Corps, its spearhead the Bavarian Leib Regiment and the Second Prussian Jägers. The Leib was commanded by Lt-Col. Ritter von Epp, later to achieve fame in the early days of the Nazi Party; while the Regimental Adjutant of the Jägers was an *Oberleutnant* Paulus whose name would forever be associated with the 'Verdun' of a generation later – Stalingrad. High above the battle, watching it as from a grandstand, a French observer in a captive balloon, Lieutenant Tourtay, saw von Epp's men storm into the village of Fleury. It was only 8.15, and the Germans had already covered nearly a mile since the attack began three hours earlier. A few minutes later, Tourtay saw twenty-four German field guns arrive at a gallop to support their tenancy of Fleury. Then the French defence began to crystallize, and shortly after 9 o'clock Lieutenant Tourtay was overjoyed to see the first French barrages of the resuscitated French artillery beginning to take effect. All that day fighting raged in Fleury, but by the evening of the 23rd it was firmly in German hands.

To the French there were moments when it looked as if, as one of the Brigadiers remarked, *'tout allait craquer'*. Every telephone call to Pétain's H.Q. at Bar-le-Duc brought worse news. There were more reports of *'défaillances'*, indicative of that physical and moral exhaustion which especially alarmed Pétain. At Thiaumont, it appeared that nearly half of the 121st Chasseurs and eighteen of its officers had been taken prisoner; it was a bad omen when distinguished units like the Chasseurs surrendered so easily. Before midday an orderly officer came with a report that Germans were now only two and a half miles from Verdun as the crow flies, and within 1,200 yards of the final ridge, the Côtes de Belleville. On his heels another arrived to tell Pétain that Ritter von Epp's men were firing their machine guns obliquely into the streets of Verdun itself, causing a minor panic. To his subordinates Pétain never revealed his alarm that day, displaying an apparent imperturbability worthy of Joffre himself and remarking only: 'We have not been lucky today, but we shall be tomorrow.'

At 3 p.m., however, he telephoned de Castelnau, gravely pessimistic, expressing fears for the safety of the great bulk of the French artillery that still lay on the Right Bank, and begging for the third time that Joffre get the Somme Offensive advanced.

Joffre and his supporters later cited this conversation as further evidence that Pétain was still contemplating a voluntary evacuation of the Right Bank, and was only forestalled by the resolution of Joffre and Nivelle. It was not so. On the Right Bank were positioned one-third of all the French guns at Verdun, and it would take an estimated three days to move them. Pétain feared – with reason – that if the German offensive continued, the defenders would be physically hurled across the Meuse, thereby losing all these guns; a sacrifice which, for France, would be second only to the capture of Verdun itself. In fact, Nivelle himself – though afterwards he was quick to claim that he had never been daunted – obviously shared Pétain's fears. He had already ordered the withdrawal of some of the guns in the Bras–Froideterre sector; in Verdun itself, the Governor was set frantically to digging trenches in the streets, fortifying houses for street fighting, and preparing Vauban's ancient citadel for siege. Even Joffre's own actions belied his subsequent claim 'I was never worried'; hastily he sent Pétain four of the divisions he so zealously had been hoarding for the Somme; in Paris, one of his officers admitted to Clemenceau that Joffre was 'prostrated' – upon which 'the Tiger' commented: 'These people will lose France!'

It was all very well for Joffre to write sanctimoniously in his Memoirs that 'Pétain had once more allowed himself to be too much impressed by the enemy.' Perhaps Pétain had fallen prey too readily to his ever-deepening pessimism. But without a shadow of doubt 23 June was a frighteningly close-run thing.

Who could tell that night that the lethal 'Green Cross' bombardment would not be repeated, that an equally potent thrust might not roll up the French defences on the morrow?

It was something only Knobelsdorf and his commanders knew. The course of German fortunes that day could hardly be better illustrated than by the letter of a twenty-five-year-old former student of Munich University, Hans Forster (killed near Verdun later in the year). Forster was an N.C.O. with the 24th Bavarian Regiment, detailed to advance between Fleury and Froideterre. Waiting in shellholes early that morning, he had noted that hardly any enemy shells fell, a pleasant contrast to the two previous days. At 7 a.m., coloured Very lights were fired, and the regiment surged forward. Within a few minutes it had reached its first objective, a French redoubt referred to as the *'A' Work*.

Forward! The French are flooding back; on the order of an officer they halt and take position again. 'Hand-grenades' is the shout among us. On all sides the defenders are falling – others surrender. One more powerful blow – the *'A' Work* is ours! ! ! We go on through a hollow. In front of us a railway embankment; to the right a curve in it. There forty–fifty French are standing with their hands up. One corporal is still shooting at them – I stop him. An elderly Frenchman raises a slightly wounded left hand and smiles and thanks me. ... Over the railway. ... In a shellhole ten yards to the left of me is our Company Commander, Lt. A. He calls out: 'It's gone wonderfully!' and laughs; then he becomes serious, for he sees that some men have gone ahead and are in danger of getting into our own fire. He stands up to shout – then – shreds of his map fly up, he clasps his hands to his breast and falls forward. Some men run to him, but in a few minutes he is dead. Forward again. No pause. Over the Fleury barbed wire; in ten minutes it's ours. With rifles slung, cigarettes in our mouths, laughing and chatting, we go on. Captured French are coming back in hundreds. ... [Though he must have been mistaken, Forster then claims to have seen, at the end of a long valley – probably the Ravine des Vignes – the suburbs of Verdun. Oh, Verdun – what rapture! we shake each others' hands with glowing faces. To the right of Fleury village stands Prince Henry [of Bavaria, later wounded in the battle], moved with joy. It is a sight – so great and sublime; time 8.20 a.m. The sun is shining. ... At about midday, the enemy gets together a counter-attack, but we overrun it and occupy a line of trenches one and a half kilometres in front of

Fleury. Gunfire is mounting. We can no longer remain in the open, and we hunt for shelters. ... That evening when we creep out of our holes we notice, to our horror, that the position was evacuated at 7 o'clock and that only our handful from the 24th and a few from the 10th were holding a line 500 yards wide. That was impossible. Lieutenant E. gave the order to move back under cover of dark, as we had been forgotten. Then, as early as 7.30 our own artillery began shooting up our positions. ... Until 3 a.m. we lay in a hole. Immense thirst. At last it rained, so we could lick the brims of our helmets, and the sleeves of our jackets. ...

Forster then headed back towards the German lines, half-carrying an N.C.O. of the Leib Regiment who had been severely wounded in the groin. As it grew light he recognized the wounded man to have been a fellow student at Munich. Together they got back safely to Fort Douaumont.

A number of factors had contributed to the ebb of the German attack that day. The effects of the 'Green Cross Gas' had been a little disappointing. French gasmasks had on the whole proved more effective (the French in fact reported only 1,600 gas casualties) than expected, and the gas tended to settle heavily in the hollows, so that French batteries on high ground were relatively protected. There had also been only enough 'Green Cross' shells to blanket the centre of the line, but the French guns on either flank were not knocked out. Above all, in their mistrust of novelty the German commanders had committed an error typical of the 1914–18 military mind; just as a hesitant Haig was later to throw away the supreme surprise value of the tank, so Knobelsdorf had decided not to risk all on Phosgene. Thus, three or four hours before the infantry went in, the gunners had been ordered to cease the gas shelling and revert to normal ammunition, giving the French a vital respite to get their guns back into action.

Tactically, too, the Germans had made the error of attacking (once again) on too narrow a front with too few reserves. This was partly due to the failure, during the preliminary offensive which began on 8 June, to consolidate their flanks by capturing Thiaumont on one side and the 'High Battery' position at Damloup on the other. Again, on the 23rd, brilliant though the German success had been in the centre, the attack had completely failed to burst the French line at the seams.

Thus the French had been able to concentrate on blocking the direct menace to Fort Souville via Fleury. By the afternoon of the 23rd, Ritter von Epp had to report that the Leib Regiment could make no further progress. It had already lost fourteen of its officers, and 550 men.

In the sultry midsummer heat of one of the hottest days of the year at Verdun, thirst set the final seal on German hopes. That afternoon, the C.O. of one of the Bavarian Leib battalions signalled back from Fleury: 'If no water can be brought up, the battalion will have to be taken out of the line.' His neighbour, Prince Henry, reported that without water he feared his battalion might suffer 'serious reverses'. During the night, Ritter von Epp sent ninety-five water carriers to the Leib Regiment from Fort Douaumont; only twenty-eight arrived. Under these conditions, the regiment was physically incapable of continuing the attack the next day.

The fact that by early June the French had regained air superiority, with all the disadvantages that entailed for the German gunners, also contributed to the day's failure. But, basically, the foundering of the German attack all boiled down to the shortage of manpower. At the critical moment in the battle, the German *Reichsarchiv* note that the French defence was stretched to such an extent that one regiment of Chasseurs was left holding 1,500 yards of line, and in their estimate the presence of just one more German unit would have led to a breakthrough. What would have happened if Knobelsdorf had had available one of the three divisions Falkenhayn had sent to Russia, or if he had not been forced to interrupt the early offensive on 12 June, can be all too readily imagined.

That evening Knobelsdorf knew that his supreme bid to take Verdun had failed. Some four thousand French prisoners were claimed (their total casualties during this battle amounted to about 13,000), but the German losses had also been depressingly high. The Fifth Army was exhausted, French resistance was stiffening, and soon the inevitable counter-attacks could be expected. There was not enough 'Green Cross' ammunition left for a second effort; nevertheless the weary, thirsty troops would have to go on battling just to hold on to the gains of the 23rd. A disappointed Kaiser returned to his H.Q. at Charleville-

Mézières, and surreptitiously the regimental colours and bandsmen were dispersed to their depots.

As night fell over the French lines, even Pétain's pessimism had lifted a little. Nivelle issued a dramatic Order of the Day, ending with the famous words:

> 'You will not let them pass!'

Mangin – who had returned from his temporary eclipse on the very eve of the battle, now promoted to command a whole sector on the Right Bank – was as impetuous as ever, and all for launching an immediate counter-attack. This time he was right. The German advance had led itself into a narrow, tongue-like salient, with its apex, at Fleury, on an exposed forward slope. The next day, French counter-attacks hacked into the salient from both sides, and massed artillery gave the thirst-crazed Bavarians a taste of what the French in their larger salient around Verdun had been experiencing ever since February. For a week Mangin attacked almost incessantly, making eight separate attempts to regain the *Ouvrage de Thiaumont*, and with the Germans striking back hard all the time. Casualties were heavy, one of Mangin's battalions losing thirteen out of fourteen officers in an abortive attack on Fleury, and the result in terms of ground reconquered was nil.

But it hardly seemed to matter any longer.

＊

For the past months British wall-scribblers had been busy chalking up exhortations (so reminiscent of the 1942–4 'Second Front' slogans) of SAVE VERDUN and STRIKE NOW IN THE WEST. Unmoved by public opinion or pressure from the French, Haig had stolidly adhered to his date of mid August for the opening of the Somme Offensive. Then on 26 May, Joffre (pushed by Pétain) had come to see him in a state of uncharacteristic agitation. If the British did nothing till August, 'the French Army could cease to exist,' shouted Joffre. Haig (according to his Diaries) had soothed him with some 1840 brandy, and subsequently agreed to have the offensive advanced to the end of June. On 24 June, following the bad news from Verdun, Premier Briand himself came to beg

Haig to bring the attack forward again. Haig said it was too late now, but he would accelerate the preliminary bombardment, and start that very day. The rumble of the British guns, which could be heard in the South of England, at German Supreme Headquarters was accompanied in the ears of Falkenhayn (who appears to have been about the only German not certain even at the eleventh hour just where the Big Push was going to be) with the sound of his whole war strategy collapsing.

For seven days the bombardment raged, the longest yet known. Then, on 1 July, the French and British infantry went over the top. Whereas, in Joffre's original plan outlined at the Chantilly Conference the previous year, Foch was to have attacked with forty divisions and Haig with twenty-five, the needs of Verdun had now whittled down the French contribution to a mere fourteen. But it was Foch's men – in the van, the famous 'Iron Corps', now recovered from its mauling before Verdun in February – who were to mark up the only real successes. They worked forward in small groups supported by machine guns, using the land with pronounced tactical skill, in the way they had learned at Verdun, and emulating where possible the German's own infiltration techniques there. On the first day they overran most of the German first line before getting stuck, and with comparatively light casualties. It was otherwise with the British forces. Led into battle largely by inexperienced officers of the 'Kitchener Army', trained by generals who believed that what had been good enough for Wellington was good enough for them, commanded by a man who – in his insular contempt for the French Army – felt there was nothing to be gained from its experiences, and weighed down by sixty-six pound packs, Haig's men advanced in a line that would have earned credit at Dettingen. At a steady walk (laden as they were it would have been impossible to run), spaced regularly – as ordered – with not more than 'two or three paces interval', they advanced across No-Man's-Land, into what Winston Churchill described as being 'undoubtedly the strongest and most perfectly defended position in the world'. The enemy machine guns (a weapon described by Haig as 'much overrated') had not been knocked out by the bombardment. Back and forth they swept across the precisely-arrayed British line, As its men fell in rows, so other lines came on at regular 100-yard intervals, displaying courage that the Germans found almost unbelievable. The majority of the attackers never even reached the forward German posts.

By the night of 1 July, Haig's army alone had lost nearly 60,000 men; among them 20,000 dead.[1] Of the day, Haig's chronicler, Colonel Boraston, had the impertinence to write that it 'bore out the conclusions of the British higher command, and amply justified the tactical methods employed.' It would have been more accurate to call it, as did a recent British writer, 'probably the biggest disaster to British arms since Hastings'. Certainly never before, nor since, had such wanton, pointless carnage been seen; not even at Verdun, where in the worst month of all (June) the total French casualty list barely exceeded what Britain lost on that *one day*. For another five months the bull-headed fight continued. Later, in defence of his Verdun operation, Falkenhayn and his supporters claimed that by thus weakening the French Army there, the Germans had been saved from disaster on the Somme; in fact, all Verdun probably did was to save the Allies from still greater losses there.

Nevertheless, at hideous cost, Britain had done her part to relieve Verdun. Honour was satisfied.

1. By comparison, the whole Battle of Alamein in twelve days cost only 13,500 British casualties, dead, wounded, and missing, and – according to Second World War standards – it was not a 'cheap' battle.

24　Falkenhayn Dismissed

> Possession of the fortress of Verdun itself has become a purely
> incidental matter as far as its strategical importance is con-
> cerned – H. H. von MELLENTHIN, *New York Times Maga-
> zine* (August 1916)

> Here are the walls upon which broke the supreme hopes of
> Imperial Germany – PRESIDENT POINCARÉ (13 September
> 1916)

The twenty-third of June 1916 represented the climax and the
crisis of the Battle of Verdun. It was also the turning point in
the Great War; though this fact may not have been so dramatically apparent as it was in the case of the defensive battles
of Alam Halfa and Stalingrad in the autumn of 1942, after
which the Axis never ceased to retreat. Nevertheless, the
failure to break through to Fort Souville and Verdun, followed
so closely by the first appearance of the new mass armies of
Britain on the Somme, ended the Germans' last real opportunity of a military knockout against the Allies. From now on
their inferior resources of manpower would force them increasingly to remain on the defensive. Russia would fall apart
under her own revolutionary stresses, thus allowing Germany
to concentrate her forces for one last desperate gamble in the
West. But – however much it may have looked like succeeding
at one moment – Ludendorff's offensive would come too late,
when Germany herself was too weak. Meanwhile the vast
weight of the United States would have been placed on the
balances of war; for where the exploits of the Lafayette
Squadron had focused American sentiments on French heroism at Verdun, the halting of the German thrust on 23 June
played its part in finally convincing hard-headed American
businessmen and politicians that the Central Powers were not
going to win the war after all.

Yet, though the critical moment had passed, that 'oak-hard'
general, Knobelsdorf, still refused to admit defeat before Ver-

dun. In keeping with the curious, and peculiarly Teutonic instinct for self-immolation and *Götterdämmerung* that loosed
off the offensives of March 1918 and the Ardennes at the end
of 1944, and enacted the melodrama of the *Führerbunker*, he
persuaded Falkenhayn to make one last attempt on Verdun.
The omens were hardly promising; along with its novelty, the
'Green Cross Gas' had lost its capacity to provoke unreason-
ing terror; some of the Fifth Army's heavy guns had already
been sent off to the Somme, and there would be no fresh reinforcements for the attack – Falkenhayn having made it clear to
Knobelsdorf that whatever he had in mind would have to be
accomplished with his own depleted forces. But Knobelsdorf
was insistent; the Fifth Army had indeed seemed to come so
close to success on the 23rd, so once again Falkenhayn ac-
quiesced.

The attack would be limited to a front even narrower than
that of the 23rd, using the equivalent of only three divisions
(of which one regiment, the 3rd Jäger, had already suffered
twelve hundred casualties during the fighting of the last
month). It was to start on 9 July, and even during the pre-
liminaries the Germans had – by a cunning ruse – registered
a useful success that dismayed the French. Almost ever since
the fall of Vaux, the Damloup 'High Battery' situated to the
south of the fort had effectively blocked the advance on Fort
Souville from the east. On the lip of a ridge commanding a
wide field of fire, the 'High Battery' was a heavily armoured
artillery position with concrete bunkers and shelters capable of
housing a company and a half of infantry. It had repulsed
countless attacks by the enemy, who had however managed to
dig themselves in uncomfortably close. In the early morning
of 3 July, troops of the German 50th Division that had taken
Vaux began firing a heavy, short-range mortar at the battery
at regular intervals. As expected, the French garrison all took
cover in their concrete shelters. Meanwhile, the German infantry crept stealthily up to within a few yards of the 'High
Battery'. At 2 a.m. the mortars took to firing bombs with their
fuses removed. The French, hearing the solid thud of these
falling unexploded assumed that they were duds and that, the
bombardment still continuing, the enemy would not yet be
attacking. But the Germans, on the sound of the first 'dud',

were already swarming over the parapet. Almost without fighting the 'High Battery', three machine guns, and a hundred men were taken.

On the night of 7 July German plans were, however, upset – once again – by the Verdun weather. After days of heat and parching thirst, the rainstorm came as bliss beyond compare to von Epp's Bavarian Leib Regiment, which, still clustered behind the railway embankment at Fleury, was to be in the van of the push on Souville for the second time. Then, as the rain continued to deluge down and the offensive was postponed for two days, the waiting troops were subjected to new miseries. The battlefield swiftly became a morass of mud, in which reinforcements stumbling lost at night were sucked down and drowned as in a quicksand. By day, lying out as it did on a slope of which every inch was observable to the French, the Leib Regiment was under strictest orders to show absolutely no movement, in order to provide at least some element of surprise for the new attack. For three days they lay in their shellholes, under intense French fire; it was particularly depressing to morale to hear wounded men howl and agonize all day in a neighbouring shell-hole, and be forbidden to go to their assistance. Roll-call on the evening of the attack showed that the leading battalion had already lost 120 men, or one-fifth of its total strength; the Regimental History states that 'It was only with great difficulty that order could be re-established during the night.'

In all the German formations spirits had seldom been lower. They were hardly revived by the spectacle of the heavy German guns once more raising a crown of volcano-like flames on battered Fort Souville.

At midnight on the 10th the 'Green Cross' shelling began. This time, benefiting from the mistakes of 23 June, the Germans continued to douse the French guns with gas until well after the infantry were actually on the move; at the same time extending the front of the bombardment. Sergeant Marc Boasson watching it through binoculars thought it

a gripping spectacle; – little by little, we saw the country disappear, the valley become filled with an ashy-coloured smoke, clouds grow and climb, things turn sombre in this poisoned fluid. The odour of gas, slightly soapy, occasionally reached us despite the distance. And at the bottom of the cloud one heard the rumble of explosions, a dull noise like a muffled drum.

In the ears of Ritter von Epp's men, the peculiar sound of the gas bombardment was sweet music; indeed, 'never before had the artillery been so blessed and idolized by the infantry.'

Still sweeter was the silence that spread, as before, among the French guns. But as the German storm-troopers advanced out into the dawn from the shell-holes, a barrage of 75s swept down all along the line, incomparably more devastating than anything experienced on 23 June. The attackers looked at each other in dismay as great gaps were torn in their formations. In a matter of minutes the 2nd Battalion of the 140th Regiment lost nearly all its officers; the C.O. of the 1st Battalion of the 3rd Jägers – which had already suffered so heavily in June and was now scheduled to lead the frontal assault on Souville – simply reported back that he could not take the responsibility for continuing, and was ordering his men to dig in. It was illustrative of how the Germans' cutting edge had been blunted over the months at Verdun.

What had gone wrong? There was a simple answer. Since the 23rd the French gunners had been equipped with new and more effective gasmasks,[1] of a design actually approved long before the first appearance of phosgene. With admirable cunning and control they had held their fire until the enemy insouciantly revealed himself.

Nevertheless, there were still the usual, unaccountable disasters and more of the disturbing *défaillances* on the French side early that day. Striking hard south-west from Damloup 'High Battery', German Jäger troops well supported with flame-throwers took the French 217th Regiment apparently by surprise. One whole battalion was encircled and rounded up, some thirty-three of its officers and 1,300 men slaughtered or captured. Its Commanding Officer, Lieut-Col. Leyrand, had a remarkable escape; captured in his command post he was en route for Fort Vaux when his two-man escort was killed by a salvo of French shells. Unwounded himself, he made his way back to his command post, where he found Germans in con-

1. French gas fatalities on the 11th are said to have totalled little more than half-a-dozen.

trol and was captured anew. That evening it was retaken by a French counter-attack; Leyrand, still unwounded, was liberated. Meanwhile, the rout of his regiment had brought the Germans on the left flank of their attack to within a few yards of the eastern end of the Tavannes Tunnel, the vital nerve centre whose western end emerged in the valley of the Meuse, close to Verdun. A flood of wounded, retching gas cases, and panic-stricken stragglers streamed towards the refuge of the tunnel, while French sappers prepared to blow it up if the German advance continued.

Something similar had happened at the other end of the line, at Fleury, where the Leib Regiment – despite its fatigue and depression – had seized a bunker containing the H.Q. of the French 255th Brigade. The commander was killed in the course of the struggle. Members of another French unit near by observed one platoon firing hard at the backs of its fellows who had thrown away their weapons and were making for the German lines. Obviously all was not well with the French defence that day. To make matters worse, two battalions Mangin sent to plug the hole left by the collapse of the 255th Brigade took the wrong direction, and they too fell victim to the oncoming Germans. Once again the Bavarian Alpine Corps had punched a dangerous hole in the French lines; but this time only some 400 yards deep.

That night, 2,400 French prisoners were counted; again a large bag considering the scale of the attack. On the 12th the battle continued afresh, but the efforts of the Germans, exhausted and with no fresh reserves to throw in, rapidly began to ebb. Still, for a few hours, confusion existed on either side as to exactly where the front line lay. Suddenly during that morning, an excited German staff officer ran to General von Dellmensingen and reported that an unidentified group of men were waving a German flag from the top of Fort Souville. The General reached for his glasses. It was true! There were Germans on the fort. Quickly he ordered the artillery to lay a protective barrage to the south of Souville. It was clear that there were no longer any French troops between the Germans and the fort. But equally there was not one single regiment available to exploit this superb opportunity.

The Germans on the glacis of the fort, about thirty of them, were in fact only leaderless fragments of the 140th Regiment, forced by the French artillery barrages to move forwards, rather than backwards with the rest of their regiment. The senior of the group was an unknown young ensign; desperately he signalled with his flag for his comrades to join him on the fort. For a while they were left undisturbed by the French. Beyond, little more than two miles away, they could see the twin towers of Verdun cathedral and the Meuse gleaming through the summer haze as it meandered in and out of the city. The Promised Land! The spires of Moscow as seen in the grey distance of autumn 1941 cannot have seemed more enthralling – nor more unobtainable – to German soldiers. Out of all the Crown Prince's legions, this was a sight that would be bestowed on these thirty alone. And it was not to last long. In Fort Souville itself the garrison had been largely knocked out, but taking shelter there were the remnants of a French regiment, some sixty men under Lieutenant Dupuy. Hearing that there were Germans on the glacis, Dupuy promptly led out his men to drive them off, in what (not knowing that this was only an isolated group) might well have been a heroically suicidal attack.

After a sharp exchange, Souville was once more undisputedly French; some ten of the Germans whose eyes had beheld the sacred city were taken prisoner, the rest killed or dispersed. In deepest frustration and despair, General von Dellmensingen saw the last flicker of German hopes at Verdun dwindle and expire.

*

The German tide receded with incomparable swiftness from its highwater mark that day. By 14 July – Bastille Day – Mangin's counter-attacks had pushed the attackers practically back to their starting-off positions of 10 July. The bid to take Verdun was finally at an end. Between 21 February and 15 July, the French had lost over 275,000 men (according to their official war history) and 6,563 officers. Of these somewhere between 65,000 and 70,000 had been killed; 64,000 men and 1,400 officers had been captured (according to the Crown Prince). Over 120,000 of the French casualties had been suffered in the last two months alone. On the German side, Falkenhayn's 'limited offensive' had already cost close on a quarter of a million men; equivalent to about twice the total complement of the nine divisions he had been willing to allocate for the battle in February. The German artillery had fired off approximately 22,000,000 rounds; the French perhaps 15,000,000. Out of their total of ninety-six divisions on the Western front, the French had sent seventy to Verdun; the Germans forty-six-and-a-half.

It was perhaps symptomatic of the whole tragedy of Verdun that this last attack need never have taken place. The Crown Prince tells us that on 11 July Falkenhayn had once more changed his mind and ordered that he should 'henceforward adopt a defensive attitude'. But it was far too late to pass on the message to the divisional staffs. The futile slaughter proceeded. And even after the German offensive was called off after 14 July, still the tragedy could not be halted; all through July, August, and part of September the hideous struggle at Verdun continued, little abated. Again it seemed as if humans had lost their power to stop the battle they had started, which went on and on, sustained by its own momentum. The French, who could never be entirely sure that 11 July did represent the Germans' last effort against Verdun and who had been pushed back so dangerously close to the city that one more breach, one more mistake, could still bring about its fall, had to fight desperately to regain breathing room. The Germans were confronted by a terrible dilemma; once their forward impetus ceased and they were forced over to the defensive, tactically they should have abandoned most of the terrain they had conquered at such hideous cost. It was largely indefensible. The Crown Prince recognized this, but even he admitted that it was impossible, because, psychologically, it 'would have had an immeasurably disastrous effect'.

Such were the symbolic proportions that names of meaningless ruins like Thiaumont and Fleury – not just *Verdun* now – had assumed in German minds. So all through the summer the ding-dong battle ensued; with the French bitterly attacking, attacking, attacking; and the Germans contesting every inch of ground, occasionally themselves attacking to regain a lost fragment. Typical of this new, transitional phase of the battle was the prolonged struggle for P.C. 119 on Thiaumont Ridge;

built as a command post for perhaps a dozen men, its recapture by the French required a whole battalion. Again and again Fleury and the Ouvrage de Thiaumont changed hands; until, by the end of the summer, all that remained of Fleury (once a village of 500 people) was a white smear visible only from the air – the sole recognizable object found on its site, a silver chalice from the church.

There were alarms on both sides. On 4 August, Private Meyer was detailed off to sing at a concert organized for the music-loving Crown Prince. But the sudden threat of a French breakthrough at Thiaumont dispatched Private Meyer's unit to plug the hole; the concert was cancelled, and the budding tenor captured by the French. On 19 July, Lloyd George told Repington of *The Times* that he was still seriously worried that Verdun might fall and the Germans 'would then shift around 2,000 guns on to our front and hammer in.' At the beginning of September, President Poincaré was to bestow the *Légion d'Honneur* upon a triumphant Verdun, but a sharper German reaction than usual re-awoke French fears to such an extent that it was felt prudent to postpone the ceremony until the new crisis had passed.

With the fighting raging back and forth over the same narrow, corpse-saturated battlefield in the blazing summer heat, the screw of horror tightened (if such a thing were possible) yet another turn. A French officer, Major Roman, describes the scene at the entrance to his dugout in July:

On my arrival, the corpse of an infantryman in a blue cap partially emerges from this compound of earth, stones, and unidentifiable debris. But a few hours later, it is no longer the same; he has disappeared and has been replaced by a *Tirailleur* in khaki. And successively there appear other corpses in other uniforms. The shell that buries one disinters another. One gets acclimatized, however, to this spectacle; one can bear the horrible odour of this charnelhouse in which one lives, but one's *joie de vivre*, after the war, will be eternally poisoned by it.

Despite their continued subjection to these vile conditions, French morale at Verdun rose perceptibly during August. Everywhere – on the Somme, in Russia, in Italy, in the Near East – the Allies were attacking, and – best of all – Verdun was no longer seriously threatened. Correspondingly, German morale sagged. In August, owing to the brutally exposed ground it was bidden to defend, Fifth Army casualties for the first time exceeded those of the French.

*

Behind the scenes, it was in August that there occurred the ultimate clash between the Crown Prince, Knobelsdorf, and Falkenhayn. Heartily relieved when Falkenhayn at last terminated the Verdun offensive, the Crown Prince was horrified to discover, after 11 July, that his Chief-of-Staff even now still cherished ambitions of taking Verdun, and was only awaiting a suitable moment to reapply pressure on Falkenhayn. The French, argued Knobelsdorf, were certain to have sent forces off to the Somme; and, pointing to the tactical difficulties that the coming of winter was bound to exacerbate, was it not better to go forward rather than back? On 15 August, Falkenhayn – following a conference with Knobelsdorf at which the Crown Prince was not present – sent a typically indeterminate memo to the Fifth Army, stating that although the offensive had ended an aggressive posture must be maintained, both for home and enemy consumption. Falkenhayn then requested an appreciation of future prospects. From this letter, the Crown Prince at once deduced that Falkenhayn had

reverted to the idea which I believed he had abandoned – of keeping open the bleeding wound in the side of the French Army.

Worse, he suspected – not without reason – that Falkenhayn and Knobelsdorf were planning a new attack behind his back.

There followed a discussion at Fifth Army H.Q., attended by the two commanders on either side of the Meuse; von François (Left Bank) and von Lochow (Right Bank). Von François thought it essential to resume the offensive, principally because to abandon it now would be 'an admission of weakness'. Von Lochow, however, had by now come round to the viewpoint that had cost his predecessor, von Mudra, his command in April. He knew the conditions on the Right Bank better than anyone, having been there since February when he commanded III Corps, and felt that even the capture of Fort Souville would only be a repetition of Vaux, leading to still more hard fighting and heavy casualties. Backing the Crown Prince, he recommended that efforts be devoted to consolidating the existing positions.

The division of opinion at Fifth Army H.Q. was reported to Falkenhayn, and back came another letter; this time characteristic of the C-in-C's hopeless indecisiveness. The future conduct of the battle Falkenhayn had started was now 'left to the Army Group Commander to decide'. Commented the Crown Prince:

Despite the cryptic nature of this document, I was secretly glad to be freed from a weight of responsibility which had become intolerable, and once more to be my own master. I knew well enough the course I was bound to choose.

The course he had chosen at last was to beseech his father in the most urgent terms to replace Knobelsdorf. Disillusioned with the failure of the Verdun operation and with the state of the war in general, for once the All-Highest listened to his son. On 23 August Knobelsdorf was sent off to command an Army Corps in Russia. His place was taken by General von Luttwitz, who, the Crown Prince says, 'entered into my ideas rapidly and without reservations.'

Von Falkenhayn's own days were numbered. In Berlin his arch-enemy, Bethmann-Hollwegg, long plotting his downfall, had been progressively feeding the flames of the Kaiser's discontent with the former favourite as the horizons of war darkened. The opportunity finally arrived on 27 August, when Rumania entered the war on the Allied side. An eventuality that Falkenhayn had predicted could not possibly occur before the Rumanian harvests were gathered in mid September, it took the German leaders thoroughly by surprise. The next day the Kaiser summoned Field-Marshal von Hindenburg, and von Falkenhayn tended his resignation. Few mourned his departure; in Vienna and at Stenay there was particular rejoicing.

When the new Commander-in-Chief and his inseparable Ludendorff paid their first visit to the Western Front (they had been on the Russian Front ever since Tannenberg in 1914), they were horrified by what they saw at Verdun.

Battles there [said Hindenburg] exhausted our forces like an open wound. Moreover, it was obvious that in any case the enterprise had become hopeless. ... The battlefield was a regular hell and regarded as such by the troops.

Verdun was hell [echoed Ludendorff]. Verdun was a nightmare for both the staffs and the troops who took part. Our losses were too heavy for us.

At once they ordered the cessation of all attacks. German losses now totalled 281,333 men; the French, 315,000.

On the other side of the lines, Pétain had been having more trouble with his impetuous subordinate, Mangin. Within three weeks of his reinstatement after the Douaumont *débâcle*, and only a few days after the collapse of the German attack on 11 July, Mangin had launched a counter-attack on a divisional scale to retake Fleury. The division chosen was the unhappy 37th African, which had given so poor an account of itself during the first days of the battle, in February, and now – with a new commander – was eager to regain its honour. But the attack was hopelessly precipitate; the divisional command had no time to become familiar with the ground, and artillery support was poorly coordinated. Once again the Verdun slopes were carpeted with the khaki-clad figures of Tirailleurs and Zouaves. After this latest Mangin fiasco, Pétain – short circuiting Nivelle – wrote him a long and unusually testy letter. Henceforth, he saw to it that there would be no more of these grandiose but ill-prepared attacks. The Second Army was to conserve its forces for the mighty counter-stroke that Pétain had had in mind ever since his appointment in the dark days of February. From early September onwards, as French offensive preparations went into top gear, and Hindenburg ordered a halt to all German activity, a sinister and uneasy calm descended over the ravaged battlefield for the first time in nearly seven months. But before Pétain's plans could reach fruition the French were to suffer one further disaster; hideous and unanticipated.

*

The Tavannes Tunnel, whose eastern exit the Germans had so nearly reached on 11 July, was merely a single-track railway tunnel on the main Metz–Verdun line. It ran for some 1,400 yards beneath the Meuse Hills, and had the enemy ever succeeded in capturing it intact it would have led them like a Trojan

Horse behind the wall of the last line of forts, straight to the heart of Verdun. On 24 February, a nervous General Herr had actually telephoned Joffre for permission to blow up the tunnel. But this was not its only significance. For the whole sector of the front from Fort Souville eastwards it had for months fulfilled the role that Fort Douaumont served for the Germans. Along its track were combined the functions of barracks, stores, and first-aid posts, of a shelter and a communication trench. Several senior command posts were located in it, and there was accommodation for some three or four thousand men. Reserves on their way to make a counter-attack lodged there, and when it failed, there they returned to seek refuge and surgery. Even the little Arab donkeys used to penetrate several hundred yards into it when shelling became too intense for them to unload outside.

In the narrow, soot-blackened tunnel, dimly lit only in certain sections, men on the move to or from the front stumbled over the bodies of the sleeping and wounded alike. Sometimes they were electrocuted by brushing up against naked power cables. The hubbub, chaos, and stench were phenomenal. Territorial Lieutenant Louis Hourticq describes the tunnel in the spring of 1916:

This subterranean existence suppresses any distinction between the day and the night ... the activity, the movement, the noise, are the same, continued without pause, without cease, from midnight to midday. ... Under lamps black with flies the surgeons sew up the torn flesh. The General Staff of a brigade is seated near by, in its little wooden cell from which radiate out runners and telephone wires.

Captain Delvert, passing through the tunnel on his way to R. 1. was struck by the filth inside it. Men unable to reach the exits (both were under incessant shell-fire) simply relieved themselves in the gutters at the side of the track. Periodically fatigue parties were detailed to sluice down these gutters; then there were cries of:

'*Attention la merde ... Otez les gamelles! Le jus coule partout.*' ;.. The joke [says Delvert] never lost its point.

At last, the Divisional Commander occupying the tunnel in July was forced to abandon cleaning operations; fearful of the spread of disease that might be caused by stirring up the polluted mire. According to Delvert,

a night passed there, and men become pale, their features drawn, they can no longer support themselves on their legs.

And yet with what joy they sought its refuge; for as Lieutenant Pierre Chaine remarked:

There one experienced the most pleasant satisfaction that one could experience under shellfire; that of having a mountain above one's head.

Despite the warning of the terrible catastrophe that had struck Fort Douaumont, in the prevailing chaos at Tavannes Tunnel it seemed inevitable that something similar would happen there sooner or later. It happened late in the evening of 4 September, probably when fire somehow broke out among a cargo of rockets that mules had just brought into the tunnel. As at Douaumont in May, in a matter of seconds a chain reaction took place; the rockets set off a grenade depot, which ignited petrol used on the lighting generator, which in turn set off more grenades. A major, one of the few surviving eyewitnesses of the disaster, told Delvert:

A shattered body flew into me, or rather poured over me. I saw, three metres away, men twisting in the flames without being able to render them any help. Legs, arms, flew in the air amid the explosion of the grenades which went off without cease.

Hourticq recalled that

our doctor, who was walking about near the exit, was hurled outside; thrown to the ground. He rose to see the mouth of the tunnel inflamed and rumbling ... a great silence followed the banging of the detonations, and fire, fed by a violent current of air, consumed during several hours everything contained in the tunnel.

Inside the holocaust, a mortal panic broke out as men found flight made impossible by the wooden bunks and partitions in the narrow tunnel, as well as by the struggling bodies of their comrades. At the eastern exit, half-asphyxiated men rushed out into the open, only to be caught in the German bombardment. They surged back again, blocking that exit until a colonel forced them out again at revolver point. Several of the terror-stricken wretches were killed by the shells. For three days the fire raged inside and none could enter. When at last it subsided, rescue parties found many charred bodies piled up beneath an airshaft, through which men had apparently tried to escape in vain. More than 500 dead were counted; the victims included a Brigade Commander and his staff, and almost the whole of two companies of Territorials.

> In February the Germans created the battle of material, but they had unfortunately forgotten to reserve exclusive rights in it – ARNOLD ZWEIG, *Education Before Verdun*

> No historical remains I have even seen since, however impressive, not even the Coliseum or the Temples of Paestum moved me so profoundly as the Forts of Vaux and Douaumont – JEAN DUTOURD, *The Taxis of the Marne*

The preparations for the French counter-offensive reveal the Verdun team of Pétain–Nivelle–Mangin working together in greater harmony than ever before. Appropriately enough, Mangin, ever straining at the leash, was to execute the attacks; Nivelle, to be responsible for all the detailed planning; Pétain, for the overall planning, for the scale and timing of the attacks – and above all for restraining his eager subordinates from the folly of yet another premature effort. This time it was going to be a set-piece battle of the kind Pétain had wanted all his army career. It would not proceed until local superiority had been achieved, especially in artillery. The frontage of the initial attack would be rather wider than that of the Germans on 23 June, and the objective – nothing less than Fort Douaumont itself. There would be three divisions in the first line, followed by three more, with a further two in reserve. From every corner of the French front, Pétain garnered his guns; over 650 in all, half of which were heavies (facing an estimated 450–500 German cannon). Above all, the 'super-heavies'. Even before Mangin's 370s had failed to make any impression on Douaumont in May, Pétain had been pestering Joffre (who once opined to Repington of *The Times* that the 'super-heavies' were 'chiefly for the diversion of the public and the press') for something more powerful. Now, at last, two brand-new 400 millimetre railway guns had arrived, and lay swaddled in camouflage netting well behind the lines. With their longer range and greater penetrating power, these Schneider-Creusot monsters – the heaviest guns France had yet used during the war – were an even deadlier version of the Krupp 'Big Berthas'. All through September and early October the ammunition trains converged on Verdun; bringing up some 15,000 tons of shells for the guns. This time, as Pétain had promised his soldiers in the past, they would not be called upon to go over the top, singing the *Marseillaise* with no cannons behind them.

The great contribution of Nivelle, the gunner, was in organizing the 'creeping barrage' behind which the attacking waves would advance – one of the first times that this technique had been tried out. The infantry were to move forward at a steady and precise 100 yards in four minutes; seventy yards behind the field-gun barrage and 150 yards behind that of the heavier guns. Troops and shellfire would advance together like a relentless flail threshing the countryside. No longer would there be that fatal tell-tale lifting of the bombardments as the infantry went in. The success of the creeping barrage (as well as the avoidance of disasters from short-falling shells that had so frequently disheartened French troops at Verdun in the past) all depended upon a liaison between infantry and artillery of an unprecedented excellence. This Nivelle planned to achieve by laying telephone wires in trenches six feet deep, that would – for once – be virtually immune to shell-fire. It was a gargantuan task.

The capture of Douaumont itself had been allotted to General Guyot de Salins's 38th Division, composed largely of Mangin's beloved African troops. Among them were two untried battalions of Senegalese; big, tough, fearless soldiers, profoundly dreaded by the Germans because of their summary ways with captives. These arrived at Verdun in September, were entranced like children by the novelty of the 'firework display', and then propelled into a minor attack to see what they could do. At once they ran amuck, beyond all control of their officers, captured some German positions and butchered the survivors. Then the Germans recovered their nerve and set up a machine gun. The wretched Africans, never having been under such fire before, incapable of understanding where all the bullets were coming from, all grouped together in their bewilderment. Those that escaped the massacre that day were quickly pulled out of the line for further intensive training. After this unfortunate incident, preparation of the infantry to be used in the attack proceeded with meticulousness similar to that being lavished on the artillery programme. At Stainville, near Bar-le-Duc, a replica of the battlefield – including Fort Douaumont in full-scale outline – had been laid out over which units were subjected to 'battle-courses' until they knew it blindfolded. Meanwhile, Pétain and Nivelle, determined that Douaumont once regained should on no account be lost again and especially mindful of the tragic lesson of Fort Vaux, summoned to Verdun a French engineer who had organized fresh-water supplies during the excavation of the Panama Canal. Within a short time he had devised an ingenious system of transportable canvas pipes for getting water across the shell-ground to the fort.

As the mighty French preparations reached their zenith, even the habitually optimistic Mangin had never been more confident. He reminded a junior officer who saw him at this time of a cat, as 'his eyes narrowed and his tongue passed over his lips' in anticipation of the losses he was about to inflict on the enemy. He had moved his H.Q. to a corn-merchant's villa in a Verdun suburb, which was lent a vaguely Arab aroma by a curtain of tent cloth hung behind his desk. In the room was a large model of the ground to be reconquered; pointing to it, he told his visitors repeatedly:

You will see my Colonials entering in Douaumont over there.

When Joffre called on the eve of the attack, he was assured

in four hours, *Mon Général*, I shall give you twenty-two battalions.

Mangin's confidence this time was widely shared in the army. General de Salins told his men dramatically:

The hour has arrived ... your victory is certain; chastisement is close for the horrid Boche.

And an officer of one of the other divisions in the first wave, noting the comforting masses of artillery and supplies, remarked bitterly:

If only we had been thus provided at the beginning of the war, we should not now be fighting in France.

It was a very different picture in the Crown Prince's camp. The elation of an army on the offensive had given way to the uncertainty of an army that has lost the initiative and knows it is about to be attacked. Aware that the new High Command was only awaiting a psychologically propitious moment before it abandoned the present forward positions at Verdun, senior officers transmitted their uneasiness to the troops. The men themselves were exhausted, many either having spent a grisly summer on the Somme, or just too long at Verdun – like the units of von Zwehl's VII Reserve Corps that had been there without relief since February. Germany's inferiority in man-power had never been more grimly apparent, and exhaustion was revealing itself in *matériel* too. Worn-out guns were drop-ping their projectiles short with a disconcerting frequency that had hitherto been largely a French preserve. Meanwhile, the misery of the men holding the exposed forward trenches grew from day to day. For weeks the French had kept up a steady bombardment – what Mangin called 'not burying the hatchet' – effectively preventing any improvement in the defences or the erection of wire. Then rain drilling into the pulverized earth had frozen in the bitter Verdun autumn weather, thawed again, and refrozen, causing the wholesale collapse of trenches quite as efficiently as Mangin's guns. Day after day the constant rain, freezing at night, was profoundly demoralizing. A steady stream hobbled to the rear on frost-bitten feet, augmented by men who had eaten putrid horse flesh in the desperate hope of being hospitalized; anything to get away from Verdun. By September, desertions had reached such unprecedented numbers that General von Lochow issued a special decree, ordering that cowardice be shown no mercy. Fifth Army officers could not remember when, since the war began, *esprit de corps* had fallen to such depths.

Inside Fort Douaumont discipline since the May catastrophe had been tightened up, stricter anti-fire precautions taken, and additional exits dug, but otherwise life had gone on much as usual throughout the summer. The fort was constantly jammed with coming and going troops (it being noticed that, very humanly, units tended to be quicker entering than leaving the blessed sanctuary of 'Old Uncle Douaumont', as it was affec-tionately called). None of this had been much interfered with yet by the non-stop French bombardment. The months' long pounding, however, had surreptitiously achieved one thing; inch by inch the protective layer of earth covering the fort (in

some places, once nearly eighteen feet deep) had been eroded
away. Unknown to its tenants, mighty Douaumont was now
like Samson with his hair partially shorn.

On 19 October, the French preliminary bombardment blasted
forth. A whole row of '*Saucisses*' seemed to be peering down on
the fort, while observation planes swarmed overhead. On the
21st, the artillery observation turret was shattered by a heavy
shell, its officer crushed under tons of concrete, without however the vitals of the fort being penetrated. Douaumont still
smiled, confident and aloof; this was all old hat. The 22nd also
passed reasonably quietly. Then shortly before midday on the
23rd the whole structure was shaken by an abnormally powerful concussion. Lights were extinguished and in the dark each
man of the garrison experienced a moment of unparalleled
private terror; was there about to be a repetition of 8 May?
Some minutes elapsed before it was discovered that a huge
shell had evidently burst inside the fort's sick bay on the upper
floor. The whole casemate had been reduced to a shambles,
and fire still raged inside. Some fifty medical personnel and
wounded had been killed. Ten minutes later, many in the fort
heard the sickening shriek of another enormous projectile on
its way down, followed by a crashing thud close at hand. A
fraction of a second later the time fuse exploded, and once
again the fort rocked. This time the barrack-room of Casemate
8 had been wiped out. It was clear that the French were using
something heavier than they had ever possessed before. At
horribly predictable intervals of ten to fifteen minutes the
400 mm. shells came down. Their accuracy was remarkable; few
missed the fort, several penetrated what remained of the earth,
and the eight-foot thick concrete carapace, before exploding
within the fort's vitals. The bakery was smashed; two successive
hits destroyed Casemates 11 and 17, and either the fourth or
fifth shot brought down the roof over the main corridor on the
upper floor, completely blocking it.

As each hit carried with it fresh disaster, the fort Command-
ant, Major Rosendahl, was having difficulty quelling panic.
With little option, he ordered the immediate evacuation of the
upper works. Nevertheless, cowering on the cellar floor where
Gardien Chenot and his Territorials had been captured in
February, the fort garrison was still not out of danger. Through

the huge hole in the roof that had been ripped above the main corridor, Hit No. 6 fell and burrowed its way right through into the principal Pioneer Depot at the bottom of the fort, which was filled with small-arms ammunition and rockets. A powerful explosion followed, asphyxiating fumes crept through the fort, and once again it seemed that the May holocaust would be repeated; for near the Pioneer Depot was a magazine full of unexpended French shells for the heavy turrets. It was the end, thought Major Rosendahl; such a risk could not be taken again. Though every exit had been effectively blanketed by French gas shells, he issued the order to abandon the fort. Only a small suicide squad stayed behind to try to extinguish the fires in the Pioneer Depot. At nightfall the French railway guns ceased their murderous work, but still the fires raged. It seemed hopeless; all the fort's water had been exhausted, and the firefighters were reduced to using the bottled mineral water stocked for the wounded. Thus during the night of the 23rd the last of Douaumont's garrison withdrew.

At least, not quite the last. There remained two solitary soldiers manning the gallery in the far north-west corner of the fort. They had not been unduly disturbed by the 400s striking elsewhere in the huge fort; they had not seen the garrison pulling out, they had received no orders to abandon their post, and – like good German soldiers – they stayed at it, alone and forgotten, for another two days. Meanwhile, at about 7 a.m. the following morning, a Captain Prollius with a small group of signallers and runners from a nearby artillery unit, wandered into the fort, and discovered (no doubt to his considerable surprise) that it was empty. Quickly he reconnoitred it to find a reason why. The fires in the Pioneer Depot were still burning, but no longer out of control and the danger of the magazines blowing up seemed to have passed. The fort was cut in two on the upper floor by the blocked corridor, but it could still be traversed via the cellar. To Prollius it appeared both feasible and – with the French attack clearly imminent – highly desirable that Fort Douaumont should still be defended; provided he could gather together enough men. All he had available were some twenty odd. Urgently he sent a runner to the rear.

Out in the open the German infantry in their shallow, partially inundated trenches had suffered as never before from the French 'softening up'. Some were luckier than others – like a wily battalion of Mecklenburgers, who, noticing that the French opposite them had pulled back from their first line of trenches just before the bombardment began (no doubt to keep out of the way of the inevitable 'shorts'!), promptly hopped in and thus escaped the worst of the shelling. For three days the dreadful bombardment continued without pause until unit after unit reported back that its capacity to resist had been reduced to virtually nil. Then, on the afternoon of the 22nd the French guns fell silent and the Germans heard the sound of cheers from the enemy assault trenches. At last the attack was about to begin! It was almost a relief. Swiftly the front line observers sent word back to their guns to begin the counter-barrage. Down came a curtain of shells on where the French assault waves should now be advancing. But they weren't! Not one man had actually left the enemy trenches.

It was all an ingenious trap laid by Nivelle. The German field-guns that had hitherto been lying silent waiting, like the kettledrums in an orchestra, for this one moment, profitlessly betrayed their positions and now drew a smothering fire from the French 155s. For yet another day and a half the counter-battery work continued, by which time only ninety German batteries out of some 158 were still in action, and many of the remainder had been savagely mauled. When the French 'softening-up' really came to an end, nearly a quarter of a million rounds had been fired. What little remained of the defending infantry's backbone began to crumble.

On the morning of the 24th a thick autumnal mist hung over the Meuse hills. It seemed as if Douaumont, sensing that its second hour of destiny was at hand, sought to avoid the issue by concealing itself in obscurity – as indeed it had done on 25 February. The German defenders enjoyed one last fleeting moment of relief; nobody could attack in this visibility. Then suddenly through the fog they heard the high-pitched French bugles, sounding the well-known call to charge:

Il y a de la goutte à boire là haut . . .

In fact, with all their training on the simulated battlefield, the weather could not have been more propitious for the

French. What were left of the German field-guns did not open fire for twelve minutes after the French had left their trenches; by this time they were already in the defenders' first line. The summer-long disputed bastions of Fleury and the *Ouvrage de Thiaumont* fell within minutes, and General de Salins's division surged on down into the Ravin de la Dame (the scene of the '*Tranchée des Baïonnettes*' in June) where they captured a Battalion Commander and his staff. The battlefield became carpeted with packs and haversacks as the French troops, exhilarated by the sense of pursuit, shed their heavy burdens. So rapid was the advance that one senior German officer was taken in his underpants. Bunkers were by-passed and left for the second waves to mop up; in one a French sergeant counted 200 prisoners. The Germans seemed to be surrendering with a readiness never encountered before. A French listening post overheard one detachment report back:

I have only one man left, all the others have run away.

Some of the Germans told their captors they had had no food for six days, and everywhere the French were impressed by the destruction their guns had executed.

For the French, the most important single factor in the attack that day was a battalion of the *Régiment d'Infanterie Coloniale du Maroc* – the distinguished regiment that alone in the French Army wore no number on its lapels, only an anchor, and that had suffered so badly in the final effort to relieve Vaux. Now it was the sole unit equipped for the kind of close-in fighting that might be expected once Douaumont was reached. Yet for one dreadful moment it seemed to have got lost in the fog. Its commander, Major Nicolai, a tall, imposing figure with fierce *gauloises* moustaches who reminded his men of a nineteenth-century cavalryman, had just arrived from Indo-China, and this was his first battle on the Western Front. Compass in hand, he had led his battalion forward into the obscurity at the prescribed 100 yards every four minutes. Soon landmarks were recognized indicating that the battalion was erring well to the left of its objective. Either the compass or the commander was at fault. An agonizing interlude; which way was Douaumont? Abruptly, as if by a miracle, the fog opened like a curtain, and there – just ahead and to the right – lay the great dome of the fort lit up in a patch of sunshine. It was an inspiring, yet rather terrifying sight. Before his men could be deterred by the menacing mass they had come to take, Nicolai ordered the battalion forward on to the fort. There was only light opposition. In a matter of minutes, the stout Battalion Adjutant, Captain Dorey, was the first officer to clamber up on to the Fort glacis, puffing and panting with the exertion. Quickly sappers and skirmishers were dispatched into the openings of the fort. Here and there resistance held up the attackers for an hour or two. But none of Captain Prollius's urgent pleas for support had been answered, and soon the French flame-throwers and grenades, striking from every quarter, had put paid to his handful of men. Early that evening Sapper Dumont, a 'fly' little Parisian soldier and *maître-ouvrier* in civil life, together with one other private, stumbled upon Prollius's command post in the cellar of Douaumont. Prollius, four officers and twenty-four men – constituting all that remained of the fort's garrison – surrendered to Dumont. Once again Douaumont was French. That it should have been both captured and recaptured virtually empty was, as a French commander remarked,

a singular fate for a fort which during eight months had been the key to a field of battle watered with the blood of hundreds of thousands of men. . . .

At his battle command post in Fort Souville, Mangin had experienced the most anxious day of his career. After the last of the *horizon-bleu* waves had been swallowed up by the fog, hours passed before any news came back. About midday the steady straggle of prisoners began, and from Souville could be seen above the mist an immense cloud of dust and smoke as the creeping barrage advanced; but no sign of the infantry behind it. Even the brigadiers had lost all touch with their subordinate formations. Exhausted, breathless runners arrived from time to time, but the picture they provided was a disjointed, and often confused one. Despite its complete superiority over Verdun, the French Airforce could offer little assistance. Courageous pilots flew their *cages à poules* at dangerously low levels in an attempt to pierce the obscurity. Some twenty planes were lost that day; many through crashing in the fog, or brought down by splinters from the ground barrage itself. Briefly Douaumont's crest was glimpsed like a reef emerging from a sea of fog, then it disappeared again.

Not until well on in the afternoon did the airforce provide the first positively encouraging news. To General Passaga, the commander of the 133rd Division – otherwise known as '*La Gauloise*' – was brought the fragment of a map dropped from an aircraft. On it was sketched the French line established level with and to the right of Fort Douaumont and scrawled across it:

La Gauloise 16 hours 30. *Vive la France!*

About the same time the anxious watchers in Fort Souville suddenly saw to their front Douaumont expose itself, clad in a beguiling rosy light as a ray of autmnal sunshine touched it. On top of the dome were three Moroccan soldiers vigorously waving their arms. It reminded one of the generals in Mangin's entourage of *le Beau Soleil d' Austerlitz*.

It was indeed as an Austerlitz that France would greet the recapture of Douaumont, but at first – having learnt prudence through past disasters – the French censors played cautious with the news until it was certain the fort would not be lost again. Already on the afternoon of the 24th a German counter-attack was thrown in, but collapsed feebly. After this no further attempts were made, and the Crown Prince acceded to losing most of the conquered terrain at Verdun; something only the deadly psychological demands posed by a *symbol* had precluded his doing upon the removal of Falkenhayn. On 2 November, the French Second Army retook Fort Vaux, which had been previously evacuated and partially demolished by its garrison. Amid the bitterest winter weather of the war, they launched the second of their major counterstrokes on 15 December ('this black day', the Crown Prince called it), recapturing Louvemont and Bezonvaux (both lost in February), and pushing the line a comfortable two miles beyond Douaumont.[1] Though a mere shadow of its former glory – open to the skies in several places and with mud and water inches deep in its corridors – the fort was safe. And with it Verdun was safe.

1. Alas, Nicolai, who also took part in this attack, now promoted Lieutenant-Colonel and decorated with the *Légion d'Honneur* for the capture of Douaumont, was killed by a German sniper.

By a strange coincidence, the French counter-offensives ended on the same day that a year earlier Falkenhayn had gained the Kaiser's approval for his 'Operation *GERICHT*'. Banking on the shortness of public memory, German propaganda did its best to play down the importance of Forts Vaux and Douaumont, but the loss of Douaumont in particular was regarded as a grave defeat throughout the army. It was, remarked one soldier, 'like losing a fragment of the Fatherland'. Said Hindenburg candidly of the October attack:

On this occasion the enemy hoisted us with our own petard. We could only hope that in the coming year he would not repeat the experiment on a greater scale and with equal success.

Compared with the incredible stubbornness they had shown during the previous months, the fight put up by the Germans in October–December had, admittedly, been half-hearted. Nevertheless, nothing could detract from the fact that France had won her most brilliant victory since the Marne. On the day of 24 October alone, Mangin's men had reconquered ground the Crown Prince had taken four and a half months to gain. They had advanced three kilometres over glutinous clay and the most shell-pocked ground ever known; an outstanding achievement by First War standards, which, had the Germans been able to emulate it on 23 June or 11 July, would have brought them to the suburbs of Verdun in one bound. Nivelle's 'creeping barrage' had proved itself an outstanding success; one of the great inventions of the war, it seemed. For once, during the French series of counter-offensives, German losses had actually been higher than the attackers'; that 11,000 prisoners and 115 guns were taken in December alone was indicative of just how far the Fifth Army had deteriorated. Nonetheless, French casualties had also been painfully severe. Nicolai's battalion of the R.I.C.M. returned from Douaumont with little more than a hundred out of 800 sent to Verdun four days earlier, and the total men consumed during the counter-offensives came to 47,000.[1] In December the relentless determination of Nivelle and Mangin to achieve their ends without regard to the cost resulted in some ominous incidents. They revealed that

1. It is again worth recalling that at Alamein Montgomery lost 13,500 men.

Verdun had left a mark on the soul of the French Army not lightly to be erased. Poincaré, arriving to decorate the troops, had stones thrown at his car, accompanied by cries of *'Embusqués!'* On the roadside out of Verdun someone had scrawled *'Chemin de l'Abattoir'*, and on the night of 10 December a whole division bound for the final offensive took to bleating like sheep. Though that same division fought heroically, it was a sinister preview of what was to come in 1917.

None of this was visible to the public of France. All it could see was a tremendous, resounding victory worthy of *La Grande Nation*. While all over the world Allied propagandists suddenly rediscovered the incomparable significance of Vaux and Douaumont (one French historian likened their recapture to Charlemagne avenging Roland on the field of Roncevaux), France jubilantly celebrated her El Alamein of the First War. She had also discovered her Montgomery, so she thought. Joffre was eclipsed; Pétain's role in preparing the way for triumphant counterstrokes was forgotten. Nivelle was the man of the moment. In a sketch glorifying the new star, *L'Illustration* wrote:

Here is a chief in the Latin sense of the word, that is to say *une tête* ... confident hope rings a carillon of bells in our hearts.

> Victory was to be bought so dear as to be almost indistinguish-
> able from defeat – WINSTON S. CHURCHILL, *The World
> Crisis*

> From Verdun, city of suffering, will stem for France a new era
> of glory – HENRY BORDEAUX, *The Captives Delivered*

Technically, the Battle of Verdun was over. But fighting
over the corpse-ridden battlefield would continue sporadically,
with occasional savage flare-ups, until the end of the war, and
the wider effects of Verdun would endure even longer.

The most immediate result of the battle was the downfall of
the once all-powerful 'Papa' Joffre. In June, the first Secret Session had revealed to French parliamentarians the full measure
of the High Command's neglect of Verdun's defences that had
cost the nation such a hecatomb of lives. Now the summit of
all Joffre's strategy, the Somme, was recognized to have been
just one more Allied failure; attended this time with even
greater casualties than the vain offensives of 1915. All through
the summer, since that Secret Session, the rumbles against
Joffre had been steadily growing louder. With the arrival of the
third winter of the war and the collapse of the Somme they had
become quite deafening. After some shabby manipulating in
the Paris *couloirs*, the old Titan who had so nearly lost France
the war, and yet without whose serene nervous system defeat
would have been equally inevitable in the early days, was
shuffled out of his post. On 27 December he was promoted
Marshal of France and then joined in obscurity the scores of
inept or unlucky commanders that he himself had *limogé* so
ruthlessly in the past. None had been speedier to recognize the
wind of change than Joffre's satraps in G.Q.G.; in a classic
passage Pierrefeu describes his leave-taking at Chantilly:

The new Marshal summoned his heads of department to the
Villa Poiret to bid them farewell. It was a sad leave-taking. . . .
The Marshal, whose rank entitled him to three orderly officers,

asked who among those present would accompany him in his retirement. Major Thouzelier alone raised his hand. The Marshal expressed his surprise at this, whereupon General Gamelin [1] said gently to him, 'General, you must not blame those who have their career to make.' And in truth, Joffre bore no ill-will. When everyone had left, the Marshal glanced once more over the villa which had housed so much glory. Then he smiled, and, giving a friendly pat to the faithful Thouzelier, he made his favourite exclamation as he passed his hand over his head. '*Pauvre Joffre! Sacré Thouzelier!*'

Well before Joffre's actual downfall, G.Q.G. had been adjusting itself to the idea of his successor. In all branches one heard glorification of the coming C-in-C. And his name? Robert Nivelle. The logical successors, de Castelnau and Foch (the latter in disfavour after the failure of the Somme) had been by-passed. So too, had been Nivelle's immediate senior, Pétain. The rejection of Pétain had resulted partly from the politicians' apprehension at having a C-in-C with such virulent declared contempt of themselves; Poincaré for one having never forgotten Pétain's unfortunate sally to the effect that 'nobody was better placed than the President himself to be aware that France was neither led nor governed.'

On the other hand, Nivelle was renowned for his ability to charm the peoples' elected. But more than that, in December 1916 France's volatile imaginaion was not seized by so self-effacingly modest a leader as Pétain. After the reconquest of Douaumont, Nivelle was the great hero, the man who would now smash through to victory. He was, says Pierrefeu with praiseworthy candour,

not only a rash commander, he was representative of the national temperament. This is the reason that he was blindly followed.

On the opening of the last of the Verdun counter-offensives, Nivelle, the artillery Colonel of 1914, left Souilly for his new command. A week later, on 22 December, Mangin also left, to take over the Sixth Army. On the eve of his departure, Nivelle repeated the slogan with which he had arrived – 'We have the formula' – and added 'the experience is conclusive. Our method

1. A generation later, amid the catastrophe of 1940, Gamelin (who in 1916 was Joffre's Chief of Operations) was to share with Joffre the experience of being sacked from the Supreme Command.

has proved itself. Victory is certain, I give you my assurance.
...' While decorating Mangin's Moroccans, he was also heard
to say 'we shall see them again in the spring.'

Pushed on by the dying d'Alenson, Nivelle at once began
to plan the great Spring Offensive, the offensive that would
end the war in one swift blow 'of violence, brutality, and rapidity', as he described it. The bull-headed attrition methods of
Joffre discarded once and for all, this decisive blow would
'erupt' through to the third and fourth enemy lines all in the
same day. The spirit of de Grandmaison would ride again,
and it would be a purely French affair. The chosen sector was
the Chemin des Dames, a long barrow overlooking the River
Aisne, one of the most strongly defended bulwarks of the
German line. The method employed would be that which had
succeeded so brilliantly at Douaumont; the saturation bombardment, followed by the 'creeping barrage'. Nivelle, however
– ignoring the lesson of the Germans' 'Green Cross' gas attacks
at Verdun – forgot one of the essential axioms of war; that
success seldom succeeds twice. The Germans had now had two
separate occasions at Verdun, in October and December, to
study Nivelle's technique – and they were never slow to learn.
Describing the evolution of a new system of defence in depth,
the Crown Prince wrote:

Had we held to the stiff defence which had hitherto been the
rule, I am firmly convinced that we should not have come through
the great defensive battles of 1917.

The superb triumph at Douaumont was to father France's
greatest disaster of the war.

Pétain and two other Army Group commanders were extremely sceptical, but the politicians (including the mistrustful
Lloyd George who had recently replaced Asquith) were
thoroughly swayed by Nivelle's charm, eloquence, and – as
usual – superlative confidence. Even the morale of the war-
weary *poilus* was raised to fresh heights by Nivelle's repeated
promises that the end of their sufferings was close at hand.
'You won't find any Germans in front of you,' he assured one
of his Army Commanders, echoing to perfection what Falkenhayn had told his generals the previous February. To the
troops as they waited to go into battle, he declared:

The hour has come. Courage. Confidence: *Nivelle*.

Meanwhile Mangin was telling his Sixth Army:

I am ready; the day after tomorrow my headquarters will be at Laon.

Unfortunately Nivelle's assurances had also reached German ears. Security had been even worse neglected than before the Douaumont fiasco the previous May, and some six weeks ahead of the offensive the defenders knew exactly what to expect. The huge weight of Nivelle's artillery preparation came down like a haymaker swung into thin air. The Germans had simply pulled back from their forward positions. On April 16 1917 the French infantry – exhilarated by all they had been promised – left their trenches with an *élan* unsurpassed in all their glorious history. They advanced half-a-mile into a vacuum, and then came up against thousands of intact machine guns. Angry, demoralized, bitterly disillusioned men flooded back from the scene of the butchery. By the following day, there had been something like 120,000 casualties. Nivelle had predicted 10,000 wounded; the Medical Services had added another 5,000 to this estimate, but in the event the offensive required over 90,000 evacuations. In the rear areas, some two hundred wounded literally assaulted a hospital train.[1] Still Nivelle, as his ambitions collapsed in fragments around him, tried to persist with the hopeless offensive. But he had broken the French Army.

Details of the slaughter on the Chemin des Dames – appalling though the truth itself was – became fiercely exaggerated. With them the kind of incidents that had occurred sporadically at Verdun multiplied throughout the army. Again the macabre, sheep-like bleating was heard among regiments sent up to the line; this time mingled with cries of 'Down with the war!' and 'Down with the incapable leaders!' Men on leave waved red flags and sang revolutionary songs. They beat up military police and railwaymen, and uncoupled or derailed engines to prevent trains leaving for the front. Interceding officers – including at least one general – were set upon.

On 3 May the mutiny proper broke out. The Nivelle Offen-

1. Typical of the chaos, in one hospital there were reported to be only four thermometers for 3,500 beds.

sive was still continuing, broken-backed, and the 21st Division (which, significantly enough, had experienced some of the worst fighting at Verdun in June of the previous year)[1] was ordered into battle. To a man it refused. The ringleaders were weeded out, summarily shot, or sent to Devil's Island. Two days later the division went back into action, and was decimated. That touched off the powder keg. Next the 120th Regiment refused to move into the line; the 128th ordered to show it an example, followed suit. Unit after unit refused duty, some of them the finest in the French Army, and over twenty thousand men deserted outright. Regiments elected councils to speak for them, ominously like the *Soviets* that had already seized power in the Russian Army, and set off to Paris *en masse*.[2] The 119th Regiment mounted machine guns on its trucks, and attempted to reach the Schneider-Creusot works, with the apparent intention of blowing it up. By June these acts of 'collective indiscipline', as the French Official War History euphemistically termed them, spread to fifty-four divisions – or half the French Army. At one time, only two out of twelve divisions in the Champagne were reckoned to be loyal, and there was not one single reliable division between Soissons and Paris. But the most astonishing feature of the whole mutiny was that no inkling of it was picked up by German Intelligence until order had been completely restored, and even Lloyd George and Haig were little better informed.

To this day, nearly half a century on, details of the French Mutinies remain veiled in exceptional mystery and secrecy, and of no aspect is less known than the true extent of the reprisals carried out in quelling them. Haig, in his diaries of November 1917, notes that he had then been told that 'there were 30,000 "rebels" who had to be dealt with.' Only a few dozen of the ringleaders were officially reported tried and shot, but how many more were shot summarily can only be guessed. From

1. So much so, that its demoralization had been reported by the G.Q.G. Liaison Officer at Second Army H.Q. (see page 266).

2. The first units to threaten to march on Paris apparently came from III Corps; the unit Nivelle had commanded on his arrival at Verdun in April 1916, and some of the worst disorders took place in Mangin's old division, the 5th. III Corps, unlike most of the other units principally involved in the mutinies, had not in fact been in the line for several weeks, and the insurrection began while the Corps was at rest camp.

time to time accounts have seeped out, unofficially, of whole
units marched to quiet sectors and then deliberately *haché* by
their own artillery. What is known is that the wretched Russian
Division in France, which news of the revolution at home and
brutal losses under Nivelle had reduced to a state of complete
rebellion, was encircled by loyal French troops and then
crushed by point-blank cannonfire.

Eventually, for all their reluctance, the French politicians
now had to turn imploringly to the one man capable of restoring order in the army. Then, for the second but not the last
time, France called for Pétain. Resisting pleas for draconian
measures from various Corps Commanders, the new C-in-C
approved only a minimum of death penalties, concentrating his
'cure' on relatively minor improvements of conditions, so
flagrantly needed in the French Army. Leave was properly
organized at last, station canteens (comparable to the British
Y.M.C.A.) were instituted, proper lavatories, showers, and
sleeping accommodation were ordered, cooks were sent to learn
how to cook, and both the quality and flow of the precious
pinard was improved. Above all, visiting a hundred divisions in
person, Pétain assured the men that there would be no more
Nivellesque offensives. Repeatedly, he said: 'We must wait for
the Americans and the tanks.' For all its simplicity, the cure was
remarkably effective, but only Pétain could have administered
it. Through his presence he made the troops feel what the
Second Army had felt while he commanded it at Verdun; that
here was a leader who would not squander their lives vainly.
Many of them never forgot it. In all his long, and later sad,
career, he never made a greater contribution to France – not
even his saving of Verdun in February 1916 – and he always
regarded his role in the Mutinies as the most anxious task of
his life.

But, for all Pétain achieved as *'le Médécin de l'Armée'* the
French Army was not the same; never again would it be able
to repeat the stubborn heroism it had shown at Verdun. As
Sergeant Boasson (who left Verdun to take part in the Nivelle
offensive) remarked:

Pétain has purified the unhealthy atmosphere. But it will be difficult for him to wipe out the impression of defiance which now rests
in the heart of the soldier towards those whom he should have

considered his leaders, his guides, his protectors, his paternal friends. ... They have ruined the heart of the French soldier.

France limped through the remainder of 1917, carrying out only a few limited, inexpensive, but highly successful operations (including one which finally dislodged the Germans from the Mort Homme, laid on by Pétain to complete the restoration of morale). But when, in 1918, the hour approached for the final offensive blow to end the war, Pétain, genius of the defence, was clearly no longer the man to execute it. Twice he had saved France, but he was not cast for the new role. Following the Mutinies, that deadly fatalistic pessimism with which the horrors of Verdun had infected him had taken an even firmer hold. When the last desperate German gamble, the Ludendorff Offensive of March 1918, was at its peak and for a moment all seemed in jeopardy, Haig commented bluntly in his diary:

Pétain had a terrible look. He had the appearance of a Commander who was in a funk and had lost his nerve.

At last, at the very eleventh hour, the Allies hit upon the best combination for the job yet found; Pétain was to remain C-in-C of all the French forces, but Foch who, though still the very spirit of *L'Attaque*, had learned more than any other Allied leader in the course of the war – was to be Supreme Commander, for the first time, of all the Allied Armies in France. Under Foch the Allies hammered forward all along the line in the summer of 1918, until even Ludendorff realized the war was lost. On 8 November, troops of the U.S. 26th Division reoccupied the Bois des Caures, where Driant and his Chasseurs had fought and died so gallantly in February 1916. Three days later, French, American, and German troops joined in celebrating the end of the war round a huge bonfire lit on the 'High Battery' at Damloup.

27   Aftermath

It seemed to us then as if a quite exceptional bond linked us
with those few who had been with us at the time. It was not
the normal sensation of affinity that always binds together men
who have endured common hardships. . . . It derived from the
fact that Verdun transformed men's souls. Whoever floundered
through this morass full of the shrieking and the dying, whoever shivered in those nights, had passed the last frontier of
life, and henceforth bore deep within him the leaden memory
of a place that lies between Life and Death, or perhaps beyond
either. . . – *Reichsarchiv*, Vol. I (WERNER BEUMELBURG,
Douaumont)

They will not be able to make us do it again another day;
that would be to misconstrue the price of our effort. They will
have to resort to those who have not lived out these days. . .
– SECOND-LIEUTENANT RAYMOND JUBERT

To Corporal Robert Perreau of the 203rd Regiment, the summit of the Mort Homme after the battle ebbed from it in the
bitter winter of 1916–17

resembled in places a rubbish dump in which there had accumulated shreds of clothing, smashed weapons, shattered helmets,
rotting rations, bleached bones, and putrescent flesh.

The following year, Lieutenant Louis Hourticq, a former
Inspector at the Paris Beaux Arts, back in the Verdun sector
for the second time, described the countryside around Douaumont with its amputated, blackened tree trunks as being 'a
corpse with tortured features'. But, superficially, the recuperative powers of Nature are immense. Soon even the blasted trees
began to put out new shoots. Staff-Sergeant Fonsagrive of the
Artillery on his return in the summer of 1917 noted that the
battlefield was carpeted with waving poppies; still, however,
there was that all-pervading smell of decomposition. Slowly
the city of Verdun, perhaps half of its houses destroyed or
damaged to some extent, came back to life. The *Verdunois*
returned whence they had been evacuated to set their town in

order and retill the ravaged fields. To nine villages around Verdun, like Fleury, Douaumont, Cumières, the inhabitants never returned. The villages had literally vanished. The deeper scars of Nature took longer, far longer to heal. At the tragic cost of still more peasant lives lost when ploughs detonated unexploded shells, Champagne, Artois, Picardy, Flanders, and even the Somme eventually came back into cultivation, with little trace of the horrors that had been enacted there. But Verdun defied man's peaceful amends longer than all of them. In places the topsoil had simply disappeared, blasted and scorched away by the endless shellfire. Nothing would grow there any more. It seemed as if the Almighty wanted Verdun preserved to posterity as the supreme example of man's inhumanity to man.

And well it might be. It is probably no exaggeration to call Verdun the 'worst' battle in history; even taking in account man's subsequent endeavours in the Second World War. No battle has ever lasted quite so long; Stalingrad, from the moment of the German arrival on the Volga to Paulus's surrender, had a duration of only five months, compared with Verdun's ten. Though the Somme claimed more dead than Verdun, the proportion of casualties suffered to the numbers engaged was notably higher at Verdun than any other First War battle; as indeed were the numbers of dead in relation to the area of the battlefield. Verdun was the First War in microcosm; an intensification of all its horrors and glories, courage, and futility.

Estimates on the total casualties inflicted at Verdun vary widely; the accounting in human lives was never meticulous in that war. France's Official War History (published in 1936) sets her losses at Verdun during the ten months of 1916 at 377,231, of which 162,308 were killed or missing,[1] though calculations based on Churchill's 'The World Crisis' (1929) would put them as high as 469,000. The most reliable assessment of German losses for the same period comes to roughly 337,000 (Churchill: just under 373,000), and contemporary German lists admitted to over 100,000 in dead and missing alone. Whatever set of figures one accepts, the combined casualties of both sides reach the staggering total of over 700,000. Nor is that all, for although strictly speaking the 'Battle of Verdun'

1. Figures of 'missing' on both sides also included those taken prisoner.

was limited to the fighting of 1916, in fact a heavy toll of lives had been enacted there long before Falkenhayn's offensive, and bitter fighting continued on its blood-sodden ground through 1917. One recent French estimate that is probably not excessive places the total French and German losses on the Verdun battlefield at 420,000 dead, and 800,000 gassed or wounded; nearly a million and a quarter in all. Supporting this figure is the fact that after the war some 150,000 unidentified and un-buried corpses – or fragments of corpses – alone were collected from the battlefield and interred in the huge, forbidding *Ossuaire*. Still to this day remains are being discovered. In comparison, it is perhaps worth recalling the overall British Empire casualties for the whole of the Second World War were: 1,246,025, of which 353,652 dead and 90,844 missing.

Who 'won' the Battle of Verdun? Few campaigns have had more written about them (not a little of it bombastic nonsense) and accounts vary widely. The volumes of the *Reichsarchiv* dealing with the battle are appropriately entitled 'The Tragedy of Verdun', while to a whole generation of French writers it represented the summit of '*La Gloire*'. The baneful results of France's immortalization of Verdun will be seen later, mean-while it suffices to say that it was a desperate tragedy for both nations. Before one considers what either side did achieve through the Battle of Verdun, what *could* they have achieved?

At the beginning of 1916, Falkenhayn could have resumed the attack on Russia, still reeling from the blows dealt it the previous year. Not only German military experts agreed with Prince Max of Baden, that

the capture of St Petersburg would have been an easy task com-pared with our efforts before Verdun. It would have struck the heart of the Russian war industry and knocked our eastern enemies out of the fight.

But Falkenhayn chose Verdun. From the preceding résumé of casualties, it is clear that his novel 'bleeding-white' experi-ment did not succeed; that it 'bled' the Germans in nearly the same proportion as the French, and in fact hit them harder because of their constant inferiority in manpower. That it could not succeed must have been abundantly clear to Falkenhayn by mid March, if not earlier. Yet he persisted. As for the Crown Prince's interpretation of 'Operation *GERICHT*', i.e.

the outright capture of Verdun, it is fair to assume that the Fifth Army *could* have taken Verdun on three separate occasions; on 25–6 February, on 8–12 June, on 23–4 June. If the Germans had taken Verdun in February, it would have constituted a great moral triumph, a dazzling military success, and one of the cheapest of the war. By itself, however, it would not then have knocked France out; although some responsible French critics felt that, had the victory been followed through, it could have led to a 'rolling-up' of the whole French front – perhaps with more disastrous consequences than in March 1918. But reserves were not available (though, at the beginning of 1916, they could still have been found) to enable the Crown Prince to break through to Verdun, let alone follow up; for the simple reason that Falkenhayn was not prepared to make a decisive issue out of Verdun, or, for that matter, any other campaign.

In mid June the conquest of Verdun might have been attended with infinitely greater calamity, because both the honour and the life-blood of France had by now been totally committed to its defence. There might have been a dramatic collapse of the whole country, possibly preceded by an acceleration of the Mutinies of 1917, but even so this could have been no more than a gamble on the part of the Germans. However, by June German losses had become so heavy that the reserves needed for the final push could not be found anywhere – especially in view of the imminence of the Allied offensive on the Somme. Although on several occasions the fate of Verdun did appear to balance on the edge of a razor, to us now it is clear that the Crown Prince was right (though tardy) in realizing by April that whatever could still be achieved there would never be worth the cost.

German military critics are more or less unanimous in condemning Falkenhayn for his inability to concentrate all at one point (in the Schlieffen-Ludendorff style), for his preference for limited, 'no risk' offensives, for being a tacit believer in the Allies' philosophy of 'attrition' (which could only work against the Central Powers), and – last but by no means least – for his boundless indecision once he had taken the plunge at Verdun.

We lost the war against an unlimited superiority, because we never succeeded in concentrating superiority at the decisive point.

So says Ludwig Gehre (*The Distribution of the German Forces during the World War – A Clausewitz Study*). And Hermann Wendt (*Verdun, 1916*):

> The soul of the German Commander-in-Chief was not up to the huge task. ... Verdun had conquered him, had become his master. ...

At the end of 1915, when Falkenhayn composed his famous Memorandum, Germany still had a good chance of winning the war; or at least of achieving a good draw via a negotiated peace. It was her last chance. Falkenhayn squandered it at Verdun. The hand he passed on to Hindenburg and Ludendorff was a losing one. He was, in the words of Captain Liddell Hart's memorable summary:

> The ablest and most scientific general – 'penny-wise, pound foolish' – who ever ruined his country by refusal to take calculated risks.

Enough has been said of the inability of the French High Command – nagged at by the ghosts of 1870 – to cede one inch of terrain for a tactical advantage; an obsession fatally shared by Hitler in Russia. The case has also been made that it might have been sensible for France to have cut her losses in February 1916, and to have abandoned the sorely neglected fortress, but honour transcended common sense. More open to argument is the issue of whether Joffre or Pétain was right in the dispute of April onwards; that is, should Verdun – once the principle of its defence *à outrance* had been embraced – or should the planned Somme offensive assume priority? Theoretically, Joffre as C-in-C was entirely justified in not being deflected from his strategy by the German initiative at Verdun, in not allowing the enemy to impose their will upon him. Had this strategy in fact led to a victorious breakthrough on the Somme, History would doubtless have rated Joffre one of her greatest marshals, but his tactics, brutally simple as they were, denied him this title. One of Falkenhayn's German apologists claims that Verdun was successful in that instead of contributing forty divisions to the Somme as agreed at the Chantilly Conference in 1915 France's contribution was in fact reduced to fourteen. But there was never a hope of a *percée* on the Somme, with or without Verdun. Joffre's rigid rationing of replacements to Pétain merely meant, by and large, that more French troops would be available to be killed on the Somme instead of at Verdun; on the other hand, it brought Pétain's defence perilously close to collapse in June, and by overtaxing the endurance of the men of the Second Army germinated the seeds of mutiny that were to sprout the following summer.

Neither side 'won' at Verdun. It was the indecisive battle in an indecisive war; the unnecessary battle in an unnecessary war; the battle that had no victors in a war that had no victors. As Prince Max of Baden noted in his memoirs,

the campaign of 1916 ended in bitter disillusionment all round. We and our enemies had shed our best blood in streams, and neither we nor they had come one step nearer to victory. The word 'deadlock' was on every lip.

By the end of 1916, territorially all the Germans had to show for ten months of battle and their third-of-a-million casualties was the acquisition of a piece of raddled land little larger in area than the combined Royal Parks of London. Falkenhayn could claim with some justification that Verdun led to the breaking of France's superbly courageous armies. However, the German Army was also never quite the same again after Verdun; as the Crown Prince admitted, 'The Mill on the Meuse ground to powder the hearts as well as the bodies of the troops.'

For the first time, the Army's confidence in its leaders was fundamentally shaken, and morale never quite recovered. Both at the front and at home, war weariness manifested itself, and it was symptomatic that Germany's first peace proposals came soon after the close of the Verdun campaign. By 1917 the Germans had, for the time being, no strength left to take advantage of Falkenhayn's 'bleeding-white' of the French Army.

One American war correspondent later assessed Verdun to be the Gettysburg of the First War, the recapture of Fort Douaumont its Pickett's Charge; and writing of the Nivelle Offensive of 1917, Waterloo was the analogy that sprang to his mind: 'the political Waterloo of Europe'.

Verdun was as much a historic turning-point for the other Allies as it was for France. One of its direct results was that from 1 July 1916 – that grim landmark in British history – the main burden of the Western Front devolved upon Britain. Verdun's role in bringing the United States a stage closer to belligerency has already been noted, and it is reasonable to add that after the Nivelle Offensive and the French Mutinies the war could no longer have been won *without* American troops. Indirectly, it was Verdun that made America's participation in the war essential and inevitable, with all its enormous implications for the future of Europe and the world.

*

Of the principal actors in the Verdun tragedy, some disappeared speedily into oblivion; others lived to play another part in European History.

The fall of Nivelle had been attended by a shaming scene at G.Q.G. when, refusing to resign, he had been literally propelled out of office, bitterly blaming Mangin for the failure on the Chemin des Dames. Afterwards he was given a command in North Africa and never again permitted to come near the Western Front. When the war ended, he made a limited return to grace; was nominated a member of the Supreme War Council in 1920, and sent to represent France in the U.S.A. at the tercentenary of the arrival of the *Mayflower* later that year. He died in 1924, still in his mid sixties, leaving no memoirs and having made no attempt to justify the calamitous offensive that bears his name and will probably be discussed as long as the war itself.

Of the Nivelle triumvirate, the shadowy *éminence grise*, d'Alenson, whom one must deem responsible for much of Nivelle's rashness, both at Verdun and subsequently, died of consumption almost immediately after the Chemin des Dames. Mangin, brought before a Court of Inquiry, was absolved from all blame but nevertheless – once again – removed from his command. True to form, he begged the Minister of War to be allowed to re-engage as a simple soldier. The boon was refused and for several months he fretted, unemployed, and pettily forbidden to reside within thirty miles of Paris. Then Clemenceau and Foch came to power, and the order went out: 'To Mangin a corps.' After six months of probation, Mangin *redemptus* was once more at the head of an Army; just in time for the great crisis of 1918. Churchill describes him superbly as

like a hungry leopard on a branch [who] sees Incomparable Opportunity approaching and about to pass below.

Opportunity arrived when Foch selected Mangin to launch the first of the victorious counter-strokes against Ludendorff's spent offensive, and the Leopard, leaping out of his lair in the Forest of Villers–Cotterets did not fail this time. A few months later Mangin rode magnificently into Metz, distributing copies of Verlaine's *Lamentation* to his troops. When peace came, he was put in charge of the French occupation of the Rhineland. Here he was seized with the inspiration to become a new 'Germanicus', the re-constructor of Germany. He became closely involved with the Rhineland separatist movement, but before his scheme could bear fruit, he died – aged only fifty-eight – in 1925. For many years rumours persisted that like Germanicus, he had been poisoned; possibly by German nationalists.

Following his downfall, Joffre's obscurity became almost complete. They gave him a small office in the *École de Guerre*, where he was attended by his faithful '*Sacré Thouzelier*' and a minute staff. Haig, in his diary, describes paying a visit to this office in October 1918:

No one hears a word of poor old Joffre now; he has quite disappeared. We found an A.D.C. in the office but were told that the Marshal does not come back after his déjeuner. I fancy the old man has this fine office, but nothing to do. Clean blotting paper and a few maps were waiting ready for use.

When the great victory cavalcade passed through the Arc de Triomphe, there were those in the crowd who wondered who was the portly peasant figure bouncing about on the reluctant chestnut, to the left of the immortal Foch. For another twelve years, Joffre pottered about in his office in the *École de Guerre*, preparing his voluminous memoirs, but otherwise showing no flicker of interest in the other post-mortems on the war in which, over so many crucial months, he had been the supreme power in France. In 1931 he died, having outlived Foch and most of the other French warlords; except de Castelnau and, of course, Pétain.

De Castelnau, denied his Marshal's baton – it was always said – because of Clemenceau's rabid anti-clericalism, retired and entered the Chamber of Deputies. Like Nivelle, he left no writings on the war,[1] a notable loss to historians, though he lived to be ninety-seven, and to see a France ruled in adversity by his nominee of February 1916.

Of the lesser figures at Verdun, many like Colonels Driant and Nicolai, Captain Cochin, Lieutenants Jubert and Joubaire, Sergeant-Major Méléra, and Sergeants Dubrelle and Boasson, either died there or on another battlefield. Among those that survived, Major Raynal, the Hero of Vaux, eventually went into politics on returning from a prisoner-of-war camp and became a pacifist. His fellow P.O.W., Captain de Gaulle, spent the years of internment developing his ideas on warfare and the French Army of the future. Officer-Cadet Buffet, who made the miraculous double journey in and out of Fort Vaux, still teaches at a school in Perpignan.

On the German side, *Oberleutnant* Brandis, after facing Nivelle on the Chemin des Dames, grew to be the idol of a whole generation of German school-children to whom he gave his sparkling lectures on the Conquerors of Douaumont. Radtke, permanently crippled by the wounds that had cost him recognition for his role on 25 February 1916, became a Prussian railway official, only emerging from obscurity to challenge von Brandis's story in the late nineteen-thirties. Now in his seventies, he lives in retirement in Berlin, still in constant touch with the elderly survivors of his platoon who shared his exploits on that incredible day. Colonel (later Major-General) Franz Ritter von Epp, commander of the Bavarian Leib in the two final assaults on Verdun, became one of the first to raise a *Freikorps* in post-war Germany, financed Hitler in his early Munich days, and was later appointed chief of the Nazi Party's Department for Colonial Policy.

Of Schmidt von Knobelsdorf, sent off to command a Corps on the Eastern Front in 1916, little was ever heard again. As far as is known, he made no attempt to answer the many vociferous German critics who after the war accused him of being chiefly responsible for the disaster at Verdun.

When Falkenhayn relinquished the Supreme Command after

1. They were almost the sole exceptions.

the Battle of Verdun, General von Zwehl noted that his hair
had turned completely white. Then there followed a brief moment of triumph. Declining the Kaiser's consolation prize for
a fallen favourite, the Ambassadorship in Constantinople, Falkenhayn was given command of the Ninth Army, which he
led in a brilliantly conceived lightning campaign against
Rumania.[1] With the collapse of Rumania, he was sent to reor-
ganize the crumbling Turkish Army in Palestine, arriving just
in time to see Allenby capture Jerusalem. He ended the war
covering the Bolsheviks in an unimportant Polish garrison post.
After the war, life for Falkenhayn consisted of giving a series
of lectures on the Rumanian Campaign at Berlin University,
and compiling his memoirs – all in that extraordinary cold and
remote third person singular. Although – uncommunicative to
the end – he never gave any clue as to his real feelings, and
until his death he still affected to believe that German losses
at Verdun had been 'not much more than a third of those of
the enemy', he appeared to be weighed down by his reflections
on the battle. Rapidly his health began to deteriorate, starting
with a breathing difficulty which doctors found hard to
diagnose. To a former A.D.C. he wrote in 1921:

My complaint is an inflammation of the kidneys with horrible
consequences, which I have been suffering from since the New Year
... the real cause of it is doubtless psychological, not physical. ...

To a relative he confided about this time that, five years after
Verdun, he still found it impossible to sleep at night. In April
1922 he died in a *Schloss* near Potsdam.

The Crown Prince too seems to have been pursued all his
life (he long outlived Falkenhayn) by the ghosts of Verdun. In
exile in Holland he sensed that even the Dutch thought of him
as 'that *Boche* – the murderer of Verdun!' For five dreary
years he lived in an abandoned parsonage on the polder of

1. Champions of Falkenhayn see proof in his Rumanian Campaign
that, under any but the impossible stalemate conditions of the Western
Front, he was indeed a great commander. They ignore however that the
actual strategy in Rumania was devised by Hindenburg–Ludendorff, not
Falkenhayn, and that, for veteran German troops, rounding up the
Rumanians (never the world's most intrepid warriors) was not far re-
moved from Kitchener's annihilation of the Khalifa's Fuzzy-Wuzzies at
Omdurman.

Wieringen, his leptic figure made to look even more bizarre by breeches, Dutch clogs, and an oversize cloth cap. Begging his cousin, King George V, for a mitigation of his circumstances, he pointed out pathetically that there was not even a bathroom in his place of exile. Then, in 1923, friends, hoping for a Hohenzollern reinstatement, spirited him back into Germany. The reinstatement never came. Instead, the Crown Prince flirted impetuously with the Nazis; then seems, with that highly-developed insight of his, to have foreseen where they would lead Germany, and swiftly recanted. Throughout the Nazi era and the Second World War he lived in retirement in Germany. In May 1945 he was arrested at Lindau by the French First Army; its commander, a General de Lattre de Tassigny, the same who as a young Company-Commander had fought at Verdun through some of the worst days of June 1916. The Crown Prince asked for an interview with de Lattre, requesting that – as he had taken no part in the recent hostilities – he be allowed to go home. De Lattre, with fresh memories of all that France had suffered at German hands, and no doubt also recalling the days when he had faced the Crown Prince on the Meuse heights, was icy:

I remind you, *monsieur*, that you had a top place on the list of war criminals.[1] You have had the extraordinary good luck of not having been shot.

Summarily dismissed, the Crown Prince retained the memory of what he conceived as a mortal insult to his dying day. That came six years later, in July 1951, strangely enough only two days before the death in prison of his erstwhile adversary, Marshal Pétain. The remaining years of his life he had shared in penury with his last mistress, a divorced hairdresser, once a Hohenzollern chambermaid.

Of the principal combatants at Verdun, there remains only Pétain, but his long and tragic subsequent career was so intertwined with the more distant effects of Verdun that he requires to be dealt with separately.

*

1. In 1918.

The consequences of the Battle of Verdun did not end with 1918. It is one of the singular ironies of history that although Falkenhayn failed to bring France to her knees, more than any isolated event of the First War, Verdun led to France's defeat in 1940.

As has already been seen, Verdun contributed to its share of 'firsts' significant to the development of warfare. Flame-throwers and Phosgene gas made their debut as assault weapons on a large scale there; for the first time it was shown that an army could be supplied by road transport; and Verdun was the forge from which originated the conception of an air-*force* in the truest meaning of the word. Tactically, at Verdun the Germans perfected their infantry infiltration techniques, which – on a much larger scale – they employed with devastating effect against Gough's Fifth Army in March 1918; the French perfected the 'creeping barrage', tried a second time with dismal results in 1917. But the full weight of the lessons of Verdun was not felt until after 1918. When the full bill of casualties then became available, military thinkers the world over were united on one point; no future war could ever be fought again like the last one. They differed only in their approach to deciding how it would be fought. The problem particularly concerned France, who, of all the belligerents, had suffered easily the highest losses in proportion to her total manpower, and the answer of that huge body of *anciens combattants* who had fought before Verdun was unhesitating. Already on 23 August 1916, G.Q.G. had pointed to it in a remarkable recantation:

One fact dominates the six-month struggle between concrete and cannon; that is the force of resistance offered by a permanent fortification, even the least solid, to the enormous projectiles of modern warfare.

After the war, France remained hypnotized by the way Douaumont and the other forts at Verdun had stood up to the months of hammering. Major Raynal is to be found writing prefaces for military books, pointing to the lunacy of making men fight 'in the open air' and recalling how his Leonidean handful inside Fort Vaux had checked the whole German advance.

In an annex to his book, *La Bataille de Verdun*, Pétain remarks pointedly:

If from the beginning we had had confidence in the skill of our military engineers, the struggle before Verdun would have taken a different course. Fort Douaumont, occupied as it ought to have been, would not have been taken … from the first it would have discouraged German ambitions. Fortification, what little there was of it, played a very large role in the victory. …

It was Pétain who systematized the new thinking. After the war, of the leaders that had emerged Marshals of France, none enjoyed more widespread prestige and affection throughout the Army than he who had entered the war as a superannuated colonel. Old age soon removed Foch from the public arena, leaving a still virile Pétain the principal arbiter of French military thought for the best part of two decades. As Inspector General of the Army, and later Minister of War, he harked back repeatedly to one of his favourite maxims:

One does not fight with men against material; it is with material served by men that one makes war.

Never again, he promised, should such sacrifices be forced upon the youth of France. As early as 1922, he was calling for the creation of a 'Wall of France' that would protect her permanently against the restive, traditional enemy. His idea of this 'Wall' as it evolved was not of clusters, or even a line, of Douaumonts; for his 400's had proved that even a Douaumont was mortal. Instead it would consist chiefly of a continuous chain of retractable gun cupolas (similar to those mounted at Douaumont and Moulainville that had proved almost indestructible), linked by subterranean passages burrowed so deep as to be beyond the reach of any projectile. For years Pétain could not persuade the governments of an impoverished France to foot the huge cost of his Great Wall. It was no coincidence that the politician eventually giving his name to it was Maginot, the ex-Sergeant who had been seriously wounded at Verdun and had led the attack on Joffre at the first Secret Session in 1916. Nor was it a coincidence that the Chief of the Army General Staff under whom the Maginot Line materialized was a General Debeney, who had commanded a division through some of the worst fighting at Verdun, on the exposed and completely unfortified Mort Homme. Among existing works to be incorporated in the Maginot Line system were Forts Vaux and Douaumont, both to some extent repaired and augmented with additional flanking turrets. As the threat of a new war approached, one French military writer declared:

The lessons of Verdun have not been lost; for the past fifteen years France has been working on her eastern frontier. ... Be confident in this fortification with the most modern techniques.

As the *poilus* took up their posts deep in the bowels of the Maginot Line in 1939, the popular cries were '*Ils ne passeront pas!*' and '*on les aura!*'

Thus, in France, since 1870 the wheel of military thinking had turned a fatal full cycle. In 1870 – in simplest terms – she had lost a war through adopting too defensive a posture and relying too much on permanent fortifications; in reaction against this calamitous defeat, she nearly lost the next war by being too aggressive-minded; and what resulted from the subsequent counter-reaction, the Maginot Line mentality, is almost too painful to recall.

*

If the effects of Verdun did not confine themselves to the period of the First War, neither were they limited to strictly military and strategic considerations. As France in the inter-war period buried herself beneath the concrete of the new super-Douaumonts of the Maginot Line, so spiritually she sought refuge behind the 'miracle' of Verdun. Because of Pétain's '*Noria*' system and the sheer length of the battle, something like seven-tenths of the whole French Army had passed through Verdun. The list of names in Verdun's Book of Honour is an impressive one; President Lebrun, Major of Artillery; President Coty, Private First Class; President de Gaulle, Captain of Infantry; Marshal Pétain, Marshal de Lattre, Admiral Darlan. ... A whole generation of French leaders passes before one's eyes. Of all the battles of the First War, Verdun was the one in which the most Frenchmen had taken part – as well as being the one that made the most profound and most painful impact. Year after year the veterans, '*Ceux de Verdun*', with their black berets, rosettes, and *rubans rouges*, made the pilgrimage in their thousands to the shrines of Verdun; to Vaux and Douaumont and the towering new *Ossuaire* that straddles the Thiaumont Ridge, its revolving beacons restlessly scanning the battlefield by night. On the anniversaries of 21 February or of the recapture of Douaumont, on Jeanne l'Arc Day, Armistice Day or 14 July, the torch-light processions filed up from Verdun to the Meuse Heights to attend sombre and moving commemorations (as often as not addressed to the Glorious Dead in the vocative). Depicting the sacredness of one of these regular pilgrimages, Henri de Montherlant wrote:

Je marchais sur cette terre humaine comme sur le visage même de la patrie.

And Anna de Noailles:

> *Passant, sois de récits et de geste économe,*
> *Contemple, adore, prie et tais ce que tu sens.*

With the passage of the years, the symbol of Verdun attained ever-increasing sanctity and at the same time it grew – more dangerously for France – to be a touchstone of national faith. This ex-Verdun generation of Frenchmen, to whom the political world since 1918 bafflingly seemed to have become more, not less, menacing, gradually arrived at the mystic belief that, since France had triumphed in this most terrible of all battles, somehow it would always be able to '*se débrouiller*'. In that grim duel, France had proved her virility; finally and for ever. (The attitude is not without its parallel in today's Micawberish Briton, who secretly reassures himself that, because of the Battle of Britain in 1940, there is bound to be another miracle somewhere round the corner that will save Britain from economic disaster, without any further undue personal effort on his part.)

Hand in hand with the mystique of the Eternal Glory of Verdun went another influence, less perceptible but infinitely more pernicious.

This war has marked us for generations. It has left its imprint upon our souls [wrote Artillery-Lieutenant de Mazenod from

Verdun in June 1916]. All those inflamed nights of Verdun we shall rediscover one day in the eyes of our children.

Two of the infantrymen who were later killed saw it more precisely, and prophetically. In a letter to his wife of 13 June 1916, Sergeant Marc Boasson admitted having had

the most horrible thought ... Germany and France will emerge from the struggle exhausted for a long time. And France for longer than Germany, her low birth rate insufficient during these last years will strike its blow amid the consequences of the war.

A month later he writes in a rage:

This is not heroism. It is ignominy. What kind of a nation will they make of us tomorrow, these exhausted creatures, emptied of blood, emptied of thought, crushed by superhuman fatigue?

Like an answering voice Jubert declared as he left for his second spell on the Mort Homme, '... they will have to resort to those who have not lived out these days....'

As the veterans of Verdun stood to attention outside the *Ossuaire* during those torchlight commemorations, and the emotive speeches brought the tears welling up, as well as the glory and the superhuman heroism, they remembered the horrors of the ceaseless shelling, the wounded men agonizingly untended, the hideous mutilations, the runners not returning, the reliefs and ration parties not arriving, the thirst, the hunger, the stench, the misery, the fear; above all, always the shells. Privately to themselves they wondered if they could do it again, if any other Frenchman could? The answer they felt was NO. No human being could do Verdun again. Then in paralysing pessimism they watched across the Rhine, at the books once entitled *The Tragedy of Verdun* now becoming replaced by themes of *The Heroic Struggle* or *Song of Heroism*; at Germany's resurgent numbers threatening to swamp France's own enfeebled birth-rate; at the memories and lessons of Verdun swept aside by the hurricane of the Nazi determination for *revanche*. During the inauguration of the *Ossuaire* in 1927, Pétain remarked that

the constant vision of death had penetrated him [the French soldier] with a resignation which bordered on fatalism.

It was a condition with which the whole generation that had fought at Verdun remained infected. Resignedly it sat down behind the new Douaumonts Maginot and Pétain had built for it as Czechoslovakia was sold down the river. Morally it had been bled white. In his book, *The Taxis of the Marne* that so savagely castigates the 'Men of Fifty' of 1940 – that is, the Verdun generation – Jean Dutourd (who was then twenty) declares brutally that France was betrayed

not by the Fifth Column. She was betrayed by you, men of fifty. She was betrayed by what should have been her vital forces.

But was it their fault that they had lost their vitality?

The German soldier of the First War – the *Reichsarchiv* admit – was more deeply affected by Verdun than by any other campaign of the war. Each post-war year the German survivors also trekked to Verdun by the hundred, trying to find the positions where they had fought so long and so desperately, or merely visiting the innumerable cemeteries with their well-tended black crosses; and one of the favourite games to a generation of German children was playing at the capture of Fort Douaumont. One might in truth add that the blood-letting, just as it had devitalized France's 'Men of Fifty', had contributed to a vacuum of leadership in Germany into which rushed the riff-raff of the Himmlers and Goebbels, but somehow Verdun itself never left quite so potent a lingering effect in Germany. It was perhaps because, inhuman as conditions at Verdun had been for the Germans, they had nearly always been one degree worse for the French; or because, relative to the number of combatants, only a quarter as many Germans as French had fought there – thus the impact of the battle was spread somewhat thinner over the post-war generation as a whole.

Most significant of all was the immense influence Verdun had upon the thinking of the *Wehrmacht* leaders, a quite remarkable number of whom were actually involved in the battle as junior officers. Von Manstein was a staff officer to General von Gallwitz during most of the campaign on the Left Bank; Paulus fought as an infantry officer through the worst fighting round Fleury from June to August. Guderian was Assistant Intelligence Officer at Fifth Army H.Q. throughout the offensive phase at Verdun; von Brauchitsch, Hitler's Army C-in-C, took part in the see-saw battles of August to September on the Right Bank, and witnessed the recapture of Fort Douaumont; Keitel, the *Wehrmacht* Chief-of-Staff from 1938 until the end of the Third Reich, was a captain on the staff of X Reserve Corps (Right Bank) in the summer of 1916. (Though they never fought in the actual battle, Rommel took part briefly in the Crown Prince's first attempts to seize Verdun in late 1914, and von Kluge was badly wounded on this front later in the war.)[1]

Militarily, as we know, the Germans solved the problem of the First War deadlock in another way to the French. Being the attackers, they had seen Verdun from a different angle. In its essentials, their problem was that which had faced Ritter von Epp, bogged down amid the limitless horrors of the shell-ground in the Thiaumont 'Quadrilateral'; how to prevent an attack losing its impetus and simply becoming ground to pieces by the enemy artillery. Having tenanted Douaumont through most of the Battle, they also sensed rather better than the French what were the Achilles Heels of permanent fortifications. The solution to both problems was provided by the *Panzer* columns of Guderian and Manstein; the lessons of the battle in which they had participated over so many months being lost upon neither of them.

On 14 May 1940, the *Panzers* smashed through at Sedan where Louis Napoleon had surrendered so ignominiously seventy years earlier. Exactly a month later German troops again stood before the gates of Verdun, led by a divisional commander who had been three times in the line there during 1916. Once again, briefly, there was heavy fighting on Côte 304 and the Mort Homme, but at 11.45 the following morning Douaumont surrendered – to a battalion commander who had served in the fort himself twenty-four years previously. None of Douaumont's new gun turrets had fired a shot. A quarter of an hour later Fort Vaux surrendered, and the German *Panzers*

---

1. Hitler, the corporal-turned-strategist, fought on the Somme but not at Verdun; nevertheless, he seems to have had some fixation about the Battle. At least one of his generals (Blumentritt) was convinced that he wanted to emulate Falkenhayn at Stalingrad, and draw the Russian armies into a 'bleeding-white' battle there – with results even more disastrous than those which overtook Falkenhayn.

rushed on to Verdun. At the Citadel a company of army bakers was taken by surprise as it leisurely baked bread for the men in the garrison, and by the afternoon of 15 June the Swastika flew over Verdun. Its conquest had lasted little more than twenty-four hours and had cost the Germans less than two hundred dead. The next day France's 'Men of Fifty', unable to help themselves, called in eighty-four-year-old Pétain as receiver in bankruptcy. An armistice was requested forthwith.

In his *éloge* to the Académie on being elected to the vacancy created by Pétain's death – one of the most difficult speeches any Frenchman could have been called on to make – André François-Poncet recounted a parable of Croesus and Solon. Croesus finds Solon weeping and asks why.

I am thinking [came the reply] of all the miseries that the Gods are reserving for you, as the price of your present glory.

Seldom have the elements of Classical Tragedy been more poignantly arrayed than in the last years of Pétain. We see the old man, about to retire twenty-six years earlier to the cottage at St Omer, now called back in his dotage to assume a responsibility Frenchmen in their prime quail before. The deep-rooted pessimism and bitterness towards Britain surges to the fore; and who indeed in France in the summer of 1940 does not believe that Britain will have 'her neck wrung like a chicken'? The huge majority of Frenchmen are solidly behind the Hero of Verdun, the man who saved the French Army in 1917 (though, in five years' time, many crying 'traitor' will conveniently try to forget this). Once again, he is the one man the Army will venerate and obey. Only an eccentric handful, brave to the point of folly, rallies to the Cross of Lorraine raised by Pétain's former subaltern and erstwhile admirer, Charles de Gaulle.

In vain the Marshal believed that France's conquerers, being themselves soldiers, would grant her an honourable peace. Pressed by Hitler to total, dishonourable collaboration, he resisted, but had little to resist with. The wily Laval treated him contemptuously as an ornamental cover to his own ambitions, presented disastrous documents for him to sign late in the evening when his old mind was befuddled. But never was he completely Laval's or Hitler's man. Derided, misguided, isolated, and betrayed he stayed on at his invidious post; 'If we leave France now, we shall never find her again,' he said repeatedly. Above all he stayed in the apparently genuine belief that somehow he alone stood for the safety of the million of his beloved soldiers captive in Germany. In his name, things were done by Vichy France that shocked the world, and especially her former Ally; but how much worse might it have been without that aged hand at the helm? Steadfastly Pétain refused to give Hitler bases in Algeria or surrender the French fleet. Though battered, his honour remained intact, accompanied to the end by a certain tragic nobility; fifty French hostages are to be shot, eighty-six-year-old Pétain offers himself in their stead as a single hostage.

Finally, as the Allies landed in North Africa, Hitler, breaking his word, invaded Unoccupied France. 'Fly to Africa,' the faithful Serrigny urged Pétain. No, he replied. If I leave, a Nazi *Gauleiter* will take over, and then what about our men in Germany?' 'A pilot must stay at the tiller during a tempest ...' You are wrong, replied Serrigny, reproaching him gently:

You think too much about the French and not enough about France.

Victorious de Gaulle returned to France; Pétain was spirited away to Germany by the Nazis. As the Third Reich collapsed, alone of the Vichy survivors he begged to be allowed to return to France to face trial.

At my age, there is only one thing one still fears. That is not to have done all one's duty, and I wish to do mine.

Through Switzerland he returned to France. He was met by General Koenig. He put out his hand. Koenig refused to take it. By edict of the man who had once applied to join the Regiment he commanded, and to whose son he was godfather, Pétain was placed on trial for his life, clad in the simplest uniform of a Marshal of France, and wearing just the *Médaille Militaire* – the only decoration shared by simple soldiers and great commanders. Urged by his lawyers to take his baton with him into court, Pétain replied scornfully 'No, that would be theatrical.' At the beginning of the trial he made one simple, dignified statement to the French people over the head of the Court, which he insisted had no power to try the Chief of

State. Modestly he outlined his career in the service of France, ending:

> When I had earned rest, I did not cease to devote myself to her. I responded to all her appeals, whatever was my age or my weariness. She had turned to me on the most tragic day of her history. I neither sought nor desired it. I was begged to come. I came. Thus I inherited a catastrophe of which I was not the author ... History will tell all that I spared you, whereas my adversaries think of reproaching me for what was inevitable. ... If you wish to condemn me, let my condemnation be the last.

Through much of the lengthy hearing he nodded and dozed. As its last witness, the defence produced a general blinded at Verdun, who admonished the court prophetically:

> Take care that one day – it is not perhaps far distant; the drama is not yet finished – this man's blood and alleged disgrace do not recoil on the whole of France, on us, and our children.

Finally Pétain spoke his last words:

> My thought, my only thought, was to remain with them [the French] on the soil of France, according to my promise, so as to protect them and to lessen their sufferings.

The Court was unmoved. France can be savage in the retribution she exacts, and now, amid the passions of victory and with the wounds of the war still unhealed, the clemency Pétain accorded the mutineers of 1917 is not for him. Guilty of High Treason is the verdict, and the ninety-year-old Marshal is sentenced to death.

Ultimately the sentence was commuted to one of life imprisonment, and for six years Pétain was confined to the Île de Yeu, off the Vendée coast; during which time he never uttered one word of recrimination. Regularly he was visited by Madame Pétain,[1] who took a room near the prison. At ninety-two, his health began to decline and Madame Pétain was allowed to move into the prison precincts. Shortly after his ninety-fifth birthday, his mind became no longer lucid and at the end of

1. As a major, Pétain has been rejected by the father of the woman he wanted to marry on the grounds that he seemed to lack prospects of advancement. She married another, was widowed by the war, and eventually married Pétain – now a Marshal of France – in 1920.

June 1951 he was freed. Within a month, he died – two days after the ex-Crown Prince – and was buried under an austere tomb in a little naval cemetery. At Verdun, his portrait in the 'Room of Honour' beneath the Citadel had been removed; his name chopped out from the head of the wooden plaque that bears the names of the 'Freemen of the City'. There are no statues – Pétain forbade the erection of any during his lifetime – but in front of the *Ossuaire* the *gardiens* will show you an empty plot of ground where Pétain had hoped eventually to rejoin his beloved soldiers.

'Perhaps,' they say, in a questioning tone, 'Perhaps, *le Maréchal* will be permitted to come back here after all.'

Postscript. On translation of *The Price of Glory* into French, there followed a long correspondence with ex-Lieutenant Kléber Dupuy (see page 298), the last French officer to stand in the way of the momentary high tide of the German advance, at Souville on 12 July 1916. Much decorated in the First World War, his subsequent career was graphically illustrative of the tragic divisions that were to plague France a generation later. After 1940, Kléber Dupuy was again decorated for his role in the Resistance, i.e. fighting *against* his former chief at Verdun, Pétain. But he never lost his respect for Pétain and, in the 1960s, he led the movement for the rehabilitation of the dead *Maréchal*; a measure adamantly opposed by Dupuy's Second World War chief, de Gaulle. In his last letter to the author, he wrote: 'My most ardent desire is to accompany the Marshal's ashes for reburial at Douaumont, and on that day I hope you will accompany me in the cortège, *bras dessus, bras dessous.*'

Alas, ex-Lieutenant Dupuy died a short time afterwards; the reburial of Pétain at Verdun has still not been permitted.

Epilogue

War is less costly than servitude, said Vauvenargues . . . the choice is always between Verdun and Dachau — JEAN DUTOURD, *The Taxis of the Marne*

Before the Second World War was ended, the sinister battle-field at Verdun claimed one more victim. The bomb plot of 20 July 1944 against Hitler had just failed and General Karl-Heinrich von Stülpnagel – the German Military Governor in Paris and one of the principal plotters – was on his way back to face trial and certain death in Germany. He asked his guard if he could go by way of Verdun, and on approaching the Mort Homme, where he had commanded a battalion in 1916, he stopped the car and got out. A short while later the driver heard a shot, and von Stülpnagel was found floating in a canal of the Meuse. The wretched man had only succeeded in putting out both his eyes; blind and helpless he was strangulated by the Gestapo.

Except perhaps deep in memories of a few old men, after 1945 the imprint of Verdun in Germany was largely erased; other more recent nightmares such as Stalingrad had replaced its image. France however has still not got the stimulating but toxic drug completely out of its system. Upon the French Army, desperately and pathetically questing after the sources of *La Gloire* as a panacea to the deadly humiliation of 1940, the influence of this drug became if anything, morally, even more potent. One of Britain's leading military writers told the author how, shortly after the Second World War ended, he was invited to attend a lengthy seminar in France at the *École de Guerre*, which was dedicated to discussing the lessons of the recent war. But, he said, to his surprise most of the time was spent in discussing the 'glories' of the previous war, 'with particular reference to Verdun'. In a sense the wheel that began to rotate after 1870 had moved through yet another quadrant; once again the ground was as disastrously fertile (and through application of the same kind of manure) as it had been when de Grandmaison and his catastrophic doctrine of *l'attaque à outrance* sprouted from it. The years when Britain was bowing to the inevitable have seen successive weak French Governments goaded on by an army desperate for *la Gloire* – anxious to win a war, any war – to commit themselves irrevocably to military 'solutions' in their overseas territories. There was first Syria and Madagascar, then Indo-China and Algeria. Alas, in Indo-China the hidden influences of Verdun overlapped once again into actual strategic considerations. After the first Viet Minh successes in 1951, de Lattre de Tassigny – who in June 1916 had held a position near to the company wiped out in the '*Tranchée des Baïonnettes*' – ordered the Delta to be surrounded 'with a belt of concrete' unmistakably inspired by Verdun's ring of forts. A few years later, after De Lattre's death, an isolated and strategically quite indefensible outpost called Dien Bien Phu was chosen as a fortress where the resurrected French Army would stake its honour and fight, if necessary, to the last man. Dien Bien Phu became a fatal symbol. With superlative courage and total abandon it did fight to the last man. Once again, as the Viet Minh swarmed over the hastily constructed bunkers, the cries of '*on les aura!*' and '*Ils ne passeront pas!*' were heard. A few months later Indo-China was lost to France. In Algeria, the same deadly influences could be detected; you do not have to scratch the surface of one of the 'Colonels of Algiers' very hard before the word VERDUN is revealed in some combination or other. Is it also just a coincidence that, at the time of the Algerian cease-fire talks, the O.A.S. should have chosen '*DE GAULLE NE PASSERA PAS*' as one of their favourite slogans?

The ghosts are not allowed to die. Every officer on both the senior and junior courses at the *École de Guerre* is still sent to Verdun for a lecture on the battle; although instructors there freely admit that it had absolutely no relevance to modern warfare. The same is true of the Artillery School at Châlons-sur-Marne. Still the torchlight pilgrimages to the *Ossuaire* continue. The ranks of '*Ceux de Verdun*' are getting a bit thin now, but already they are reinforced by the *anciens combattants* of another war who turn to Verdun, rather than to Bir Hakim or Strasbourg, as a touchstone of faith. And yet another generation is being steeped in the tradition. During the Verdun pilgrimages one is struck by the long silent files of children that throng into the little chapel at the *Ossuaire* to take part in special commemoration services, and in even the smallest villages of France the anniversary of 21 February 1916 is often celebrated by schoolchildren being marched in procession to the village war memorial.

After 1945, Verdun became again a sleepy garrison town, with one of the vilest climates in France. Early in the morning the bugles calling reveille up in the Citadel still sound thinly over the town, and only an insensitive soul can hear them without a shudder of association. For the tourist who happens to wander into this part of France, the shops of Verdun still display tasteless mementoes of the battle, such as candles moulded in the shape of shells; as indeed, shockingly enough, does a horrid little boutique within the *Ossuaire* itself. But the less obvious reminders are now unlikely to reveal themselves to the casual eye. As you approach Verdun from Bar-le-Duc, without the wreathed helmets on each kilometre stone it would be hard to believe that this narrow, insignificant secondary road was the *Voie Sacrée* along which poured the lifeblood of France in such immense draughts; harder still to imagine its deserted stretches jammed with primitive military transports, bumper to bumper, night and day. At Stenay, the dreary little Meuse town where the Crown Prince and Knobelsdorf had their headquarters, you can, if you peer about, still see, unaffected after nearly fifty years, German signs left behind by the Fifth Army. At Souilly, there is nothing to indicate that this was once Pétain's H.Q. in the first stages of the battle. The *Mairie* is the *Mairie* once more, but if you enter and ask about *le Maréchal* an old soldier working in the secretariat with the gold thread of the *Médaille Militaire* in his buttonhole will delightedly show you the humble office, the worn leather chair.

Closer to Verdun, in the Meuse villages, the signs abound; the viciously heavy barbed wire used on the farms, the wall of the cowsheds made from the thick dugout corrugated iron, the scarecrow using a German helmet. The villages themselves, like those all over France, are still half-empty as the hangover of a war that decimated the peasant population; and (or does one imagine it?) enveloped in a sourness and mournful gloom that is not to be found elsewhere in France, like a blight over the countryside. Still, it is said, there is more danger of infecting a small cut, more tetanus, indigenous to the Verdun area than to any other part of the country. And everywhere, everywhere there are the cemeteries, large and small, French with white crosses, German with black, but all well cared for.

If you sit long enough on one of the forts on the Bois Bourrus, gazing at the superb panorama of the battlefield, perhaps a young shepherd with a torn trilby will come up to you, and divining your thoughts will remark scornfully:

They must have been mad, *ces gens-là.*

Then, casting a shell fragment at his flock, he is off. Most of the infertile battlefield on the Right Bank is now shrouded over with a merciful cloak of secondary-growth trees and shrubs, dense hawthorn and wild roses. It is almost impenetrable. Where you can find your way inside it, you at once feel rather than see that literally every inch of the ground is pock-marked. Suddenly you may come across apple-trees blossoming in the wilderness, and you know you are on the site of one of the nine vanished villages. At some, like Ornes, there are still the vaguely identifiable fragments of tiles and remnants of houses heaped into crude trenches; at others, like Beaumont and Fleury, there is a small shrine or a monument to guide you, otherwise not a brick.

The slopes of the Mort Homme are covered with a forest of young firs, planted in the 1930s when all other attempts at cultivation had failed. The wind whistles through the trees and the birds sing, and that is all. It is the nearest thing to a desert in Europe. Nobody seems ever to visit it. Even lovers eschew the unchallenged privacy of its glades. The ghosts abound; it is one of the eeriest places in this world. A grown man will not willingly repeat the experience of getting lost in the labyrinth of firecuts that crisscross the deserted plantations.

Everywhere in the spooky jungles the pathetic relics, the non-perishable debris of battle still lie; the helmets, the rusted water-bottles, the broken rifles, the huge shell fragments – and, still, the bones. The wild boar of the Meuse are extremely partial to them; and every day the French Army Chaplain at the *Ossuaire* explores the battlefield, looking for the tell-tale sign of diggings. Barely a week goes by without the discovery of some new 'unknown soldier' often part of some all-too-easily reconstructed tragic scene; perhaps half-hidden in a shell-hole the tableau of three skeletons – of two stretcher-bearers and the casualty they were carrying, all killed by the same shell.

Little enough of this is seen by the casual visitor to Verdun, who is funnelled to the *Ossuaire*, to the '*Tranchée des Baïonnettes*', and above all to Forts Vaux and Douaumont. On the crumbling outside wall of Vaux, near a memorial to Raynal's last pigeon, a cracked and modest little plaque placed there by an anonymous mother may move you:

To my son, since your eyes were closed mine have never ceased to cry.

Inside they will show you Raynal's office and sell you a copy of his book. At Douaumont, the elderly *Gardiens* – all survivors of the battle – grumpily escort visitors round the tour they have made ten thousand times, accompanied with their own curious version of history that has evolved over the years, with the frequently interjected, melancholy litany of '*très grandes pertes, très grandes pertes*'. When there are no visitors, they can very likely be found up on the glacis, collecting *escargots* in old German helmets for their supper. Up there, standing on the 155 millimetre turret, like a ghost in modern dress, is a young *poilu* with slung rifle, a *Gitane* suspended from his lip, eyeing disdainfully the old men at their snail hunt. He is supposed to be sentry to the rifle range now carved out of the desert beyond the fort, over which Kunze and Radtke must have crept to enter Douaumont on that fateful day of February 1916.

•

A few years ago a colonel in the new German *Luftwaffe* told the author how he had been travelling from Germany to attend a N.A.T.O. meeting in Paris, and had taken the route through Verdun.

On the hills outside the city, I was held up by roadworks. A bulldozer was at work, cutting a new road, and as its blade entered the earth out tumbled German steel-helmets of the First War. It was a strange sensation. Here I was, a German officer on my way to sit in conference with our French allies. ... I could hardly believe that all this had happened only forty-four years ago, even just within my lifetime. It was more like watching archaeologists dig up the very distant past.

The folly, the waste, and the stupendous courage of the men who fought at Verdun indeed seem to belong to an age a thousand years removed from our own; the world of Falkenhayn and Nivelle, of the murderous rivalry between the Gaul and Teuton supermen, to have disappeared in the mists of Ancient History. How much longer will the ghosts of Verdun continue to torment France? When will they be exorcized? Will it be when the last of the old warriors guarding Douaumont and its memories have moved on to their Valhalla? Or will France have to wait until the eerie forests on the Mort Homme mature and are hewn down, and farms and happy villages once again populate its dead slopes?

Index

Index of Army Units

FOR THE BEST IN PAPERBACKS, LOOK FOR THE

In every corner of the world, on every subject under the sun, Penguin represents quality and variety – the very best in publishing today.

For complete information about books available from Penguin – including Puffins, Penguin Classics and Arkana – and how to order them, write to us at the appropriate address below. Please note that for copyright reasons the selection of books varies from country to country.

In the United Kingdom: Please write to *Dept E.P., Penguin Books Ltd, Harmondsworth, Middlesex, UB7 0DA.*

If you have any difficulty in obtaining a title, please send your order with the correct money, plus ten per cent for postage and packaging, to *PO Box No 11, West Drayton, Middlesex*

In the United States: Please write to *Dept BA, Penguin, 299 Murray Hill Parkway, East Rutherford, New Jersey 07073*

In Canada: Please write to *Penguin Books Canada Ltd, 2801 John Street, Markham, Ontario L3R 1B4*

In Australia: Please write to the *Marketing Department, Penguin Books Australia Ltd, P.O. Box 257, Ringwood, Victoria 3134*

In New Zealand: Please write to the *Marketing Department, Penguin Books (NZ) Ltd, Private Bag, Takapuna, Auckland 9*

In India: Please write to *Penguin Overseas Ltd, 706 Eros Apartments, 56 Nehru Place, New Delhi, 110019*

In the Netherlands: Please write to *Penguin Books Netherlands B.V., Postbus 195, NL–1380AD Weesp*

In West Germany: Please write to *Penguin Books Ltd, Friedrichstrasse 10–12, D–6000 Frankfurt/Main 1*

In Spain: Please write to *Longman Penguin España, Calle San Nicolas 15, E–28013 Madrid*

In Italy: Please write to *Penguin Italia s.r.l., Via Como 4, I-20096 Pioltello (Milano)*

In France: Please write to *Penguin Books Ltd, 39 Rue de Montmorency, F-75003 Paris*

In Japan: Please write to *Longman Penguin Japan Co Ltd, Yamaguchi Building, 2–12–9 Kanda Jimbocho, Chiyoda-Ku, Tokyo 101*

A CHOICE OF PENGUINS

The Secret Lives of Trebitsch Lincoln   Bernard Wasserstein

Trebitsch Lincoln was Member of Parliament, international spy, right-wing revolutionary, Buddhist monk – and this century's most extraordinary conman. 'Surely the final work on a truly extraordinary career' – Hugh Trevor-Roper. 'An utterly improbable story ... a biographical coup' – *Guardian*

Out of Africa   Karen Blixen (Isak Dinesen)

After the failure of her coffee-farm in Kenya, where she lived from 1913 to 1931, Karen Blixen went home to Denmark and wrote this unforgettable account of her experiences. 'No reader can put the book down without some share in the author's poignant farewell to her farm' – *Observer*

In My Wildest Dreams   Leslie Thomas

The autobiography of Leslie Thomas, author of *The Magic Army* and *The Dearest and the Best*. From Barnardo boy to original virgin soldier, from apprentice journalist to famous novelist, it is an amazing story. 'Hugely enjoyable' – *Daily Express*

The Winning Streak   Walter Goldsmith and David Clutterbuck

Marks and Spencer, Saatchi and Saatchi, United Biscuits, GEC ... The UK's top companies reveal their formulas for success, in an important and stimulating book that no British manager can afford to ignore.

Bird of Life, Bird of Death   Jonathan Evan Maslow

In the summer of 1983 Jonathan Maslow set out to find the quetzal. In doing so, he placed himself between the natural and unnatural histories of Central America, between the vulnerable magnificence of nature and the terrible destructiveness of man. 'A wonderful book' – *The New York Times Book Review*

Mob Star   Gene Mustain and Jerry Capeci

Handsome, charming, deadly, John Gotti is the real-life Mafia boss at the head of New York's most feared criminal family. *Mob Star* tells the chilling and compelling story of the rise to power of the most powerful criminal in America.

FOR THE BEST IN PAPERBACKS, LOOK FOR THE 🐧

A CHOICE OF PENGUINS

Return to the Marshes Gavin Young

His remarkable portrait of the remote and beautiful world of the Marsh Arabs, whose centuries-old existence is now threatened with extinction by twentieth-century warfare. 'A talent for vivid description rarely found outside good fiction' – Jonathan Raban in the *Sunday Times*

Manhattan '45 Jan Morris

Disembarking with the victorious GIs returning after the war, Jan Morris takes us on a wonderfully nostalgic exploration of Manhattan in 1945; an affectionate portrait of an unrepeatable moment in history.

Britain's Poisoned Water Frances and Phil Craig

Every day millions of British families drink water containing toxic chemicals. But what are we doing about it? This startling investigation is essential and shocking reading for anyone concerned about our environment, our health, and the health of our children.

How I Grew Mary McCarthy

Mary McCarthy's account of her formative years possesses all the insight, wit and intelligence of her classic *Memories of a Catholic Girlhood* and her international bestseller *The Group*. 'Rich, generous stuff … it leaves one licking one's lips for what is yet to come' – Penelope Lively

Who Should be Sleeping in Your Bed – and Why James Oliver

Should a Little Princess be faithful to a Wimp? This series of simple quizzes and personality profiles devised by clinical psychologist James Oliver will show you why infidelity happens – and how to make sure it doesn't happen to you.

The Big Red Train Ride Eric Newby

From Moscow to the Pacific on the Trans-Siberian Railway is an eight-day journey of nearly six thousand miles through seven time zones. In 1977 Eric Newby set out with his wife, an official guide and a photographer on this journey. 'The best kind of travel book' – Paul Theroux

Riding the Iron Rooster   Paul Theroux

An eye-opening and entertaining account of travels in old and new China, from the author of *The Great Railway Bazaar*. 'Mr Theroux cannot write badly ... in the course of a year there was almost no train in the vast Chinese rail network on which he did not travel' – Ludovic Kennedy

The Markets of London   Alex Forshaw and Theo Bergstrom

From Camden Lock and Columbia Road to Petticoat Lane and Portobello Road, from the world-famous to the well-kept secrets, here is the ultimate guide to London's markets: as old, as entertaining and as diverse as the capital itself.

The Chinese   David Bonavia

'I can think of no other work which so urbanely and entertainingly succeeds in introducing the general Western reader to China' – *Sunday Telegraph*. 'Strongly recommended' – *The Times Literary Supplement*

The Diary of Virginia Woolf
Five volumes edited by Quentin Bell and Anne Olivier Bell

'As an account of intellectual and cultural life of our century, Virginia Woolf's diaries are invaluable; as the record of one bruised and unquiet mind, they are unique' – Peter Ackroyd in the *Sunday Times*

Voices of the Old Sea   Norman Lewis

'I will wager that *Voices of the Old Sea* will be a classic in the literature about Spain' – *Mail on Sunday*. 'Limpidly and lovingly, Norman Lewis has caught the helpless, unwitting, often foolish, but always hopeful village in its dying summers, and saved the tragedy with sublime comedy' – *Observer*

Ninety-Two Days   Evelyn Waugh

With characteristic honesty, Evelyn Waugh here debunks the romantic notions attached to rough travelling. His journey in Guiana and Brazil is difficult, dangerous and extremely uncomfortable, and his account of it is witty and unquestionably compelling.

A CHOICE OF PENGUINS

The Russian Album   Michael Ignatieff

Michael Ignatieff movingly comes to terms with the meaning of his own family's memories and histories, in a book that is both an extraordinary account of the search for roots and a dramatic and poignant chronicle of four generations of a Russian family.

Beyond the Blue Horizon   Alexander Frater

The romance and excitement of the legendary Imperial Airways East-bound Empire service – the world's longest and most adventurous scheduled air route – relived fifty years later in one of the most original travel books of the decade. 'The find of the year' – *Today*

Getting to Know the General   Graham Greene

'In August 1981 my bag was packed for my fifth visit to Panama when the news came to me over the telephone of the death of General Omar Torrijos Herrera, my friend and host...' 'Vigorous, deeply felt, at times funny, and for Greene surprisingly frank' – *Sunday Times*

The Search for the Virus   Steve Connor and Sharon Kingman

In this gripping book, two leading *New Scientist* journalists tell the remarkable story of how researchers discovered the AIDS virus and examine the links between AIDS and lifestyles. They also look at the progress being made in isolating the virus and finding a cure.

Arabian Sands   Wilfred Thesiger

'In the tradition of Burton, Doughty, Lawrence, Philby and Thomas, it is, very likely, the book about Arabia to end all books about Arabia' – *Daily Telegraph*

Adieux: A Farewell to Sartre   Simone de Beauvoir

A devastatingly frank account of the last years of Sartre's life, and his death, by the woman who for more than half a century shared that life. 'A true labour of love, there is about it a touching sadness, a mingling of the personal with the impersonal and timeless which Sartre himself would surely have liked and understood' – *Listener*

A CHOICE OF PENGUINS

The Assassination of Federico García Lorca Ian Gibson

Lorca's 'crime' was his antipathy to pomposity, conformity and intolerance. His punishment was murder. Ian Gibson – author of the acclaimed new biography of Lorca – reveals the truth about his death and the atmosphere in Spain that allowed it to happen.

Between the Woods and the Water Patrick Leigh Fermor

Patrick Leigh Fermor continues his celebrated account – begun in *A Time of Gifts* – of his journey on foot from the Hook of Holland to Constantinople. 'Even better than everyone says it is' – Peter Levi. 'Indescribably rich and beautiful' – *Guardian*

The Hunting of the Whale Jeremy Cherfas

'*The Hunting of the Whale* is a story of declining profits and mounting pigheadedness ... it involves a catalogue of crass carelessness ... Jeremy Cherfas brings a fresh eye to [his] material ... for anyone wanting a whale in a nutshell this must be the book to choose' – *The Times Literary Supplement*

Metamagical Themas Douglas R. Hofstadter

This astonishing sequel to the bestselling, Pulitzer Prize-winning *Gödel, Escher, Bach* swarms with 'extraordinary ideas, brilliant fables, deep philosophical questions and Carrollian word play' – Martin Gardner

Into the Heart of Borneo Redmond O'Hanlon

'Perceptive, hilarious and at the same time a serious natural-history journey into one of the last remaining unspoilt paradises' – *New Statesman*. 'Consistently exciting, often funny and erudite without ever being overwhelming' – *Punch*

When the Wind Blows Raymond Briggs

'A visual parable against nuclear war: all the more chilling for being in the form of a strip cartoon' – *Sunday Times*. 'The most eloquent anti-Bomb statement you are likely to read' – *Daily Mail*

PENGUIN POLITICS AND SOCIAL SCIENCES

Political Ideas David Thomson (ed.)

From Machiavelli to Marx – a stimulating and informative introduction to the last 500 years of European political thinkers and political thought.

On Revolution Hannah Arendt

Arendt's classic analysis of a relatively recent political phenomenon examines the underlying principles common to all revolutions, and the evolution of revolutionary theory and practice. 'Never dull, enormously erudite, always imaginative' – *Sunday Times*

The Apartheid Handbook Roger Omond

The facts behind the headlines: the essential hard information about how apartheid actually works from day to day.

The Social Construction of Reality Peter Berger and Thomas Luckmann

Concerned with the sociology of 'everything that passes for knowledge in society' and particularly with that which passes for common sense, this is 'a serious, open-minded book, upon a serious subject' – *Listener*

The Care of the Self Michel Foucault
The History of Sexuality Vol 3

Foucault examines the transformation of sexual discourse from the Hellenistic to the Roman world in an inquiry which 'bristles with provocative insights into the tangled liaison of sex and self' – *The Times Higher Educational Supplement*

A Fate Worse than Debt Susan George

How did Third World countries accumulate a staggering trillion dollars' worth of debt? Who really shoulders the burden of reimbursement? How should we deal with the debt crisis? Susan George answers these questions with the solid evidence and verve familiar to readers of *How the Other Half Dies*.

PENGUIN POLITICS AND SOCIAL SCIENCES

Comparative Government S. E. Finer

'A considerable *tour de force* ... few teachers of politics in Britain would fail to learn a great deal from it ... Above all, it is the work of a great teacher who breathes into every page his own enthusiasm for the discipline' – Anthony King in *New Society*

Karl Marx: Selected Writings in Sociology and Social Philosophy
T. B. Bottomore and Maximilien Rubel (eds.)

'It makes available, in coherent form and lucid English, some of Marx's most important ideas. As an introduction to Marx's thought, it has very few rivals indeed' – *British Journal of Sociology*

Post-War Britain A Political History Alan Sked and Chris Cook

Major political figures from Attlee to Thatcher, the aims and achievements of governments and the changing fortunes of Britain in the period since 1945 are thoroughly scrutinized in this readable history.

Inside the Third World Paul Harrison

From climate and colonialism to land hunger, exploding cities and illiteracy, this comprehensive book brings home a wealth of facts and analysis on the often tragic realities of life for the poor people and communities of Asia, Africa and Latin America.

Housewife Ann Oakley

'A fresh and challenging account' – *Economist*. 'Informative and rational enough to deserve a serious place in any discussion on the position of women in modern society' – *The Times Educational Supplement*

The Raw and the Cooked Claude Lévi-Strauss

Deliberately, brilliantly and inimitably challenging, Lévi-Strauss's seminal work of structural anthropology cuts wide and deep into the mind of mankind, as he finds in the myths of the South American Indians a comprehensible psychological pattern.

PENGUIN HISTORY

The Germans Gordon A. Craig

An intimate study of a complex and fascinating nation by 'one of the ablest and most distinguished American historians of modern Germany' – Hugh Trevor-Roper

Imperial Spain 1469–1716 J. H. Elliot

A brilliant modern study of the sudden rise of a barren and isolated country to the greatest power on earth, and of its equally sudden decline. 'Outstandingly good' – *Daily Telegraph*

British Society 1914–1945 John Stevenson

A major contribution to the *Penguin Social History of Britain*, which 'will undoubtedly be the standard work for students of modern Britain for many years to come' – *The Times Educational Supplement*

A History of Christianity Paul Johnson

'Masterly … It is a huge and crowded canvas – a tremendous theme running through twenty centuries of history – a cosmic soap opera involving kings and beggars, philosophers and crackpots, scholars and illiterate *exaltés*, popes and pilgrims and wild anchorites in the wilderness' – Malcolm Muggeridge

The Penguin History of Greece A. R. Burn

Readable, erudite, enthusiastic and balanced, this one-volume history of Hellas sweeps the reader along from the days of Mycenae and the splendours of Athens to the conquests of Alexander and the final dark decades.

A History of Latin America George Pendle

'Ought to be compulsory reading in every sixth form … this book is right on target' – *Sunday Times*. 'A beginner's guide to the continent … lively, and full of anecdote' – *Financial Times*

PENGUIN HISTORY

The Penguin History of the United States   Hugh Brogan

'An extraordinarily engaging book' – *The Times Literary Supplement*. 'Compelling reading ... Hugh Brogan's book will delight the general reader as much as the student' – *The Times Educational Supplement*. 'He will be welcomed by American readers no less than those in his own country' – J. K. Galbraith

The Making of the English Working Class   E. P. Thompson

Probably the most imaginative – and the most famous – post-war work of English social history.

The Waning of the Middle Ages   Johan Huizinga

A magnificent study of life, thought and art in 14th- and 15th-century France and the Netherlands, long established as a classic.

The City in History   Lewis Mumford

Often prophetic in tone and containing a wealth of photographs, *The City in History* is among the most deeply learned and warmly human studies of man as a social creature.

The Habsburg Monarchy 1809–1918   A. J. P. Taylor

Dissolved in 1918, the Habsburg Empire 'had a unique character, out of time and out of place'. Scholarly and vividly accessible, this 'very good book indeed' (*Spectator*) elucidates the problems always inherent in the attempt to give peace, stability and a common loyalty to a heterogeneous population.

Inside Nazi Germany   Conformity, Opposition and Racism in Everyday Life
Detlev J. K. Peukert

An authoritative study – and a challenging and original analysis – of the realities of daily existence under the Third Reich. 'A fascinating study ... captures the whole range of popular attitudes and the complexity of their relationship with the Nazi state' – Richard Geary

7.95

BY THE SAME AUTHOR

The Fall of Paris

The Siege and the Commune 1870–71

'Mr Horne has a great canvas and he has taken his opportunity. *The Fall of Paris* is compulsively readable' – *The Times*

'Mr Horne has thrown open to the public this dazzling and terrifying year of history' – *New Statesman*

'It would be difficult to show more skill in organizing material drawn from so many sources. This is indeed the most enthralling historical work' – *Daily Telegraph*

To Lose a Battle

'Mr Horne follows his line unfalteringly. All the details are there: the small, fleeting triumphs, the greater intelligence . . . that make war so fascinating and so terrible. Mr Horne's great gift is his ability to hold his readers in the grip of such feelings, constantly shifting his focus from the minor battlefield incident to the high military or political decision without mystifying or fatiguing them' – *Economist*